Anonymous

Dodd, Talbott and Parsons' Indianapolis City Directory

and business mirror for 1862

Anonymous

Dodd, Talbott and Parsons' Indianapolis City Directory
and business mirror for 1862

ISBN/EAN: 9783337291464

Printed in Europe, USA, Canada, Australia, Japan

Cover: Foto ©Andreas Hilbeck / pixelio.de

More available books at **www.hansebooks.com**

The most Popular Establishment in the City is the
FASHIONABLE HAT STORE OF
H. BAMBERGER

No. 16 E. Washington St.,

Where old and young, rich and poor, citizens and strangers, go to purchase their

Hats, Caps, Furs & Straw Goods,

As the assortment is extensive, prices to suit the times. Quality of goods as represented, and New Styles always predominating.

CALL AND SEE BEFORE PURCHASING ELSEWHERE.

P. S.---The Wholesale Department of this Establishment is a new feature, and Country Merchants will always find a full stock at Cincinnati prices.

Successive years at Mechanic's Institute, Cincinnati.

MRS. A. THOMSON & SON,
WHOLESALE NEWS AND
STATIONERY DEPOT,

7 Pennsylvania St., one door N. Odd Fellows' Hall.

The following is a partial list of our Newspapers and Magazines—

New York Ledger,
New York Mercury,
New York Weekly,
New York Clipper,
New York Herald,
New York Tribune,
New York Illustrated News,
Frank Leslie's Illustrated,
Harper's Weekly,
Scientific American,
Boston Pilot,
Irish American,
New York Budget,
New York Comic Monthly,
New York Vanity Fair,
New York American Union,
New York True Flag,
New York Flag of Our Union,
New York Yankee Notions and Nick Nax,
Literary Companion, House-Hold Journal,
Wide World,
Wilkes' Spirit of the Times,
Waverly Weekly,
Harpers' Magazine,
Godey's Magazine,
Peterson's Magazine,
Continental Magazine,
Ballou's Dollar Magazine,
Arthur's Magazine,
Waverly Magazine,
Atlantic Magazine,
Monthly Novelette,
M'me Demorest's Mirror of Fashions,
Le Bon Ton, Paris Fashions.

Also, School Books, Dairies, Blank Books, Note Paper, Letter Paper, Envelopes, Pencils, Pens, Inks, &c.

D. J. CALLINAN,
Dealer in
STAPLE AND FANCY
DRY GOODS,
CLOAKS, SHAWLS,
EMBROIDERIES, LACE GOODS,

Ribbons, Straw Goods, Hosiery, &c.,

No. 28 East Washington Street, North Side,

INDIANAPOLIS, IND.

First Premium awarded the Wheeler & Wilson Sewing Machine for three

DODD, TALBOTT & PARSONS'

Indianapolis City Directory

AND

BUSINESS MIRROR,

FOR 1862.

PUBLISHED ANNUALLY.

H. H. DODD & CO.,
BOOK AND JOB PRINTERS AND BOOK BINDERS.

Successive years at the United States Fair.

H. H. DODD & CO.,	H. H. DODD & CO.,
PRINTERS,	**BOOKBINDERS,**
NO. 18 EAST WASHINGTON STREET,	NO. 18 EAST WASHINGTON STREET,
INDIANAPOLIS, IND.	INDIANAPOLIS, IND.

A Wheeler & Wilson Sewing Machine with Hemmer, for $50.

CITY DIRECTORY. 7

METROPOLITAN HALL,

INDIANAPOLIS, IND.

VALENTINE BUTSCH, - - Proprietor.

This Hall can, after the 1st of March, 1862, be rented for Concerts, Lectures, Panoramic or other Exhibitions, at reasonable rates. The proprietor has an annual license for exhibitions in the Hall, and no additional charge will be made for license. A faithful Janitor is always in attendance to attend to the warming and lighting of the Hall.

Address,

VALENTINE BUTSCH.

INDIANAPOLIS, IND.

81,000 Wheeler & Wilson's Sewing Machines in use in this country.

BOSTON STORE,

No. 10 E. Washington St.,
INDIANAPOLIS, IND.

DRY GOODS,
CARPETS,
CLOAKS, FURS, &c.,
CHEAP FOR CASH.
WILLIAM ZEIGLER, Proprietor.

INDEX TO ADVERTISEMENTS.

	PAGE.
ALE AND PORTER—	
Wright, Downer & Co.	178
AGRICULTURAL IMPLEMENTS—	
Hasselman & Vinton	58, 59
Glazier Charles	86
Grosvenor & Turner	11
Redstone, Bros. & Co.	243
ARTISTS, PHOTOGRAPH, AMBROTYPE AND DAGUERREOTYPE—	
Bruening E. & J.	80
Hays & Runnion	20
Morris J. C	68
Weeks & Cox	110
ATTORNEYS—	
Caven John	36
Dye J. T.	24
Hamlin C.	122
Leathers & Carter	38
Peelle & Davis	26
BAKERY—	
Cunningham F. P.	32
BARBERS—	
Franklin W. H.	20
Henning & Stelzell	94
BILL POSTER—	
Smith S	242
BILLIARD ROOMS—	
Exchange	90
St. Charles	44
Union Hall	46
BOOK BINDERS—	
Braden Wm	132
Campbell & Boyles	72
Dodd H. H. & Co.	100
BOOK PUBLISHERS—	
Asher & Co.	outside front cover
Clarke & Co.	86
Dodd H. H. & Co	100, 130
Merrill & Co.	126, 128
BOOK STORES—	
Bowen, Stewart & Co	80
Merrill & Co.	126, 128
Werden & Co.	24
BOOTS AND SHOES—	
Deters J. H., (Cincinnati)	148
Knodle A. & Son	20
BUTCHERS—	
Blanc, Borst & Lake	38
Roos & Schmalzried	68
CARPETS AND MATTING—	
Fletcher H. A. & Co.	112
Boston Store	8
CIGARS AND TOBACCO—	
Frost J. M.	96

	PAGE.
Heidlinger J. A.	70
Ludden & Lee	74
Meyer G. F.	132
Schnull A. & H.	70
COAL OIL AND LAMPS—	
Browning Robert	180
Rockey H. S.	92
Vickers W. B.	outside front cov
CONFECTIONERY—	
Beebe & Hawes	52
Cunningham F. P.	32
COMMISSION AND PRODUCE—	
Glazier C.	86
Schnull A. & H.	70
Wallace A.	124
CROCKERY AND GLASSWARE—	
Hawthorn & Buchanan	86
DENTISTS—	
Frink S. C.	28
DRUGS—	
Browning Robert	180
Egner & Wocher	72
Hannaman William	34
Lowry W. M.	28
Vickers W. B.	outside front cov
DRY GOODS—	
Bee-Hive, L. H. Tyler	front edge.
Boston Store, W. Zeigler	opp. index
Callinan D. J.	opp. title page.
Fletcher H. A. & Co	112
New York Store, W. & H. Glenn & Co.	54, 55
EXPRESS COMPANIES—	
Adams	outside front cover.
American	inside front cover.
United States	inside front cover.
FANCY GOODS—	
Parker R. R.	76
Parker Edgar	78
FLOURING MILLS—	
Bates City	44
FOUNDRIES—	
Hasselman & Vinton	58, 59
FURNITURE—	
Spiegle, Thoms & Co.	46
GROCERS—	
Beebe & Hawes	52
Birch J. & Co	104
Culver E.	30
Danforth & Simpson	96
Holmes C. L.	94
Hogshire & Hunter	40
Schnull A. & H.	70

For four successive years at the Ohio State Fair.

INDIANAPOLIS

Spencer & Soewell 34
Thompson Mary 18
Van Houten & Graham 76
Wallace Andrew 124

GUNS AND PISTOLS—
Parker Edgar 78
Wilson J. B. 72

HALLS—
Metropolitan 7

HARDWARE—
Wilson J. B. 72
Wood A. D. 104

HATS AND CAPS—
Bamberger H....opp. inside ft. cover.
Brown W. P. 26

HOSIERY—
Parker R. R. 76

HOT AIR FURNACE—
Cox Charles 94

HOTELS—
Farmers' Hotel 42
Macy House 32
Ohio House 78
Ray House 242
Union Hall 46
Union House 68

ICE—
Butsch Joseph 38
Pitts G. W 266

INSURANCE—
Dunlop J. S. 26
Hayden J. J. (Phœnix) 185, 186
Spann John S......outside back cover

IRON RAILING AND BANK VAULTS—
Williamson & Haugh 266

LEATHER, HIDES AND OIL—
Fishback John 42

LIME, CEMENT AND COAL—
Butsch V. 22

LITHOGRAPHERS AND ENGRAVERS—
Middleton, Strobridge & Co., Cincinnati 154

LIVERY STABLES—
Allen & Hinesley 78
Johnston O. W 64
Wood & Foudray 66

MACHINE SHOPS—
Hasselman & Vinton 58, 59
Redstone, Bros. & Co. 243

MATHEMATICAL INSTRUMENTS—
Steffens C. W. & Co. 122

MERCHANT TAILORS, &C.—
Gapper Fred 44
Gramlin J. & P 20
Kahn A. 180
Moritz, Bros. & Co. 76
Sprague & Co., Cin....outside b'k cov

MILK—
Reily John O. 30

MUSIC AND MUSICAL INSTRUMENTS—
Willard & Stowell 84, 85

MUSIC TEACHER—
Schonacker H. J. 132

NEWSPAPERS—
American 62
Cincinnate Dailies 104
Journal Co. 56
Sentinel 60

NEWSPAPERS AND PERIODICALS—
Thomson Mrs. A. & Son..op. title page

NURSERY AND GREEN HOUSE—
Loomis W. H 66

OPTICIAN—
Moses L. W.......outside front cover

OYSTERS—
Beebe & Hawes 52
Hugg M. 92

PAINT AND COLOR WORKS—
Drake C. B. & Co 22

PAPER DEALERS—
Braden Wm 132
Bowen, Stewart & Co. 80

PATENT MEDICINES—
Frost J. M 96

PHYSICIANS—
Barnes H. F. 24
Fishback Charles 72
Jameson & Funkhouser 18
Merrill J. F. 30

PRINTERS—
Cameron W. S. 50
Cullum & Stanage 14
Dodd H. H. & Co. 130
Landon & Hastings 180

REAL ESTATE—
Barnitz & Murphy 22
Dunlop J. S. 26
Eldridge Jacob 242
Hamlin L. H. & C. 122
Smith Francis 38

RAIL ROADS—
Indianapolis & Cincinnati 82
Peru & Indianapolis 88
Jeffersonville 94
Terre Haute & Richmond 102
Madison & Indianapolis 106
Indiana Central 108

RESTAURANT—
Burt's 13

SADDLE AND HARNESS MAKER—
Hinesley A. J. 48

SADDLERY HARDWARE—
Hinesley A. J. 48

SALOONS AND RESTAURANTS—
Crystal Palace 42
Exchange 15
Florances 90
Hugg Martin 92
Hofmeister C. 68
Lang Louis 36
Little's Hotel 34
Magnolia 48
Nebraska 48
Palmer House 40
Pearl Street 241
Sandford Caylor 18
St. Charles 44
Union Hall 46
Washington Hall 32

SAW MANUFACTORY—
Atkins E. C. 13

SEAL AND PRESS MAKER—
Hall Mrs. C. F., Cincinnati ... 148

SEWING MACHINES—
Wheeler & Wilson...foot lines & 244
Singer Sewing Machine Co...219, 220

SPICE MANUFACTORY—
Dixon G. R., Cincinnati 150

STEREOTYPE FOUNDRY—
Fleming Geo. H......inside back cover

Wheeler & Wilson's Sewing Machines warranted for three years.

CITY DIRECTORY.   11

P. P. STEWART'S CELEBRATED COOKING STOVE.

MUNSON & JOHNSTON,
Wholesale and Retail dealers in
COOKING, PARLOR AND HEATING STOVES,
Manufacturers of
TIN, SHEET IRON AND COPPER WARE,
No. 62, first door East of Odd Fellows' Hall, INDIANAPOLIS.

☞ The attention of Builders is particularly called to our Tin Roofing, Guttering and Spouting. Satisfaction warranted.

JULIUS A. GROSVENOR.   WILLIAM H. TURNER.

GROSVENOR & TURNER,
GENERAL
Commission Merchants,
Dealers in
AGRICULTURAL IMPLEMENTS,
Grain Seeds, &c.,
NO. 84 WEST WASHINGTON STREET,
Theater Building, Second door East of the State House,
INDIANAPOLIS, IND.

The Wheeler & Wilson Hemmer is the only Hemmer that will Fell.

	PAGE.		PAGE.
STONE CUTTER—		UNDERTAKERS—	
Smith, Ittenbach & Co	18	Weaver & Williams	92
STOVES AND TINWARE—		VINEGAR—	
Cox Charles	94	Schnull A. & H	70
Munson & Johnston	11	Schofield T. B. & Co	22
SUNDAY SCHOOL BOOKS—		WALL PAPER—	
Clark & Co	86	Bowen, Stewart & Co	80
TEAS—		Werden & Co	24
Ludden & Lee	74	WATCHES AND JEWELRY—	
TOYS, WOODEN AND WILLOW-WARE—		Feller George	36
Klotz Emil	16	McLene J	230
Mayer Charles	178	Bingham W. P. & Co	outside b'k cov
Parker Edgar	78	WINDOW SHADES, CURTAINS AND FIXTURES—	
TRUNK MAKER—		Fletcher H. A. & Co	112
Becker H	44	Werden & Co	24
TYPE AND STEREOTYPE FOUNDRIES—		WINES AND LIQUORS—	
Cincinnati	152	Culver E	30
Franklin, Cincinnati	146	Hugg Martin	24
Hills, O'Driscoll & Co., Cin	150	Schnull A. & H	70

CONTENTS.

	PAGE.		PAGE.
Alphabetical Arrangement of Names	16	Indianapolis Rolling Mill Company	274
Banks and Bankers	275	Libraries	277
Business Mirror	245	Masonic	270
Churches and Pastors	262	Odd Fellows	273
City Officers	267	Post Office	270
County Officers	269	Railroads	277
Courts	269	State Benevolent Institutions	279
Educational	275	School Trustees	268
Fire Department	268	Township Officers	269
Gas Company	275	Typographical Union	279
Halls and Public Buildings	276	Young Men's Christian Association	279

A Wheeler & Wilson Sewing Machine will last a life-time.

E. C. ATKINS,

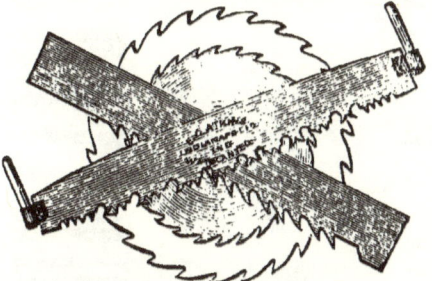

MANUFACTURER OF
EVERY DESCRIPTION OF SAWS.

Patent Ground Circular Saws,
Extra Tempered Mill and Muley Saws,
Tuttles's Patent Cross-Cut Saws,
Single Hook Cross-Cut Saws.

SHEFFIELD WORKS, 155 S. Illinois Street,

INDIANAPOLIS, IND.

Special attention paid to Repairing. Breakage in repairing at owner's risk.

BURT'S DINING HALL,

No. 13 South Illinois Street,

FOUR DOORS BELOW PALMER HOUSE.

WARM MEALS AT ALL HOURS.

Oysters and Game in their Season.

HOURS FOR REGULAR MEALS

Breakfast	6 to 9 A. M.
Dinner	12 M. to 2 P. M.
Supper	6 to 8 P. M.
Regular Meals	25 Cents.

ICE CREAM AND FRUITS IN THEIR SEASON.

SPECIAL APARTMENTS FOR LADIES.

N. B. No Liquors Sold on the Premises.

---

350 families in Indianapolis and vicinity use Wheeler & Wilson.

INDIANAPOLIS

PRICES REDUCED
AT THE
RAILROAD PRINTING OFFICE.

CULLUM & STANAGE,
(Successors to John Fahnestock,)

JOB PRINTERS AND ENGRAVERS,
No. 19 West Washington Street, INDIANAPOLIS.

Printing in Colors Neatly Executed.

Wheeler & Wilson's Sewing Machines have been awarded the First Premium

EXCHANGE Restaurant and Saloon,

C. W. Hall's Block,
No. 23 North Illinois Street, Indianapolis, Ind.

FISH, GAME, OYSTERS,

And other Delicacies in their Season, Served in the best Style to Order, at All Hours.

CHOICE DOMESTIC AND IMPORTED

WINES, LIQUORS AND CIGARS,

KEPT CONSTANTLY ON HAND.

For four successive years at the Am. Institute, New York.

NEW YORK BAZAAR,

EMIL KLOTZ, Proprietor,
37 East Washington Street,
INDIANAPOLIS, IND.

Wholesale and Retail dealer in

FANCY GOODS,
NOTIONS,
TOYS, FANCY HARDWARE,
GROCERIES,
CIGARS & TOBACCO,
Wooden & Willow Ware,
CUTLERY,
FIRE ARMS,
AND
AMMUNITION.

Full assortment and best quality of Goods at Lowest Prices.

EMIL KLOTZ.

The Wheeler & Wilson Hemmer makes hems of any width.

DODD, TALBOTT & PARSONS'
Indianapolis City Directory
FOR 1862.

ABBREVIATIONS.

Bds., *boards*; cor., *corner*; res., *residence*; col., *colored*; wid., *widow*; opp., *opposite*; bet., *between*; ave., *avenue*; E., W., N., S., *East, West, North, South*. The word *street* is implied.

A

Abbett Charles H., physician, 20 Virginia ave.
Abbett L., physician, 20 Virginia ave., office in basement.
Abbett Wm. A., salesman, Fancy Bazaar, bds. 20 Virginia ave.
Abrams John, clerk, 74 E. Washington, res. 133 Noble.
Abromit Adolphus, clerk at Arsenal, res. 153 S. Tennessee.
Acher Frank, dealer in patent medicines, res. 101 S. New Jersey.
Achey Henry, tavern keeper, res. 5 Kentucky ave.
Achey John H., bds. 5 Kentucky ave.
Adair J. S., res. Macy House.
Adams Charles T., laborer, bds. 124 N. West.
ADAMS EXPRESS, John H. Ohr, agent, 12 E. Washington.
ADAMS GEO. H., book-keeper Asher & Co., res. 149 N. Pennsylvania.
Adams Hubbard, watchman, res. 85 S. New Jersey.
Adams Jno. W., (Mauldin & Co.,) bds. Pyle House.
Adams Levi P., cooper, bds. at Thos. H. Adams'.
Adams Martha, dress-maker, res. 199 N. Ala.
Adams Reuben, deputy sheriff, res. 71 S. New Jersey.
Adams Thos. H., cooper, N. Illinois, bet. second and third.
Adams W. L., salesman, 26 and 28 W. Washington, res. 60 E. North.

350 families in Indianapolis and vicinity use Wheeler & Wilson.

220 East Wash. St.,

OPEN NIGHT AND DAY.

SANDFORTH CAYLOR, - Proprietor.

CHARLIE D. LOVETT, Barkeeper.

SMITH, ITTENBACH & CO.,
STONE CUTTERS,

No. 170 South Delaware Street.

Keep constantly on hand all kinds of STONE, and will promptly fill all orders in city or country, of any style.

WORK WARRANTED.

JAMESON & FUNKHOUSER,
Physicians & Surgeons,

No. 5 South Meridian St.,

INDIANAPOLIS, IND.

MARY THOMPSON,

No. 66, Corner of South and Delaware Streets,

Keeps constantly on hand a supply of

DRY GOODS AND GROCERIES.

Cash Paid for Produce.

The Wheeler & Wilsons's Hemmer makes hems of any width.

Aderson Wm, salesman, 27 W. Washington.
ÆTNA BUILDING, N. Pennsylvania, bet. Washington and Market.
ÆTNA INS. CO., William Henderson, Agent, Ætna Building, Pennsylvania.
Ætna Mills, J. Skillen & Bro., Proprietors, W. Washington.
Affenstranger Cyrus, blacksmith, res. 149 N. West.
Afton A., newspaper carrier, res. 13 Central.
Aigen Patrick, night policeman, res. 8 Michigan Road.
Aikens Mrs. Martha, seamstress, res. Hosbrook.
Albert John W., saddle and harness maker, 103 E. Washington, res. 210 N. Alabama.
Albrecht Geo., varnisher, at Spiegel, Thoms & Co., res. 95 Davidson.
Albro Henry, machinist, Root's foundry, 252 S. Delaware.
Aldag August, shoemaker, 137 E. Washington, res. 40 Spring.
Aldag Charles L., shoemaker, 137 E. Washington, res. 32 N. Liberty.
Aldag Louis, shoemaker, res. 30 N. Liberty.
Aldene Mrs. E., dress-maker, res. 35 W. New York.
Aldridge John, carpenter, res. Davidson, bet. Michigan and Vermont.
Alexander Geo., bds. 27 Indiana ave.
Alexander John E., silversmith, W. Indianapolis.
ALFORD, MILLS & CO., wholesale grocers, 36 E. Washington.
Alford Thos. G., (Alford, Mills & Co.,) res. 83 N. Alabama.
Alhand J. L, wagon-maker, res. 164 N. Noble.
Allaire Andrew B., blacksmith, bds. 138 N. Alabama.
Allaire Peter A., brick-mason, res. 138 N. Alabama.
Allaire Jas. P., brick-layer, res. 138 N. Alabama.
ALLEN REV. ARCHIBALD C., presbyterian, res. 38 E. New York.
Allen Emory, (col.,) teamster, res. 133 N. Alabama.
Allen Henry, (Allen & Hinesley,) res. 66 W. Vermont.
Allen James, pressman Cullum & Stanage.
Allen Johanna, (wid.,) washer, 17 Virginia ave.
Allen Joseph, wood chopper, res. North, bet. Blackford and California.
Allen Robert, res. 114 W. New York.
Allen William, machinist Bellefontaine car shop, res. 105 Meek.
ALLEN & HINESLEY, livery and sale stable, rear of Palmer House, Pearl.
Allred Garretson W., City Sexton, res. South, bet. Missouri and California.
Altamon Samuel, (Osgood, Smith & Co.,) res. 205 N. Illinois.

A. KNODLE & SON,
Manufacturers and Dealers in
BOOTS AND SHOES,
No. 32 East Washington Street,
INDIANAPOLIS, INDIANA.
All kinds of Work and Repairing done to order.
TERMS, POSITIVELY CASH.

HAYS & RUNNION'S
FINE ART GALLERY,
No. 32½ East Washington St., opposite Glenn's Block.
PHOTOGRAPAS
Life and Miniature size, Plain or in Oil Colors.
PHOTOGRAPHS IN INDIA INK.
Ambrotypes, Ferrotypes, &c.

J. & P. GRAMLING,
MERCHANT TAILORS,
And Dealers in
READY-MADE CLOTHING,
GENTS' FURNISHING GOODS, TRUNKS AND VALISES.
No. 41 East Washington St.,
INDIANAPOLIS, INDIANA.

WILLIAM H. FRANKLIN,
FASHIONABLE BARBER,
Cor. Washington and Meridian Sts.,
UNDER BRANCH BANK,
INDIANAPOLIS: IND.

Hair Cutting, Hair Dyeing, Shaving, Shampooing, &c., done by experienced workmen.

A Wheeler & Wilson Sewing Machine with Hemmer, for $50.

Altland Samuel T., carpenter, res. 171 N. New Jersey.
Altmonds Harmin, clerk, 134 W. Washington.
Alvey J. H., book-keeper, 71 W. Washington, bds. Palmer House.
Alvord E. S., res. 54 N. Pennsylvania.
Ambrose Mary, Superioress of Sisters of Providence, cor. Georgia and Tennessee.
AMERICAN EXPRESS COMPANY, cor. Washington and Meridian, J. Butterfield, Agent.
AMES A. S., Baptist Minister, res. 11 W. Market.
Amos Edward R., res. N- Pennsylvania.
Ames James, piano manufacturer, 1 Blake's Building. res. 155 Michigan.
Amos Thomas D., policeman, res. 73 Spring.
Amos William, brick mason, res. 143 N. Noble.
Anaker John, laborer, res. 70 N. Noble.
Anckenbrook Henry, drayman, res. 273 S. Delaware.
Anderson Mrs., es. 53 E. Market.
Anderson George, carpenter, bds. 53 E. Market.
Anderson George P., (Bates City Mills,) res. 5 E. New York.
Anderson G. P., insurance agent and notary public, 44 N. Pennsylvania, res. 5 E. New York.
Anderson James, ostler, bds. Farmer's Hotel.
Anderson James, carpenter, bds. 53 E. Market.
Anderson James W., messenger American Express Company, res. 111 N. East.
Anderson Jerome S., El de la Hom House, bds. 42 N. Mississippi.
Anderson James, carpenter, res. 52 Indiana avenue.
Anderson Robert J., bricklayer, res. 156 N. Delaware.
Anderson Samuel, (col.,) wood sawyer, res. 63 S. Noble.
Anderson Thomas, laborer, res. 84 Indiana ave.
Anderson William, clerk, bds, 53 E. Market.
Anderson William, cooper, res. 188 E. St. Clair.
Andra John, saddler and harness maker, 171 E. Washington, res. 152 E. New York.
Andrew John, saddler and harness maker, 169 E. Washington, res. 151 New York
ANDREWS L. N., general freight agent Peru & Indianapolis railroad, office at depot, res. 73 N. Delaware.
Anta Jacob, blacksmith, res. 199 S. Delaware.
Anthony David, carpenter, res. 131 E. New York.
Applegate B., book-keeper, cor. Washington and Delaware, bds. Bates House.
Appleton Eliza, (col.,) washer, res. 123, E. St. Clair.
APPLETON JAMES R., (H. H. Dodd & Co.,) res. 100 W. Vermont.
Archey David, (col.,) res. 136 N. Delaware.

81,000 Wheeler & Wilson's Sewing Machines in use in this country.

INDIANAPOLIS

T. B. SCHOFIELD. JAMES ROSS.
THOMAS B. SCHOFIELD & CO.,
Manufacturers and Wholesale Dealers in
CIDER, GRAPE AND FAMILY
Vinegar.
ALSO, DEALERS IN
OLD RYE, BOURBON, &c.
No. 49 South St.,

VALENTINE EUTSCH,
Keeps on hand a fresh and large stock of
Lime, Cement and Coal.
Office opposite Madison Depot,
Orders promptly filled in any part of the city or country.

C. B. DRAKE & CO.,
NO. 47 SOUTH STREET, Manufacturers of
WHITE LEAD & COLORS
And Dealers in
VARNISH, OILS, &C.
City and Country Orders Solicited.

CHARLES BARNITZ. TOBIAS MURPHY.
BARNITZ & MURPHY,
Real Estate, Collecting, and
GENERAL INTELLIGENCE AGENCY,
Will sell, buy and exchange Houses, Lots, Farms, improved or unimproved. We also rent houses. All business properly attended to.
Room No. 8 Temperance Hall, West Wash. St.

The First Premium awarded the Wheeler & Wilson Machine

Armburster John J., clerk Meikel's brewery, res. West, bet. Maryland and Georgia.
Armon Pat., ostler for Wm. Wilkinson.
Armstrong George F., express messenger, res. Tennessee, S. of Garden.
Armstrong John, salesman New York York Store, bds. 109 E. South.
Armstrong John N., laborer, res. 47 McCarthy.
ARMSTRONG REV. WILLIAM, Agent American Bible Society, res. 186 N. Illinois.
Armstrong & Perine, coal dealers, 12 W. Maryland.
Arnhilter Henry, harness maker, bds. 151 New York.
Arnold B. F., law student, bds. 44 N. Pennsylvania.
Arnold Mrs. Jane, (wid.) res. cor. Fletcher's ave. and Pine.
Arnold Peter, laborer, res. 7 N. New Jersey.
Arthur Thomas, machinist, Washington Foundry. res. 117 S. Tennessee.
Ash Richard, laborer, res. 99 E. Louisiana.
Ash Richard, res. alley, bet. Noble and Benton.
Asher John R., (A. & Co.,) bds. S. Pennsylvania.
ASHER & CO., book publishers and sellers, 3 Odd Fellows' Hall. (See card outside front cover.)
Ashmer J. G., artist, res. 69 N. Tennessee.
Askin Patrick, laborer, res. Michigan, bet. Liberty and East.
Asmus Fred., carpet weaver, res. 74, W. Michigan.
Asper Harman, laborer, res. E. Wyoming.
Aston Joseph, horse dealer, res. 9 Kentucky ave.
Astor Saloon and Restaurant, Fey & Runman, 9 N. Pennsylvania.
Athon James S., physician and surgeon, res. 82 N. New Jersey.
Atkins E. C., saw manufacturer, 155 S Illinois, res. 29 Madison ave.
Atkinson Eliza, (wid.,) res. 73 E. Merrill.
Atkinson Joseph H., road master on the Bellefontaine R. R., res. 233 S. Delaware.
Atkinson Thomas J., painter, res. 11 Massachusetts ave.
Aubrey Thomas, harness maker, 103 E. Washington, bds. East Street House.
Augelman William, cigar maker, 35 W. Washington, res. 70 N. Mississippi.
Aumann Christ., wood chopper, res. 143 E. Georgia.
Austemyre Andrew, laborer, res. 17 Central.
Austen John J., gardener, res. 77 E. Market.
Austin Mrs. Myra, (wid.,) res. 13 Central.
Avels Margaret, grocery, res. 277 S. Delaware.
Averill Martin V., candidate for orders, bds. cor. Delaware and New York.

For four successive years at the Ohio State Fair.

MARTIN HUG,
Wholesale Dealer in
FOREIGN AND DOMESTIC
LIQUORS,
BRANDIES, WINES, &C.,
No. 140 West Washington Street. near the State House,
INDIANAPOLIS, INDIANA.

ELIAS WERDEN.   DAN'L G. WILLIAMS.

WERDEN & CO.,
Wholesale and Retail Dealers in
Medical, School, Blank Books,
AND STATIONERY.
Also, Manufacturers and Importers of Wall and Window Paper, Oil and Linen Shades, Window Fixtures, Cord and Tassels.
No. 26 East Washington St. opposite Glenn's Block,
INDIANAPOLIS, IND.
Wall Paper and Window Shades hung on short notice.

JOHN T. DYE,
Attorney & Counsellor at Law,
INDIANAPOLIS, INDIANA.

Office in Blackford's Building, corner of Washington and Meridian sts. Residence 154 West New York st.

DR. HENRY F. BARNES,
Physician and Surgeon,
INDIANAPOLIS, IND.

OFFICE, Diagonal Cor. of Washington St. and Kentucky Ave. opposite Bates and Palmer Houses.

Wheeler & Wilson's Sewing Machines awarded the first premium for five

Avery John L., carpenter, shop cor. North and Alabama, res. 104 N. Alabama.
Avery John P., medical student, res. 104 N. Alabama.
Avery Leonard S., res. 140 N. Tennessee.
Avil Joseph, hack driver, 259 S. Pennsylvania.
Ayres David, wood sawyer, res. 67 Hosbrook.
Ayres Milton, plow maker, res. 13 Henry.
Ayres William S., carpenter, res. cor. Tennessee and First.

B

Backesto J. P., physician, res. 28 N. Illinois.
BACON DAN., bds. Bates House.
Bacon Elisha W., painter, res. 131 N. Alabama.
Bacon John L., blacksmith, bds. 131 N. Alabama.
Bacon T. L., book-keeper, bds. 59 E. New York.
Bacon William M., painter, res. North, bet. Alabama and New Jersey.
Baer Mrs. (wid.,) res, W. Georgia.
Baggs Frederick, clerk State Auditor's office, res. 59 E. Ohio.
Bailey —, carpenter, res. 8 Bates.
Bailey William, moulder for Root, Bennet & Co., res. 173 S. Mississippi.
Bailey William, tailor, 63 E. Washington.
Baine R. T., machinist, bds. Farmer's Hotel.
Baker Mrs. A., (Mrs. A. B. & Co.,) res. 26 S. Illinois.
Baker Mrs. A. & Co., milliners and dealers in fancy goods, 24 S. Illinois.
Baker J. A., clerk, 32 W. Washington, res. 26 S. Illinois.
Baker John, harness maker, 34 W. Washington, bds. Pyle House.
Baker James M., (Baker & McIver,) res. 26 S. Illinois.
BAKER & McIVER, manufacturers and dealers in hats, caps and furs, 22 E. Washington.
Baldwin J. Herman, Fancy Bazaar, 6 E. Washington, res. 83 E. New York.
Balke Charles, saloon, 175 E. Washington, res. same.
Ball C., railroader, res. 91 Indiana ave.
Ball John, porter, Morris House.
Ballard Austin, seal and press maker, res. 5 Circle.
Ballard G. M., teacher at Institute for the Blind.
Ballingers Elijah M., carpenter, res. 150 N. East.
Ballinger Edward B., student at law, with R. L. Walpole.
Balls Chas., baggage master Lafayette R. R., res. 91 Indiana ave.
Ballweg Fred., laborer, res. 59 N. Mississippi.

Successive years at Mechanic's Institute, Cincinnati.

JOHN S. DUNLOP,
INSURANCE AND REAL ESTATE AGENT,
Note and Stock Broker and Notary Public,
INDIANAPOLIS, IND.,

Represents the following well known and reliable Insurance Companies:

	ASSETS.
Lorillard Fire Ins. Co., N. Y.,	$600,000.
Security Fire Ins. Co., N. Y.,	700,000.
Continental Fire Ins. Co., N. Y.,	1,050,000.
Springfield Fire Ins. Co., Springfield, Mass.,	450,000.
Market Fire Ins. Co., N. Y.,	300,000.
New England Fire Ins. Co., Hartford, Conn.,	225,000.
Mutual Life Ins. Co., N. Y.	8,000,000.

Office, third door North of North-West Corner Washington and Meridian Streets.

INDIANAPOLIS
SILK AND FUR HAT
MANUFACTORY,
No. 20 Kentucky Avenue, next to the State Treasury Building.

Hats made to order, and guaranteed to fit the most difficult shaped heads.

W. P. BROWN.

W. A. PEELLE, (Sec. of State.)   EDWIN A. DAVIS.

PEELLE & DAVIS,
ATTORNEYS AND COUNSELLORS AT LAW,
INDIANAPOLIS, INDIANA,

Over the office of the Secretary of State.

☞ Particular attention given to Securing and Collecting Debts throughout the State.

A Wheeler & Wilson Sewing Machine will last a life-time.

Ballweg Ambrose, U. S. Arsenal, 7 Madison ave.
Bals Charles, (Ruschaupt & B.), res. 56 E. St. Joseph.
Bals Christ., clerk, 82 E. Washington.
Bals Henry, (retired,) res. 51 Union.
Balwig & Kindler, gun and locksmiths, res. 17 Kentucky ave.
Bamberger David, res. 207 Crawfordsville Road.
BAMBERGER HERMAN, wholesale and retail dealer in Hats, Caps, Furs, &c., old Sentinel building, 16 E. Washington, res. W. side New Jersey, bet. Market and Ohio.
Bamberger Isaac, clerk, 3 E. Washington.
Banaclaus Rebecca, (wid.,) res. 45 E. Louisiana.
BANK OF THE STATE OF INDIANA, cor. Illinois and Kentucky ave. H. McCulloch, Pres't., James M. Ray, Cashier.
Banister S. L., shoemaker, res. 122 S. Noble.
Banks F. R., railroader, res. 66 S. Noble.
Bannon Andrew, moulder, res. 194 E. Ohio.
Bannister Purcell, stencil cutter, res. 31 Indiana ave.
Barbee Robert B., wagon maker, res. 165 N. East.
Barbee Sampson, res. N. Orient.
Barbour Lucian, (B. & Howland.) res. 107 N. Alabama.
Barbour Samuel, proprietor Barbour House, 29 and 31 N. Alabama.
BARBOUR & HOWLAND, attorneys at law, N. W. cor. Washington and Meridian.
Barger John, wagon maker, W. Indianapolis.
Barker Jerry, clerk, 56 E. Washington, bds. 149 N. Delaware.
BARKER THOS. D., (Featherston & B.,) res. 149 N Delaware.
Barkley James, laborer, res. 75 E. Merrill.
BARNARD J., agent for Downer, Bemis & Co.'s Champaigne Ale, 20 S. Meridian, res. 207 N. Illinois.
Barnett David, works in post office, bds. 123 N. New Jersey.
Barnett Isaac, res. 66 N. East.
Barner S., Union Dining Hall, 55 W. Washington, res. same.
Barnes A., clerk American Express Office, res. 24 S. Meridian.
Barnes Ellis, foreman Journal Office, res. 113 N. East.
BARNES H. F., physician, office Blake's building.
Barnes Jerome B., hack driver, res 216 S. Alabama.
Barnes William, patent agent, res. 66 N Delaware.
Barnham Wm., blacksmith, cor. Vermont and California.
Barnitz Charles, (Barnitz & Murphy,) res. 148 N. Illinois.
BARNITZ & MURPHY, real estate agents, 8 Temperance Hall.
Barnitz J. W., physician and taxidermist, bds. 148 N. Illinois.
Barnitt Thomas, grocer, 170 E. Washington, res. 183 Market.

The Wheeler & Wilson Hemmer is the only Hemmer that will sell.

S. C. FRINK,
DENTIST,

Office No. 4 Yohn's Block, Cor. Wash. & Meridian Sts.,
INDIANAPOLIS, INDIANA.

Would return his most sincere thanks to his friends and the public for their patronage of the past, hoping by a faithful performance of all work entrusted to him as a Surgeon or Mechanical Dentist, still to merit a continuance of the same.

He will be happy to meet, not only his old friends, but new ones—having added much to his facilities for the convenience and comfort of his numerous patrons, and also for the quick dispatch of all kinds of Dental work. From one tooth to a whole set inserted in a few hours. Every operation for the preservation and beauty of the human teeth, will be performed in the most careful and thorough manner.

CHLOROFORM GIVEN WHEN REQUIRED.

OFFICE HOURS FROM 8 A. M., TO 5 P. M.
Also, his celebrated

Oriental Tooth Powder,
For cleansing and beautifying the teeth, always on hand. Prices to correspond with the times, and all work warranted.

W. M. LOWRY,
DRUGGIST,

No. 49 Massachusetts Avenue,
INDIANAPOLIS, INDIANA.

General dealer in all kinds of Medicines,—Allopathic, Botanic, Eclectic and Concentrated, and all the most popular Patent Medicines of the day. Pure Drugs, Chemicals, Perfumery, Stationery, Toys, Notions and Fancy articles,

TOBACCO AND CIGARS,

Coal Oil, Burning Fluid, Candles, Soap, Teas, Brooms, Spices, Candies, Cider Vinegar, Paints, Oils, Dye Stuffs, Window Glass, Putty, Brushes, Bird Seed, Matches, Lamp Chimneys and Wicks, and in short almost any thing that may be found in a well filled

DRUG AND VARIETY STORE.

Physicians' Prescriptions filled with accuracy and dispatch. Pure Wines and Liquors for Medical Purposes.

Excelsior Weather Strips, and "Right" for sale.

First Premium awarded the Wheeler & Wilson Sewing Machine for three

Barnett Thomas, jr., clerk, 170 E. Washington, bds. 183 Market.
Barr Jabob, venitian blind maker, shop 86 N. Alabama, res. same.
Barrett Michael, laborer.
Barrett Patrick, laborer, res. 82 S. Noble.
Barrett Z. E., conductor Bellefontaine Railroad, bds. Palmer House.
Barry E. H., Grand Secretary Odd Fellows, res. cor. Tennessee and First.
Barry Ellen, (wid.,) 306 S. Delaware.
Barry John, laborer, res. 64 Huron.
Barry Thomas G., salesman, 40 E. Washington, bds. cor. First and Tennessee.
Barst Frederick, butcher, res. 65 E. Merrill.
Bart Daniel, milkman, res. 69 E. St. Marys.
Barth George, res. 198 Virginia ave.
BARTH REV. JOHN H., Methodist, res. 121 N. Alabama.
Barth Lewis A., porter E. C. Mayhew & Co., res. 198 Virginia ave.
Bartlett John M., cook Spencer House, res. 173 N. Mississippi.
Bartlett Joseph L., trader, res. 121 S. Tennessee.
Barwell Thomas, painter, bds. 151 N. Liberty.
Bass Love, (col.,) eating saloon, res. 22 Bates.
Bassett Mrs. Amanda, res. 20 E. Ohio.
Bassett H. H., clerk Frank Smith, res. cor. Pennsylvania and Ohio.
Bassett John, baker, res. 165 S. Delaware.
Bassett William, with J. F. Johnston, res. cor. Meridian and Maryland.
BATES CITY MILLS, J. Wash. Jefferies, proprietor, cor. Noble and Washington.
Bates Harvey, Sr., res. 67 E. Market.
BATES HARVEY, JR., (Wright, B. & Maguire,) res. cor. Madison ave. and Lincoln.
BATES HOUSE, cor. Washington and Illinois, William Judson, proprietor.
BATES HOUSE HAIR DRESSING SALOON, Henning & Stelzell, proprietors, Bates House, Illinois.
BATES HOUSE SALOON, under Bates House, Illinois.
BATTELLE REV. C. D., minister Wesley Chapel, res. 2 Circle.
Batty Edwin, carpenter, res. Broadway.
Batty John H., commissary 19th regiment U. S. A., res. 156 E. New York.
Bawde Andrew, in Central depot, res. 29 S. Alabama.
Bauer Mrs. J. V. R., res. 63 N. Illinois.

SUGAR GROVE DAIRY,
One Mile North of City.

JOHN O. REILY, - - Proprietor.

MILK, delivered in any part of the city at reasonable rates.

CALIFORNIA HOUSE,

By ADAM KISTNER,

No. 136 Illinois Street, near the Union Depot,
INDIANAPOLIS, IND.

FARE—Per Meal, 25 Cents; Per Day, 75 Cents. Wagon Yard for the Accommodation of Travelers.

JOHN F. MERRILL, M. D.,
156 West Washington St.

DR. MERRILL devotes his time exclusively to the treatment of Chronic Diseases, Scrofula, Rheumatism, Diseases peculiar to Females, Affections of the Liver, Secret Diseases, Fistula, Self Abuse, Female Obstructions, from whatever cause produced; Fits, Enlargement of Spleen, Scald Head, &c.—Diseases examined by Uriscopia, or Chemical Examination of the Urine, is desired. Remedial Agents wholly Eclectic. Office accessible day or night. No boys around.

ELIHU CULVER,
DEALER IN
GROCERIES & LIQUORS,
WHOLESALE AND RETAIL,
No. 142 West Washington Street, Indianapolis.

Wheeler & Wilson's Sewing Machines have been awarded the First Premium

Baugh Casper, butcher, res. 14 W. Garden.
Baxter William, (col.,) wood chopper, res. Howard.
Baylor James J., U. S. A., res. 258 S. Delaware.
BAYMILLER CHARLES P., local editor Daily State Sentinel, bds. 90 Massachusetts ave.
Beach W. B., res. 106 N. West.
Beal J. A. attorney at law, 6 Glenns' Block, res. 82 N. East.
Beale J., painter and paper hanger, res. 175 E. South.
Beam David, (Byrkit & B.,) carpenters, res. 125 S. Tennessee.
Beard Amos, plow maker, bds. 28 Indiana ave.
Beard Benjamin F., plow maker, bds. 28 Indiana ave.
Beard Salmon, (B. Starr & Co.,) res. 28 Indiana ave.
BEARD, STARR & CO., plow makers, 2 N. Tennessee.
Beasley John E., shoemaker, 32 E. Washington, res. 105 N. Tennessee.
Beatty Charles, assistant real estate agent, 13 S. Illinois, bds. 50 S. Mississippi.
BEATY DAVID S., President Indianapolis Gas Light and Coke Company, office Hubbard's Block, res. 80 E. Michigan.
Beck C., gunsmith, 15 S. Meridian, res. 80 N. New Jersey.
BECK E., proprietor Crystal Palace Saloon, 44 W. Washington.
Beck Frederick, butcher, cor. Bluff Road and McCarthy res. in rear.
Beck Jacob, gunsmith, res. cor. Alabama and St. Clair.
Beck John, cigar maker, 10 Bates House, bds. Union Hall.
Beck John A., watchmaker, Odd Fellows Hall, bds. W. H. Campbell.
Beck Jos. A., conductor Terre Haute Railroad, res. 69 W. South.
Beck Samuel, gunsmith, 86 E. Washington, res. 21 S. Delaware.
BECKER H., manufacturer and dealer in trunks, valises, &c., 30 W. Washington, res. 139 South Tennessee.
Becker Jacob, (Tapking & B.,) res. N. Pennsylvania, opp. Blind Asylum.
Beckman John, laborer, res. 208 S. Alabama.
BEECHWOOD NURSERY, J. F. Hill & Co., proprietors, office 44 N. Pennsylvania.
Beebe R., (B. & Hawes,) bds. Morris House.
BEEBE & HAWES, wholesale and retail grocers. 9 W. Washington.
Beehimer S. B., carpenter, 28 E. Georgia.
BEE HIVE DRY GOODS STORE, 2 W. Washington, Louis H. Tyler, proprietor.
Beerman John, porter Union Depot, res. 112 S. Noble.

For four successive years at the Am. Institute, New York.

F. P. CUNNINGHAM'S
Confectionary, Bakery and Ice Cream Saloon,

No. 43 Cor. Market and Illinois Streets,

INDIANAPOLIS, IND.

Every kind of Taffy kept constantly on hand. Oysters, Pigs' Feet, Chickens, Ham and Eggs, Sardines, &c.

Warm Meals at all hours, for 25 cents.

WASHINGTON HALL SALOON
AND RESTAURANT.

78 and 80 West Wash. St., INDIANAPOLIS, IND.

DIETZ & DAVIS, - **Proprietors.**

Beer, Wines, Ale, Liquors and Cigars always on hand. Oysters and Game in every style.

MACY HOUSE,
Cor. of Illinois and Market Streets,
INDIANAPOLIS, IND.

This is a new and first class House in all its departments, well situated, being in the center of the business part of the city, and well merits a liberal share of public patronage.

Terms, One Dollar per Day,
AND REASONABLE PER WEEK.

J. EDWARD REDFORD, Prop'r.

Wheeler & Wilson's Sewing Machines warranted for three years.

Beever E., carpenter, res. 182 Massachusetts ave.
Behimer Daniel, carpenter, res. 6 Willard.
Belger Joseph, carpenter, res. 154 E. New York.
Bell A., watch maker, 37 W. Washington, bds. E. Washington.
Bell Miletus, physician and surgeon, res. 124 N. Delaware.
Bell William, teamster, res. 74 N. Blackford.
Bellefontaine Railroad Line, office cor. Louisiana and Meridian.
Belles John, machinist, Western Machine Works.
Bellis Samuel, dealer in sewing machines, res. 110 N. New Jersey.
Bellous Elihu, blacksmith Western Machine Works, res. 171 N. Alabama.
Belzer George, laborer, res. 213 N. Alabama.
Belzner Michael, laborer, res. 193 S. Pennsylvania.
Bemiss D. S., book-keeper, Bates City Mills, bds. Little's Hotel.
Bender David, proprietor National Hotel, W. Washington.
Bender T., currier for John Fishback.
Bender Tobias, laborer, res. 131 E. Market.
Benham A. M., salesman 4 Bates House, bds. Macy House.
Benjamin D. O., (D. O. B. & Son,) res. 166 S. Alabama.
BENJAMIN D. O. & SON, Capital City File Works, Pennsylvania, one square E. of depot.
Benjamin Theodore, (D. O. B. & Son,) res. 166 S. Alabama.
Benjamin Thomas, file cutter, bds. 166 S. Alabama.
Benner James, laborer, res. 360 Virginia ave.
Bennet William, wood chopper, W. Indianapolis.
Bennett W. H., (Root, B. & Co.,) res. 119 N. Pennsylvania.
Benson Henry, egg packer, res. 51 Benton.
Benton Harvey, boiler maker Lawrenceburg car shop, res. E. National Road.
Berger Edward, cigar maker, bds. 41 Spring.
Berger V., porter Macy House.
Bergner G., assistant teller Indianapolis Branch Banking Company, bds. 93 Washington.
Beringer Joseph, bar-keeper St. Charles Saloon, bds. 157 Alabama.
Berry G. W., brakeman Central Railroad, res. 53 Benton.
Berry I. N., clerk Hoosier Woolen Factory, res. 244 W. Washington.
Berry John, laborer, res. 75 W. Vermont.
Berry Mary, res. 212 E. St. Clair.
Berry Michael, stone cutter, res. 46 Spring.
Berry Richard, laborer, res. 276 S. Delaware.
Berryman Eli, laborer, res. Duncan.
Berryman John, wagon maker, res. 50 S. Noble.

3

The Wheeler & Wilson Hemmer makes hems of any width.

LITTLE'S HOTEL SALOON
AND
RESTAURANT,

Under Little's Hotel,

Cor. of East Washington and New Jersey Streets,

INDIANAPOLIS, IND.

JOHN LEDLIE, - - - Proprietor.

A VERY FINE SELECTION OF

WINES, LIQUORS AND CIGARS

ALWAYS ON HAND.

Oysters & Game in their Season.

WM. HANNAMAN,
—DEALER IN—
PURE DRUGS
AND MEDICINES,

40 East Washington St., - - - INDIANAPOLIS.

Prescriptions carefully compounded by experienced clerks at all hours.

SPENCER & SOCWELL,
—DEALERS IN—
GROCERIES & PRODUCE,

No. 202 EAST WASHINGTON STREET.

Orders from the Country promptly filled and attended to.

Wheeler & Wilson's Sewing Machines awarded the first premium for five

Berryman William, blacksmith, res. 46 S. Noble.
Berwer John, huckster, res. 90 Davidson.
Bese Frederick, laborer, res. 144 N. Liberty.
Beskeng Christ., laborer, res. 58 Huron.
BESSONIES AUGUSTUS, Priest of St. Johns Church, res. Georgia, bet. Tennessee and Illinois.
Bettes W. R., clerk J. K. Sharpe, res. 24 Massachusetts ave.
Bevington Albert, plasterer, res. 192 N. Noble.
Biddle Wm., res. Orient.
Bidin C. W., dress maker, 165 E. Washington, res. same.
Biedenmeister, C. A., res. 59 N. East.
Bigelow Ira P., plasterer, res. 178 E. New York.
Bigelow J. S., deputy U. S. Marshall, res. cor. Tennessee and St. Clair.
Biner Wm. P., cigar maker for Chas. C. Hunt, res. Delaware, opp. Court House.
Bingham Jos., model maker, res. 50 Benton.
BINGHAM J. J., (Elder, Harkness & B.,) editor of Daily State Sentinel, res. 88 Maryland,
BINGHAM, W. P., (W. P. B. & Co.,) res. 53 N. Meridian.
BINGHAM W. P. & CO., watch makers and jewelers, 20 E. Washington.
Binkley Saml., prop. Marion Agricultural Works.
Bippus John, tailor, 16 N. Pennsylvania, res. 16 S. Pennsylvania.
Birch James, (B. & Farmer,)
Birch & Farmer, wholesale and retail grocers, 79 E. Washington.
Bird Abram, res. 95 N. Illinois.
Birk John, light factory, res. 154 N. New Jersey.
Birt David H., saddle and harness maker, res. Winston, bet. Michigan and Vermont.
Birkenmayer P. S., res. 60 N. Meridian.
Bisbing Chas., blacksmith, bds. 124 N. West.
Bisbing Jacob, depot marshal, res. 124 N. West.
Bishop Mrs, res. 193 N. New Jersey.
Bishop Wm., rolling mill, res. 17 Willard.
Blach Maria, res. 14 S. East.
Black Geo. H., carpenter, res. 121 W. Georgia.
Black James, res. 129 N. West.
Black John, Indiana Central R. R., bds. Bates House.
BLACKFORD'S BLOCK, S. E. cor. of Washington and Meridian.
Blades Cassunder, res. Tennessee, 1 square S. of Garden, near the Rolling Mill.
Blæs Nicholas, saloon, 48 S. Delaware.
Blain Jas. W., painter, res. 86 N. Mississippi.

Successive years at Mechanic's Institute, Cincinnati.

LOUIS LANG'S
RESTAURANT
AND SALOON,
No. 17 E. Washington St.,
INDIANAPOLIS, IND.

Choice Wines, Liquors and Cigars,
ALWAYS ON HAND.
OYSTERS AND GAME IN THEIR SEASON.

GEORGE FELLER,
—DEALER IN—

WATCHES, CLOCKS,
AND JEWELRY.
REPAIRING DONE ON SHORT NOTICE.
No. 67 WEST WASHINGTON ST.

JOHN CAVEN.
Attorney and Counselor at Law,
OVER No. 19 EAST WASHINGTON STREET,
INDIANAPOLIS, IND.

☞ Also, special attention given to the Collection of Claims throughout the State.

Wheeler & Wilson's Sewing Machines warranted for three years.

Blain Thos., works Washington Foundry, res. 95 W. New York.
Blair James M., harness maker, 198 W. Washington, res. same.
BLAKE'S BUILDING, cor. Washington and Kentucky ave.
Blake Jas. R.. clerk Rolling Mill, bds. 186 N. Tennessee.
Blake Jas., 186 N. Tennessee.
Blake John, plaining mill, res. 134 N. West.
Blake Wm., Quartermaster U. S. Army, res. 201 N. Tennessee.
Blake W. P., plumber, res. 134 N. West.
Blanc, Borst & Lake, Bates House meat market, 16 Bates House, Illinois.
Blanc John, (B., Borst & Lake,) res. 74 S. New Jersey.
Blanchard W. A., book-keeper McTaggart, Coffin & Co., bds. Bates House.
Bland Hiram, carpenter, res. 166 S. New Jersey.
Blank Antoine, clerk 142 E. Washington, bds. same.
Blank Peter, clerk 142 E. Washington, bds. same.
Blats F., cook Capital Saloon.
Blauvelt Daniel, horse farrier, res. 23 S. Delaware.
Blessing Benjamin, watchman Cincinnati Depot, res. 229 S. Alabama.
BLIND ASYLUM, North, bet. Pennsylvania and Meridian.
Blonge John, butcher at Bates House, res. 57 S. New Jersey.
BLOOD REV. CALEB, baptist, res. 11 Fort Wayne ave.
Bloom S., salesman, 3 E. Washington, bds. Palmer House.
Blue Cyrus, carpenter, res. 153 N. East.
Bly John, res. 119 E. Market.
Bly Perry, switchman, res. 32 N. East.
Blythe Samuel, laborer, res. 115 S. Alabama.
Boardman David, superintendent woolen factory, res. 125 W. New York.
Boaz Mrs. C. T., (wid.,) res. 20 W. North.
Boaz W. T., cashier I. & C. R. R., res. 20 W. North.
Bobbs Mrs. Elizabeth, res. 81 N. Pennsylvania.
Bobbs John S., physician and surgeon, office over Harrison' Bank.
Bock Christian, carpenter, res. 140 N. Alabama.
Bockemyer Henry, laborer, 334 Virginia ave.
Boden Ezra, laborer, 51 McCarthy.
Bodenhamer Wm., printer Journal Office, bds. Illinois.
Bodenmuller Leonard, blacksmith, res. 152 E. New York.
Boeen James, R. R. man, res. cor. Winston and Biddle.
Bœhm Gottlob C., works 17 Kentucky ave., bds. 28 Kentucky ave.
Bœnter Philip, in the army, res. 58 Hosbrook.

A Wheeler & Wilson Sewing Machine will last a life-time.

BATES HOUSE
MEAT MARKET
UNDER BATES HOUSE,
ILLINOIS STREET, - - INDIANAPOLIS, IND.

BLANC, BORST & LAKE, Propr's.

The best quality of Meats of all kinds always on hand.

JOSEPH BUTSCH,
ICE DEALER,
RESIDENCE, 48 WEST SOUTH STREET,

Will deliver ICE at all hours, to any part of the city on short notice, and the most reasonable terms. Having put up about 400 tons, he can supply all demands.

W. W. LEATHERS.   GEORGE CARTER.

LEATHERS & CARTER,
ATTORNEYS AT LAW & NOTARIES PUBLIC,
Office, No. 86 East Washington Street, North side, up-stairs, in the second building West of the Court House Square, INDIANAPOLIS.

Will practice Law in the Federal and State Courts; also, make Deeds, Mortgages, Leases, &c.; take Depositions, and attend promptly to the Collection of Claims and Settlement of Estates, and all kinds of Probate Business.

REFERENCES BY PERMISSION.—Hon. Sam. E. Perkins, Judge Supreme Court, Hon. John Coburn, Judge Court of Common Pleas, John C. New, Clerk of Circuit Court, Fletcher & Sharpe, A. & J. C. S. Harrison, Bankers, H. A. Fletcher, Merchant, Indianapolis; Hon. Henry S. Lane, U. S. Senator, Crawfordsville, Ind.

FRANCIS SMITH,
(LATE DELZELL & SMITH,)

Solicits the patronage of his friends in all kinds of business connected with a general

REAL ESTATE AGENCY.
NO SALE, NO PAY.

My stock of Farms, Houses, Vacant Lots, Business Houses, and Suburban Residences, is equal to any in the State. HOUSES TO RENT.

Office, No. 37 East Washington Street,
Second Door East of Glenns' Block, - - INDIANAPOLIS, INDIANA.

Bœrum Joseph S., mail agent Bellfontaine R. R., bds. 200 N. Illinois.
Bœs Wm., land office, res. 261 S. Pennsylvania.
BŒTTICHER JULIUS, editor and proprietor of Indiana Volksblatt, 130 E. Washington, res. same.
BOHLEN D. A., architect, Ætna Building, res, 41 Huron.
Bohlster Fred., wood sawyer, res. 89 W. New York.
Bolan Michael, works Rolling Mill, res. 39 Henry.
Bolan Wm., works carriage shop, res. 107 E. Vermont.
Bolen Wm., pressman Cullum & Stanage.
Bollinger James, salesman 70 E. Washington, bds. Ray House.
Bollman Fred., Cincinnati bakery and confectionery, 87 E. Washington, res. same.
Bolton Mrs. S. T., (wid.,) res. 58 S. Tennessee.
Bolty Henry, cooper, res. 184 N. Noble.
Bomheffer Henry, carpenter, 236 Madison ave.
Bond A., shoemaker, res. 20 W. St. Clair.
Boney Christian, carpenter, res. 18 N. East.
Bonham ——, 1st engineer Identical Mills.
Bonham P. H., engineer Hudnut's Hominy Mill, res. 114 E. Georgia.
Bonnet John H., fireman Central R. R., res. 55 Benton.
Boohome Wm., chair maker, bds. Meridian.
Bookter George, weaver, res. cor. California and Maryland.
Boots Mrs. Mary, (wid.,) res. Hosbrook.
Boots Wm., wood chopper, res. city limits.
Borst Frederick, (Blanc, B. & Lake,) res. 67 Merrill.
BOSTON STORE, Wm. Zeigler, proprietor, 10 E. Washington.
Bottcher Conrad, wood sawyer, res. 172 N. New Jersey.
BOUCHET ED., fancy dyer and scourer, one door N. of Bates House, res. same.
Bouf John, butcher, Eagle Grocery, cor. Illinois and Indiana ave., bds. 28 Kentucky ave.
Bourke Thomas, laborer, res. 266 Madison ave.
Bouryer Adrien, bar-keeper, 260 S. Delaware.
Bouvard Hannah, (wid.,) res. 136 N. Mississippi.
Bouyer William, (col.,) white washer, res. 53 W. Georgia.
Bovey Adrian, tinner, Root, Bennett & Co.
Bowen S. T., (B., Stewart & Co.,) res. 126 N. Illinois.
BOWEN, STEWART & CO., wholesale and retail books, stationery, &c., 18 W. Washington.
Bower Thomas, laborer, res. 21 on alley E. of S. East.
Bowler Martin, res. 2 Huron.
BOWLES THOMAS H., attorney at law, 10 E. Washington, bds. Bates House.

A. KAHN,
WHOLESALE & RETAIL CLOTHIER,
And Dealer in
Gents' Furnishing Goods, &c., &c.

8 East Washington St.,
INDIANAPOLIS, INDIANA.

HOGSHIRE & HUNTER,
Wholesale and Retail Grocers,
And Dealers in
PROVISIONS, COUNTRY PRODUCE, &C.
25 West Washington St.,
INDIANAPOLIS, IND.

PALMER HOUSE
SALOON,
Newly fitted up under the management of
R. F. YOUNG.
Choice Wines,
LIQUORS & CIGARS,
Constantly on hand.

Oysters and Game in their Season.

---

350 families in Indianapolis and vicinity use Wheeler & Wilson.

Bowman A., salesman 26 and 28 W. Washington, res. 50 W. Vermont.
Bowman Henry, tailor, 158 E. Washington.
Bowman Henry, brick moulder, res. 72 S. Noble.
Boyd D. M., groceries and provision, 39, res. 37 S. Meridian.
Boyd James, butcher, shop cor. North and Pennsylvania, res. 118 N. Alabama.
Boyd James T., physician and surgeon, res. 108 Indiana ave.
Boyles M. W., (Campbell & B.,) res. 60 Ohio.
Bracken Edward, cooper, res. 133 W. Maryland.
Bracken Thomas A., carpenter, res. St. Joseph, bet. Illinois and Meridian.
Brademier Christian, boss of repairs, Madison Railroad, res. 53 Union.
Brademier John F., teamster, res. Michigan, bet. New Jersey and East.
BRADEN WILLIAM, paper and stationery, 24 W. Washington, res. 191 W. Washington.
Braden David, U. S. A., res. 75 W. New York.
Bradford Dr. A., bds. Ohio House.
Bradley J. H., res. 69 N. Pennsylvania.
Bradley J. W., constable, res. 69 Benton.
Bradley James, laborer, res. 13 Union.
Brado Joseph, with M. H. Good.
Brado Thomas, grocer, res. cor. East and South, and Virginia ave.
Bradshaw James M., res. 57 N. Meridian.
Bradshaw John A., res. 12 E. Vermont.
Bradshaw J. William, res. 70 N. East.
Bradshaw Margaret, (wid.,) res. 161 S. Alabama.
BRADSHAW WILLIAM A., general freight agent Indiana Central Railway, res. 70 N. East.
Brady Patrick, fireman I & C. R. R., res. near cor. Orient, S. E. Michigan Road.
Bradymier Henry, laborer, res. 227 S. East.
Bragumier Thomas, student, bds. cor. Illinois and First.
Brah L., baker and grocer, 46 Ft. Wayne ave., res. same.
Braining Humphrey, carpenter, res. 295 S. Delaware.
Bramwell Z. T., railroader, res. 66 E. Merrill.
Bramwell John M., book-keeper 22 W. Washington, res 48 S. Mississippi.
BRANCH OF THE BANK OF THE STATE OF INDIANA, cor. Washington and Meridian, George Tousey, President; David E. Snyder, Cashier.; V. T. Malott, Teller.
Brand J. G., grocer, 25 Bluff Road, res. in rear.
Brando John H., Indiana Central R. R., res. 25 E. Georgia.
Brandt Christ., drayman for Root, Bennett & Co.

The Wheeler & Wilson Hemmer is the only Hemmer that will Fell.

CRYSTAL PALACE
RESTAURANT,

No. 44 West Wash. St.,

INDIANAPOLIS, IND.

EDWARD BECK, Prop'r.

JOHN FISHBACK,
Cash Dealer in
Hides, Oils and Leather,
Corner Meridian and Maryland Sts.
INDIANAPOLIS, INDIANA.
☞ Cash paid for all kinds of Leather in the rough.

FARMERS' HOTEL,
One Square North of Union Depot,
INDIANAPOLIS, IND.

H. E. BUEHRIG, Prop.   -   WM. QUINN, Clerk.

BOARD, ONE DOLLAR PER DAY.

81,000 Wheeler & Wilson's Sewing Machines in use in this country.

Brandum Samuel, Oriental hair-dressing saloon.
Branger Frederick, carpenter, res, 9 McCarthy.
Branian Andrew, workman at Rolling Mill, res. Missouri, S. of Canal.
Brannigan Patrick, laborer, bds. 43 Massachusetts ave.
Braty John, plow maker for Beard, Starr & Co., bds. Ohio House.
Bray John S., policeman, res. 94 N. East.
Bredemayer Christian, laborer, res. 146 Davidson.
Breen Michael, railroader, res. 169 Railroad.
Brenard William, ostler, Exchange stables.
Brenman John, porter at Postoffice, res. 356 Virginia ave.
Bretney William, Deputy Marshal, res. 48 S. Meridian.
Bretz Adam, grocer, 44 Louisiana, res. 40 S. Illinois.
Brewer Frederick, laborer, res. Winston, bet. Biddle and North.
Brewing William, mattress maker, res. 63 N. West.
BRENNINGER AUGUSTUS, grocer, W. Washington, res. same.
Bridehop Richard, teamster, res. 115 E. New York.
Briggs Mrs. Elizabeth, res. 269 Massachusetts ave.
Brigham Charles E., printer Sentinel office, bds. S. New Jersey, bet. South and Merrill.
Bright Mrs. E., boarding house, 45 N. Pennsylvania.
Bright Major, res. 45 N. Pennsylvania.
Brimmerman Caston, carriage maker, res. 9 Ft. Wayne ave.
Brimmerman Frederick, carriage maker, res. 123 N. Alabama.
Bringer William, cooper, res. 163 N. New Jersey.
Brink A. D., salesman 29 W. Washington.
Brink Frederick, driver for Speigel, Thoms & Co., res. 184 E. Vermont.
Brink William, tailor, res. bet. Davidson and Railroad.
Brinker August, grocery, 94 W. New York, res. same.
Brinkley Benj., wagon maker, Marion Agricultural Works, res. Tennessee, bet. Merrill and Norwood.
Brinkleman Emil, painter, workman at Washington Foundry, bds. 28 Kentucky ave.
Brinkman & Ruschaupt, livery and sale stable, 17 S. Delaware.
Brinkman C., (B. & Ruschaupt,) bds. 61 N. New Jersey.
Brinkmeyer George, salesman 82 W. Washington, res. 80 Davidson.
Brinkmeyer George, saloon keeper, res. 129 Davidson.
Brinkmeyer J. C., (J. C. B. & Co.,) res. 152 Liberty.
BRINKMEYER J. C. & Co., importers and wholesale dealers in foreign and domestic liquors, tobacco and cigars, 82 W. Washington.

Upwards of 100 W. & W. Machines in use in Ind'p'lis making army clothing.

BATES CITY MILLS,
COR. WASHINGTON AND NOBLE STS.,
INDIANAPOLIS, INDIANA.

ST. CHARLES RESTAURANT,
BILLIARD SALOON & SHOOTING GALLERY,
NO. 86 E. WASHINGTON ST.
INDIANAPOLIS, INDIANA.

Choice Wines, Liquors and Cigars; Oysters and Game in their season.

F. GŒPPER'S
CLOTHING
And Merchant Tailoring Establishment,
No. 15 E. WASHINGTON ST.,
ONE DOOR EAST OF HARRISON'S BANK,
INDIANAPOLIS, IND.

Keeps constantly on hand a well assorted stock of ready-made Clothing and Furnishing Goods, which he sells at the lowest prices.

H. BECKER,
TRUNK
MANUFACTURER,
No. 30 West Washington Street,
Under Temperance Hall,
INDIANAPOLIS, IND.

Trunks, Valises, Ladies' Bonnet Boxes, Carpet Bags, &c., wholesale and retail. Trunks made to order. Trunks repaired on fair and reasonable terms.

Wheeler & Wilson's Sewing Machines have been awarded the First Premium

Brinkmeyer John, liquors, Washington, res. 152 N. Liberty.
Brinkmire Fred., laborer, res. 127 Davidson.
Brison Mrs. Julia, seamstress, res. 130 Davidson.
Brison J. W., assistant in Quartermaster's department, bds. Oriental House.
Bristor Samuel M., carriage maker, res. 51 N. Delaware.
Brit Thos., workman at Rolling Mill, bds. 188 S. Tennessee.
Britney W. H., telegraph operator, Bellefontaine Railroad Line, bds. 48 S. Meridian.
Brittingham Mrs. Hettie, res. 18 N. Illinois.
Broadrich Mrs. Mary,(wid.,) res. 9 N. Ellsworth.
Broden James, moulder, res. 119 E. New York.
Broden John, res. 117 E. New York.
Broden Michael, printer, bds. 117 E. New York.
Broder Mrs. Ellen, res. Mississippi, bet. South and Henry.
Brodrick Patrick, bar-keeper Exchange restaurant.
Brok Richard, drayman, res. E. Wyoming.
Broking Charles, drayman, res. 27 Union.
Bronson G. W., principal 5th ward school, res. Oak near Church.
Bronson Robert T., carpenter, res. 103 N. Alabama.
BROOKS REV. ASAHELL L., Fourth Presbyterian, res. 89 E. Ohio.
Brooks Bennet, carpenter, res. Massachusetts ave. near North.
Brooks Bryant, barber, bds. 116 Georgia.
Brooks Mrs. Hannah, (wid.,) W. Indianapolis.
Brooks Mrs. Helen, dress-maker, res. 14 N. New Jersey.
Broomer Francis, laborer, 180 S. Pennsylvania.
Broomer Frederick, painter, res. 173 E. Ohio.
Brotz Adam, grocery, res. 82 S. Illinois.
Brotz John, blacksmith, 86 W. Washington, bds. 28 Indiana ave.
Brough G. W., butcher, res. 32 Davidson.
BROUGH JOHN, general superintendent Bellefontaine R. R., bds. Morris House.
Brouse Andrew, carpenter, res. 60 E. New York.
Brouse C. W., salesman, 70 E. Washington, bds. 38 E. Market.
Brouse David W., carpenter, bds. 60 E. New York.
BROUSE REV. J. A., Methodist, res. 38 E. Market.
Brown Arnst, res. 168 N. Noble.
BROWN AUSTIN H., local editor Indianapolis Daily Journal, and attorney for soldiers' claims, res. S. Meridian.
Brown C. F., superintendent Indianapolis gas light and coke company, bds. Long's boarding house, Maryland.
Brown E. A., conductor B. & I. R. R., bds. Bates House.

C. SPIEGEL,   F. THOMS,   H. FRANK,   A. SPIEGEL.

SPIEGEL, THOMS & CO.,

MANUFACTURERS,
WHOLESALE & RETAIL
Dealers in all Kinds of

FURNITURE,
AND CHAIRS.

Warerooms, No. 73 W. Washington St.,
INDIANAPOLIS, INDIANA.

Union Hall
111, 113, 115 and 117, East Washington Street,
INDIANAPOLIS, IND.

MATTHIAS EMMENEGGER, - Prop'r.

Boarders kept

By the Day or Week.

Three first class

Billiard Tables.

CHOICE WINES,
LIQUORS
And Cigars,
ALWAYS ON HAND.

First Premium awarded the Wheeler & Wilson Sewing Machine for

Brown George, carpenter, res. 168 N. Alabama.
Brown H. C., carpenter, res. Illinois, cor. Fourth.
Brown H. M., conductor Jeffersonville R. R., bds. Palmer House.
BROWN IGNATIUS, attorney at law and notary public, 19½ E. Washington, res. 151 East.
Brown I. F., tinner 5 Virginia ave., res. 168 N. Alabama.
Brown James, paper hanger, res. 135 N. Alabama.
Brown James H., druggist, res. 70 N. Alabama.
Brown Jerry, (col.,) engineer Sentinel office, res 151 N. Alabama.
Brown John, plasterer, res. 182 N. Liberty.
Brown John, shoemaker, shop and res. Tennessee, S. of Garden.
Brown John G., grocer, 150 N. New Jersey, res. 144 N. New Jersey.
Brown John H., tinner, bds. 168 N. Alabama.
Brown John L., County Treasurer, office county building, res. 67 N. New Jersey.
Brown John W., baker, shop 150 N. New Jersey, res. same.
Brown J. W., res. 22 N. Meridian.
Brown Latham B., bds. 15 S. Mississippi.
Brown Mrs. Mary, washer, res. 149 E. Market.
BROWN P. A., attorney at law, 24 E. Washington, res. 130 N. New Jersey.
Brown Pat., laborer, res. 174 S. Delaware.
Brown Phillip, lumber merchant, res. 275 Massachusetts ave.
BROWN R. D., State Librarian, res. 15 Mississippi, Hammond's Block.
Brown Richard, machinist, res. 51 N. New Jersey.
Brown Ryland T., professor natural science North Western Christian University, res. Ft. Wayne ave.
Brown Samuel, (col.,) white-washer, res. alley, bet. Illinois and Tennessee.
Brown Willis, farmer, res. 116 W. Georgia.
BROWN W. P., fur and silk hat manufacturer, 20 Kentucky ave., bds. Tully House, 79 S. Illinois.
Browning Edmond, land office agent, res. 88 Virginia ave.
Browning George T., clerk Quartermaster's department, res. 107 Indiana ave.
BROWNING ROBERT, wholesale and retail druggist, 22 W. Washington, res. 102 N. Illinois.
Brubaker H. W., clerk 18 S. Meridian, res. 127 N. Pennsylvania.
Brueggemann William, tailor, res. 192 E. Ohio.
Bruening E., (E. & J. B.,) bds. at Walks.
BRUENING E. J., daguerrean artists, 6 E. Washington.

Successive years at the United States Fair.

MAGNOLIA SALOON
AND
RESTAURANT,
No. 9 South Illinois Street,
INDIANAPOLIS, IND.

S. A. FLAGG, - - - Proprietor.

The very best quality of all kinds of

Liquors & Cigars

ALWAYS ON HAND.

A. J. HINESLEY,
SADDLE & HARNESS MAKER,

Keep constantly on hand all kinds of Ladies' and Gentlemen's Riding Saddles, Bridles, Martingales, Whips, Spurs and Stirrups, Coach, Buggy, Express and Wagon Harness, Horse Clothing of every description, for all seasons, Fly Nets and Rubber Covers, together with a large and well assorted stock of

SADDLERY HARDWARE.

Military Equipments made to order at short notice. Country harness makers will find here a good assortment of everything connected with the business, which we will sell at CINCINNATI OR NEW YORK PRICES. ☞ REPAIRING DONE AT SHORT NOTICE.

34 West Washington St., - - INDIANAPOLIS.

NEBRASKA SALOON,
No. 12 Louisiana Street, Opposite Union Depot,
INDIANAPOLIS, IND.,
NALTNER & NALTNER, Propr's.

Keep constantly on hand a general assortment of the best

LIQUORS, WINES, BEER AND ALE,

Mixed Drinks, Cigars, Tobacco, &c.

A Wheeler & Wilson Sewing Machine with Hemmer, for $50.

Bruening J. (E. & J. B.,) bds. at Walks.
Bruff Geo. W., butcher, res. 32 Davidson.
Bruff John. railroader, res. 217 S. Alabama.
Brummer Prof. C., res. 12 E. Michigan.
Brumley Wm., laborer, 192 N. New Jersey.
Brundage E. C., clerk Beebe & Hawes, res. 167 E. Market.
Bruner Charles, manufacturer and dealer in boots, shoes, &c., 33 W. Washington, res. 112 S. New Jersey.
Brunes Henry, laborer, res. 186 N. New Jersey.
Brunger James, boss weaver Ohio Premium Woolen Factory.
Brunkum Henry, laborer, res. W. Elizabeth.
Brunner Roman, machinist, res. 14 S. Illinois.
Bryant Alexander, foreman Bellefontaine car shop, res. 173 S. New Jersey.
Bryant B. F., salesman 17 E. Washington, res. 111 W. South.
Bryant's Commercial College, Ætna Building, Wm. Purdy, Principal.
Bryant James, res. 113 W. South.
Bryant James G., bds. Mrs. Smith, Alvord's Block.
Bryant W. L., res. 111 and 113 W. South.
Bryant William, wood-chopper, res. 111 W. South.
Brykit William, workman at woolen factory, res. 135 W. Market.
Bryson James W., superintendent U. S. warehouse, bds. Oriental House.
Bachann James M., (Richmond & B.,) res. 14 Fletcher's ave.
Buchanan Cyrus F., carpenter, res. 14 S. West.
Buchanan G. W., U. S. A., res. 83 S. East.
Buchanan James M., wagon maker, Fletcher's ave.
Buchanan John, laborer, res. W. of Terre Haute depot.
Buchanan John A., mailing clerk postoffice, res. 26 S. Mississippi.
Buchanan Oliver, brickmason, res. 52 Indiana ave.
Buchanan Thomas, (Hawthorne & B.,) res. E. Washington.
Buche Fred., boots and shoes, 104 S. Illinois, res. same.
Bucher Henry, saloon 51 South, res. in rear.
Buchholtz Fred., cigar maker, 35 W. Washington.
Buchhorn Christ., wagon maker, 156 S. Delaware, res. bet. Alabama and New Jersey.
Buck Charles, railroader, res. Biddle, near city limits.
Bucker John, marble dresser, res. 57 St. Joseph.
Buckharst Fred., cigar maker, res. 197 N. Illinois.
Buckley John, ostler, bds. 20 S. Pennsylvania.
Buckmar Frank W., bds. Palmer House.
Bucksot William, res. 84 E. Market.
Buckstatler Martin, confectioner, bds. 50 W. South.
Buckstatler Mrs. Sarah, (wid.,) res. 50 W. South.

A Wheeler & Wilson Sewing Machine will last a life-time.

Capital Steam Printing House.

WILLIAM S. CAMERON,

BOOK AND CARD PRINTER.

POSTERS, LEASES,
BILL HEADS,
Cards, Contracts,
LABELS, RECEIPTS,
CIRCULARS,
Deeds, Mortgages,

PLAIN OR IN COLORS.

☞ No Newspaper in connection with this Establishment.

No. 8 PEARL STREET, INDIANAPOLIS, IND.

All Work Done When Promised.

NEATNESS.   DISPATCH.

First Premium awarded the Wheeler & Wilson Sewing Machine for three

Budane Louis, tailor, res. 190 Pennsylvania.
Budd Milton, brick maker, res. Winson, cor. North.
Buddenbaum Henry, carpenter, res. 206 E. Ohio.
Budenz Henry, (H. B. & Co.,) 144 W. Washington, res. 190 S. Pennsylvania.
Budenz Lewis, (H. B. & Co.,) res. 190 S. Pennsylvania.
Budenz H. & Co., merchant tailors, 144 W. Washington.
BUEHRIG H. E., proprietor Farmers' Hotel, cor. Illinois and Georgia.
Buehrig William, bds. Farmers' Hotel.
Buenagel Fr., baker Union Steam Bakery.
Buff N. G., attorney at law, res. 177 South.
Bufkins John C., district prosecuting attorney, office 43½ E. Washington, res. 129 Massachusetts ave.
Bugby L. M., warehouse, res. 38 S. Pennsylvania.
Bugg Nathan, (col.,) cook Morris House.
Buist Thomas, 125 N. Illinois.
Buler John, blacksmith, bds. National Hotel.
Bulker Myrer, laborer, McCarthy, near Virginia ave.
Bullard Charles G., furniture finisher, res. S. East, S. of South.
Bullard Talbot, physician and surgeon, 23 S. Meridian, res. 87 E. Ohio.
Bullard Wm. R., physician, 23 S. Meridian, bds. 87 E. Ohio.
Bunink William, laborer, res. 93 Bluff Road.
Bunte John B., carpenter, res. 118 N. Mississippi.
Burch Wm., grocer, res. Orient.
Burdick Wm. P., merchant, res. 101 N. Meridian.
Burges C. N., printer Journal office, res. 121 N. East.
Burgess Lloyd A., saddler, 20 W. Washington, res. 164 N. Tennessee.
Burgess Samuel J., harness maker at Sulgrove & Reynolds', res. 164 N. Tennessee.
Burgner John, basket maker, res. 17 Chatham.
Burgoyne Stephen, cigar maker, 38 Louisiana opp. Union depot, bds. California House.
Burk Eli, saloon, W. Indianapolis.
Burke Frederica, (wid.,) res. 105 E. South.
BURK GEORGE, eating saloon, 13 W. Washington, res. 107 E. Ohio.
Burk Henry, workman at Washington Foundry, res. 156 S. Tennessee.
Burk John, coal dealer, res. 148 N. Tennessee.
Burk William, tailor, 144 E. Washington.
Burk William, bds. 148 N. Tennessee.
Burke Henry, stone mason, res. 274 S. Delaware.
Burke L. L., printer Sentinel office, bds. Pyle House, cor. Illinois and Maryland.

BEEBE & HAWES,

Wholesale and  Retail Dealers in

Fancy & Staple Groceries,
PROVISIONS AND CONFECTIONERIES.
FRUIT AND GAME IN THEIR SEASONS.

Head Quarters for Mann & Co.'s Baltimore Oysters.

CASH PAID FOR COUNTRY PRODUCE.

Orders from the Country promptly filled. Goods delivered free of charge.

DEPOT, No. 9 West Washington St.

The First Premium awarded the Wheeler & Wilson Machine

Burkhart Andrew J., painter, res. 146 N. Mississippi.
Burley G. W., salesman Boston Store, bds. 15 E. Ohio.
Burnes John, teamster, Carlisle Model Mills.
Burnett J. C., assistant deputy Auditor of State, res. 123 N. Delaware.
Burnett W. H., res. 119 N. Pennsylvania.
Burnham N. G., physician and surgeon, 4 Yohn's Block, res. same.
Burns John, blacksmith, shop 158 S. Delaware, bds. Market, bet. Noble and Davis.
Burns Michael, laborer, res. 46 Massachusetts ave.
Burns Patrick, laborer, res. 1 Willard.
Burns W. V., attorney, 38½ W. Washington, res. 231 N. Tennessee.
Burns William, rope maker, res. S. West.
Burrows G. W., auction and sale stable, 14 N. Pennsylvania, res. 142 Virginia ave.
Burst Thos., res. 125 N. Illinois.
Burt A. S., Burt's Restaurant, 13 S. Illinois, res. same.
Burt Gabriel, (col.,) laborer, res. Seventh.
Burt's Restaurant, A. S. Burt, proprietor, 13 S. Illinois.
Burton George K., cooper, 78 N. West, res. 78 N. Mississippi.
Burton John C., clerk 3 Bates House, res. 221 New Jersey.
Busch Adam, carpenter, res. 148 N. Mississippi.
Busch Christian, boots and shoes, 138 W. Washington, res. same.
Busee Samuel, railroader, res. 60 W. Louisiana.
Bush George B., physician, res. 143 Virginia avenue.
Bush George M., (B & Hannum,) bds. Oriental House.
BUSH JACOB, ten-pin alley and billiard saloon, 246 and 248 E. Washington, res. 250 E. Washington.
BUSH & HANNUM, City Saloon, 53 and 55 S. Illinois.
Bussell E. T., solicitor of patents, res. 19 S. Mississippi.
Bussell Wm. M., receiving clerk at arsenal, bds. 19 S. Mississippi.
Bussey John, Verandah saloon, opp. Union depot, res. 144 W. Maryland.
Busswell John, carpenter, 90 S. Delaware, res. cor. Buchannan and Wright.
Butch Peter, U. S. A., res. 26 Union.
Butler Charles, compositor at Cameron's job office.
Butler John, brakeman I. & C. R. R., res. 20 Lord.
Butler Mrs. Margaret, book-folder, res. 117 N. Alabama.
Butler Ovid, res. Forest Home ave., near University.
Butler Ovid D., assistant deputy clerk, res. 119 N. New Jersey.
Butler Scott, tinner, 69 W. Washington.
Butsch George M., grocer, res. 173 S. Delaware.

GLENNS' BLOCK,
INDIANAPOLIS, IND.

(*See Engraving, opposite page.*)

This new and elegant block, erected and owned by Wm. Glenn, H. Glenn, and R. P. Glenn, is situated on the south side of Washington, between Meridian and Pennsylvania streets, occupying the site of the old Browning Hotel, afterwards called the Wright House. It is three and a half stories high, being 68 feet front on Washingon street, and extending back to Pearl street, containing three store rooms and eight offices; the side stores are $17\frac{1}{2}$ feet wide and 132 feet deep. The center store, known as THE NEW YORK STORE, is occupied by the proprietors of the block, W. & H. Glenn & Co., and is $32\frac{1}{2}$ feet in width by 132 feet in depth. This store is the mammoth dry goods establishment of the State. The offices are occupied by the city authorities, namely: His Honor the Mayor, City Treasurer, City Clerk, Civil Engineer, Street Commissioner, Chief Fire Engineer, City Attorney, City Marshal and Police, with a chamber for the meetings of the City Council. Store south of entrance in American Alley, is occupied by the Cincinnati Gas Fitting Co. The office, corner of Pearl street and American alley, is occupied by T. A. Goodwin, publisher of the *Indiana American*, the only evening paper in the city. One store, (that on the east), is occupied by Merrill & Co., dealers in law books, stationery, &c. The one on the west side is occupied as a shoe store by Cady & Co. The appearance of this block is very attractive, chaste and elegant, without a fault, and is an ornament to our main street. It was rebuilt at a cost to the Messrs. Glenn of forty-five thousand dollars.

Wheeler & Wilson's Sewing Machines have been awarded the First Premium

GLENNS' BLOCK, INDIANAPOLIS, INDIANA.

For four successive years at the Am. Institute, New York.

INDIANA STATE JOURNAL
MAMMOTH STEAM
Printing Establishment

SOUTH-EAST COR. MERIDIAN AND CIRCLE STREETS, INDIANAPOLIS, IND.

THE JOURNAL OFFICE IS PREPARED TO DO ALL KINDS OF

BOOK AND JOB WORK
NEATLY, PROMPTLY AND ACCURATELY,

Being supplied with a number of fast Presses, running by steam. Every description of Printing can be done on short notice and quick time. We have in successful operation one of GEO. P. GORDON'S FIRE-FLY PRESSES, CAPABLE OF PRINTING FROM 8,000 TO 20,000 CARDS PER HOUR. We can furnish Printed Cards, when ordered in large quantities, at cheaper rates than other establishments in Indiana can buy the unprinted Cards at Stationery Stores.

ADVERTISING.

THE DAILY AND WEEKLY JOURNAL furnish the best medium in the State for Merchants and others to advertise their business through. It circulates in every county in the State, and has the heaviest local circulation of any paper published in Indianapolis.

JOURNAL COMPANY, Indianapolis, Ind.

The Wheeler & Wilson Hemmer makes hems of any width.

CITY DIRECTORY.   57

Butsch John, res. 42 W. South.
BUTSCH JOSEPH, ice dealer, res. 48 W. South.
BUTSCH VALENTINE, lime and coal merchant, opp. Madison depot, N. side of South, res. 42 W. South.
Butterfield Cyrus, printer, bds. Tully House.
Butterfield E. L., printer, bds. 149 N. East.
BUTTERFIELD J., agent American and United States Express Companies, bds. 95 N. Tennessee.
Butterfield John W., printer, res. 73 N. New Jersey.
Butterfield J. M., apprentice Journal office, bds. 149 N. East.
Butterfield Moreno, patent honey maker, res. 149 N. East.
Byram N. S., (Tousey & B.,) res. 84 E. Ohio.
Bynon Thomas, wood sawyer, res. 241 Massachusetts ave.
Byrkin Phillip, carpenter, res. 81, N. New Jersey.
Byrkit Frank, clerk, 14 Illinois, res. 81 South.
Byrkit John W., carpenter, (B. & Beam,) res. Norwood, bet. Illinois and Tennessee.
Byrkit Ed., works for Byrkit & Beam, bds. 68 S. Tennessee.
Byrkit Martin, (B. & Beam,) res. 68 S. Tennessee.
BYRKIT SOCRATES M., wood engraver, 19 W. Washington, bds. 81 N. New Jersey.
Byrkit & Beam, planing mill and sash and blind factory, 60 S. Tennessee.

C

Cader John, shoemaker, res 89 S. East.
Cady Mrs. Abby A., res. 4 Circle.
Cady David L., (C. & Co.,) res. 92 N. New Jersey.
CADY & CO., manufacturers and dealers in boots and shoes, Glenns' Block.
Cahill Michael, laborer, res. 52 N. Liberty.
Cahill John S., Wabash, bet. Liberty and Noble.
Cain John, broker, office in Dodd & Co.'s building, res. cor. East and Wood.
Cain Dennis, works Washington Foundry, res. 88 E. Georgia.
Cain Geo. W., book-binder, works H. H. Dodd & Co.'s, bds. 135 West Market.
Cairns John, laborer, res. 100 E. Market.
Calaban Michael, laborer, res. 23 E. Georgia.
Calaghan Stephen, salesman New York Store, bds. Macy House.
Cale Dennis, porter Bates House.
Calhaine James (col.,) cook Telegraph Restaurant.
CALIFORNIA HOUSE, Adam Kistner, proprietor, 136 and 138 S. Ill.

Upwards of 100 W. & W. Machines in use in Ind'p'lis making army clothing.

Wheeler & Wilson's Sewing Machines awarded the first premium for five

CITY DIRECTORY.   59

LEWIS W. HASSELMAN.   ALMUS E. VINTON.

HASSELMAN & VINTON,
MANUFACTURERS OF
Agricultural Implements,
Horse Powers, Threshers and Separators, Sugar Mills,

Steam Engines,
Grist and Saw Mill Machinery, Shaftings, Pulleys, Hangers, Gearing, Castings of all kinds, Wrought-Iron Work, Bridge Bolts and Castings,

BOILERS AND CHIMNEYS,
Sheet-Iron Work, Water Wheels, Foundry and Machine Work in general.

[See Engraving, opposite Page.]

Successive years at Mechanic's Institute, Cincinnati.

DAILY AND WEEKLY
INDIANA
State Sentinel
STEAM PRINTING HOUSE,

South-West Cor. of Washington and Meridian Sts.,

INDIANAPOLIS, IND.,

ELDER, HARKNESS & BINGHAM, - - Proprietors.

THE WEEKLY INDIANA STATE SENTINEL

Is the largest

Family Newspaper
PRINTED IN THE WEST.

Weekly Sentinel, one year, in advance, - - - $1 00
Daily Sentinel, one year, in advance, - - - 6 00

Possessing facilities unsurpassed by any Establishment in the West, we are prepared to do all kinds of

BOOK & JOB PRINTING

On the most reasonable terms. Our assortment of Types and Printing Material is large and complete, with

Steam Power Presses
OF THE LATEST IMPROVEMENT.

Orders for all kinds of Plain and Decorative Job Printing and Book Work are solicited, which will be promptly filled.

The Wheeler & Wilson Hemmer is the only Hemmer that will Fell.

Callaghan Julia A., (wid.,) res. 241 Dennis, rear.
Callahan Michael, laborer, res. 27 N. Ellsworth.
Callaham John, at engine house, res. 101 E. South.
CALLINAN DANIEL J., dealer in dry goods, &c., (see card) 28 E. Washington, bds. Dr. Gatlin.
Cambron George, brick moulder, res. 285 S. East.
CAMERON WM. S., book and Job printer, 8 E. Pearl, res. 116 N. Alabama.
Camilla, Sister of Providence, N. E.cor. Georgia and Tennessee.
Campbell Andrew, tailor, res. West, bet. Maryland and Georgia.
Campbell Charles, res. 2 North.
Campbell Sam. L., book-binder, bds. 2 North.
Campbell Samuel, messenger Indianapolis Branch Banking Co., res. 11 Virginia ave.
Campbell Thos. S., (C. & Boyles,) res. 79 N. Meridian.
Campbell Wm., bds. 8 Virginia ave.
Campbell W. H., clerk in post office, res. 8 Virginia ave.
Campbell W. L., lawyer, (at Sinking Fund,) bds. 24 N. Mississippi.
CAMPBELL & BOYLES, book-binders, 27 E. Washington.
Canby John, assistant superintendent Bellefontaine R. R., Line, res. Bellefontaine, Ohio.
Cane Patrick, soldier, res. 265 S. Delaware.
Cauley Thos. res. 31 South.
Cannall Augustus, marble dresser, res. 227 S. Alabama.
Cantrill D. M., printer Journal Office, res. 50 W. Vermont.
CAPITAL STEAM JOB OFFICE, Wm. S. Cameron proprietor, 8 E. Pearl.
Cardell William, clerk 72 E. Washington, bds. with E. E. Holland.
Carico John, carpenter, res. 54 Indiana ave.
Carlisle D. W., agent Central R. R., res. 46 W. Walnut.
Carlisle Hamilton, flour packer Carlisle's Model Mills.
Carlisle John, (John C. & Son,) res. 204 W. Washington.
Carlisle John & Son, flour and feed store, 68 W. Washington.
Carlisle's Model Mills, John Carlisle, proprietor, 254 W. Washington.
Carlisle H. D., (John C. & Son,) res. 240 W. Washington.
CARMICHAEL J. D., proprietor Palmer House, cor. Washington and Illinois.
Carney Wm., porter Farmers' Hotel.
Carper Thomas, railroader, res. W. Market.
Carr Michael, shoemaker, bds. Pat. Burns.
Carral W. H., farmer, res. 176 E. South.
Carroll Miss Annie, cloak maker with Miss Moon.

Wheeler & Wilson's Sewing Machines warranted for three years.

INDIANAPOLIS

THE
INDIANA AMERICAN,
DAILY AND WEEKLY.

THE INDIANA AMERICAN BEING THE ONLY

Regular Evening Paper,

IN INDIANAPOLIS.

And being devoted largely to Family Reading, it has such a circulation among families as constitutes it an excellent

ADVERTISING MEDIUM.

TERMS OF ADVERTISING REASONABLE.

THE WEEKLY

Circulates among the principal

Farmers and Workingmen

Of the State, more exclusively than any other Weekly.

A Wheeler & Wilson Sewing Machine with Hemmer, for $50.

Carroll Grunull, Carroll's Saloon, 11 N. Illinois, bds. same.
Carroll Miss Belle, private school under Associate Reformed Church, Ohio, bet. Pennsylvania and Delaware.
Carter Alex., (col.,) laborer, res. Howard.
Carter Charles E., policeman, res. 89 N. Illinois.
Carter George, (Leathers & C.,) res. 113 N. Alabama.
Carter Henry, carpenter, res. W. Georgia, bet. Missouri and West.
Carter John, salesman Boston Store, bds. 15 E. Ohio.
Carter L. L., cooper, W. Indianapolis.
Carton Andrew, laborer, res. on S. East.
Cartright Mrs. Alice, res. 131 W. Vermont.
Case John B., engineer, res. 75 N. Noble.
Cassady Isaac N., produce dealer, res. 165 N. Liberty.
Casselbaum Frederick, wood sawyer, res. Winston, N. of Biddle.
Casselberry Mary, dressmaker, res. 181 Massachusetts ave.
Castlin L., barkeeper East Empire Saloon, bds. 24, cor. Market and New Jersey.
Cathcart Andrew, res. 162 S. New Jersey.
Cathcart Robert W., clerk Merrill & Co., bds. 162 S. New Jersey.
Catlin Ebenezer, laborer, res. W. Market.
Catterson Abe., policeman, res. 56 S. Noble.
Catterson Cy. W., carpenter, res. 91 N. Meridian.
Catterson James, policeman, res. 241 Indiana ave.
Catterson R. F., tinner, 69 W. Washington, bds. Pyle House.
Cattizer Caroline, (wid.,) res. Stephens.
Cattizer Kinder, at peg and last factory, res. Stephens.
Caughlin Patrick, laborer, res. 78 S. Noble.
Caulfield Miss Rosanna, school teacher, bds. 104 N. Mississippi.
CAVEN JOHN, attorney at law, 19½ E. Washington, bds. Bates House.
Cavenaugh Mat., laborer, res. Missouri, S. of South.
Caylor Anthony, pedlar, res. 158 N. Noble.
Caylor Frank, hackman, res. 74 N. Noble.
Caylor Otho, coffee stand in East market, res. 125 E. Market.
CAYLOR SANTFORD, saloon, 220 E. Washington, res. same.
Central Restaurant, 6 W. Washington, Henry Shaub, proprietor.
Ceritzer Henry, laborer, res. 262 Madison ave.
Chaboude Lewis, barkeeper Beck's Saloon, res. 264 S. Delaware.
Chamberlin Jas., farmer, res. cor. Tennessee and Second.
Chambers Abram, engineer, res. 79 Massachusetts ave.

81,000 Wheeler & Wilson's Sewing Machines in use in this country.

OLIVER W. JOHNSTON,
LIVERY, SALE

AND
BOARDING STABLES,
PEARL STREET,

Between Illinois and Meridian,

INDIANAPOLIS, IND.

CARRIAGES AND HORSES
BOUGHT AND SOLD.

Carriages to let at all times.

Chambers Mrs. Frances, Bee-Hive Store, bds. 31 N. Meridian.
Chandler Eliza Mrs., res. 72 W. Maryland.
Chandler George, printer Journal office, bds. 72 W. Maryland.
Chandler Henry C., printer, 8 E. Washington, bds. 258 W. Washington.
Chandler Thomas, res. 169 N. Mississippi.
Chandler Thomas E., (Wiggins & C.,) res. 258 W. Washington.
Chandler Wm. G., pattern maker, bds. 258 W. Washington.
Chapman D. C., painter, res. 65 S. Pennsylvania.
Chapman Major Geo. H., U. S. A., res. 37 W. Ohio.
Chapman R., W. Indianapolis.
Chapman Samuel, peddler, res. 19 Bates.
Chapman Thomas, carpenter, res. Spring, cor. North.
Charles John, Central Mills, res. 105 N. Meridian.
Charles Thomas, hack driver, res. 75 E. Georgia.
Chase A. E., mail agent, res. 99 Virginia ave.
Chase James F., conductor on the Bellefontaine R. R., res. 235 S. Delaware.
Chase Joseph W., Madison R. R., res. 223 S. Delaware.
Cheeks Omer, farmer, res. 121 Bluff Road.
Chester Albert A., stair builder, res. Duncan.
Childers J. P., pump maker, shop in rear of German Catholic Church, res. 151 S. Noble.
Chipman L., clerk B. F. Tuttle's store, res. 128 N. Tennessee.
Chism Robert, (col.,) res. 190 W. North.
Chites John, porter Little's Hotel.
Chittenden William G., laborer, res. East, bet. Liberty and Noble.
Chollette Jacob H., book-keeper, res. 22 N. Mississippi.
Chrech Frederick, carpenter, res. 215 S. Delaware.
Christ Henry, servant Mrs. Morris.
CHRISTIAN RECORD, Journal Building, A. D. Goodwin, publisher.
Christman Otto, superintendent Crystal Palace saloon, bds. same.
CHRISTY ALBERT, dealer in groceries, fruits of all kinds, cakes, candies, cigars, tobacco, nuts, crackers, flour, &c., 14 Louisiana, opp. Union depot.
CHRISTY A., grocery and produce store, cor. Illinois and Maryland, res. 55 South.
Church J. A., (J. A. C. & Co.,) res. Pine, near Fletcher ave.
Church Joseph A. & Co., flour and feed store, 5 S. Delaware.
Churchman F. M., clerk Fletcher's Bank, res. 8 E. Michigan.
CHURCHMAN W. H., Superintendent of Institute for the Blind, res. at Institute.

INDIANAPOLIS

WOOD & FOUDRAY,
LIVERY, SALE
AND
BOARDING STABLES,
No. 10 N. Pennsylvania Street,
INDIANAPOLIS, INDIANA.

Dealers in

MULES & HORSES.

Horses and Carriages to let day and night.

HORSES BOARDED BY THE DAY OR WEEK.

W. H. LOOMIS'
Woodlawn Green House,
NO. 189 VIRGINIA AVENUE.

Green House Plants, Boquets, Roses
AND HARDY SHRUBS.
Also, Fruit and Ornamental Trees for sale
At Reduced Cash Prices.

The largest collection of new Hardy Grape Vines, offered in the West, among them will be found the famous Delaware, Diana, Anna, Logan, Lenoir, Rebecca Allen's Hybrid, Cuyahoga, and

Thirty Other Varieties.

Descriptive, wholesale, and other Catalogues furnished on application.

Address, W. H. LOOMIS,
No. 189 Va. Avenue,
INDIANAPOLIS, IND.

The First Premium awarded the Wheeler & Wilson Machine

CITY SALOON, 53 and 55 S. Illinois, Bush & Hannum, proprietors.
CLAFLIN C. C., agent Wheeler & Wilson's sewing machines, 19 W. Washington, res. 110 N. Meridian.
Clark ——, U. S. A., res. 122 W. Ohio.
Clark Alfred D., clerk at Bowen, Stewart & Co.'s, bds. 67 N. Mississippi.
Clark A. M., house painter, res. 67 N. Mississippi.
Clark Absalom, washerman, res. 28 W. North.
CLARK EDWARD, President and Agent of the Indiana and Illinois Central Railway Company, 24½ E. Washington, res. 36 N. Delaware.
Clark Hugh, carriage maker, res. 35 E. St. Clair.
Clark H., laborer, res. 139 W. New York.
Clark Mrs. Maria, (wid.,) bds. 95 W. Vermont.
Clark Rueben O., res. 98 W. Michigan.
Clark S. A., carriage trimmer, res. 96 N. East.
Clark W. T., agent for Merchants' Despatch, 31 W. Washington, bds. 79½ E. Washington.
CLARKE E. W., Baptist minister, res. 73 S. Noble.
Clarke Edward W., (M. G. C. & Co.,) res. 51 N. Pennsylvania.
Clarke John, book-keeper, Clarke & Co.
Clarke M. G., (Clarke & Co.,) res. 169 N. Pennsylvania.
Clarke M. G. & Co., publishers and proprietors of Witness, Odd Fellows' Hall.
Clarke William C., (C. & Co.,) bds. 169 N. Pennsylvania.
CLARKE & CO., book publishers and agents for S. S. books, Odd Fellows Hall.
Clawson Albert, blacksmith, bds. 28 Indiana ave.
Clay Hillery, deputy clerk United States Court, bds. 139 N. New Jersey.
Clayton C. J., peddler, res. 3 Willard.
Cleary Patrick, porter Bates House.
Cleaver John W., bricklayer, res. 197 N. Noble.
Cleaver Jefferson, bricklayer, alley bet. New York and Ohio.
Clem Aaron, (Clem & Bro.,) res. cor. Massachusetts ave. and Alabama.
Clem William F., (Clem & Bro.,) res. 110 N. Alabama.
Clem & Bro., grocers, cor. Massachusetts ave. and Alabama.
Clemens John, carpenter, res. Illinois, bet. First and Second.
Clemm John E., clerk Quartermaster's Department, res. 82 N. Delaware.
Clever W., messenger Adams Express Company, bds. Palmer House.
Clifton Joseph B., laborer, res. 174 N. New Jersey.
Cline Andrew, engineer, res. 96 E. Louisiana.

For four successive years at the Ohio State Fair.

CHRISTIAN HOFMEISTER,
SALOON AND RESTAURANT.

Choice Wines, Liquors, Ale, Beer and Cigars always on hand. Oysters and Game in their season.

75 East Washington St.,
INDIANAPOLIS, INDIANA,

J. C. MORRIS'
Photographic Temple of Art,

26 & 28 W. Washington St., over Fletcher's store,

INDIANAPOLIS, INDIANA.

Photographs Plain or in Oil, or in Water Colors. Ambrotypes, Melainotypes, &c., &c.

UNION HOUSE,
(NEAR THE UNION DEPOT.)

Corner of Illinois and South Streets,

INDIANAPOLIS, IND.,

Seventy-five cents per day. Twenty cents per meal. Supper lodging and breakfast, sixty cents.

STEPHEN MATTLER, - - Proprietor.

JACOB ROOS.   CHARLES SCHMALZRIED.
ROOS & SCHMALZRIED,
Dealers in all kinds of

FRESH & SALT MEATS,
No. 89 South Illinois Street,
Between Georgia St. and Union Depot,
INDIANAPOLIS, INDIANA.

Wheeler & Wilson's Sewing Machines awarded the first premium for five

Cline Chas. H., U. S. A., res. 150 N. Mississippi.
Cline Joel, miller, res. 191 S. Alabama.
Cline Peter, teamster, res. S. West.
Clinton Harton, Capt. U. S. A., res. 32 E. Georgia.
Cloffi Conradt, watchman B. & I. R. R. depot. res. 7 Huron.
Close John, (C. & Bro.,) bds. Macy House.
Close Wm. H., (C. & Bro.,) bds. Macy House.
Close & Bro., (col.,) barbers, 4 N. Pennsylvania.
Coach Henry, res. cor. Fletcher ave. and Pine.
Coburn Mrs. Ann, res. 185 N. East.
Coburn Mrs. Sarah, res. 47 N. Delaware.
Coburn Ellen, works at arsenal, bds. 34 N. Ellsworth.
Coburn John, Colonel 33d Regiment Indiana Volunteers, res. 60 E. Ohio.
Coburn J. F., machinist at Indianapolis and Cincinnati machine shop, res. 103 S. Alabama.
Coburn William, bar-keeper Empire saloon, bds. Morris House.
Cochran Milton, cooper, res. Michigan Road.
Cochran Wm., carpenter, res. Eddy, S. of Garden.
Coen John, paper hanger and boarding house keeper, res. 107 S. Tennessee.
Coffer Hannah, (wid.,) res. 123 E. McCarthy.
Coffin Eli, cigar maker, res. 167 E. Ohio.
Coffin Stephen, (McTaggart C. & Co.) res. 20 Delaware.
Coffman Adam, laborer, 105 Madison ave.
Coffman Jacob, carpenter, res, 171 S. New Jersey.
Coffman Samuel J., carpenter, res. 163 N. Mississippi.
Cogan Mary, (wid.,) res. 64 E. Merrill.
Cogil ——, res. 186 Virginia ave.
Cogill John, workman at arsenal, res. 61 S. New Jersey.
COLCLAZER REV. J., Methodist, res. 35 N. Pennsylvania.
Colclazer J. H., watchmaker, 20 E. Washington, bds. 35 N. Pennsylvania.
Coldwell James T., blacksmith, 67 S. Pennsylvania.
Cole D. G., res. 135 N. East.
Cole John, farmer, W. Indianapolis.
Cole O. F., salesman, 30 W. Washington, res. 51, cor. Ohio and Alabama.
Coleman Henry, hack driver, res. 66 Indiana ave.
Colley S. A., attorney at law, 10½ S. Meridian, res. 164 N. New Jersey.
Collins Cornelius, laborer, res. 100 E. Market.
Collins E. J., carpenter, res. 67 Spring.
Collins John, carpenter, res. 37 S. Illinois.
Collman Henry, boarding house, res. 28 S. Pennsylvania.
Collup Frederick, grocer, 166 E. Washington, res. same.
COLLY I. J., detective police, res. 49, cor. Ohio and Noble:

Successive years at Mechanic's Institute, Cincinnati.

A. & H. SCHNULL,
WHOLESALE GROCERS,
PRODUCE & COMMISSION MERCHANTS,
Importers of and dealers in
WINES, LIQUORS,
AND
CIGARS,
FOREIGN FRUITS,
NUTS,
SARDINES,
&c., &c.

RECTIFIED WHISKY AND VINEGAR MANUFACTORY.
COR. WASHINGTON AND DELAWARE STREETS,
INDIANAPOLIS, IND.

Cigars, Fine Cut & Plug Tobacco
WAREHOUSE.

JOHN A. HEIDLINGER,
Manufacturer and Wholesale Dealer in
CIGARS,
And direct importer of the
Choicest Brands
OF
HAVANA CIGARS,
AND
COMMISSION MERCHANT.
No. 3 Palmer House, and No. 10 Bates House,
INDIANAPOLIS, IND.

Wheeler & Wilson's Sewing Machines have been awarded the First Premium

Colsby Henry, (col.,) whitewasher, res. 156 N. Missouri.
Colstock Henry, carpenter, res. 22 W. North.
Colstock John A., street commissioner, bds. 22 W. North.
Colton Wm., engineer, res. 27 S. Liberty.
Combs Hawkins, laborer, res. 136 E. McCarthy.
Comegys Levi, carpenter, shop 62 N. Delaware, res. same.
Compagne Henry J., laborer, res. 40 Huron.
Comsky James, hack driver, res. 257 S. Delaware.
Conaty James B., bonnet bleacher, 22 S. Illinois, res. same.
Conkle John, laborer, res. 30 Union.
Conly John, workman at Rolling Mill, res. 166 S. Mississippi.
CONNER A. H., Postmaster, bds. Bates House.
Conner Daniel, laborer, res. 25 Railroad.
Conner James, laborer, res. 21 E. Georgia.
Connor John, laborer, res. 199 E. Ohio.
Conner John, laborer, bds. 184 S. Tennessee.
Conner Lawrence, ostler, 14 N. Pennsylvania, bds. Scarry House.
Conner Michael, U. S. A., res. 181 S. New Jersey.
Conner Michael, laborer, res. 101 E. Louisiana.
Conraigan James, railroader, res. E. end of Maryland.
Conroy Patrick, tailor, res. West, bet. Maryland and Georgia.
Converse Joel, express-man, res. 153 N. East.
Cood Charles, collar maker, res. Pennsylvania.
Cook Francis, laborer, res. 210 S. Tennessee.
Cook Fred., (Wm. C. & Co.,) res. 36 Liberty.
Cook Fred., driver Adams Express Company, bds. Spencer House.
Cook Henry, brick mason, bds. 20 Chatham.
Cook Henry, laborer, res. John near Winston.
Cook Henry, laborer, res. 45 E. Georgia.
Cook H. P., clerk at M. H. Good's, bds. 10 W. Market.
Cook Miss Jane, res. 22 Indiana ave.
Cook Jesse M., carpenter, res. 111 E. New York.
Cook Mrs. J., boarding house, 44 N. Pennsylvania.
Cook John, machinist, bds. 20 Chatham.
Cook Mrs. Mary, res. 20 Chatham.
Cook M. R., painter 31 S. Meridian, res. 75 W. Maryland.
Cook R., meat market, 3 N. Illinois, res. 22 Indiana ave.
Cook Thomas, laborer, res. 31 Central.
Cook William, (Wm. C. & Co.,) res. East, S. of Washington.
COOK WILLIAM & CO., dealer in dry goods, groceries, boots, shoes, &c., 189 E. Washington.
Coolmam William, cigar maker at G. Meyers, 25 W. Washington, res. 70 N. Mississippi.
Cooly Charles, res. Biddle, near city limits.
Coon Peter, res. 10 N. East.

J. B. WILSON,

Wholesale and retail

DEALER IN

HARDWARE

Silver Plated Ware, Window Sash, Glass, Mill & Cross Cut Saws,

R. R. Lanterns, And Coal Oil Lamps.

No. 60 W. Washington St.

7 SHOT REVOLVER,

MADE BY THE

Manhattan Fire Arms Manufacturing Co.,
NEW YORK.

Weighs 10 ounces; *loaded* in half the time, and shoots with double the force of other kinds. The charges may remain in the Pistol for years without injury or be withdrawn without danger. The workmanship is superior, and the price moderate. *For Sale by*

J. B. WILSON, Indianapolis, Ind.

TOM S. CAMPBELL.   M. W. BOYLES.

CAMPBELL & BOYLES,
Book Binders, Job Rulers
AND
BLANK BOOK MANUFACTURERS,
No. 37 East Washington St.,
(2 doors east of Glenns' Block, up stairs,)
INDIANAPOLIS, IND.

EGNER & WOCHER,
DRUGGISTS AND APOTHECARIES,

Dealers in

Glass, Paints, Varnishes, &c.

81 Washington St.,

INDIANAPOLIS, IND.

CHARLES FISHBACK, M. D.,
PHYSICIAN AND SURGEON,
Res. 40 E. New York, Office 22 E. Market, St.,
INDIANAPOLIS, IND.,

The Wheeler & Wilson Hemmer makes hems of any width.

Coon Phillip, bar-keeper Court House Saloon.
Cooney Dennis, laborer, res. 9 N. East.
Coons Mrs. Elizabeth, res. 83 Davidson.
Cooper Albert, laborer, res. 275 S. Delaware.
Cooper Charles A., auctioneer, res. 11 E. North.
Cooper Hamilton, tailor, res. W. Market.
Cooper J., boots and shoes, 53 E. Washington, res. 81 N. Alabama.
Cooper John, blacksmith, res. 229 S. Delaware.
Cooper Nathan, (col.,) wood sawyer, res. 145 N. Tennessee.
Cooper W. H., clerk for William Wise, 74 W. Washington, bds. 229 S. Delaware.
Copeland Jesse, builder, res. 128 E. Market.
Copeland J. W., dealer in millinery goods 7 S. Meridian, res. 105 S. New Jersey.
Copeland S. P., bonnet presser, res. 101 N. Mississippi.
Corbit Mrs. Mary A., (wid.,) res. 136 N. Mississippi.
Cordey William, res. 84 N. Meridian.
Corkran John, laborer, res. Water, N. of McCarthy.
Corliss C., physician, 7 E. Maryland.
Cornelius Deborah, (wid.,) 237 S. Alabama.
Cornelius Wm., plasterer, res. 116 E. McCarthy.
Corner James, carpenter, res. Biddle, near city limits.
Corwine Benjamin F., res. Plumb near University.
Cosby Richard, carpenter, res. 58 Huron.
Costelo John, foundryman, res. W. Market.
Coster Charles H. M., laborer, res. 115 N. Alabama.
Coster D., farmer, res. 37 N. Noble.
Coster David W., carpenter, res. 71 Spring.
Costigan F., bds. Oriental House.
Cottman John A., U. S. A., res. 159 W. Vermont.
Cotton Randolph J., jailer, bds. 18 N Alabama.
Cottrell Thomas, (C. & Knight,) res. 102 S. New Jersey.
Cottrell & Knight, gas fitters and coppersmiths, 94 S. Alabama.
Coughlin Wm., (Merritt & C.,) woollen factory, res. 127 W. New York.
Coumbe E. J., baker, at Union Steam Bakery.
Court House Saloon, cor. Washington and Alabama, C. Monninger, proprietor.
Cousins Samuel, saloon-tender, res. 190 W. North.
Covington Susan, (wid.,) res. 144 W. Market.
Cox A. J., (Weeks & C.,) res. 205 S. Alabama.
COX CHARLES, dealer in stoves, tin and sheet-iron ware, 11 W. Washington. res. 43 S. Meridian.
Cox Charles H., salesman, 11 W. Washington, bds. 43 S. Meridian.
Cox David, tinner, 11 W. Washington.

CHINA TEA STORE!

No. 14 Bates House, Illinois Street.

INDIANAPOLIS, IND.

LUDDEN & LEE, - - - - - Proprietors.

WE ARE RECEIVING EVERY WEEK FRESH INVOICES OF EVERY VARIETY OF

Green & Black Teas.

Strangers visiting the City will find it to their advantage to call and inspect our variety of choicest

Imperial, Gunpowder, Young Hyson & Oolongs

N. B.—WE PROMISE TO

SELL TEAS 30 PER CENT. LOWER

Than any other House in the State.

First Premium awarded the Wheeler & Wilson Sewing Machine for three

Cox Edward, finisher Ohio Premium Woolen Factory.
Cox J., landscape and portrait painter, Ray's Building, res. 41 S. Meridian.
Cox Jas., shoemaker, bds. with Knight.
Cox Jefferson R., carpenter, res. 188 S. East.
Cox Mrs. Sophia, (wid..) res. 148 W. Market.
Cox Wm. C., (Tomlinson & C.,) res. 144 N. Illinois.
Coyner Martin, contractor, res. 209 E. St. Clair.
Craft Smith, blacksmith, res. 210 Indiana ave.
Craft W. H., watchmaker and jeweler, 2 Odd Fellows Hall.
Craig Wm., school teacher, bds. 45 N. Pennsylvania.
Craighead Mary Jane, (wid.,) res. 18 Maryland.
Crane Alex G., speculator, res. cor. Washington and Tennessee.
Crane J. D., New York picture gallery, 19 W. Washington, res. Lafayette.
Crane L., porter Farmers' Hotel.
Crane Worth, artist, New York picture gallery, bds. Pyle House.
Crapo R. P., (R. P. C. & Co.,) bds. Pyle House.
Crapo R. P. & Co., dealers in ambrotype and photographic goods, Journal Building.
Crawford Eli, moulder, 250 S. Delaware.
Crawford Mary C., seamstress, bds. 132 E. North.
Crean Dennis, porter Farmers' Hotel, res. 204 S. Delaware.
Creamer Sarah, (wid.,) res. 199 S. Pennsylvania, rear.
Cremer James, (col.,) laborer, res. 124 W. New York.
Cressharber Sebastian, boiler-maker, res. 231 S. Alabama.
Cressner Theodore, book-keeper Indiana Daily State Sentinel Office, res. 133 N. West.
Crimer Henry, butcher, shop cor. East and North, res. 71 E. St. Mary.
Criqui M., merchant tailor and clothier, 84 E. Washington, res. 173 E. Ohio.
Crossland J. A., fancy dry goods, 75 W. Washington, res. 224 N. Illinois.
Cropper Alexander, hack driver, alley, bet. Market and Washington.
Cropsey J. E., cabinet maker, res. 62 N. Missouri.
Crouch G. W., (G. W. & J. C.,) livery and sale stable, 24 S. Pennsylvania, bds. Little's Hotel.
Crouch G. W. & J. C., livery stable, 24 S. Pennsylvania.
Crouch J., (G. W. & J. C.,) bds. Little's Hotel.
Crouch John, laborer, res. cor. Michigan and Tennessee.
Crozier Geo., watchman Glenns' Block, res. 89 N. Meridian.
Crug G., grocery, res. 24 E. Georgia.
CRYSTAL PALACE SALOON AND RESTAURANT, E. Beck, proprietor, 44 W. Washington.

Successive years at the United States Fair.

MORITZ, BROTHER & CO.,
CLOTHIERS
AND
MERCHANT TAILORS,

ALSO, DEALERS IN

CLOTHS, CASSIMERES AND VESTINGS,

No. 3 E. Washington St., Blackford's Building,

AND

No. 19 West Washington St., Sherman's Building,

INDIANAPOLIS, IND.

For Hosiery, Knitting Materials,

AND

GENTS' FURNISHING GOODS,

Go to R. R. PARKER,

Sign of the "Big Stocking,"

No. 30 WEST WASHINGTON ST.

ALSO, DEPOT FOR THE ENAMELED PAPER COLLARS.

VAN HOUTEN & GRAHAM,

Wholesale and Retail

GROCERS

AND DEALERS IN

Provisions, Country Produce, &c.,

South-East Cor. Illinois and Market Streets,

INDIANAPOLIS, IND.

A Wheeler & Wilson Sewing Machine with Hemmer, for $50.

Cuhn Wm., baker, res. 64 N. East.
Culon Chas., attorney at law, res. Cumberland, bet. Alabama and Delaware.
Culley Daniel B., res. 156 N. Pennsylvania.
Culley David V., president board of school trustees, res. 13 E. Ohio.
Culley Mrs. Mary tailoress, res. 119 S. Tennessee.
Cullum Eberle, (C. & Stanage.) res. St. Clair, bet. Michigan Road and Diagonal.
CULLUM & STANAGE, R. R. steam printers and engravers, office 19 W. Washington.
Cully D. T., salesman, 3 Palmer House, bds. 26 Illinois.
Cully Ed., clerk, bds, 76 N. Illinois.
CULVER ELIHU, wholesale and retail grocer, 142 W. Washington, res. same.
Cummins James, eating house, 194 W. Washington, res. same.
Cummings John H., teamster, res. Indiana ave.
CUNNINGHAM F. P., bakery and confectionery, 43 N. Illinois, res. same.
Cunningham Hugh, res. 45 S. East.
Curby Susannah, (wid.,) res. 15 Central.
Curby Thomas, cooper, res. 15 Central.
Curran David, printer, Journal Office, bds. 6 Noble.
Curren Mrs. Anne, washer, res. 144 E. New York.
Curry Hamilton, (col.,) cook, res. 97 Massachusetts ave.
CURTIS ANDREW, justice of the peace, 39 E. Washington, res. 159 Virginia ave.
Curtis Charles, engineer Wm. Henderson steam fire engine.
Curtis Casper T., artist, res. Water, N. of McCarty.
Curtis Joseph, (col.,) cook Bates House, res. 101 W. North.
Curtis Truman M., engineer, res. Water, N. of McCarty.
Curzon Joseph, architect, Journal Building, res. 218 N. Illinois.
Cussan Garret, clerk, res. 62 Indiana ave.
Cutting A., willow basket and broom maker, res. 177 N. Delaware.
Cutts H. P., blacksmith, res. Indiana ave.

D

Daggett W., wholesale and retail confectionery and tea store, 22 S. Meridian, res. same.
Dahne William, laborer, res. Winston, bet. New York and Vermont.
Dailey John, laborer, res. W. St. Clair.
Daily Condy, huckster, res. 144 N. Liberty.

ALLEN & HINESLEY'S

LIVERY AND SALE STABLE,

Pearl St., in rear of Palmer House, INDIANAPOLIS.

Every description of vehicles usually found in Livery Stables always on hand. Horses kept by the Day, Week or Month.

GUN MATERIALS AND FANCY GOODS.

EDGAR PARKER,

DEALER IN

GUNS, PISTOLS,

GUN MATERIALS,

Bird Cages, Fancy Baskets, Hobby Horses, Toys & Fancy Goods of all kinds,

25 South Illinois Street, - - - INDIANAPOLIS.

OHIO HOUSE,

No. 31 West Market Street,

INDIANAPOLIS, IND.

MARTIN NEIMAN, - - - - - Proprietor.

☞ This House is convenient to the business part of the city. Boarders kept by the day or week.

A Wheeler & Wilson Sewing Machine will last a life-time.

Daily C. R., U. S. A., res. 309 Virginia ave.
Daily Michael, haberdasher, 192 S. Delaware.
Daily Patrick, clerk, res. 190 S. Delaware.
Daily William, res. 153 N. Liberty.
Daily Elisha W., res. 113 N. Tennessee.
Dain Robert C., paper hanger, bds. 108 St. Joseph.
Dain Mrs. P., res. 18 Michigan Road.
Dain E. J., auctioneer, bds. Little's Hotel.
Dame Jason, marble worker and dealer, 67 E. Washington, res. 8 East.
Dana Mrs. E. S., res. 33 Meridian.
Danals Samuel, railroader, res. 63 S. New Jersey.
Dancy Frank, pattern maker, res. 184 S. Alabama.
Danforth A. J., (D. & Simpson,) res. 112 N. Pennsylvania.
DANFORTH & SIMPSON, wholesale and retail dealers in groceries, produce, &c., 3 Odd Fellows' Hall.
Daniels Mrs. C. F., dress maker, res. 60 N. Delaware.
Daniels Samuel, res. 71 S. New Jersey.
Danmier Frederick, drayman, res. 146 E. Ohio.
Danway Andrew, laborer, W. Indianapolis.
Daragh William, merchant tailor, res. 56 S. Illinois.
Darby John, hominy maker, Railroad City Mills, res. 33 W. Ohio.
Darnall W. W., Captain 11th Regiment Indiana Volunteers, res. 71 N. Delaware.
Darnell C., carpenter, res. Illinois, bet. Fifth and Sixth.
Darnell John, railroader, res. 23 Harrison.
Darnley Francis, railroader, res. 22 Henry.
Darragh William, cuttlery, 3 E. Washington, res. cor. Willow and Garden.
Darrow George, wood sawyer, res. 149 S. Mississippi.
Darrow Ben. C., (Cady & Co.,) res. 161 N. New Jersey.
Darrow James R., auctioneer, res. 67 N. East.
Dash John, laborer, res. 116 S. Noble.
Daugherty J. F., clerk postoffice, res. 61 Massachusetts ave.
Daumont P. A., jeweler, 9 S. Meridian, res. 32 E. Market.
DAUMONT S. H., watch maker, hair braider, and dealer in clocks, watches, jewelry, silver and plated ware, 9 S. Meridian.
Daven Peter, laborer, res. 83 Huron.
Davenport John, engineer planing mill, res. 58 Indiana ave.
David Mrs. Ann, seamstress, res. 20 N. East.
David Thomas, (Rigg & D.,) res. 83 South.
David William, res. Illinois, N. of Fourth.
David Wm. C., Florance's saloon, bds. Acy Wright.
Davidson A. H., farmer, E. end of Market.
Davidson John, collector for Journal Company, res. 85 Davidson.

Upwards of 100 W. & W. Machines in use in Ind'p'lis making army clothing.

PHOTOGRAPHIC ART GALLERY

OF
E. & J. BRUENING,
No. 6 EAST WASHINGTON ST.,
INDIANAPOLIS, IND.

AMBROTYPES, MELAINOTYPES,
PLAIN PHOTOGRAPHS,

In the most elegant style, equal to the best made in France.

PHOTOGRAPHS FROM MINIATURE TO LIFE SIZE,
COLORED IN OIL.

Daguerreotypes or Ambrotypes copied into Plain Photographs of any size,

By E. BRUENING, Artist, from Dusseldorf.

Prices moderate and perfect satisfaction warranted.

BOWEN, STEWART & CO.,
BOOKSELLERS
AND
STATIONERS,

And Dealers in

WINDOW PAPER, WALL PAPER,
PRINTING PAPER AND PRINTERS' MATERIALS,

No. 18 WEST WASHINGTON STREET,

INDIANAPOLIS, INDIANA.

---

350 families in Indianapolis and vicinity use Wheeler & Wilson.

Davis Mrs. Maria, tailoress, res. 79 N. New Jersey.
Davis Allen, brakeman Bellefontaine R. R., res. 54 Benton.
Davis Amos, (col.,) wood sawyer, res. Sixth, bet. Mississippi and Missouri.
Davis Benjamin, railroader, res. 51 E. Lonisiana.
DAVIS C. B., insurance agent, Odd Fellows' Hall, res. 137 N. Pennsylvania.
Davis Charles W., clerk Union Hall Billiard Room.
Davis D. W., cook St. Nicholas Saloon.
Davis Edwin A., (Poelle & D.,) attorney at law, bds. Bates House.
Davis Edward, constable, res. 123 N. Pennsylvania.
Davis E. W., (Deitz and D.,) res. 78 and 80 W. Washington.
Davis F. A. W., teller Indianapolis Branch Banking Co., bds. cor. Market and Meridian.
Davis Fleming, railroader, res. 124 S. Noble.
Davis George, blacksmith, bds. 179 E. Market.
Davis Haldan, city policeman, res. 159 N. Delaware.
Davis J., foundry, res. 64 N. Meridian.
DAVIS JAMES, boots and shoes, 137 E. Washington, res. 5 N. Noble.
Davis James, foundryman, bds. 13 N. New Jersey.
Davis John G., clerk Odd Fellows' Hall, bds. Mrs. Campbell's.
Davis Joseph S., messenger Adams Express Co., bds. Palmer House.
Davis Joseph W., bell and brass foundry, res. 129 Virginia ave.
Davis Milton, laborer, res. cor. McCarty and Union.
Davis Richard M., shoemaker, res. bet. East and Noble, and Washington and Market.
Davis Robert F., sawmaker, bds. Ray House.
Davis Thomas, butcher, shop 6 S. Alabama, res. 83 South.
Davis Thomas, shoemaker, bds. 5 N. Noble.
Davis T. J., (Kellogg & D.,) bds. Palmer House.
Davis William, 26th Ind. Volunteers, res. 221 N. Noble.
Davis William C., salesman Bee-Hive store, bds. at Macy House.
Davis Wm. H., carpenter, works at Wright's pump shop, E. Maryland, res. 46 W. Maryland.
Dawes A. C., traveling agent E. C. Mayhew & Co., bds. Palmer House.
Dawson David S., blacksmith, works Jones & Vanblaricum's, Maryland, E. of Meridian, res. 41 W. Georgia.
Dawson George, tinner, res. 183 N. New Jersey.
Dawson Riley, miller, res. 72 E. St. Clair.
DAY REV. HENRY, pastor Baptist Church, bds. Mrs. McCarty, cor. Meridian and Merrill.

G

Wheeler & Wilson's Sewing Machines warranted for three years.

INDIANAPOLIS & CINCINNATI

SHORT LINE RAILROAD.

Shortest Route by 30 Miles.
The only Route Without Change of Cars.

Three Trains leave Indianapolis daily, on the arrival of Trains from Peru, Lafayette and Terre Haute.

Through to Cincinnati in advance of all other Routes.

Connecting at Cincinnati with all the Great Eastern and Southern Railroad Lines, and with Steamers on the Ohio River.

The Line of the Indianapolis and Cincinnati Railroad commences at Indianapolis, the Capital of Indiana, and passing through the towns of **SHELBYVILLE, GREENSBURG, LAWRENCEBURG AND NORTH BEND,** (In view of the Residence and Tomb of the late General Harrison,) terminates at Cincinnati, the Queen City of the West.

This Road was projected with a view to accommodate the travel and trafic, which, coming from the North-West, seeks, through the Railroad City, (Indianapolis,) a direct avenue to the great Commercial Metropolis of the West.

For this purpose the two cities have been connected by a direct line of Railroad of uniform gauge, 110 miles in length, built in a style second to no other road in the Union, being first class in all its equipments for the transportation of passengers and freight in the shortest time and at low rates.

With favorable and reliable arrangements with all connecting Roads, throughout the entire West, this Line guarantees unusual care and the amplest accommodations to its patrons.

SLEEPING CARS ATTACHED TO ALL NIGHT TRAINS.

The Company's exclusive Telegraph Line is used, when necessary, to govern the movement of Trains, and Loughridge's Celebrated Patent Car Brakes are attached to all Passenger Trains, by which they can be perfectly controlled; besides all the other modern improvements necessary for the comfort and safety of Passengers, the managers of this road have liberally provided.

☞ **FARE THE SAME AS BY ANY OTHER ROUTE.**

BAGGAGE CHECKED THROUGH.

H. C. LORD, President.
W. H. L. NOBLE, General Ticket Agent.

First Premium awarded the Wheeler & Wilson Sewing Machine for three

Day L., (W. F. Oglesby & Co.,) bds. 91 N. Tennessee.
Day W. W., butcher, res. E. St. Clair.
Deader William, laborer, res. 117 Union.
Dearboag Christian, laborer, res. 129 E. McCarty.
Deaker Casper, wood sawyer, res. 85 E. St. Mary.
Decker Conrad, blacksmith, res. 140 Davison.
Decker John, res. 227 N. Alabama.
Decker John B., watchmaker and jeweler, 184 E. Washington, res. same.
Deenen James M., clerk 46 Fort Wayne ave., res. 157 N. New Jersey.
Deer John, laborer, res. 230 N. Alabama.
Deery Edward, laborer, res. Jackson, near city limits.
Deery John, laborer, res. Jackson, near city limits.
De Ford Wm., R., (De F. & Quimby,) res. 113 Massachusetts ave.
Defrees John D., sup't gov. printing, Washington, D. C., res. 54 S. Meridian.
De Ford & Quimby, attorneys at law, 35½ E. Washington.
Dehart Austin, teamster, res. 137 N. Mississippi.
Deisier John, Jefferson House, 31 South, res. same.
Deitz Peter, laborer, res N. Blake.
Deleny Michael, railroader, res. 73 N. Noble.
Deller Frederick, painter, res. 102 N. Noble.
Delvo Eugene, stone cutter, res. 3 Elm.
Delzell Hugh, lieutenant Ind. Vol.
Delzell Samuel, sutler U. S. A., res. 91 N. Alabama.
Demos L., saddler, res. 13 W. St. Clair.
Demmy Martin, saddler at Sulgrove & Reynolds, 8 Huron.
Demmy Wm. H., harnessmaker, 20 W. Washington, bds. 8 Huron.
Demotte Wm., teacher Deaf and Dumb Asylum, res. E. National Road.
Demunn Geo., section boss Bellefontaine R. R., res. 12 Bates.
Deneen Amanda, seamstress, res. 157 N. Alabama.
De Nene William, salesman New York Store, bds. Spencer House.
Deniston Mrs. E. A., (wid.,) res. 73 N. Missouri.
Denk Andrew, res. 137 Indiana ave.
Denner Andrew, teamster, W. Indianapolis.
Dennes Mrs. Elvira, res. 78 N. East.
Dennis Peter, soldier, res. 221 S. Delaware.
Dennison O. E., printer, bds. Pyle House, cor. Illinois and Maryland.
Denniston Mrs. E. A., (wid.,) milliner and dressmaker, res. 73 N. Missouri.
Denwald Mathew, drayman, res. 71 Davidson.
Depot Bakery, J. C. Wineberger, prop'r, opp. Union Depot.

Successive years at the United States Fair.

CITY DIRECTORY.   85

WILLARD & STOWELL,

Keep constantly on hand an Extensive assortment of

Melodeons,

OF THE BEST MANUFACTURERS.

N. B.—Piano-Fortes Tuned & Repaired. Old Piano-Fortes taken in Exchange for New Ones.

PIANO-FORTES TO RENT

A LARGE ASSORTMENT OF

GUITARS, VIOLINS, FLUTES, FLUTINAS, ACCORDEONS, DRUMS, FIFES, &c., GUITAR AND VIOLIN STRINGS OF THE BEST QUALITY. ALSO,

INSTRUCTION BOOKS,
OF ALL KINDS.

For four successive years at the Ohio State Fair.

CHARLES E. HAWTHORN. THOMAS BUCHANAN.
HAWTHORN & BUCHANAN,
IMPORTERS OF
CHINA, GLASS
AND
QUEENSWARE,
No. 83
E. Washington St.,
INDIANAPOLIS, IND.

Also, Manufacturers and Dealers in

STONEWARE.

CLARKE & CO.,
ODD FELLOWS' HALL,
INDIANAPOLIS, IND.
SUNDAY SCHOOL AND RELIGIOUS BOOKS.
PUBLICATIONS OF THE
American Sunday School Union, American Tract Society, Am. Bap. Pub. Society, Sheldon & Co., Henry Hoyt, and Methodist Book Concern. Agents for the State for Horace Waters' DAY AND SABBATH SCHOOL BELL.

CHARLES GLAZIER,
(Late Bradshaw & Glazier,)
COMMISSION MERCHANT,
DEALER IN
FLOUR, GRAIN, HAY, BUTTER,
Dried Fruit, Seeds, and Produce Generally. Also, Agent for the New York Reaper,
No. 16, Cor. Pearl and Meridian Sts., Indianapolis.

Particular attention given to the sale and purchase of Flour, Grain and Produce.

Wheeler & Wilson's Sewing Machines have been awarded the First Premium

Dupez Aug., currier Mooney & Co.'s.
Dernham Max, agent Eagle Clothing Store, 1 W. Washington, res. 28 N. Mississippi.
Derringer David, carpenter, res. Howard.
Deshley John. cabinet maker, res. Pennsylvania.
Despa Aernest, painter. res. 30 Loukabee.
Dessar A., (D. & Bro.,) res. Illinois, second door from cor. of Illinois and Vermont.
Dessar David, (D. & Bro.,) bds. Illinois, second door from cor. of Illinois and Vermont.
DESSAR & BRO., merchant tailors and clothiers, 6 E. Washington.
Detricht William, bds. 14 W. Georgia.
Devall A. A., (wid.,) res. 112 Virginia ave.
Devening Daniel, wood sawyer, res. S. West.
Devennish John J., moulder, res. 140 E. New York.
Devennish ——, cutter, res. 139 E. South.
Devinnish Solomon, tailor, res. 169 South.
De Ware James, machinist, res. 172 E. Ohio.
Dezeng Charles E., clerk, 14 W. Washington, bds. 132 N. Illinois.
Dickens Ephraim, res. 99 Indiana ave.
Dickey Mrs. Rebecca, seamstress, res. 133 E. New York.
Dickison J. C., res. 109 S. Alabama.
Dickison J. L., physician, res. 135 S. Alabama.
Dickman Frederick, carpenter, res. 41 N. East.
Dickman Francis, farmer, Illinois, cor. Sixth.
Dickman Fred., salesman 29 W. Washington.
Dickson Andrew, New York Store, bds. Palmer House.
Dickson Carlos, book-keeper, 26 and 28 W. Washington, bds. 36 Meridian.
Dickson George, (col.,) carpenter, res. 123 Ohio.
Diefert Alec, butcher, 167 S. Delaware.
Dieter Jacob, cigar maker, 35 W. Washington.
Dieter Ernst, shoemaker, res. 133 Railroad.
Dietz Adam, Paradise Garden, cor. Alabama and Ft. Wayne, res. same.
Dietz George, (D. & Davis,) 78 and 80 W. Washington.
DIETZ & DAVIS, Washington Hall Saloon, 78 and 80 W. Washington.
Dietzel Adam, ostler, res. 77 N. Davidson.
Dilgr Adam, barber Bates House hair-dressing saloon, bds. with Mrs. Walk.
Dill Mrs. Gertrude, res. 11 E. North.
Dill Miss Lizzie St. C., authoress, bds. 11 E. North.
Dill A. M., saddler, res. 69 E. Merrill.
Dill Henry C., printer, bds. 11 E. North.

For four successive years at the Am. Institute, New York.

PERU & INDIANAPOLIS

1862. **1862.**

RAILROAD.

This Road is seventy-three miles in length, runs through the center of Marion, Hamilton, Howard and Miami counties, and extends from Indianapolis to Peru, passing through the flourishing towns of Noblesville, Cicero, Tipton, Sharpsville and Kokomo, connecting at Peru with the Toledo, Wabash and Western Railroad East for Toledo and Detroit, and West for Logansport, Delphi, Lafayette, and towns in Eastern Illinois. Also, connects at Kokomo with the C. & C. Air Line R. R. for Chicago, and towns and cities in the North-West. Connects at Indianapolis with

MADISON AND INDIANAPOLIS,
TERRE HAUTE & RICHMOND,
Terre Haute, Alton and St. Louis, and
JEFFERSONVILLE AND INDIANAPOLIS,

And the other numerous Railroads diverging from Indianapolis for all points South and West. This is the most direct route from Louisville and Southern towns to TOLEDO, DETROIT, AND MONTREAL.

FREIGHT AND PASSENGERS carried as low as by any other Route.

This is 62 miles shorter to the Lakes from Indianapolis than by any other road. This Company have excellent facilities for transporting FREIGHT and PASSENGERS, and the road is in good running condition and a safe and reliable route.

DISTANCES.

INDIANAPOLIS to	Miles.		Miles.
James' Switch	6	Sharpsville	46
Phipp's	9	Fairfield	50
Castleton	11	Kokomo	54
New Britton	17	Cassville	59
Noblesville	22	Miamitown	57
Cicero	28	Leonda	63
Arcadia	31	Peru	73
Buenna Vista	34	Fort Wayne	129
Tipton	39	Toledo	223
Jacksons' Mill	42	Chicago	182

OFFICERS.

DAVID MACY, General Agent and Superintendent.
C. B. ROBINSON, Assistant Superintendent.
THEO. P. HAUGHEY, Secretary, Treasurer, and General Ticket Agent.
L. N. ANDREWS, General Freight Agent.
F. GILMON, Master Machinist, (Peru, Indiana.)

Dill James, bds. 11 E. North.
Dill John P., bds. 11 E. North.
Dilley John, boarding house, 72 S. Illinois.
Dillon Daniel, laborer, res. 21 Benton.
Dillon John B., historian, bds. 88 Virginia ave.
Dillon Patrick, Wright's Bowling and Billiard Saloon, bds. near Rolling Mill.
Dillon Mrs. Sarah, (wid.,) seamstress, res. 26 Willard.
Dinsmore J. J., teacher of penmanship, Bryant's Commercial College, bds. with Mrs. Cook.
Dippel Joseph, laborer, res. 111 N. Noble.
Dipple John, waiter Little's Hotel.
Dipple Henry, bar-keeper National saloon.
Dirkert Jacob, cabinet maker, res. 128 N. West.
Disler Mrs. Mary, (wid.,) res. 163 S. Tennessee.
Diver James, clerk, res. 44 Massachusetts ave.
Dixon James, laborer, bds. 13 S. Illinois.
Dixon James, workman at arsenal, res. Missouri, S. of South.
Doarr George, waiter at Spencer House, res. S. Illinois, S. of Pogue's Run.
Dobson Mrs. Catherine, res. 170 W. Market.
DODD H. H., (H. H. D. & Co..) res. 168 W. New York.
DODD H. H. & CO., book and job printers, and book binders, 18 E. Washington.
Dodd Joshua, auctioneer. res. 51 Indiana ave.
Dodd John W., res. 128 N. Illinois.
DODD, TALBOTT & PARSONS, directory publishers, old Sentinel Building, 18 E. Washington.
Dodge W. C., engineer Bellefontaine R. R., res. 227 S. Delware.
Dodson Wm., engineer Terre Haute R. R., bds. 107 S. Tennessee.
Doerr George, hotel waiter, res. 34 S. Illinois.
Doggett G. R., harness maker, 20 W. Washington. bds. Little's Hotel.
Doggett Richard, shoemaker, res. 69 W. Vermont.
Doherty M., (McTaggart & D.,) res. near Underhill's Mill.
DOHN PHILLIP, manufacturer and dealer in furniture, 21 S. Meridian, res. same.
Dolus John, laborer, res. 56 Hosbrook.
Domon Emile, clerk California House.
Donaldson C. S., wholsale dealer in teas, cigars and tobacco, 71 W. Washington, res. 222 Illinois.
Donnan Mrs. Barbara, (wid.,) boarding house, 74 N. Tennessee.
Donohue James, railroader, bds. 95 Bates.
Donough Daniel B., book-keeper, 14 W. Washington, bds. 21 Kentucky ave.

Successive years at Mechanic's Institute, Cincinnati.

EXCHANGE
BILLIARD ROOMS,
EXCHANGE BUILDING,

Illinois Street, opposite the Bates House,

INDIANAPOLIS, IND.

Chauncey Montgomery, Prop'r.

THE EXCHANGE IS THE

FINEST BILLIARD ROOM

In the State, and second to none in the Western Country.

FLORANCE'S
SALOON,

No. 13 North Illinois St.,
INDIANAPOLIS, IND.

Florance Richter, - Proprietor.

THE VERY BEST

Wines, Liquors and Cigars,

ALWAYS ON HAND.

Donovan Ephraim, res. 184 N. East.
Donovan James, drayman, res. W. North.
Doogan Thomas, shoemaker, res. 152 E. North.
Doran Michael W. E., pattern maker, res. cor. Pine and Forest ave.
Dorr George, waiter Spencer House.
Dorsey N. J., physician and surgeon, 48 N. Pennsylvania, res. same.
Dorsey Thomas, laborer, res. 104 N. Mississippi.
Doty David D., (D. & Lee.) res. Danville, Indiana.
Doty John, teamster, W. Indianapolis.
DOTY & LEE, State House Saloon, opp. State House.
Dougherty Charles, grocer, res. 245 S. Delaware.
Dougherty Joab, cabinet maker, res. 49 N. New Jersey.
Dougherty Zedick, physician, res. California, bet. Washington and Market.
Doughty John G., Quartermaster U. S. A.
Doughty Lafayette, driver of engine Henderson, res. 50 N. Delaware.
Douglass George, at Douglass' book-bindery, bds. 130 W. New York.
Douglass James G., book-binder, Journal Building, res. 130 W. New York.
Douglass Mrs. John, (wid.,) res. 130 W. New York.
Douglass S. M., principal station baggage master at Union Depot, bds. 130 W. New York.
Downer W. S., (Wright & D.,) bds. Adam Gold, W. Washington.
Downey John, stone cutter, 127 E. Washington, res. 11 E. Georgia.
Downey M., marble worker and dealer, 127 E. Washington, res. same.
Downey Mrs. Mellissa, res. 43 N. Pennsylvania.
Downey James E., works at arsenal, bds. 34 E. Market.
Downing John P., clerk, 20 S. Meridian.
Downs Charles, blacksmith, res. 71 N. Missouri.
Doxon Mrs. Mary, res. 66 N. East.
Draeger Charles, watchmaker 67 W. Washington, res. 59 Georgia.
Drake E. B., (E. B. D. & Co.,) bds. 88 N. Alabama.
Drake Edward, foundryman, Root, Drake & Co., bds. 91 N. Alabama.
Drake R. H., book-binder, Journal Building, bds. Macy House.
DRAKE E. B. & CO., manufacturers of whitelead and colors, 47 South. (See card.)
Drechsel Geo., plow stalker, bds. East Street House.
Dreher Mathias, salesman 70 E. Wash. res. 46 N. Liberty.

H. S. ROCKEY,
Wholesale and Retail dealer in
COAL OIL LAMPS,
WICKS, &c.
No. 13 South Meridian Street,
INDIANAPOLIS, IND.

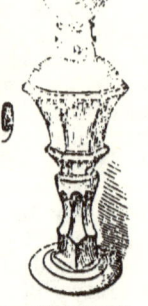

MARTIN HUG,
CAPITAL SALOON,
No. 14 East Washington St., INDIANAPOLIS, IND.

CHOICE WINES,
LIQUORS AND CIGARS,
Oysters and Game in their Season.
WARM MEALS AT ALL HOURS.

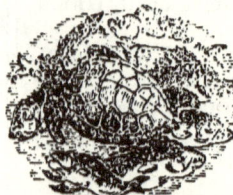

WEAVER & WILLIAMS,
UNDERTAKERS,
No. 72 West Washington Street,
INDIANAPOLIS, IND.

BURIAL CASES,
Metalic, Wooden and Terra Cotta,
FURNISHED AND PREPARED FOR TRANSPORTATION.
Orders punctually attended to day or night.

Upwards of 100 W. & W. Machines in use in Ind'p'lis making army clothing.

Dresback C. Henry, messenger American Express Company, bds. Morris House.
Drew John A., (S. W. D. & Son,) res. 76 N. Tennessee.
Drew Samuel W., (D. & Son,) res. Massachusetts ave., near Michigan.
Drew S. W. & Son, carriage makers, E. Market Square
Drinkut Wm., watchman, res. 89 S. New Jersey.
Driscoll Jerry, workman at Rolling Mill, res. 22 Willard.
Drought John, laborer, res. Canal, S. of South.
Drum ......, carpenter, res. ... S. New Jersey.
Drum J. ..., res. ... Pennsylvania.
Drum Jas. A., Quartermaster 19th Regiment Indiana Volunteers.
Drum Robert, teamster, res. 122 N. East.
Drum Wm. H., res. 238 S. Alabama.
Duffy John, tailor, res. cor. Maryland and West.
Duffy James, laborer, res. 35 N. Ellsworth.
Dugan Peter, tailor, bds. Little's Hotel.
DUGAN THOMAS, French boot manufacturer, 4 Blake's Building, 4th store. res. 152 N. Ohio.
Duke Mrs., (wid.,) W. Indianapolis.
Duke James, res. First, bet. Meridian and Illinois.
Dukwater Jacob, railroader, E. end of Market.
Dulz John P., clerk 256 E. Washington, bds. same.
Dumont E., Brigadier General U. S. A., res. 60 N. Alabama.
Dumont Eugene A., book-keeper Western Machine Works, bds. N. W. cor. Louisiana and New Jersey.
Dumont John J., (D. & Sinker,) res. S. W. cor. Louisiana and New Jersey.
Dumont & Sinker, Western Machine Works, cor. Pennsylvania and Railroad.
Dunbar Melzar, mason, res. 178 S. Pennsylvania.
Dunbar James, res. 117 W. North.
Duncan Harry, bds. 13 Kentucky ave.
Duncan John, laborer, res. 153 East.
Duncan Robert, 2nd engineer Identical Mills.
Duncan Robert B., attorney at law, office Hubbard's block, res. Ft. Wayne ave.
Dunlap James, artist, 137 E. Washington.
Dunlap Livingston, physician, res. 12 Virginia ave.
Dunlop John, Sr., res. 72 N. Meridian.
DUNLOP JOHN S., general insurance and real estate agent, cor. Meridian and Washington. res. 114 N. Meridian.
Dunlop Robert, works Goldsmith's nursery, res. 83 Huron.
Dunmire Anthon, laborer, res. 5 Railroad.
Dunn Mrs. E. A., (wid.,) res. 26 and 28 W. New York.
DUNN JACOB P., notary public, office Indianapolis Branch Bank, res. 80 E. Market.

850 families in Indianapolis and vicinity use Wheeler & Wilson.

CITY GROCERY.

C. L. HOLMES,
Wholesale and Retail

GROCER, PRODUCE
AND COMMISSION MERCHANT,
And Dealer in

FOREIGN FRUITS, &c.,
NO. 31 WEST WASHINGTON STREET,
First door West of Charles Meyer,

INDIANAPOLIS, IND.

CHARLES COX,
Manufacturer of

Tin and Sheet-Iron Ware,
And Dealer in

PARLOR, COOKING AND HEATING STOVES,
Hot-Air Furnaces,
FOR HEATING PUBLIC AND PRIVATE BUILDINGS.
No. 11 WEST WASHINGTON STREET,
INDIANAPOLIS, IND.

HENNING & STELZELL,
Proprietors of

BATES HOUSE
AND
PALMER HOUSE
Hair-dressing
SALOONS,
NOS. 12 ILLINOIS ST.,
And 1 Palmer House.

Cold, Warm and Shower Baths. Hair-cutting and Shampooing done by the best workmen.

A Wheeler & Wilson Sewing Machine will last a life-time.

Dunn John C., plumber and gas fitter, 24 Kentucky ave. res. Mississippi, N. of St. Clair.
Dunn W. A., clerk Wright, Bates & Maguire, res. 20 S. Mississippi.
Dunn William, porter 6 Bates House, res. 6 S. Tennessee.
Durham George W., bricklayer, 142 E. Ohio.
Durie Henry, engineer, res. 149 E. Ohio.
Durninger ——, plasterer, res. 17 E. George.
Dury John, salesman 5 W. Washington, res. 72 N. East.
Duthie James, helper Central car shop, res. 12 Bates.
Duvall D. C., grocer, res. 113 N. Illinois.
Duvall David, clerk 31 W. Washington, res. 113 N. Illinois.
Duvall Joseph P., butcher, 260 Madison ave.
Duzen William, cabinet maker, res. 132 E. North.
Dwyer Thomas, laborer, res. 51 E. Market.
Dwyer William, shoemaker, 308 S. Delaware.
DYE JOHN T., attorney at law, Blackford's Building, res. 154 W. New York. (See card.)
Dyer Stephen, railroader, res. 234 Indiana ave.

E

Eads Miranda, school teacher, bds. 31 N. Ellsworth.
Eagle John H., foreman Journal office, res. 142 N. Alabama.
EAGLE SALOON, 130 E. Washington, Christ. Wriedt, proprietor.
Early Peter, workman at Rolling Mill, res. 63 Bluff Road.
Early Peter, U. S. A., res. 178 S. East.
East Empire Saloon, Charles Lauer, proprietor, 162 E. Washington.
Eastman Henry, U. S. A., res. 191 S. Delaware.
Ebert John, carpenter and builder, 32 Kentucky ave., res. South. second house W. of Canal.
Eckhart Wm. A., salesman 19 W. Washington, bds. Farmers' Hotel.
Eden Charlton, carpenter, res. 86 E. Ohio.
Edger Mrs. Margaret, res. 88 N. New Jersey.
Edwards E., boarding house, 53 S. Illinois.
Edmonds William, (V. K. Hendricks & Co.,) 76 W. Washington, res. 85 N. Meridian.
EVERSON GEO. V., produce dealer, bds. 42 W. Maryland.
Egner Franz, (E. & Wocher,) bds. Union Hall.
EGNER & WOCHER, wholesale and retail druggists, 81 E. Washington.
Ehmann Thomas, teamster, res. Tennessee, bet. Fourth and Fifth.
Eilaling Dedroch, drayman, res. 13 E. McCarthy.

INDIANAPOLIS

J. M. FROST,

Manufacturer and Wholesale Dealer in

PATENT MEDICINES,

PROPRIETOR OF

FROST'S LONDON PILLS,
FROST'S LINIMENT,
FROST'S PAIN RELIEF,
EGYPTIAN SALVE,
OTTAR OF ROSES.

Also, Wholesale Dealer in Foreign and Domestic

CIGARS, TOBACCO, &c.

No. 95 East Washington Street,

INDIANAPOLIS, IND.

AGENTS WANTED, to whom a good commission or salary will be given.

A. J. DANFORTH. F. F. SIMPSON.

DANFORTH & SIMPSON,

Wholesale and Retail Dealers in

Groceries, Produce, &c.

No. 3 Odd Fellows' Hall,

INDIANAPOLIS, IND.

Goods delivered free to any part of the city. Particular attention given to keeping choice Teas, Coffee, Sugars, &c., &c.

A Wheeler & Wilson Sewing Machine with Hemmer, for $50.

Einatz Anthony, res. 127 N. Delaware.
Ekin Capt. James A., U. S. Quartermaster, bds. Bates House.
Elbersmeier Henry, laborer, res. 152 N. Noble.
Elbreg George, marble cutter, bds. Kinder House.
ELDER JOHN R., (E., Harkness & Bingham,) res. 78 N. New Jersey.
Elder E. A., clerk postoffice, res. 98 N. West.
Elder William G., boarding house, res. 89 E. Market.
ELDER, HARKNESS & BINGHAM, proprietors of Daily and Weekly Indiana State Sentinel, S. Meridian, opp. old postoffice.
Eldridge Jacob, real estate agent, 13 S. Illinois, res. 50 S. Mississippi.
Elff Frank, barber, shop Washington, res. 49 E. Maryland.
Ellenbogen Elias M., salesman 4 W. Washington, bds. Macy House.
Ellicott Mrs., washer, res. 91 Railroad.
Elliott Mrs. M., (wid.,) res. 81 S. New Jersey.
Elliott Byron K., attorney at law and notary public 24½ E. Washington, bds. Oriental.
ELLIOTT C. A., wholesale grocer and dealer in liquors, cor. Meridian and Maryland, res. 77 N. Illinois.
Elliott Capt. John, bar-keeper City Saloon, bds. Oriental House.
Elliott Harvey J., conductor I. & C. R. R., res. 141 E. South.
ELLIOTT J. F., general agent I. M. Singer's Sewing Machines, 3 Odd Fellows' Hall, Washington, res. 33 N. Delaware.
Elliott J. T., clerk Oriental House.
Elliott Russell, salesman Boston Store, bds. Pyle House.
Elliott S. T., bds. Little's Hotel.
Elliott S. W., adjutant 56 regiment, bds. Oriental House.
Elliott Thomas B., flour, grain and produce, cor. S. Alabama and Ind. & Cin. R. R.
Elliott W. J., proprietor Oriental House, Illinois, bet. Maryland and Georgia.
Ellis Henry, carpenter, bds. 142 N. New Jersey.
Ellsworth Henry, attorney at law, res. 88 N. Meridian.
Ellsworth S. W., conductor Laf. & Ind. R. R., bds. Bates House.
Elms Charles, fireman Bellefontaine R. R., res. 34 E. Georgia.
Elmer J. W., clerk Madison Depot, res. 140 E. McCarty.
Elstrod Henry, wood sawyer, res. 143 N. Liberty.
Ely Ephraim, carpenter, W. Indianapolis.
Emerson R., carpenter, res. 141 W. Ohio.
Emett Robert, laborer, res. 7 E. New York.

7

350 families in Indianapolis and vicinity use Wheeler & Wilson.

Jeffersonville
RAILROAD.

The Great Southern United States Mail and Express Route,

FROM INDIANAPOLIS
TO THE
SOUTH & SOUTH-WEST,

VIA LOUISVILLE, KENTUCKY,

Connecting with Trains on the

LOUISVILLE AND NASHVILLE RAILROAD,

AND WITH

Louisville & Memphis and Louisville & New Orleans

LINE PACKETS,

For Nashville, Chattanooga, Memphis, Vicksburg, Jackson, Huntsville, New Orleans, and all the Principal Southern Cities.

TWO TRAINS LEAVE INDIANAPOLIS DAILY,
(SUNDAYS EXCEPTED.)

Passengers from the North, East and West, will find the route by the way of Indianapolis & Jeffersonville Railroad, the most expeditious route to the Principal Cities in the West and South-West.

THROUGH TICKETS sold in all the principal Railroad and Ticket Offices in the Eastern and Northern States. Remember the route, via Indianapolis and Louisville, via Jeffersonville Railroad.

A. S. CROTHERS, Sup't.

H. H. REYNOLDS, Gen'l Ticket Agent.

J. G. WHITCOMB, Agent, Indianapolis.

Wheeler & Wilson's Sewing Machines awarded the first premium for five

EMMENEGGER MATHIAS, proprietor Emmenegger's Union Hall, 107, 109, 111 and 113 E. Washington.
Emmerich Henry, (E. & Reese,) res. 91 W. Washington.
Emmerich & Reese, wholesale and retail grocers, 91 and 93 W. Washington.
EMPIRE SALOON, R. Beebe, proprietor, 23 W. Washington.
Enda Herman, dyer, Ohio Premium Woolen Factory.
Enderlin John, confectioner, Union Steam Bakery.
Enderschord Harman, works Ohio Woolen Factory, bds. 83 Illinois.
Indicut Isham, (col.,) saloon-tender, res. 68 W. Vermont.
Engel John, butcher, res. 152 E. Market.
English John, ostler Exchange Stables.
English Joseph K., city treasurer, office Glenns' Block, res. 113, cor. Michigan and East.
Ennes Philip, grocer, res. 229 Massachusetts ave.
Ennis William, cabinet maker, res. 225 N. Noble.
Ennis Louis, butcher, Central Meet Market, res. 223 N. Noble.
Enter Wegant, hat house, res. Missouri, bet. Georgia and South.
Erling George, res. 96 E. Maryland.
Ernst Frederick, drayman, res. 23 Union.
Esemann Joseph, wood sawyer, corporation line, Madison Lane.
Eske Christ., engine house, res. 344 Virginia ave.
Espy Mrs. Margaret, (wid.,) res. 85 S. Tennessee.
Etherington Benj., machinist, Lawrenceburg car shop, res. 91 Bates.
Etherton Samuel, laborer, res. W. Market.
Etsler Charles, bds. 156 N. East.
Etsler Lloyd, res. 156 N. East.
Etswahn Ed., res. 89 W. New York.
Eugel Jacob, cartman, works V. Butsch & Co., res. 35 Spring.
Eulalia, Sister of Providence, cor. Georgia and Tennessee.
Euller George, shoemaker, bds. 101 Spring.
Eurich John, (E. & Schaffer,) res. Illinois.
EURICH & SCHAFFER, St. Nicholas Saloon, 7 N. Illinois.
Evans David B., labarer, bds. 19 William.
Evans George T., (J. P. E. & Co.,) bds. Macy House.
Evans H. W., works Lawrenceburg car shop, res. E. National Road.
Evans J. L., (J. L. & W. N. E.,) res. Noblesville, Ind.
Evans J. L. & W. N.,) wholesale boots and shoes, 3 Bates House.
Evans John, shoemaker, shop and res. 65 E. end W. South.

.Successive years at Mechanic's Institute, Cincinnati.

BOOK BINDERY.

H. H. DODD & CO.,

No. 18 East Washington Street,

INDIANAPOLIS, IND.

BLANK BOOKS OF EVERY DESCRIPTION,

Made to Order on Short Notice.

PRINTING AND BINDING FOR PUBLISHERS,

Upon the most Liberal Terms.

Evans J. P. & Co., Capital Steam Flour Mills, cor. Market and Missouri.
Evans O. F., book-keeper, 30 S. Meridian, bds. Macy House.
EVANS REV. THOMAS, United Brethren, res. 27 N. Liberty.
Evans W. N., (J. L. & W. N. E.,) res. Noblesville, Ind.
Evers John, mattress maker, res. 191 E. Washington.
Everson Erastus, bds. 42 W. Maryland.
Everson George V., egg and produce dealer, under Metropolitan Hall, W. Washington, res. 42 W. Maryland.
Everling Ernos, porter New York Store, res. 109 E. South.
Everling Mary, (wid.,) res. 27 N. Ellsworth.
Eviler Mrs. M., res. 101 Railroad.
Ewing B., (J. & B. E.,) res. 20 Virginia ave.
Ewing J., (J. &. B. E.,) res. 20 Virginia ave.
Ewing J. &. B., physicians, 18 Virginia ave.
EXCHANGE BILLIARD ROOM, Exchange Building, Chauncey Montgomery, proprietor.
EXCHANGE BUILDING, Charles W. Hall, proprietor, Illinois, opp. Bates House.
EXCHANGE LIVERY AND SALE STABLE, Charles W. Hall & Co., proprietors, Illinois, opp. Bates House.
EXCHANGE RESTAURANT, Chas. W. Hall, proprietor, Illinois, opp. Bates House.
EXLINE REV. GEO. A., minister English Luthran Church, res. Illinois, bet. Second and Third.

F

Faber August, saloon, 73 S. Illinois, res. same.
Fack Frederic, bar-keeper, State House Saloon, res. same.
FAHNESTOCK JOHN, engraver on wood, 19 W. Washington, res. 71 N. Alabama.
Fahnestock Mrs. O., dress maker, 18 S. Illinois, res. same.
Fahnestock Dr. S., physician and surgeon, 2 second story Glenns' Block, res. 71 N. Alabama.
Fahrbach Philip, brick-layer, res. 42 W. South.
Fahrion Christian, cabinet maker, 61 E. Washington.
Fairbank Andrew, plasterer, res. 148 S. New Jersey.
Fairley John P., bds. Palmer House.
FAIVIE F. J., salesman, cor. Illinois and Maryland, bds. Pyle House.
Falkner Mumford, teamster, W. Indianapolis.
Farion George, with Fred. Rusch, res. 45 Union.
Farley Richard, laborer, res. 147 N. Tennessee.
Farley Thomas, saw maker, bds. Spencer House.
Farll Ferguson, works Crossland's store, res. 39 W. St. Clair.

TERRE HAUTE & RICHMOND

RAILROAD.

Trains leave Terre Haute for Indianapolis daily, (Sundays excepted,) as follows:

First Express Train,

Leaves Terre Haute at 1.45 A. M., and arrives at Indianapolis at 4.50 A. M.

Second Express Train,

Leaves Terre Haute at 3.55 P. M., and arrives at Indianapolis at 9.00 P. M.

These trains make close connections at Indianapolis with Trains for

NEW YORK, BOSTON, PHILADELPHIA,

Baltimore, Washington City, Cincinnati, Louisville, &c.

Mail Train

Leaves Terre Haute at 8.05 A. M., and arrives at Indianapolis at 11.32 A. M.; stops at all way stations; connects at Indianapolis with Trains for

Cincinnati, Cleveland, Columbus and Madison.

☞ Passengers will please procure Tickets before entering the Cars. Through Tickets for all the Eastern Cities, &c., to be had at the Ticket Office. Freight Trains leave daily, except Sunday.

FREIGHT ARRANGEMENTS.

Quick time is made by Express Freight Trains from St. Louis to the East. Only one change between St. Louis and Pittsburg, Buffalo and Cleveland. Stock Shippers will find this the most Superior Route to the East. Any arrragements can be made with James Beebe, corner of Second and Poplar streets, St. Louis, Missouri, in Valentine & Co.'s Freight House.

E. J. PECK, President.

CHAS. WOOD, Secretary.

First Premium awarded the Wheeler & Wilson Sewing Machine for three

Farmer J. B., (Birch & F.,) res. 280 R. R. ave.
FARMERS' HOTEL, H. E. Buehrig, proprietor, cor. Illinois and Georgia.
Farmers'.Hotel Saloon, H. E. Buehrig, proprietor.
Farrall Fergus, porter 75 W. Washington, res. St. Clair.
Farrell Miss C. J., dress maker, res. 21 S. Delaware.
Farrell John, clerk post office, res. Davidson, bet. New York and Vermont.
Farreon Geo., teamster 81 and 83 Masonic Hall.
Farrow James, painter, res. 54 E. St. Mary.
Fassett A. H., machinist, bds. 258 W. Washington.
Fatout J. L., (J. L. & M. K. F.,) bds. 85 Indiana ave.
Fatout M. K., (J. L. & M. K. F.,) res. 85 Indiana ave.
Fatout J. L. & M. K., carpenters and builders, 109 Indiana ave.
Fatter George, tailor, Duncan, bet. Delaware and Alabama.
Faulkner Isaac B., traveling agent for William Sheets, bds. Pyle House.
Fawler Benjamin, res. 21, alley E. of S. East.
Fay Henry, wagoner for Meikel's brewery, res. W. Maryland, bet. West and Missouri.
Feakner Gotleib, railroader, res. S. West.
Fearnly John, (F. & Greer,) carpenter, 68 S. Delaware, res. outside corporation.
Feary Henry, printer, Sentinel Office, bds. 154 E. North.
Feary Jeremiah E., carpenter, 7 Virginia ave., res. 154 E. North.
Feathering George, farmer, res. 199 E. Ohio.
Featherston Wm. E., (F. &. Barker,) res. 115 Massachusetts ave., bet. Michigan and North.
Featherston & Barker, auctioneers and commission merchants, 56 E. Washington.
Feeling Frederic W., grocery, res. 125 E. South.
Fegen John, tailor, bds. 87 E. Washington.
Feigh Conrad, wood sawyer, res. 72 N. Noble.
FELLER GEORGE, watchmaker and jeweler, and silverware manufacturer, 67 W. Washington, res. same.
Feltbutsch John, laborer, res. 83 Davidson.
Felter Thos., laborer, res. 3 Bates.
Fenling Joseph, City Bakery, 201 E. Washington.
Ferdinand Zimmer, barber shop, 62 South.
Ferguson A. L., pressman Journal Office, bds. 43 Georgia.
Ferguson C. A., watchmaker and jeweler, 7 W. Washington, res. 13 W. Ohio.
Ferguson Jas. C., pork packer, res. 28 N. Meridian.
Ferguson Kilby, attorney at law, 24½ E. Washington, res. S. E. cor. McCarty and East.
Ferguson L. A., clerk 8 S. Meridian, bds. 112 Virginia ave.

Successive years at the United States Fair.

FRANCIS A. RATTI,
SOLE AGENT FOR THE
Cincinnati Daily Papers,

Delivered to Subscribers upon the arrival of the MORNING TRAIN from Cincinnati.

Commercial, - - 12 1-2 Cents	Large Gazette, - - 15 Cents
Enquirer, - - - - 12 1-2 Cents	Small Gazette, - - 10 Cents

Per Week, payable at the end of every Two Weeks.

Orders left at Cameron's Job Office, 8 East Pearl St., will be attended to.

House-Building and House-Furnishing
HARDWARE,

Of every style and price, Cheap for Cash,
71 East Washington St., Sign of BIG PAD-LOCK,

J. BIRCH & CO.,
Wholesale and Retail Dealers in
Groceries, Provisions,
COUNTRY PRODUCE, ETC.
79 East Washington St., - - INDIANAPOLIS.

☞ Fruits of all kinds constantly on hand. ☜

Upwards of 100 W. & W. Machines in use in Ind'p'lis making army clothing.

Ferguson R., cutter Dessar & Bro., res. 104 N. Meridian.
Ferito Patrick, laborer, res. 50 Bates.
Ferling Charles (Lenruger & F.,) res. 96 Maryland.
Ferree J. D., printer American Office, res. 138 E. Ohio.
Ferris Mrs. Mary, (wid.,) res. 103 W. South.
Ferrita Maurice, school teacher, res. 76 Bluff Road.
Ferry Jas., messenger Adams Express Co., res. 68 W. Vermont.
FERTIG FRANK, house, sign, plain and ornamental painter, also grainer, 6 E. Washington, res. 41 South.
Ferthnicht Ernst, (Heithum & F.,) res. Virginia ave.
Fetrow Alexander, carpenter, res. 72 S. East.
Fey & Remman, Astor Saloon Restaurant, 9 N. Pennsylvania.
Fike Peter, teamster, 53 Madison ave.
Findley William, superintendent Exchange Buildings, bds. 44 N. Pennsylvania.
Findling Valentine, plasterer, res. Alabama, bet. St. Clair and Wood.
Finger Ibert, currier, res. W. North.
Fink Daniel, candy maker, res. 34 Louisiana.
Fink John F., machinist, Western Machine Works.
Finn John, cooper, res. 14 Union.
Finn John, laborer, res. 217 S. Delaware.
Finter Friedrick, baker, res. 77 Ft. Wayne ave.
Fintson James P., carpenter, res. 130 E. Ohio.
Fiscus Andrew, brick-layer, res. Davidson, bet. New York and Michigan.
Fiscus John, brick mason, res. Davidson, bet. New York and Michigan.
Fiscus Thomas W., brick mason, res. 136 E. St. Clair.
Fiscus William, brick mason, res. 155 E. New York.
Fish A. A., photograph artist, cor. Meridian and Washington, res. same.
Fish Mrs. Elizabeth, res. 116 N. Mississippi.
Fish John L., mailing clerk P. O., res. 11 E. Michigan.
Fish William, printer Journal office, bds. 11 E. Michigan.
FISHBACK CHARLES, physician, office 22 E. Market, res. 48 E. New York.
FISHBACK JOHN, wholesale and retail dealer in hides, leather, &c., 30 S. Meridian, res. 49 S. Meridian.
Fishback Wm. P., (Harrison & F.,) res. 137 Virginia ave.
Fisher Adam, laborer, res. in rear of 6 Bluff Road.
Fisher Andrew, furniture store, 78 E. Washington, res. 120 N. East.
Fisher A., painter, res. 120 N. East.
Fisher Benjamin, barber, cor. Louisiana and Illinois, res. 147 S. Mississippi.

A Wheeler & Wilson Sewing Machine will last a life-time.

MADISON

AND
INDIANAPOLIS R. R.

Daily Trains leave Union Depot, Indianapolis, for

Madison, Cincinnati & Louisville.

This is the Shortest Railway Line from Indianapolis to Cincinnati and Louisville, connecting at Madison with

UNITED STATES MAIL STEAMERS,

For Cincinnati, which connect with the Express Trains leaving in the morning for the East, and by the Kentucky Central Railroad for the South.

RETURNING, Arrive at Indianapolis at 10.50 A. M., making connections with all Trains leaving for the

EAST, NORTH AND WEST.

☞ Fare to Cincinnati, or from Cincinnati to Indianapolis, $3 00. To Louisville, $3 50.

NO CHARGE FOR MEALS OR STATE-ROOMS

On the Steamers, or for Baggage or Omnibus at Madison. Shippers and Merchants west, will find it to their interest to travel over and ship by this line.

D. C. BRANHAM, Sup't.
T. P. MATTHEWS, Gen. Freight and Ticket Ag't, Madison.
R. E. ROCKWELL, Freight Ag't, Indianapolis.

The Wheeler & Wilson Hemmer makes hems of any width.

FISHER CHARLES, justice of the peace, res. 16 W. North.
Fisher Charles, cooper, res. 37 Spring.
Fisher Charles, tailor, 69 E. Washington.
Fisher George, shoemaker, res. 224 N. New Jersey.
Fisher Matthew, head waiter Bates House.
Fisher Matthew, shoemaker, res. 64 Bluff Road.
Fisher W. G., tinner, 177 E. Washington.
Fisher W. I., shoemaker, lives around town.
Fisher William, U. S. A., res. 129 Blake.
Fisk Hiram, blacksmith, res. 79 Davidson.
Fitch William, policeman, res. 65 N. West.
Fitchey Michael, carpenter, res. 115 W. Maryland.
Fitzgerald John, tinner, 62 E. Washington, res. 308 Delaware.
Fitzgerald William, laborer, res. in rear of 208 S. Delaware.
Fitzgibbon M., (M. F. & Co.,) res. cor. Mississippi and W. Washington.
FITZGIBBON & CO., wholesale grocers and commission merchants, Meridian, opp. Union Depot.
Flacck John, cigar maker, 18 E. Washington, bds. Union Hall.
FLAGG S. A., proprietor Magnolia Saloon, 9 S. Illinois, bds. 10 Mississippi.
Flaherty Caleb, wood-hauler, res. 35 Hosbrook.
Flaherty John, laborer, res. 20 Garden.
Flaig Matthew V., carpenter, 22 Kentucky ave., bds. South, second door W. of Canal.
Flaper ——, farmer, res. Illinois, N. of Sixth.
Flatauer M., (F. & Jackson,) res. Ohio.
Flatauer & Jackson, dealer in dry and fancy goods, 75 E. Washington.
Flatauor Michael, peddler, res. Wabash, bet. Liberty and Noble.
FLEMING GEO. H., editor and publisher of "Indiana's Home-Life and Camp-Life," bds. Palmer House.
Fleming Peter, laborer, res. 16 S. Noble.
FLETCHER'S BANKING OFFICE, S. A. Fletcher, proprietor, 30 E. Washington.
Fletcher Calvin, Sr., (F. & Sharpe,) res. N. Pennsylvania.
Fletcher David, laborer, res. 187 S. New Jersey.
Fletcher H. A., (H. A. F. & Co.,) bds. Bates House.
FLETCHER H. A. & CO., wholesale and retail dealers in staple and fancy dry goods, carpets, oil cloths, &c., 26 and 28 W. Washington.
Fletcher H. F., messenger American Express Company.
Fletcher John, well-digger, 330 S. Delaware.
FLETCHER MILES J., Superintendent of Public Instruction, bds. Bates House.

THE GREAT
CENTRAL ROUTE.

1862. 1862.

Indianapolis & Columbus
SHORT LINE.

Three Daily Trains to Columbus without Change of Cars.

Indiana Central Railway.

This line is the Great Central Short Line from St. Louis to Dayton, Columbus, Pittsburg, Cleveland, New York, Boston, and all intermediate points, and is the most desirable route in its facilities and accommodations to passengers and shippers.

Passengers having tickets via this route, can take choice of the four Great Eastern Lines.

Only One Change of Cars between Indianapolis,

PITTSBURG, WHEELING AND CLEVELAND.

Being of uniform guage with all Railroads East of Indianapolis, this route offers unparalleled inducements to Shippers of Live Stock and Freight.

Passengers desiring to take advantage of the Short Line must be particular to call for tickets via

Indianapolis, Dayton & Columbus

The only direct route to Zanesville, Newark, Steubenville, Pittsburg, Wheeling, &c.

CINCINNATI,

The only route through Richmond, Hamilton, &c. Two daily trains connect at Cincinnati with Kentucky Central Railroad for Cynthiana, Lexington and Paris. Also with River Packets for Parkersburg, Marietta, &c.

SECURE YOUR TICKETS VIA INDIANA CENTRAL.

HORACE PARROTT, Gen'l Ticket Agent.

H. G. CAREY, Superintendent.

Wheeler & Wilson's Sewing Machines warranted for three years.

FLETCHER S. A., proprietor Fletcher's Bank, 30 E. Washington, res. 88 E. Ohio.
Fletcher S. A., Jr., teller Fletcher's Bank, res. 187 Virginia ave.
Fletcher William, shoemaker, 32 E. Washington, res. 7 North.
Fletcher William, res. 267 Virginia ave.
Fletcher Zach., cabinet maker, res. 64 W. Vermont.
FLETCHER & SHARPE, Indianapolis Branch Banking Company, cor. Washington and Pennsylvania.
Flinn Joanna, (wid.,) res. 234 Madison ave.
Flinn James, laborer, res. 196 S. East.
Flinn Pat., res. Canal, S. of South,
Flitz Charles, (Runer & F.,) res. 100 Bluff Road.
FLORANCE'S SALOON, Florance Richter, proprietor, 13 N. Illinois.
Flours Samuel, carpenter, res. 105 E. South.
Flowers A. B. J., pattern-maker, res. 131 W. Maryland.
Flynn Byron P., laborer, res. 15 S. Alabama.
Fobes Albert D., deputy clerk Supreme Court, State House.
Fogan James B., stone cutter, bds. Farmers' Hotel.
Fogerty William, workman at Rolling Mill, res. 12 Willard.
Fogle Frederick, plasterer, res. Winston, near Railroad.
Folay Patrick, railroader, res. 78 E. Louisiana.
Foley Charles, student, bds. 86 Massachusetts ave.
Foley James, ostler, 14 N. Pennsylvania, res. Virginia ave.
Foley Margaret, (wid.,) boarding house, 196 S. Delaware.
Foley Tim., works for J. K. Sharpe, res. S. E. Michigan Road.
Follett Nathaniel, head miller Bates City Mills, bds. Little's Hotel.
Foltz Frederick, res. 113 N. Alabama.
Foos Thomas J., bakery 84 N. Mississippi, res. same.
Foote Jeremiah, res. 10 E. Michigan.
Forbes Matthew, engineer Bellefontaine R. R., res. 68 Spring.
Ford Charles J., clerk Werden & Co., bds. Palmer House.
Ford John, traveling agent, res. 23 W. Michigan.
Forsha Joseph, W. Indianapolis.
Forshee George W., blacksmith, res. 93 Massachusetts ave.
Forsyth Foster, salesman Bee-Hive, bds. 71 N. Pennsylvania.
Forsyth William, U. S. Quartermaster's office, res. 71 N. Pennsylvania.
Forstride Louis, shoemaker, bds. Farmers' Hotel.
Forwinger J., tailor, 84 E. Washington.
Foster Alford, boiler maker Lawrenceburg car shop, res. 15 Lord.
Foster E. J., salesman 26 and 28 W. Washington, bds. Palmer House.

81,000 Wheeler & Wilson's Sewing Machines in use in this country.

THE OLD AND RELIABLE
METROPOLITAN
FINE ART
GALLERY,

College Hall Building, 34 1-2 E. Washington,

INDIANAPOLIS, INDIANA,

IS THE PLACE TO GET THE BEST

PHOTOGRAPHS

OF ALL SIZES, FROM

CARD VISITE to LIFE-SIZE.

ALSO,

DAGUERREOTYPES,

Ambrotypes,
Malainotypes,
Ferrotypes, &c.,

AT LOW PRICES. REMEMBER, THIS IS THE ONLY GALLERY WHERE THE

GENUINE DAGUERREOTYPE

IS MADE. ANY SMALL PICTURE ENLARGED TO

LIFE-SIZE, and COLORED IN OIL by Superior Artists.

WEEKS & COX.

The First Premium awarded the Wheeler & Wilson Machine

FOSTER REV. JAMES, pastor of Universalist Church, bds. 8 Virginia ave.
Foster R. Sanford, Lieutenant Colonel 13th Regiment Indiana Volunteers.
Foster William R., at Deaf and Dumb Asylum.
Foster Wallace S., Lieutenant 13th Regiment Indiana Volunteers.
FOUDRAY JOHN E., (Wood & F.,) res. 109 N. New Jersey.
Foudray Mrs. Martha, res. 3 Massachusetts ave.
Foulton John, res. 145 Virginia ave.
Foulke Mrs. Elizabeth, dressmaker, bds. 79 Massacusetts ave.
Foust Mrs. Daniel, res. 85 Illinois.
Fox Barney, laborer, res. 66 Hosbrook.
Fox Joseph, waiter Union Hall.
Fox Martin, bar-keeper Capital Saloon.
Frailing Patrick, laborer, res. 288 Virginia ave.
Frances Mrs. Sarah, seamstress, res. 6 S. Pennsylvania.
Francis William, brakesman I. & C. R. R., res. 100 Bates.
Franco Alex., res. cor. Mississippi and Washington.
Frank Henry, (Spiegel, Thoms & Co.,) res. cor. Spring and Vermont.
Frank Joseph, laborer, res. near Virginia ave,
Frank Samel, salesman Glaser & Bro., bds. Pyle House.
Frankem Jonathan, clerk I. L. Frankem's stove store, 49 and 51 E. Washington, res. 155 N. Illinois.
Frankem I. L., stove store, 49 and 51 E. Washington, res. 155 N. Illinois.
Frankenstein George, Morris House shaving saloon, res. opp. Madison Depot.
Franklin Anderson, (col.,) laborer, res. 73 W. Vermont.
FRANKLIN WM. H., barber under Branch Bank, res. 126 W. Ohio. (See card.)
Franstein George, barber shop Morris House, res. 33 South.
Franz Peter, well digger, res. 159 Railroad.
Franzman Adam, salesman 70 E. Washington, bds. at Beck's.
Frauer I. C., German Druggist, 185 E. Washington, res. same.
Fraug F. E., cabinet maker, bds. cor. Alabama and Washington.
Frazee Samuel, res. 104 N. Illinois.
Frazier John H., deputy U. S. Marshal, res. 144 E. North.
Frazier William, bridge builder, res. bet. New York and Vermont.
Frederick Godfrey, laborer, res. 39 S. Illinois.
Freeman John, (col.,) oyster saloon under telegraph office, res. N. Meridian.
Freeman N. B., salesman E. C. Mayhew & Co., res. 71 W. New York.

TRADE PALACE.

H. A. FLETCHER & CO.,

Dealers in

RICH,

FANCY

AND STAPLE

DRY GOODS,

CARPETS,

FLOOR OIL CLOTHS,

Cocoa Matting,

MATS, RUGS, DAMASKS,

SHADES, GILT CORNICE,

AND

HOUSE FURNISHING GOODS GENERALLY.

RAY'S STONE BLOCK,

Nos. 26 and 28 West Washington Street,

INDIANAPOLIS, INDIANA.

Carpets cut and made to order. Oil Cloths put down, and Cornice and Shades put up.

The Wheeler & Wilson Hemmer is the only Hemmer that will Fell.

FREE PRESS, (German) daily and weekly, Richard Heninger, proprietor.
FRENCH CHARLES G., jeweler and watchmaker, 37 W. Washington, res. E. Washington.
FRENZEL JOHN P., Kansas Eating Saloon 83, drinking saloon 85 S. Illinois, res. same.
Frick Philip, tinner, 177 E. Washington.
FRICKE REV. CHARLES, German Lutheran, res. 13 N. East.
Friday Michael, carpenter, res. 167 E. Michigan.
Frink E. O., dentist, 4 Yohn's Block, bds. 118 N. Pennsylvania.
FRINK S. C., dentist, 4 Yohn's Block, Meridian, res. 118 N. Pennsylvania.
Fritz Joseph, currier for Mooney & Co.
Frizzell Allen, carpenter, res. Mississippi, bet. First and Second.
Froelking John F., watchman Bellefontaine depot, 253 S. Pennsylvania.
Frommier Henry, clerk 16 W. Washington, res. 76 N. Mississippi.
FROST J. M., manufacturer and wholesale dealer in patent medicines, also dealer in foreign and domestic cigars, 95 E. Washington, res. 150 N. Pennsylvania.
Frost Nicholas, laborer, res. 162 S. Tennessee.
Frushour Casper, brick-layer, res. 146 S. New Jersey.
Fry Mrs. R. N., res. 122 N. Illinois.
Fugate James L., salesman 21 W. Washington, res. 65 W. New York.
Fuller J. M., attorney at law, res. 14 E. Ohio.
Fulmore Charles, railroader, res. 2 E. Louisiana.
Fulweiler John, res. 114 W. Georgia.
FUNKHOUSER D., (Jamison & F.,) office 5 S. Meridian.
Furchtniht Ernst, cabinet maker for Spiegel, Thoms & Co., res 279 Virginia ave.

G

Gaear David, tailor, res. Tennessee, bet. Fourth and Fifth.
Gaebert Henry, laborer, res. 41 Union.
Gaff Andrew, butcher, bds. 179 E. Market.
Gaff Andrew, butcher, shop Noble, near Market, res. 60 E. St. Joseph.
Gaff Henry, wood cutter, res. 64 E. St. Joseph.
Gahm John, grocer, cor. North and Indiana ave.
Gale John, laborer, Root, Bennett & Co.
Galivan Michael, policeman, res. 25 Henry.

Upwards of 100 W. & W. Machines in use in Ind'p'lis making army clothing.

Gall Dr. A., office Glenns' Block, res. 37 N. New Jersey.
Gall Edwin, clerk, 28 E. Washington, bds. 37 N. New Jersey.
Gall John, machinist, Western Foundry, res. 38 S. Illinois.
Gallagher Francis, laborer, res. 42 Massachusetts ave.
Gallatin Albert, (col.,) whitewasher, N. Missouri, bet. Vermont and Michigan.
Gallegar Mrs. Mary, washer, res. 33 E. Market.
Galloway John A., painter, res. 36 N. Illinois.
Gallup E. P., (W. P. & E. P. G.,) bds. Bates House.
Gallup W. P., (W. P. & E. P. G.,) bds. Bates House.
Gallup W. P. & E. P., grain dealers, commission merchants and agents for Fairbanks' scales, 74 W. Washington.
Gamble James, carpenter, res. bet. East and New Jersey, and Washington and Market.
Gamerdinger Jacob, striker Lawrenceburg car shop, res. E. National Road.
Ganber John, blacksmith for Beard, Starr & Co., bds. Ohio House.
Gansberg Frederick, at Union Depot, res. 318 Virginia ave.
Ganter C., bakery, 181 E. Washington, res. same.
Ganter Daniel, baker, bds. 181 E. Washington.
Gardiner Richard C., comb maker, 25 N. Alabama, res. same.
Gardner Conrad, butcher, res. 155 N. Mississippi.
Gardner S., sash maker, res. W. James.
Garin Francis, blacksmith, 43 McCarthy.
Garety Michael, driver Adams Express, res. Vermont.
Garlick H. M., clerk American Express office, bds. 11 W. Market.
Garner Conrad, butcher, res. 155 Mississippi.
Garner L. W., watch-maker, 7 W. Washington, bds. Pyle House.
Garrett Joseph, workman at brass foundry, res. 219 S. East.
Garther Thomas, messenger Adams Express Company, bds. Palmer House.
Gartner Joseph, tinner, W. Washington, res. 155 Mississippi.
Garver Matthias, teamster, bds. 48 W. South.
Gaston Edward Y., (H. R. G. & Co.,) res. 37 Kentucky ave.
Gaston Hiram R., (H. R. G. & Co.,) res. 27 Kentucky ave.
Gaston H. R. & Co., carriage makers, Kentucky ave.
Gaston John M., physician and surgeon, 22 E. Market, res. 77 N. New Jersey.
Gaston Sim., bar-keeper Johnston's saloon, bds. Bender House.
Gates Charles, bar-tender Spencer House, res. 14 Willard.
Gates D. S., messenger American Express Company.
Gates John J., blacksmith, res. 85 E. Market.
Gates M., blacksmith, res. 42 cor. Ohio and Alabama.

Gatling R. J., real estate agent, Blackford's Building, res. 44 S. Meridian.
Gaudge John, workman at Rolling Mill, res. Missouri, S. of South.
Gay Alfred, agent Central Canal Company, res. 20 N. West.
Gaylord S. B., messenger American Express Company, bds. Morris House.
Gearlage Barnhart, laborer, res. 16 S. Alabama.
Geiger Fred., locksmith, bds. 49 S. Illinois.
Geisel George, blacksmith, res. 49 Ft. Wayne ave.
Geisel John, blacksmith, res. 121 Davidson.
Geisel Henry, blacksmith, 158 S. Delaware, res. E. Market, bet. Noble and Davis.
Geisendorff Ed., woollen factory, res. 170 W. New York.
Geisendorff G. W. & Co., manufacturers of woolen and dealers in dry goods, 63 W. Washington.
Geisendorff W., (G. W. G. & Co.,) res. 270 W. Washington.
Geiss Frank, book-binder Journal Building, bds. Macy House.
Gilder Miss L., teacher McLean's Seminary, bds. same.
Gentile Amos, U. S. A., res. W. Indianapolis.
George Aurelia, bds. 22 N. Mississippi.
George Austin R., salesman 3 Bates House, bds. 16 N. Mississippi.
George Frederick, cashier W. & H. Glenn & Co., res. 113 E. Vermont.
George James, grocer 132 W. Washington, res. same.
George Ophelia, bds. at 22 N. Mississippi.
George Otis, 1st carpenter at theater, bds. 22 N. Mississippi.
George R., res. 16 Mississippi.
Gerard Elias, shoemaker, 12 S. Illinois.
Gerard Wm., res. 44 Bates.
Gerandy Nicholas, tailor, res. 92 Davidson.
Gerhausen John, baker Union Steam Bakery.
Gerheler Christian, wood sawyer, res. 75 Fort Wayne ave.
German Dry Goods Store, 43 and 45 E. Washington, Krause & Willenberg, proprietors.
German John, railroader, res. E. Wyoming.
German and English Free School, Maryland, bet. Alabama and Delaware.
Gerper Frederick, laborer, res. 172 Virginia ave.
Gerrett David, carpenter, res. 18 N. New Jersey.
Geetig Henry, barber, Odd Fellows' Hall, res. 113 E. Market.
Gerstner A. G., merchant tailor and clothier, 158 E. Washington, res. same.
Gettenby Jas., laborer, res. Garden, E, of Tennessee.

Gibbons R. R., second miller Bates City Mills, res. N. W. cor. Noble and Washington.
Gibbs Reuben (col.,) barber, res. 154 S. Illinois.
Gibson John, baggage master, T. & R. R. R., res. 199½ S. Pennsylvania, up stairs.
Gibson William, huckster, res. 70 Bluff Road.
Gibson William S., periodical depot, Pennsylvania, near Washington, res. Bluff Road.
Giel Conrad, pump maker, res. 216 E. Washington.
Giesesking Frederick, blacksmith, res. 38 Davidson.
Giesesking William, res. 40 Davidson,
Gietber Frederick, laborer Lawrenceburg depot, res. 92 Union.
Gilkey Oliver, carpenter, bds. 31 Indiana ave.
Gillespie Mrs. Jane, res. 44 N. Delaware.
Gillett John, traveling agent C. O. & P. C & C. R. R., res. 16 W. Michigan.
Gillinn John, farmer, res. 211 S. Alabama.
Gillit Horace S., teacher Deaf and Dumb Asylum, res. Orient.
Gilmore Daniel F., brick layer, res. cor. Stephen and Virginia ave.
Gilson F. A., sutler of 13th Indiana Volunteers, res. 59 E. Market.
Gimbael Martin, cabinet maker and dealer in furniture, 147 E. Washington, res. Market.
Gimbel Jacob, laborer, res. 129 E. Market.
Gimber John, blacksmith, bds. East Street House.
Gimbil Michael, clerk 90 E. Washington, res. 336 S. Delaware.
Girten Harry, blacksmith, bds. 93 Massachusetts ave.
Gitzendanner William, confectioner Union Steam Bakery.
Givens John, at Walpole's office.
Glaser Julius, (G. & Bros.,) res. 15 East.
Glaser & Bros., merchant tailors and clothiers 2 Bates House, Washington and Illinois.
Glass Christian C., lawyer, res. 47 N. Noble.
Glass Henry, teamster, W. Indianapolis.
Glasser Anthony, butcher.
GLAZIER CHARLES, commission merchant and dealer in flour, grain, hay, butter, &c., 16 cor. Pearl and Meridian, res. 100 Virginia ave.
Glazier Daniel, engineer fire department, res. 109 S. New Jersey.
Glazier Frank, engineer fire department, res. 192 W. Maryland.
Glear Frederick, carpenter, res. 63 Union.
Glear William, laborer, res. 59 Union.

A Wheeler & Wilson Sewing Machine with Hemmer, for $50.

Glenn Amanda, (wid.,) res. 243 S. Delaware.
GLENNS' BLOCK, E. Washington, S. side, bet. Meridian and Pennsylvania.
Glenn H., (W. & H. G. & Co.,) bds. 73 N. Meridian.
Glenn R. P., (W. & H. G. & Co.,) bds. 73 N. Meridian.
Glenn Wm., (W. & H. G. & Co.,) res. 73 N. Meridian.
GLENN W. & H. & CO., wholesale and retail dry goods, &c., Glenn's Block, East Washington.
Glessing T. B., scenic artist, 62 Tennessee.
Glore W. W., with M. H. Good, bds. Palmer House.
Glumpp Fred., brewer, res. W. Maryland, bet. Missouri and West.
Goddard Samuel, stone-cutter, res. 18 S. West.
Godfard George, telegraphic operator Terre Haute Depot, bds. 107 S. Tennessee.
George George, shoemaker, 176 E. Washington.
Gaeken Wm., mechanic,, res. 31 S. Liberty.
Gœpper Andrew, butcher, res. 152 W. Michigan.
GŒPPER F., merchant tailor and clother, 15 E. Washington, res. 61 Illinois.
Gœtz Charles, bar-keeper, Spencer House Saloon.
Goff Eliza, washing and sewing, res. 127 N. West.
Gold Adam, grocer, &c., opp. Hoosier Woolen Factory, res. same.
Gold J. Sooy, book-keeper Wright & Downer, bds. Adam Gold, W. Washington.
Gold Samuel, grocery clerk, bds. opp. Hoosier Whoolen Factory.
Golden Dennis, laborer, res. 296 Virginia ave.
Golding Thomas, teamster, res. Dunlop.
Goldman Jacob, rag-pedlar, res. 203 S. Delaware.
Goldsberry L. D., manufacturer and dealer in stoves and tinware, 182 E. Washington, res. E. Maryland.
Goldston M., (Goldston & Carfunkel,) bds. 16 S. Pennsylvania.
Goldston & Carfunkel, manufacturers of ladies' hoop skirts, 12 S. Pennsylvania.
Golly Theodore, shoemaker, works 103 W. Washington, res. 89 W. Market.
Golzenleuchter John, wood sawyer, res. 169 Railroad.
Good Edward, machinist, works Washington Foundry, res. S. Illinois, S. of Pogue's Run.
Good M. H., staple and fancy dry goods, 5 E. Washington, bds. Bates House.
Goodman Anthony, merchant tailor, 16 N. Pennsylvania, res. 56 Market.
Goodperle Peter, works for Spiegel, Thoms & Co., res. N. Noble.

Goodwin A. D., publisher Christian Record, Journal Building.
GOODWIN E., editor Christian Record, office Journal Building, res. Jackson, near University.
Goodwin Geo. K., at Arsenal, res. 9 W. Market.
GOODWIN T. A., editor and proprietor Indiana American, 11 E. Pearl, res. Washington, near Deaf and Dumb Asylum.
Goram Geo. L., brick-layer, res. 179 N. Mississippi.
Gordon C. L., house carpenter, res. Missouri, S. of South.
Gordon Mrs. T., res. 69 Indiana Av.
Gordon Geo., res. 63 Indiana ave.
Gordon Geo., trader, 69 Indiana ave.
GORDON GEO. E., attorney at law, Odd Fellows' Hall, res. 92 N. Pennsylvania.
Gordon James, bds. 69 Indiana ave.
Gordon Jonathan W., major 11th regiment regular U. S. A., bds. Bates House.
Gore James, bds. 74 N. Delaware.
Gorney G. R., 209 E. Washington.
Gorrell Willis A., book-keeper, 83 E. Washington, bds. 78 Massachusetts ave.
Gorrell Mrs. Isabella J., res. 78 Massachusetts ave.
Gosman Wm., carpenter, res. 4th, bet. Tennesssee and Mississippi.
Gosnell Grunberry, moulder at Root, Bennett & Co., res. 171 S. Mississippi.
Gosney George, in real estate office, res. 91 Indiana ave.
Gosney G. K., clerk, res. 91 Indiana ave.
Goth Peter, clerk, bet. St. Clair and Ft. Wayne ave.
Goth Valentine, cooper, res. 77 Spring.
Goth John, works Bellefontaine car shop, res. 60 Davidson.
Gott John, tailor, res. 150 N. Liberty.
Gott Thos., constable, res. 147 S. Tennessee.
Gould Delos, bds. 43 W. Michigan.
Gould O., government inspector, bds. Palmer House.
Gousner Henry, bar-keeper, 75 E. Washington.
Gowens Simeon, (col.,) res. cor. Ohio and West.
Grab John, stone-mason, res. 149 N. Liberty.
Grabhorn Henry, varnisher, res. Fourth, bet. Tennessee and Michigan.
Grader Herman, confectioner, Union Steam Bakery.
Graham John J., (Van Houten & G.,) res. 155 Virginia ave.
Graham Samuel, conductor Lafayette R. R., res. 207 N. Tennessee.
Graham Thomas, laborer, res. 25 Railroad.
Graham W. A., (Reynolds & G.,) res. 83 N. New Jersey.

Graham W. S., deliveryman American Express Co., res. Meridian.
Graham Wm., brick-maker, (Smith & G.,) res. 26 Huron.
Graham Wm., res. 45 S. Meridian.
Gramling A., res. 116 Noble.
Gramling J., (J. & P. G.,) res. 116 Noble.
Gramling P., (J. & P. G.,) res. 118 Noble.
GRAMLING J. & P., merchant tailors, and dealers in clothing, E. Washington.
Granby Wm., in Root's foundry, res. 46 Hosbrook.
Grannong John, shoemaker, bds. 51 S. Illinois.
Grant George, blacksmith, res. 67 Bluff Road.
Grant Geo. H., agent for the Eclectic School Books, 18 W. Washington, bds. Bates House.
Grant Thos., engineer Terre Haute R. R., res. 151 S. Tennessee.
Grant Wm., engineer, res. W. South, bet. Mississippi and Missouri.
Graphorn Henry, varnisher, Spiegel, Thoms & Co., res. Mississippi.
Grater Harman, cooper, res. 144 E. Market.
Gray Alice, school teacher, res. 64 E. South.
Gray Jonathan, brick-mason, res. 203 N. Noble.
Gray J. W., foreman E. C. Mayhew's shoe store, res. 81 W. South.
Gray John W., shoe maker, at Cady & Co's., res. 71 South.
Gray Patrick, works rolling mill, res. 180 S. Tennessee.
Gray S. R., teamster, res. Elizabeth.
GRAY WILLIAM, bakery, 64 South, res. in rear.
Graydon A., clerk, 88 E. Washington, bds. 184 E. Ohio.
Graydon Alexander, sen., res. 184 E. Ohio.
Greany John, laborer, res. 192 S. Tennessee.
Greegor J. W., butcher, Central Meat Market, bds. 68 N. East.
Green A., clerk, 8 N. Pennsylvania, bds. Scary House.
Green Allen T., painter, res. 297 Virginia ave.
Green George, grocery, 133 cor. Tennessee and South, res. same.
Green George. tailor, 19 W. Washington, res. 133 cor. South and Tennessee.
Green James, laborer, res. 141 N. West.
Green Michael, laborer, res. 241 S. Pennsylvania.
Green Molly, res. 13 N. New Jersey.
Greene James, res. 93 N. Meridian.
Greene N. S., clerk, 18 W. Washington, bds. 93 N. Meridian.
Greenard James, shoemaker, res. 150 W. Washington.
Greenart Henry, tailor, 15 E. Washington.
Greenwald Henry, cigar box maker, res. 79 Davidson.

Greenleaf Edward, master machinist, Western Machine Works.
Greenleaf Edward, machinist, res. 280 Massachusetts ave.
Greer James, poet, res. 160 S. Mississippi.
Greer W. H., carpenter, res. 180 S. Mississippi.
Greff John, butcher, res. 238 Madison ave.
Gregg James, wagon maker, res. 36 N. Illinois.
Greggory David, fur dealer.
Grein Henry, baker, bds. 214 E. Washington.
Grein John, baker, 214 E. Washington. res. same.
Grein John, jr., baker, bds. 214 E. Washington.
GREUZARD L. S., house, sign and ornamental painter, 136 E. Washingeon, res. 134 E. Washington.
Gresh Beniville F., prof. of music, res. 27 Kentucky ave.
Greshimer M., salesman cor. Washington and Meridian, res. 28 N. Mississippi.
Gridley F. R., watchmaker, Bates House, Washington, bds. Morris House.
Griffin B., drayman, res. 71 N. Bright.
Griffin Dennis, laborer, res. Missouri, S. of South.
Griffin James, laborer, res. Water, N. of McCarty.
Griffin James, messenger in State House, res. 300 S. Delaware.
Griffin Martin, laborer, res. 177 S. East.
Griffin Michael, drayman, res. 67 Bright.
Griffin Mike, U. S. A., 18 W. Washington, res. 37 Bright.
Griffin Patrick, laborer, res. 316 S. Delaware.
Griffith George W., plasterer, res. 22 N. New Jersey.
GRIFFITH H., retired, res. 52 N. Illinois.
Griffith J. R., res. 32 S. Mississippi.
Griffith P. H., professor, bds. 5 N. Illinois.
Grigsby Jas., tanner, res. S. E. Michigan Road.
Grigwaugh August, tailor, res. E. Washington.
Griner John, shoemaker, bds. 51 S. Illinois.
Grisheimmeir Moritz, clerk Eagle Clothing Store, 1 W. Washington, bds. 28 N. Mississippi.
Grissen John, cartman, res. N. Blake.
Groeshel Charles, tailor, res. 131 N. Noble.
Grore Joseph, tinner, 62 E. Washington, bds. Lynch's.
Grooms A. C., book-keeper Journal Office, res. 87 Indiana ave.
Grosch John, ale-bottler, res. 113 N. Noble.
Grosvenor Julius A., (G. & Turner,) res. 15 W. Ohio.
GROSVENOR & TURNER, general commission merchants, and dealers in agricultural implements, 84 W. Washington.
Grote Henry, laborer, 17 S. Delaware, res. N. Alabama, bet. Washington and Market.

---

350 families in Indianapolis and vicinity use Wheeler & Wilson.

Grout J. B., boots and shoes, 3 W. Washington, res. cor. Illinois and Maryland.
Grube Jacob, carpenter, res. Illinois, S. of Pogue's Run.
Gruenstein George, undertaker, res. 114 E. Market.
Grunart H., shoemaker, bds. 150 W. Washington.
Gulick John F., (Morningstar & G.,) res. 120 East.
Gulick Samuel, scenic and banner painter. Leave orders at postoffice.
Gulliver Wm., (col.,) barber, res. 63 Kentucky ave.
Gump Jacob, blacksmith, bds. 106 St. Joseph.
Gustin L., physician and surgeon, office cor. Louisiana and Illinois, res. 17 W. Georgia.
Gustin L. Q., traveling agent, bds. 17 W. Georgia.
Gutkeucht W., bakery, 134 S. Illinois, res. same.
Gutkneght Rudolf, shoemaker, 124 N. Mississippi, res. same.
Guth Edward, machinist, res. 32 S. Illinois.
Guthridge J. W., agent N. Y. & E. R. R., res. 12 Indiana ave.
Gutnicht John, painter, res. 105 Ft. Wayne ave.
Gutperle Peter, clerk, res. 116 N. Noble.

H

Haas E., proprietor St. Charles Saloon, 86 E. Washington, res. 157 S. Alabama.
Haas Geo., Indianapolis Bakery, 246 W. Washington, res. same.
Habeniy Henry, laborer, res. 103 W. New York.
Hackett Wm., brick-mason, res. 22 S. Liberty.
Hackleberg Samuel, huckster, res. 39 cor. Maryland and Meridian.
Hadley Wm., deputy assessor, res. 151 N. Delaware.
Hodrahand T., boiler-maker, Western Machine Works.
Hœerl Wm., salesman German Dry Goods Store, res. 14 Georgia.
Hagar Edward C., book-keeper Fletcher's Bank, bds. 21 S. Delaware.
HAGERHORST C. F., clerk 34 N. Illinois, res. 23 Indiana ave.
Hagerhorst Christina, res. 156 S. Tennessee.
Haggart Wm., L. & I. R. R., res. 122 N. Blake.
Hahn Charles F., dealer in produce, 41 N. Alabama, res. same.
Hahn H., East Street House, S. of Pogue's Run, S. East.
Hahn Jas., baker Union Steam Bakery.
HAHN LOUIS, meat market, 105 W. Washington, res. 120 N. Mississippi.

The Wheeler & Wilson Hemmer is the only Hemmer that will Fell.

C. W. STEFFENS. E. F. STEFFENS.

CHARLES W. STEFFENS & CO.,

MATHEMATICAL,

Optical and Philosophical

INSTRUMENT MAKERS,

And Manufacturers of F. Yeiser's

PATENT SOLAR CHRONOMETERS,

No. 8 Blackford's Building.

South-East Cor. Washington and Meridian Sts.,

INDIANAPOLIS, IND.

All Kinds of Small Machinery, Models, &c., neatly done. Repairing Promptly Attended to.

L. H. & C. HAMLIN, | **C. HAMLIN,**
REAL ESTATE AGENTS, | **ATTORNEY AT LAW, AND NOTARY PUBLIC,**

Room No. 8, 3d Floor Old Sentinel Building,

No. 18 East Washington Street,

INDIANAPOLIS, IND.

This is a Real Estate and Law Firm, and are doing a large business in both branches. C. Hamlin will practice in the Courts of this and those of the adjoining counties, also, in the Supreme Court. They have now a large selection of different sized good Farms in this and the adjoining States; also, a great variety of City Property.

But just at this time, and during the war, they are giving particular attention to SOLDIERS' CLAIMS.

Those desiring to place their business in the hands of active business and accommodating young men, can not do better than to secure the services of this firm.

First Premium awarded the Wheeler & Wilson Sewing Machine for three

Hahn Philip, musician, res. 52 S. Delaware.
Hains H. M., candy maker, 22 S. Meridian, bds. same.
Haisch John, printer Indiana Volksblatt.
Hale Chas. H., 1st. lieutenant U. S. A., bds. Bates House.
Haley Ann, (wid.,) res. 49 S. New Jersey.
Haley Oliver, laborer, res. Wabash, bet. East and Liberty.
Halford E. W., 19 W. Washington, bds. 72 N. Alabama.
Hall Charles W., (Chas. W. H. & Co.,) bds. Bates House.
HALL CHAS. W. & CO., proprietors Exchange Livery
    Stables, Illinois, opp. Bates House.
Hall Eli A., res. 148 N. Pennsylvania.
Hall Harry L., conductor I. & C. R. R., bds. Bates Houes.
Hall James, tailor, res. Pennsylvania.
Hall James, fireman Peru R. R., bds. Virginia ave.
Hall Lytle, pump maker, res. 33 S. Delaware.
Hall Martin, wagon master in Reynold's Brigade, Virginia,
    res. 40 E. Louisiana.
Hall R. H., (Rand & H.,) res. 47 N. Meridian.
Hall T. W., bds. Pyle House.
Hall Thomas Q., pedlar, res. 118 N. East.
Hall Wm., machinist saw shop, res. 99 Bates.
Hall Wm. S., merchant, bds. 13 Kentucky ave.
Hallahin Jeremiah, laborer, res. W. Elizabeth.
Halpin M. H., printer Journal Office, bds. Mrs. Kinder.
Halpin Wm., head waiter Oriental House.
Hambaugh Thomas waiter Little's Hotel.
Hamill Daniel, expressman, res. 133 Blake.
Hamilton A., tinner, 62 E. Washington, res. 184 N. Alabama.
Hamilton David, compositor Capital Job Office.
Hamilton F. W., deputy county auditor, res. 48 California.
Hamilton H., U. S. A., res. West Market.
Hamilton Harvey, wood chopper, res. 129 E. North.
Hamilton John, works Bellefontaine car shop, bds. Mrs.
    Sarah Hamilton, S. E. Michigan Road.
Hamilton John A., res. 52 Benton.
HAMILTON JNO. W., attorney at law, and county libra-
    rian, Blackford's Building, res. E. National Road.
Hamilton Mrs. Sarah, (wid.,) res. S. E. Michigan Road.
Hamilton Thos., (col.,) barber, res. Tennessee.
Hamilton Wm. H., book-binder Wm. Sheets.
Hamlin C., (L. H. & C. H.,) attorney at law and notary
    public, bds. Little's Hotel.
Hamlin Mrs. Catherine, (wid.,) res. 57 Kentucky ave.
Hamlin E. S., attorney at law, bds. Little's Hotel.
Hamlin L. H., (L. H. & C. H.,) res. Virginia ave.
HAMLIN L. H. & C., real estate agents, 8 third floor old
    Sentinel Building, (see card.)
Hammel Andrew, blacksmith, res. 215 Massachusetts ave.

PRODUCE, FORWARDING & COMMISSION
MERCHANT,

DEALER IN

Fish, Rosin, Tar, Nails, Cheese, Flaxseed, Grain, Flour, &c. Also, Sole Agent for the sale of Lake and Kanawha Salt, Louisville Cement, Jersey City and Newark Lime and Plaster,

No. 38 Virginia Avenue and No. 51 Delaware Street,

Residence, No. 34 North Delaware Street,

INDIANAPOLIS, IND.,

☞ Particular attention given to the sale and shipment of Flour and Grain, and liberal advances made on same.

81,000 Wheeler & Wilson's Sewing Machines in use in this country.

Hammond A. A., (M. Fitzgibbon & Co.,) res. cor. Mississippi and Washington.
Hammond John, laborer, res California, bet. Washington and Market.
Hammond Philip, in rolling mill, bds. 188 S. Tennessee.
HAMMOND U. J., attorney at law and notary public, 19½ E. Washington, bds. 73 N. Meridian.
Handy Adolphus, brick-mason, res. 273 S. Delaware.
Handriban Mrs. Eliza, (wid.,) res. 20 Elm.
Hanna John, constable, res. 191 E. St. Clair.
Hanna S. C., book-keeper 75 W. Washington, bds. Bates. House.
Hannah Samuel, treas. Ind. Central R. R., res. N. Meridian.
Hannah V. C., pay-master, res. S. of Pogue's Run, Virginia ave.
HANNAMAN WILLIAM, wholesale and retail druggist, 40 E. Washington.
Hannum Orrin, (Bush & H.,) bds. Oriental House.
Hanning J. F., laborer, res. 30 N. Noble.
Hanning J. G., (Ramsey & H.,) res. cor. Vermont and Ellsworth.
Hanning Michael, machinist, res. 93 St. Joseph.
Hanrahan P., boarding house, res. 184 S. Tennessee.
Hanshield Charles, engineer, res. 35 S. Liberty.
Hanthorn Mrs. Mary A., seamstress, res. Bates, E. of Noble.
Hannsen J. F., porter Bates House.
Hanway Samuel, mail agent, res. 75 N. New Jersey.
Happe George, saloon-keeper, 81 S. Meridian.
Harbert Enoch, butcher, res. W. St. Clair.
Harbine Mrs. Elizabeth, res. 91 N. Alabama.
Harbison Alex., engineer Journal Office, bds. 70 W. Vermont.
Harbison Robt., brakeman Laf. R. R., bds. 70 W. Vermont.
Harbison Mrs. Sarah, (wid.,) res. 70 W. Vermont.
Hard Abraham, butcher, res. 128 N. Alabama.
Hardin J. Samuel, baker for H. M. Haynes.
Harding Thos. W., 106 N. Pennsylvania.
Hardesty Wm., patent dealer, res. Illinois, bet. Second and Third.
Hardy Robert Boyd, salesman New York Store, bds. Morris House.
Harkman Charles, baker, res. 63 N. New Jersey.
Harkness John, (Elder, H. & Bingham,) res. 77 N. Pennsylvania.
Harlan George, cabinet maker at Sloan & Ingersoll's, res. 78 N. Tennessee.
Harlan J. J., agent for Grover & Baker's sewing machines, Yohn's Building, res. 7 Ohio.

A Wheeler & Wilson Sewing Machine will last a life-time.

MERRILL & CO.,
PUBLISHERS

AND

BOOKSELLERS,

Wholesale and Retail Dealers in

LAW BOOKS,
SCHOOL BOOKS,
GENERAL LITERATURE,

BLANK BOOKS

AND

STATIONERY,

GLENNS' BLOCK,

NO. 25 EAST WASHINGTON STREET,

INDIANAPOLIS, INDIANA.

Harlington Patrick, grocer, res. 50 E. Louisiana.
Harman Jacob, livery, res. 112 E. Market.
Harman Patrick, ostler for Wilkison, 10 E. Pearl, res. 108 Davidson.
Harman Valentine, grocer, W. Indianapolis.
Harmenick Mrs. C., res. 13 Railroad.
Harmining Christ., waiter Spencer House.
Harness Solomon, laborer, res. 23 McCarthy.
Harper Mrs., (wid.,) works at arsenal, res. 142 N. West, up stairs.
Harper Henry, cooper, res. 92 Bluff Road.
Harper John L., book-keeper, E. C. Mayhew & Co., res. 115 N. Illinois.
Harper W. S., pressman Cameron's job office.
Harran Joseph, waiter Bates House, res. 123 W. Maryland.
Harrington Dennis, laborer, 260 S. Delaware.
Harrington James, cabinet maker for Sloan & Ingersoll, bds. Ohio House.
HARRINGTON PATRICK, groceries, wines and liquors, 58 South, res. cor. East and Cincinnati R. R.
Harrington Patrick, laborer, res. Willard.
Harris Berg., (col.,) laborer, res. N. Missouri, bet. Vermont and Michigan.
Harris Charles E., carpenter, res. Wabash, bet. New Jersey and East.
Harris Charles A., baggage master St. Louis and Indianapolis Railroad, bds. Oriental House.
Harris Mrs. Elizabeth, washer, res. 77 N. East.
Harris E., Paris dye house, 19 S. Meridian, res. same.
Harris George, clerk, 83 E. Washington.
Harris Henry, mechanic, res. 189 S. Noble.
Harris Isaac, miller, Railroad City Mills, res. cor. Vermont and California.
Harris Joseph, grocer.
Harris Joseph, dyer, scourer and dealer in second hand clothing, 38 S. Illinois and E. Washington, res. 111 Illinois.
Harris Lazarus, (col.,) cook, res. 143 E. New York.
Harris M. B., (col.,) porter 18 W. Washington, res. 85 Canal.
Harris Mumford, porter, res. 66 Powell.
Harrison A. I., with Wm. Sheets, bds. cor. Pennsylvania and Ohio.
Harrison Alfred, Harrisons' Bank, res. 61 N. Meridian.
HARRISONS' BANK, 19 E. Washington, A. & J. C. S. Harrison, proprietors.
Harrison Benjamin, (H. & Fishback,) res. 127 N. Alabama.
Harrison John S., dyer, 19 S. Meridian.

For four successive years at the Am. Institute, New York.

INDIANAPOLIS

BOOKS! BOOKS!
BOOKS!!

WHETHER YOU LIVE IN

CITY, TOWN OR COUNTRY,

YOU WILL WANT

Books, Paper

PENS, PENCILS, PICTURE FRAMES, &C.,

And by calling at the Store of

MERRILL & CO.,

GLENNS' BLOCK,

No. 25 E. Washington St.,

INDIANAPOLIS, INDIANA,

You can get all these things of the best quality at Wholesale and Retail Prices.

The Wheeler & Wilson Hemmer makes hems of any width.

Harrison John C. S., Harrisons' Bank, res. 63 N. Meridian.
Harrison Thomas, U. S. A., res. 23 S. Illinois.
Harrison Wm. M., U. S. A., res. 61 W. New York.
HARRISON & FISHBACK, attorneys at law 62 E. Washington.
Hart James, grocer, 230 E. Washington, res. same.
Harter John A., tinner, res. 139 N. Delaware.
Harteway Henry W., drayman, res. 124 Davidson.
HARTH M., proprietor Spencer House, cor. Illinois and Louisiana.
Harting Frederick, (H. & Bro.,) res. 25 S. Illinois.
Harting Henry, (H. & Bro.,) res. 25 S. Illinois, up stairs.
Harting William, laborer, 94 Union.
Harting & Bro., brewers, 25 S. Illinois.
Hartman Christian, bds. 34 S. Illinois, S. of Pogue's Run.
Hartman Christian, laborer, res. 139 E. Ohio.
Hartman Matthew, plasterer, res. 110 N. Alabama.
Hartman Oswald, shoemaker, bds. 34 S. Illinois, S. of Pogue's Run.
Hartman Charles, cook Bates House.
Hartmann O., shoemaker, 64 E. Washington.
Hartpence Walter, printer for Cullum & Stanage, bds. 197 E. Washington.
Hartwell E., bds. Bates House.
Harvey A. C., 169 N. Noble.
Harvey A. D., salesman 3 Bates House, bds. Pyle House.
Harvey John, salesman New York Store, res. Massachusetts ave.
HARVEY J. S., State Treasurer, res. 54 S. Meridian.
Harvy S. L., deputy Treasurer of State, bds. 54 S. Meridian.
Haselden Charles, cordwainer, res. 71 W. Vermont.
Hasket Elijah, pump maker, 26 Kentucky ave., bds. 28 Kentucky ave.
Hasler E. A., salesman New York Store, res. 106 Tennessee.
Hass Edward, saloon keeper, res. 157 S. Alabama.
Hasselman L. W., (H. & Vinton,) res. 38 S. Meridian.
HASSELMAN & VINTON, Washington Foundry and Machine Shop, opp. Union Depot.
Hassion John, ostler, bds. Ohio House.
Hassler E. A., clerk New York Store, res. 106 N. Tennessee.
Hassman Henry, laborer, cor. Pennsylvania and South.
Hasson Charles, res. 117 N. Meridian.
Hastings Edwin L., (Landon & H.,) printer Journal office, res. 87 cor. Tennessee and New York.
Hatfield Frederick, laborer, res. 192 E. St. Clair.
Hatten Thoms, salesman 30 S. Illinois, bds. 66 Delaware.
Hattendorf Henry, tailor, res. Liberty, bet. New York and Vermont.

H. H. DODD.   C. P. HUTCHINSON.   J. R. APPLETON.   J. J. PARSONS.

H. H. DODD & CO.,

(SUCCESSORS TO BINGHAM & DOUGHTY,)

𝕭ook and 𝕵ob 𝕻rinters,

PUBLISHERS, AND

BLANK BOOK MANUFACTURERS.

HAVING IN CONSTANT USE SIX STEAM PRESSES, ENABLES US TO FURNISH ALL DESCRIPTIONS OF BOOK AND JOB PRINTING PROMPTLY, AND IN THE NEATEST POSSIBLE MANNER. PARTICULAR ATTENTION PAID TO PRINTING IN COLORS. THE LARGEST ASSORTMENT OF POSTER TYPE IN THE STATE.

INDIANAPOLIS:
NO. 18 EAST WASHINGTON STREET,
Formerly Sentinel Building.

Upwards of 100 W. & W. Machines in use in Ind'p'lis making army clothing.

Haueisen William, salesman 20 W. Washington.
Hauf Valentine, laborer, res. 71 Davidson.
Haufler John, laborer, res. Meridian.
Haufman George, collar maker, 80 S. Delaware, res. in rear.
Haug Michael, plow maker, res. 9 N. Liberty.
Haugh Adam, cancer doctor, res. 6 N. Meridian.
Haugh Benjamin, iron rail manufacturer, res. 164 N. Pennsylvania.
Haugh E., (Williamson & H.,) iron railing manufacturers, 2 N. Delaware, res. 116 E. Vermont.
Haugh J. R.. teller Fletcher's Bank, res. 6 N. Meridian.
HAUGHEY THEODORE P., general ticket agent P. & I. R. R., res. 100 N. Pennsylvania.
Hautendurf Henry, tailor, 144 E. Washington.
Haupt Robert, dry goods, res. 95 Ft. Wayne ave.
HAVEN REV. JAMES, minister Strange Chapel, res. 107 N. Tennessee.
Haver Charles, laborer, res. 79 E. Merrill.
HAWES GEO. W., (Beebe & H., & H. & Co.,) bds. Morris House.
HAWES & CO., family grocery, 3 N. Illinois, opp. Bates House.
Hawthorn Charles E., (H. & Buchanan,) res. 83 E. Washington.
Hawthorn & Buchanan, wholesale and retail china, glass and queensware dealers, 83 E. Washington.
HAY REV. L. G., Presbyterian, res. 130 N. Tennessee.
Hay Wm. H., assistant quartermaster U. S. A., bds. Jacob Landis', 18 W. Maryland.
Hay C., bds. 130 N. Tennessee.
HAY'S ACADEMY, under Masonic Hall, Tennessee.
Haydon Henry S., farmer, res. Michigan Road.
Hayden J. J., insurance and general collecting agent, cor. Meridian and Washington, res. 154 W. New York.
Hayden N., bds. 44 N. Pennsylvania.
Hayden N. P., telegraphic operator, bds. 58 N. Illinois.
Haynes H. M., baker and confectioner, 40 W. Washington, res. same.
Haynes Lewis, agent for Fairbank's scales, bds. Bates House.
Haynes Philip, superintendent for H. M. Haynes, bds. 40 W. Washington.
Haynes William, printer Journal office, bds. Mrs. Smith's.
Hays B. S., (H. & Runnion,) res. 132 N. Alabama.
Hays Mrs. Catherine, seamstress, res. 30 Davidson.
Aays Mrs. Elizabeth, (wid.,) res. 74 W. Vermont.
HAYS & RUNNION, photographists, 32½ E. Washington.
Hayworth Isaac, U. S. A., res. 95 W. Market.

81,000 Wheeler & Wilson's Sewing Machines in use in this country.

GEO. F. MEYER,

MANUFACTURER AND DEALER IN

ALL KINDS OF
CHEWING AND SMOKING TOBACCO,
CIGARS AND SNUFF,

Sign of "Big Indian Chief,"

No. 35
West Washington St.,
INDIANAPOLIS, IND.

☞ All Goods warranted of the best quality. Orders solicited and promptly attended to.

MR. H. J. SCHONACKER,
Would respectfully inform the Citizens of Indianapolis, that he is prepared to give
Instruction upon the Piano Forte,
At the residence of those who desire the services of an able teacher.

Having had considerable experience and complete success in teaching this difficult instrument, he would be happy to obtain a share of public patronage.
No pains will be spared on his part to give satisfaction and ensure a fine execution. Pianos tuned and repaired.

FOR TERMS APPLY AT MESSRS. W. H. TALBOTT & CO.'S JEWELRY STORE, NO. 24 EAST WASHINGTON STREET.

REFERENCES.
MR. CHARLES BRUMMER,   MR. J. J. PARSONS,   MR. H. BULLOCK.

WILLIAM BRADEN,
Blank Book Manufacturer,
AND DEALER IN
BLANK BOOKS, PAPER & STATIONERY,
No. 24 West Washington St.,
INDIANAPOLIS, IND.

☞ All kinds of Blanks on hand, or printed to order. ☜

The Wheeler & Wilson Hemmer makes hems of any width.

Hazzard Col. Geo. W., res. 59 N. Meridian.
Healey Oliver, engineer Cameron's job office.
Healy Mrs., dressmaker, res. 11 N. Alabama.
Heaf August, dyer, 10 S. Pennsylvania, res. same.
Hearth John G., carpenter, res. 127 N. East.
Hecklebird Samuel, res. 33 S. Meridian.
HECKMAN REV. G. C., pastor 3d Presbyterian Church, res. 134 N. Tennessee.
Heckmann ——, flour and feed store, 266 E. Washington, res. same.
Hedderich Peter, machinist, res. 66 N. Noble.
Hedge Lanson, railroader, res. 225 S. Delaware.
Hedges Elijah, cabinet maker, 72 W. Washington, bds. West.
Hedges Mrs. Ellen, res. 89 N. Illinois.
Hedges Isaac, clerk, Bowen, Stewart & Co., res. 103 N. Tennessee.
Heffer August, boot and shoemaker, 103 W. Washington, res. 89 Market.
Heffner Ferdinand, shoemaker, bds. 89 Market.
Heinbaugh Fred., cooper, res. 99 Meek.
Heibner Jacob, laborer, res. 59 Mississippi.
Heidenrich Christ., tailor, res. 50 Huron.
HEIDLINGER J. A., wholesale manufacturer and dealer in cigars, tobacco, snuff, &c., 3 Palmer and 10 Bates House, res. cor. Washington and Delaware.
Heim Jacob, butcher, res. Point, bet. National Road and Michigan Road.
Heiner John, clerk 16 Meridian, bds. 206 Merrill.
Heiser John, laborer, res. 172 N. Noble.
Heitcomb George, tailor, Glaser & Bro., res. 113 New York.
Heithum Charles, (H. & Fertheucht,) res. Virginia ave.
Heithum & Fertheucht, furniture manufacturers and dealers, res. 61 E. Washington.
Heldebrand Henry W., carpenter, res. cor North and New Jersey.
Helfra Andrew, cigar maker, bds. Farmers' Hotel.
Helin Adam, carpenter, res. 62 N. Noble.
Helin John, grocer, 104 Davidson, res. same.
Helmer John, laborer, res. 121 Bluff Road.
Helwig Charles, carpenter and builder, res. 113 E. Ohio.
Helyrune Christian, drayman, res. 23 E. Wyoming.
Henderson D., res. 52 Bates.
Henderson George, wood sawyer, res. 226 N. New Jersey.
Henderson Wm. W., plasterer, res. 147 E. New York.
HENDERSON WILLIAM, attorney at law and agent for the Ætna Insurance Co., Ætna Building, Pennsylvania, res. 163 N. Illinois.

The Wheeler & Wilson Hemmer is the only Hemmer that will Fell.

Hendrick Edward O. H., res. 128 Davidson.
Hendricks I. C., soldier, res. 207 S. Alabama.
HENDRICKS THOS. A., attorney at law, Ætna Building, bds. Bates House.
Hendricks V. K., (V. K. H. & Co.,) bds. 37 W. Ohio.
HENDRICKS V. K. & CO., wholesale dealers in boots and shoes, 76 W. Washington.
Hennessy Daniel, laborer, res. 65 N. Bright.
Henn Charles, plainer, res. 148 Davidson.
Hennay Tom., tailor, 3 E. Washington.
Hennessy John F., waiter Spencer House.
HENNING FRED. A., (H. & Stelzell,) res. 63 N. Illinois.
HENNING & STELZELL, proprietors of Bates and Palmer House hair dressing saloons.
Henninger Chas.. (H. & Co.,) res. S. Illinois.
Henninger Charles & Co., cigars and Tobacco, 87 S. Illinois.
Henninger Gustave. (H. & Co.,) res. Illinois.
HENNINGER C. & CO., manufacturers and dealers in cigars and tobacco, 42 E. Washington.
Henninger Charles, (C. H. & Co.,) bds. 71 S. Illinois.
HENNINGER R., proprietor Indiana Free Press, res. 104 Michigan. cor. Massachusetts ave.
Henrich Joseph, boots and shoes, res. 126 Davidson.
Henry John, laborer, res. 61 E. St. Joseph.
Henry Mary, (wid.,) res. 182 S. East.
Hensan Charles, grocer, 50 Bluff Road, res. same.
Henshaw Wm., laborer, res. 170 Virginia ave.
Hepp John, carpenter, res. Pratt, bet. Illinois and Meridian.
Herald and Era, (weekly,) 2 S. Meridian, M. G. Lee, proprietor.
Herdin Azra, carpenter, res. 87 E. Market.
Herdin Edwin, carpenter, bds. 87 E. Market.
Hereha John, laborer, res. 196 S. Tennessee.
Hereth J. C., saddles, harness, &c., 103 E. Washington, res. Noble, bet. Market and Ohio.
/Hereth A., saddler, 103 E. Washington, bds. Little's Hotel.
/Hereth Peter, carpenter, res. cor. Vermont and Spring.
Hering Philip, tuner and repairer of musical instruments, 4 Bates House, res. 85 South.
Heritage Samuel, res. 7 E. New York.
Herman Jacob, bar-keeper Nebraska Saloon, bds. cor. Meridian and Indiana ave.
Herman John, cabinet maker, res. Winston, bet. Ohio and New York.
Herner John, bds. 70 N. East.
Herni Henry, shoemaker, 32 E. Washington, res. Stevenson.
Herreth Henry, carpenter, res. 31 N. Noble.
Herreth John, saddler, res. 29 N. Noble.

First Premium awarded the Wheeler & Wilson Sewing Machine for three

CITY DIRECTORY. 135

Herron James, U. S. A., res. Dunlop.
Herron Fred. M., watchmaker, bds. Mrs. McCready, Market.
Herth L., carrier, res. 181 E. Vermont.
Hertkem Philip, expressman, res. city limits, near Biddle.
Hervey Samuel, clerk 14 N. Pennsylvania, bds. 142 Virginia ave.
Hessa Fanny, (wid.,) res. 68 E. Merrill.
Hessling Bernherd, tailor, res. 141 E. Market.
Hetchel John, ostler, res. Wabash, bet. New Jersey and East.
Hetchbeth John, (col.,) laborer, res. Howard.
Hetselgesser Samuel, miller, res. 148 S. Illinois.
Hetterich Fred., yardman Spencer House.
Heustis B., conductor I. & C. R. R., bds. Bates House.
Hewitt Charles, student at law, 84 E. Washington, bds. 44 E. Pennsylvania.
Hewling J. P., res. 65 N. Pennsylvania.
Heynes James, mill-wright, res. 26 N. Delaware.
Hiatt John R., bar-keeper Pearl Street Saloon, bds. same.
Hick Wm., laborer, 17 S. Delaware, bds. Farmers' Hotel.
Hidkin John, cabinet maker, works Spiegel, Thoms & Co., res. Winston, bet. Ohio and New York.
Hidlelbergen Nanna, washer, res. 332 S. Delaware.
Hietkem George, tailor, res. 113 E. New York.
Higby Richard, baggage master St. Louis and Ind. R. R., bds. Oriental House.
Hight Ferd., actor Metropolitan Theater, res. 259 S. Pennsylvania.
Higgens John, tailor, 59 E. Washington.
Higgins Wm., silver-plater, res. 125 Massachusetts ave.
Higgins W. W., Palmer House Dining Saloon, res. Illinois.
Hilbert Thomas J., wood sawyer, res. 97 E. Market.
Hild August, laborer, res. 163 N. Noble.
Hildebrand Jacob S., book-keeper 21 W. Washington, res. 111 Illinois.
Hiles Isaac, carpenter, res. 156 W. Vermont.
Hill G. W., saw mill, cor. East and Georgia, res. 68 S. East.
Hill George, (col.,) cook, res. 105 W. North.
Hill James, teamster Ætna Mills.
Hill James, clerk Skillen's flour mill, W. Washington, res. 46 W. Marylrnd.
Hill James B., (J. F. H. & Co.,) bds. 38 N. Alabama.
Hill J. F., (J. F. H. & Co.,) res. 38 N. Alabama.
HILL J. F. & CO., proprietors of Beech-wood Nursery, 44 N. Pennsylvania.
Hill John, actor, bds. 13 Kentucky ave.
Hill John H. & Co., Beech-wood Nursery, office 44 N. Pennsylvania, res. 38 N. Alabama.

Successive years at the United States Fair.

Hill J. O., at saw mill with G. W. Hill, bds. 68 S. East.
Hill W. O., clerk 63 W. Washington, res. 26 N. Pennsylvania.
Hillgemann Herman, shoemaker, 198 Massachusetts ave.
Hillis L. H., saddler 103 E. Washington, bds. 179 E. Market.
Hillman Charles, works in foundry, res. Water, near McCarty.
Hillman Fred., laborer, res. Water, near McCardy.
Hillman Wm., blacksmith, shop 306 Virginia ave., res. 310 Virginia ave.
Hills Lucean, freight agent Bellefontaine R. R. Line, res. 20 N. Meridian.
Hilt F. L., coach blacksmith, res. 35 W. New York.
Hilt C. W., U. S. A.
Hinckley David J., clerk Bellefontaine R. R. Line, bds. Meridian.
Hinde E., grocer, 155 E. Washington, res. East.
Hinde P. J., grocer Little's Hotel, res. 37 N. East.
Hinds Jesse, brick-mason, res. 74 N. East.
Hinds Solomon, brick-layer, res. 83 N. New Jersey.
Hines E., music and dancing master, res. 71 Indiana ave.
HINESLEY A. J., dealer in saddles, harness, whips, &c., 34 W. Washington, res. 119 Massachusetts ave.
Hinesley John, laborer, res. 80 W. Vermont.
Hinesley Wm., (Allen & H.,) res. 73 W. New Jersey.
Hinkle Christ., spinner Ohio Premium Woolen Factory.
Hinninger George, blacksmith, res. 51 E. St. Joseph.
Hinton Wm., pedlar, res. 263 Massachusetts ave.
Hirshler Abraham, book-keeper 3 E. Washington, bds. Morris House.
Hitchcock A., speculator, res. 119 N. Alabama.
Hitchcock F., carpenter, res. 213 N. Noble.
Hiser H., plasterer, res. 177 Railroad.
Hiss Henry, clerk 140 E. Washington, bds. same.
Hiser Andrew, laborer, res. 295 S. Delaware.
Hodges Richard, carpenter, res. 82 E. St. Joseph.
Hodgson Isaac, architect, 14 Yohn's Block, res. 135 N. Meridian.
Hœfgen Samuel B., attorney at law, 19½ E. Washington, bds. Little's Hotel.
Hœfner August, shoemaker, 103 W. Washington, res. 89 W. Market.
Hœg Michael, blacksmith, 86 W. Washington, res. 11 Liberty.
Hœlsmith Frederick, laborer, res. John, near Winston and city limits.
Hofaling Fred., watchmaker, res. 42 Spring.
Hofferberth Wm., laborer, res. 69 N. Bright.

Hoffman Casper, blacksmith, res. 224 N. Alabama.
Hoffman Henry, boot and shoemaker, 27 Union, res. in the rear.
Hoffmeyer Henry, tailor, 63 E. Washington, res. 203 Delaware.
HOFMEISTER CHRISTIAN, saloon, 75 E. Washington, res. same.
Hofmeister Christian, (C. & N. H.,) res. 82 N. Noble.
Hofmeister & Nicholas, grocers, res. 82 N. Noble.
Hogan John, works J. K. Sharpe, res. near cor. Orient and S. E. Michigan Road.
Hogshire Wm. R., (H. & Hunter,) bds. Palmer House.
HOGSHIRE & HUNTER, wholesale and retail grocers, 25 W. Washington.
Hohl Christ. C., grocery and saloon, 77 E. Washington, res. same.
Holbrook H. C., clerk 37 E. Washington, bds. 77 N. Alabama.
Holbrook Thomas E., res. 77 N. Alabama.
Holddy Louis, cook Crystal Palace Saloon, bds. same.
Holdskom Charles,, whip maker, 20 W. Washington, res. cor. Mississippi and New York.
Holey L., railroader, res. S. E. Michigan Road.
Holhoger E., bar-keeper, res. 5 Willard.
Holland Bell, bds. 53 N. East.
Holland Charles, U. S. A., res. Market, bet. West and California.
Holland Charles E., clerk 72 E. Washington, res. Alabama.
Holland John, carpenter, res. 217 S. Delaware.
Holland John, laborer, res. 177 S. East.
Holland John W., wholesale and retail grocer and commission merchant, 72 E. Washington, res. 58 N. Illinois.
Holland F. R., clerk, bds. with C. E. Holland.
Holland T. F., book-keeper 72 E. Washington, bds. with T. Smith.
Holler Philip H., stone mason, res. 218 N. Noble.
Holler Philip, railroader, res. 117 N. Noble.
Holley Theodore, shoemaker, res. 89 W. Market.
Holliday Cotz H., clerk Indiana Central R. R., res. 117 E. Ohio.
Holliday E. G., clerk Ætna Insurance office, res. N. Illinois.
HOLLIDAY REV. F. C., res. 117 E. Ohio.
Halliday Gideon, lightening rod manufacturer, res. 42 Pratt.
HOLLIDAY REV. WILLIAM, Presbyterian, res. 102 N. Alabama.
Holliday William J., (Murphy & H.,) res. 145 S. Pennsylvania.
Hollocher G. E., head waiter Morris House.

For four successive years at the Ohio State Fair.

HOLLOWAY C. B., salesman 3 Bates House, res. 48 N. Tennessee.
Holloway S. B., res. 133 N. Mississippi.
Holloway L.. clerk 37 E. Washington.
Holloway William R., Private Secretary Governor Morton, bds. at Mrs. Kinder's.
Holman G. G., res. 60 N. Pennsylvania.
Holman M. C., broom maker, res. 152 N. Pennsylvania.
Holmes Mrs. Mary, boarding house, res. 51 N. East.
HOLMES C. L., wholesale and retail grocer, 31 W. Washington, bds. 42 N. Mississippi.
Holmes Henry, plasterer, res. California, bet. Maryland and Georgia.
Holmes J., res. 101 N. Meridian.
Holmes Samuel, egg packer, &c., 188 E. Washington, bds. 30 East.
Holt Mrs. Louisa, res. 87 N. East.
Holzer John, porter Union Steam Bakery.
Homburg Dr., physician and surgeon, Ray's Building.
Homer Jeremiah, 17 Virginia ave.
Honay Thomas, tailor, res. 182 S. Tennessee.
Hooker Henry, clerk, res. 145 E. South.
Hooker E. M. B., 20th Regiment Indiana Volunteers.
Hoolihan James, railroader, res. Howard.
Hooper Walter, blacksmith, res. 112 N. East.
Hoosier Woolen Factory, G. W. Geisendorff & Co., proprietors, N. S. of Washington, near White River Bridge.
Hoover Andrew, blacksmith, bds. 123 N. Alabama.
Hoover William, blacksmith, bds. bet. New York and Noble.
Hopkins J. H., traveling agent, res. 60 S. Illinois.
Horn Henry J., at City grocery, 31 W. Washington, res. 42 N. Mississippi.
Hornaday John E., carpenter, res. 159 N. Alabama.
Horner D. H., salesman New York Store, bds. Morris House.
Horsman Isaac, salesman New York Store, res. 124 E. Michigan.
Hosbrook Daniel B., surveyor, res. 108 N. Mississippi.
Hoshour Samuel K., prof. N. W. C. University, res. N. New Jersey, bet. Market and Ohio.
Hoskins Joseph, railroader, res. 96 E. McCarty.
Hoskins Robert, teamster, res. 160 E. Ohio.
Hoslup Isaiah, master mechanic, res. 221 S. East.
Hosmer Geo., machinist, res. E. National Road.
Hoss David, laborer, res. 350 Virginia ave.
Hoss Fred., wood sawyer, res. 66 W. Ohio.
Hoss Geo., professor college, res. Jackson, near University.
Hossfelt Charles, clerk 212 E. Washington, res. same.
Hotz George, (Geo. H. & Co.,) bds. Farmers' Hotel.

Wheeler & Wilson's Sewing Machines warranted for three years.

CITY DIRECTORY. 139

Hotz Geo. & Co., meachant tailors and clothiers, 69 S. Illinois.
Houston C. B. clerk, 66 E. Washington, res. 51 E. Ohio.
Howard Mrs., (wid.,) res. 45 S. East.
Howard Charles L., sawyer, res. 39 N. East.
Howard E., (E. H. & Son,) res. 52 S. Illinois.
HOWARD DR. E. & SON, cancer physicians, 52 S. Illinois.
Howard Henry, carpenter, res. 194 E. St. Clair.
Howard L. B., salesman 5 W. Washington, res. 115 Ohio.
Howard Law. N., (E. H. & Son,) res. 52 S. Illinois.
Howard S. W., clairvoyant physician, res. 13 S. Mississippi.
Howard Michael, res. 22, in alley S. of S. East.
Howell Margaret, res. 6 S. Pennsylvania.
Howes Henry, carpenter, res. 50 Indiana ave.
Howland J. D., (Barbour & H.,) N. E. cor. Vermont and Tennessee.
Howland Michael, brick-mason, res. cor. Illinois and Fourth.
Hoyt Harriet, boarding house 27 S. Delaware.
Hubbard Wm , laborer, res. 283 Virginia ave.
Hubbard Garrison, teamster, res. 41 S. Illinois.
Hubbard W. S., res. 9 Circle.
Hudnut Howard, with Theodore Hudnut, bds. N. Illinois.
Hudnut Theodore, Identical Mills, S. Pennsylvania, res. N. Illinois, outside city limits.
Huey M. S., cabinet maker, 97 E. Washington. res. 84 W. Georgia.
HUFF JOHN E., bakery and confectionery, 200 W. Washington, res. same.
Huffer James M., saddler, 20 W. Washington, res. 134 E. Market.
Huffer James M., pedlar, res. 134 E. Market.
Huffman Henry, cooper, res. 153 W. Michigan.
Huffman Henry, tanner, res. 197 E. Washington.
Huffman Huffman. laborer, res. 68 S. Noble.
Huffman Michael, blacksmith, res. 63 Bluff Road.
Huffner August, shoemaker, 89 W. Market.
Hug Joseph. bar-keeper Capital Saloon.
HUG MARTIN, wholesale liquor store and proprietor Capital Saloon, 14 E. Washington, res. 45 N. New Jersey.
Hugh Slavens, drayman, res. 157 S. Tennessee.
Hughes David, hackman, res. 233 S. Pennsylvania.
Hughes David, carpenter, res. 268 S. Delaware.
Hughes Mrs. M., washer, res. 31 N. Liberty.
Hughey Wm., res. 86 E. Louisiana.
Hughes William, bds. 232 S. Pennsylvania.
Hugo Charles plasterer, res. 33 N. Noble.
Hugo Martin, wholesale and retail liquors, 140 North.
Hull A. D., cigar maker, 112 E. Washington.

A Wheeler & Wilson Sewing Machine with Hemmer, for $50.

Hull David, cigar maker, res. 52 N. East.
Hull Wm., res. Tennessee, bet. Fifth and Sixth.
Hume James M., (H. A. Fletcher & Co.,) res. 77 N. Mississippi.
HUME MADISON, Baptist minister, res. 75 N. Mississippi.
Hume Newton, salesman, 70 E. Washington, bds. 75 N. Mississippi.
HUMORIST MONTHLY, Landon & Hastings, publishers, 8 E. Washington.
Humphrey C. F., watch-maker, 37 W. Washington, bds. E. Washington.
Humphrey Samuel, cooper, res. Indiana ave.
Hume H. H., bds. Spencer House.
Hunt Abe, cigar maker for C. C. Hunt.
Hunt Albert, plow maker at Beard, Starr & Co.'s, bds. 28 Indiana ave.
Hunt Allen L., captain 26th regiment Ind. Vol., res. 166 N. East.
Hunt Charles C., manufacturer, wholesale and retail dealer in cigars and tobacco, 61 E. Washington, res. same.
Hunt David B., clerk, U. S. Mustering Office, res. 78 Massachusetts ave.
Hunt George, dentist, res. 40, N. East.
Hunt George, telegraph messenger, bds. 6 Circle.
Hunt Jesse, watchman at arsenal, res. 7 N. Ellsworth.
Hunt Mrs. Julia A., (wid.,) res. 6 Circle.
Hunt Phineas G. C., M. D., res. Market, bet. Pennsylvania and Delaware.
Hunt Thomas E., res. 100 W. Michigan.
Hunt William, cigar maker for C. C. Hunt.
Hunter M., (Hogshire & H.,) bds. Palmer House.
Hunter Maston, Kentucky Union Saloon, 81 E. Washington.
Hunter Ralph, fireman Engine No. 5, res. 72 S. East.
Hurley John, drayman, res. 131 N. Mississippi.
Hurley Patrick, currier for Mooney & Co.
Hurley Patrick, teamster, res. cor. Bright and North.
Hurly Moses F. huckster, res. 81 Bluff Road.
Hurrle Ignatius, tailor, res. 7 Railroad.
Husbar Henry, U. S. A., res. 83 W. Maryland.
Husted Hiram, carpenter, res, 19 McCarty.
Hustes John, engineer switch pony, Terre Haute Railroad, bds. 107 S. Tennessee.
Hutchins H. H., book-keeper, 90 E. Washington, res. 148 Virginia ave.
HUTCHINSON C. P., (H. H. Dodd & Co.,) bds. 45 N. Pennsylvania.
Hulsman M., saw filer, S. Pennsylvania, res. Maryland.

Hutton Mrs. Eliza Jane, (wid.,) res. Tennessee, bet. Third and Fourth.
Hutton Thomas, carpenter, res. 95 W. Vermont.
Hutsell John, ostler, Little's Hotel.
Hyatt James M., school teacher, res. Harrison, E. of Pine.
HYDE ABNER R., proprietor Little's Hotel, cor. Washington and New Jersey.
HYDE REV. NATHANIEL A., pastor 1st Con. Church, bds. 10 E. Market.
Hyde & Weathers, meat market, 173 E. Washington.
Hymbaugh Joseph, laborer, res. 44 S. East.
Hyner Andrew, railroader, res. 34 S. Noble.
Hyner Jacob, U. S. A., res. 112 E. McCarty.
Hyser Edward, res. 243, N. New Jersey.

I

Identical Mills, Theodore Hudnut, proprietor, S. Pennsylvania.
Idler Clinton, machinist T. H. R. R. shop, res. cor. South and Mississippi.
Igoe Martin, quartermaster 35th Regiment, res. 17 E. Loukabee.
Iliff Charles, clerk 22 E. Washington, bds. 39 N. Alabama.
Iliff James, clerk Glaser & Bro., bds. 37 N. Alabama.
Iliff Richard W., painter, res. 39 N. Alabama.
ILLINOIS & INDIANA CENTRAL RAILWAY, office 24½ E. Washington, Ed. Clark, agent.
Imbry Charles A., brewer, res. 193 S. Pennsylvania.
Imes Solomon, res. Illinois, bet. First and Second.
Ince Joseph, shoemaker, 38 W. Washington, res. 176 Massachusetts ave.
Ingerman William, works at arsenal, res. W. Indianapolis.
Ingersol H. W., furniture dealer, 78 E. Washington, res. 152 S. New Jersey.
Inglekink Frederick, works Madison depot, res. 73 Bluff Road.
Inglekink William, switchman Terre Haute depot, res. 90 Bluff Road.
INDIANA AMERICAN, T. A. Goodwin, editor and proprietor, Pearl, rear of Gleenns' Block, daily and weekly.
INDIANA CENTRAL RAILWAY, ticket and general offices cor. Virginia ave. and Delaware.
INDIANA CENTRAL RAILWAY, freight depot Delaware, cor. Louisiana.
INDIANA CENTRAL RAILWAY, engine house on track, bet. Noble and Benton.

INDIANA FREE PRESS, 83 E. Washington, R. Heninger, proprietor, German weekly.
INDIANA'S HOME-LIFE AND CAMP-LIFE, published weekly at $2 a year, office 18 East Washington.
INDIANA SCHOOL JOURNAL, monthly, publication office Journal Building, cor. Circle and Meridian.
INDIANA STATE SENTINEL, Meridian, bet. Washington and Pearl, Elder, Harkness & Bingham, proprietors, daily and weekly.
INDIANA U. S. ARSENAL, Market, bet. Tennessee and Mississippi.
INDIANA VOLKSBLATT, 132 E. Washington, Julius Bœtticher, proprietor, German weekly.
INDIANAPOLIS BAPTIST FEMALE INSTITUTE, cor. Pennsylvania and North, Rev. G. Williams, principal.
INDIANAPOLIS BRANCH BANKING COMPANY, S. W. cor. Washington and Pennsylvania, Calvin Fletcher, President; T. H. Sharpe, Cashier.
INDIANAPOLIS GAS LIGHT AND COKE COMPANY, D. S. Beaty, President; Samuel Vanlaningham, Secretary; office Ray's Building.
INDIANAPOLIS GYMNASIUM, cor. Meridian and Maryland, up stairs.
INDIANAPOLIS JOURNAL COMPANY, Journal Building, cor. Circle and Meridian, daily and weekly, J. M. Tilford, President.
INDIANAPOLIS McLEAN FEMALE INSTITUTE, Meridian, cor. New York, Rev. C. Sturdevant, principal.
INDIANAPOLIS, PITTSBURG & CLEVELAND RAILROAD LINE, part of Bellefontaine line, office cor. Meridian and Louisiana.
INDIANAPOLIS ROLLING MILL, cor. Merrill and Mississippi, J. M. Lord, President.
INDIANAPOLIS & CHICAGO AIR LINE, via Kokomo and C. & C. air line; office at Peru & Indianapolis R. R. office.
INDIANAPOLIS & CINCINNATI RAILROAD, offices cor. Delaware and Louisiana.
INDIANAPOLIS & CINCINNATI FREIGHT DEPOT, S. Delaware, bet. Maryland and South.
INDIANAPOLIS & LAFAYETTE RAILROAD, freight office, N. of North, bet. Missouri and Mississippi.
INDIANAPOLIS, PITTSBURG & CLEVELAND RAILROAD, office cor. Meridian and Union track.
Inkle John, carpenter, res. cor. Bates and Cady.
Irick Rebecca, milliner, 234 N. New Jersey.
Irick William, brick-layer, res. 172 N. New Jersey.
Irick William H., brick-layer, res. 156 N. New Jersey.

Irons Mrs. Catherine, (wid.,) seamstress, res. 119 W. Maryland.
Irven Ann M., (wid.,) res. 18 S. East.
Irvin C. A., brick mason, res. S. of Wyoming.
Irwin Joseph, bds. 13 W. Ohio.
Irwin Mrs. Martha, res. 42 E. New York.
Isensee Albert F. W., bell-hanger and locksmith, 17 Kentucky ave., bds. 28 Kentucky ave.
Isgrig James, carpenter, res. Illinois, bet. Fifth and Sixth.
Ittenbach Frank, stone cutter, (Smith, I. & Co.,) 208 S. Delaware.

J

Jackson A. S., tinner, Root, Bennett & Co.
Jackson D., Jackson's Museum, 19 W. Washington, res. 112 Mississippi.
Jackson E. S., tinsmith, 70 S. Delaware.
Jackson House, Hugh Marmont, proprietor, 136 W. Washington.
Jackson Henry, blacksmith, 86 W. Washington, bds. 28 Indiana ave.
Jackson Morris, (Flatauer & J.,) res. Ohio.
Jackson's Museum, 19 W. Washington.
Jackson Wiliam, roofing, res. 26 N. Liberty.
Jackson W. N., Union Railway Company, bds. Dr. Gatling.
Jacobs Valentine, Captain 19th Indiana Regiment, res. 58 E. Maryland.
Jacups William, laborer, res. Ash, near University.
James Allen, laborer, res. 123 E. St. Clair.
James John, tinner, Root, Bennett & Co.
James T. S., (W. W. J. & Co.)
James W. W., (W. W. J. & Co.,) res. 168 N. Tennessee.
James W. W. & Co., marble works, 58 S. Meridian.
JAMESON REV L. H., minister Christian Church, res. 97 W. South.
JAMESON P. H., (J. & Funkhouser,) res. 51 cor. Ohio and Alabama.
JAMESON & FUNKHOUSER, physicians and surgeons, 5 S. Meridian.
Jasper Oliver, (col.,) wood chopper, res. Seventh.
JEFFERIES J. WASH., proprietor Bates City Mills, cor. Noble and Washington, bds. Little's Hotel.
Jenison Geo. M., (W. H. Talbott & Co.,) res. 9 W. Ohio, near Meridian.
Jenison Mrs. Harriet, (wid.,) res. 9 W. Ohio.
Jenison O. F., opp. 24 East Washington, bds. 9 W. Ohio.

Jenkins A. W., grocer, cor. Pennsylvania and North, res. same.
Jenkins Ebenezer, painter and glazier, rear of Bates House, res. 32 E. Ohio.
Jenkins John, clerk 120 N. Pennsylvania, res. 126 Market.
Jenks W. R. C., printer, Journal Office, res. 24 N. Pennsylvania.
Jennings Patrick, teacher, res. 25 N. Liberty.
Jennings Wm., tinner, 69 W. Washington, res. 55 E. Ohio.
Jerard Ittenbach & Co., grocers, 180 S. Delaware.
Jerrel Miss M., teacher McLean's Seminary, bds. same.
Joachime Augustus, tallow chandler, res. 93 W. Maryland.
Joennivolas Joroin, carpenter, res. Winston, bet. North and Michigan.
John Charles, boarding house, 199 E. Washington.
John Samuel, book-binder, bds. 67 N. East.
John Samuel, bds. 14 W. Georgia.
Johnson Mrs., dress maker, 12½ S. Pennsylvania.
Johnson Aaron, clerk, res. Mississippi, N. of St. Clair.
Johnson Benjamin, soldier, res. 25 Central.
Johnson Ben. F., saloon, 212 W. Washington.
Johnson Ben. F., clerk 4 Blake's Building, bds. 58 N. Mississippi.
Johnson C., tailor, 19 W. Washington, bds. cor. Garden and Willard.
Johnson C. A., photographer, &c., 33 W. Washington.
Johnson C. R., wood dealer, bds. Ohio House.
Johnson D. R., student with Dr. Boyd.
Johnson Eleanor, (wid.,) res. California, bet. Market and Washington.
Johnson George, clerk Wood's hardware store, res. 240 S. Alabama.
Johnson G. H., salesman City Hardware Store, 12 W. Washington, res. 240 S. Alabama.
Johnson Geo. H., laborer, res. Illinois, bet. Second and Third.
Johnson G. W., grocer, Mississippi, N. of St. Clair.
Johnson Hubbard, salesman 70 E. Washington, bds. 121 E. Ohio.
JOHNSON ISAAC E., attorney at law and loan office, 4 Blake's Building, res. 58 N. Mississippi.
Johnson John, merchant tailor, 48 S. Illinois, res. Mississippi.
Johnson J. F., wholesale and retail grocer, 31, cor. Meridian and Maryland, res. 11 Maryland.
Johnson John S., farmer, res. 74 Bluff Road.
Johnson M. L., captain Co. I, 51st regiment, res. 41 N. New Jersey.
Johnson Philip, carpenter, res. 155 N. East.

Johnson Thomas, (col.,) cook Little's Hotel.
Johnson T. D., salesman New York Store, res. 107 W. Ohio.
Johnson Wm., grocery, 167 Tennessee, cor. Garden, res. same.
Johnson Wm., laborer, res. 160 N. Blake.
Johnson Wm. W., printer, res. 112 E. Vermont.
JOHNSTON O. W., livery and sale stable, 11 and 13 W. Pearl, res. 172 E. South.
Johnston Mrs. Fidellie, sewing, res. 148 N. East.
Johnston George, blacksmith, res. 74 E. Louisiana.
Johnston John F., dentist, res. and office 11 E. Maryland.
Johnston S. A., book-keeper, 62 E. Washington, bds. 86 E. Vermont.
Johnston William J., (Munson & J.,) res. 86 Vermont.
Jolly Jas., watchman Lawrenceburg car shop, res. 11 Lord.
Jolly John, works Lawrenceburg car shop, res. 11 Lord.
Jones ——, res. 36 Liberty.
Jones A., (J., Vinnedge & Co.,) res. 79 N. Pennsylvania.
Jones A., Jr., (J., Vinnedge & Co.,) bds. Bates House.
Jones A. M., clothes inspector, res. 139 E. South.
Jones Alex., (col.,) farmer, res. Illinois, N. of Sixth.
Jones B. D., sutler 52d Regiment, res. S. E. cor. Alabama and Vermont.
Jones Edward, railroader, res. 44 S. Noble.
Jones Edwin E., salesman, 20 S. Meridian.
Jones Fleming, broom-maker, Illinois, N. of Sixth.
Jones George W., farmer, res. Illinois, N. of Sixth.
Jones J. W., checker T. H. freight depot.
Jones Jesse, res. 106 N. Illinois.
Jones J. M., inspector U. S. warehouse.
JONES JOHN P., clerk of Supreme Court, res. Tennessee, N. of St. Clair.
Jones Johnny, salesman 17 W. Washington, bds. 79 Pennsylvania
Jones Lewis, harness maker, 34 W. Washihgton, res. 56 Indiana ave.
Jones Mrs. Mary A., (wid.,) res. 154 W. Vermont.
Jones N. R., conductor Terre Haute Railroad, res. 49 W. Georgia.
Jones Sheridan, (col.,) laborer, res. Howard.
Jones Spicer, sutler 47th regiment, res. 206 N. Illinois.
JONES, VINNEDGE & CO.'S shoe house, 17 W. Washington.
Jones William, (col.,) barber, bds. Little's Hotel.
Jones William, meat market, 122 S. Illinois, bds. Station House.
Jonte Emuel, cook Spencer House.

10

350 families in Indianapolis and vicinity use Wheeler & Wilson.

FRANKLIN TYPE AND STEREOTYPE FOUNDRY,

168 Vine Street, bet. Fourth and Fifth Streets,

CINCINNATI, OHIO.

R. ALLISON, - - Superintendent.

Manufacturers of and dealers in

NEWS, BOOK AND JOB TYPE,

PRINTING PRESSES, CASES, GALLEYS, &c.,

Inks & Printing Material

Of every description.

STEREOTYPING

OF ALL KINDS,

Books, Music, Patent Medicine Directions, Jobs, Wood Cuts, &c., &c.

Brand & Pattern Letters

OF VARIOUS STYLES.

ELECTROTYPING

IN ALL ITS BRANCHES.

The Wheeler & Wilson Hemmer makes hems of any width.

Jordan Gilmer, clerk Washington City, res. 104 W. Tennessee.
Jordan Joseph, laborer, res. 133 Bluff Road.
Jordan Samuel J., tailor, res. 157 S. Mississippi.
Jordan Thos., flour and grain dealer, 18 S. Meridian, res. 92 E. Market.
Jose N., furniture store, 4 S. Pennsylvania, res. out of city.
Joseph J. G., salesman 2 Palmer House, bds. same.
Joseph R. C., retired, res. 158 W. New York.
Jude James, laborer, res. 21 E. Wyandott.
Judson Charles E., book-keeper Bates House.
Judson William, proprietor Bates House, cor. Washington and Illinois.

K

Kabis Leopold, clerk with R. Beebe, Empire Saloon.
Kahle Samuel F., cabinet maker, res. Orient.
KAHN A., clothier and dealer in furnishing goods, 2 Palmer House, bds. Morris House.
Kahn Jacob, Union clothing store, 46 E. Washington, bds. Oriental House.
Kahn Lewis, butcher, res. 120 N. Mississippi.
Kahra Michael, bar-keeper Lou. Lang's saloon, bds. same.
Kaiser Adam, shoemaker, bds. Kentucky ave.
KALL LEWIS, renovater and exchanger of clothing of all kinds, 93 E. Washington, res. 63 East.
KANSAS EATING AND DRINKING SALOON, 83 and 85 S. Illinois, John P. Frenzell, proprietor.
Karnes Joseph, carpenter, res. 58 Davidson.
Karrle Christ., boot and shoemaker, 64 E. Washington, res. 72 S. Delaware.
Karnatz John, shoemaker, res. 114 N. Alabama.
Karrle Joseph, manufacturer and dealer in boots and shoes, 64 E. Washington, res. 35 South.
Karvauwn Patrick, railroader, res. cor. Missouri and Georgia.
Kasser Frederick, painter, res. 55 W. Liberty.
Kaskell Thurlow, carpenter, res. 82 W. Maryland.
Kaskell William H., bds. 82 W. Maryland.
Katahar Michael, laborer, res. Bates.
Kaufmann Moritz, butcher, res. 131 N. East.
Kantman M., well-digger, res. 58 Massachusetts ave.
Keane Mrs. A., (Lynch & K.,) res. 43 N. Tennessee.
Keating Miss L. U., wood dealer, res. 20 Elm.
Keating Jeffrey, laborer, res. 288 S. Delaware.
Keating Michael, laborer, res. 31 South.

The Wheeler & Wilson Hemmer is the only Hemmer that will Fell.

HEAD-QUARTERS FOR FASHIONABLE
BOOTS & SHOES,
JOHN H. DETERS,
53 West Fourth Street, CINCINNATI. O.,

Has now on hand the most extensive, varied, and elegant assortment of Boots and Shoes in the City. Articles manufactured at his establishment are superior to any made in this country as regards their beauty, shape, workmanship and durability. His stock comprises Ladies', Gentlemens,' Misses,' Boys,' Youths,' and Childrens,'

BOOTS AND SHOES,
OF EVERY STYLE,

And in infinite variety, all made by artistic workmen. Doing a large business and selling strictly for cash, enables him to sell his goods very cheap.

N. B.---A large stock of Military Boots and Shoes constantly on hand.

MRS. C. F. HALL,
SEAL ENGRAVING,
At No. 14 West Fourth St., CINCINNATI, O.

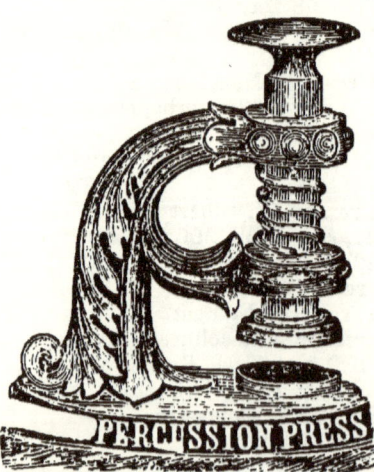

Notarial, Court, Corporation, State, Ecclesiastical, College, Society, I. O. O. F., Masonic, I. O. S. M., Library, and all others of an official character engraved and adjusted to latest Improved Presses. Also every variety of Business Seals, with Percussion and Lever Presses, for Merchants, Bankers, Manufacturers, &c.

Percussion Press, with Seal of Fifty Letters..................$5 00
Lever Press, with Seal of Fifty Letters...................... 6 00
Devices Extra.
Court Seal and Press.......$10 to $25
Wax Seals for public and private use. Wedding and Visiting Cards neatly engraved and printed. Address,

Mrs. C. F. HALL,
No. 14 West Fourth Street,
CINCINNATI, O.

A Wheeler & Wilson Sewing Machine with Hemmer, for $50.

Keatinge Joseph J., newspapers and periodicals, 19 S. Illinois, res. same.
Keefer Jacob, machinist Washington foundry, res. 155 S. Mississippi.
Keeler William, coffee vender, ress. 44 Spring.
Keeling John, salesman New York Store, res. 109 S. East.
Keely Mrs. Elinor, res. alley, bet. New York and Ohio.
Keely George L., press boy, bds. 105 N. Noble.
Keely Henry S., printer Dodd & Co., bds. 159 E. Ohio.
Keely Isaac I., bricklayer, res. 105 N. Noble.
Keely Isaac I., physician and surgeon, bds. 62 E. Michigan.
Keely John, bricklayer, res. 48 N. East.
Keely Oliver S., bricklayer, res. 159 E. Ohio.
Keely Samuel, bricklayer, res. 177 N. Noble.
Keely William, carpenter, res. 62 E. Michigan.
Keely William H., grocer, cor. Market and Noble, res. E. 165 Ohio.
Keen Ennis, tailor, 69 S. Illinois, bds. Farmers' Hotel.
Keen H. W., (Tarlton & K.,) res. 122 N. Illinois.
Keenan Thos., res. 61 S. Noble.
Keesee George, laborer, res. 201 Indiana ave.
Keesee William N., carpenter, res. 144 Blake.
Kehoe Thomas, laborer, res. 84 N. Tennessee.
Keiffer John G., wood sawyer, res, 86 St. Joseph.
Kline Nicholas, shoemaker Massachusetts ave., res. Spring.
Keiser Adam, shoemaker, bds. 28 Kentucky ave.
Keishner F., currier for John Fishback.
Kecker Sophie, washer, res. 186 N. New Jersey.
Kelb Henry, laborer, res. 98 St. Joseph.
Kelkauf Frederick, central depot, res. 115 Union.
Kelleher James, shoemaker, res. 9 N. New Jersey.
Keller Daniel, stone-mason, bds. 174 N. East.
Keller John, laborer, res. 28 Forest.
Keller Lewis, salesman New York Store, res. 109 S. East.
Keller Mrs. Mary, washer, res. alley, N. bet. New Jersey and East.
Keller James ostler, res. 175 E. St. Clair.
Keller Z. P., machinist, res. 84 S. East.
Kelley Dennis, harness maker, res. 82 N. Tennessee.
Kelley Mrs. Mary, (wid.,) res. 73 N. Missouri.
Kellish Martin, butcher Bates House Meat Market.
Kellish Michael, butcher Bates House Meat Market.
Kellogg Henry S., salesman 71 E. Washington, bds. 87 Meridian.
Kellogg Newton, edge tool maker, res. S. E. cor. Market and West.
Kellogg W. H., (K. & Davis,) bds. Pyle House.
Kellogg & Davis, fine art gallery, 8 E. Washington.

Upwards of 100 W. & W. Machines in use in Ind'p'lis making army clothing.

GEO. R. DIXON.   I. W. PARKER.

GEO. R. DIXON & CO.,

OHIO MUSTARD MILLS,

WHOLESALE DEALERS IN

FRESH ROASTED & GROUND COFFEE, SPICES,

Mustard, Pepper Sauce, Tomato Catsup,

BAKING POWDER,

Peanuts, Indigo, Nutmegs, &c.,

Highest Cash Prices paid for Mustard Seed.

Nos. 243, 245 & 247 Sycamore Street,

CINCINNATI, OHIO.

D. HILLS & CO.   C. F. O'DRISCOLL.

HILLS, O'DRISCOLL & CO.,

Stereotype and Electrotype,

FOUNDRY,

DEALERS IN

PRINTING MATERIALS

No. 141 MAIN STREET,

CINCINNATI, OHIO.

Stereotyping and Electrotyping of all kinds; Books, Music, Pamphlets, and Jobs of every description done at short notice and in the best manner. Colored and Black Inks of all kinds for sale.

Wheeler & Wilson's Sewing Machines awarded the first premium for five

CITY DIRECTORY. 151

Kelly Elisha, E., (col.,) laborer, res. N. Mississippi.
Kelly James, huckster, res. 66 Bluff Road.
Kelly John B., painter, 278 Madison ave.
Kelly Jonathan, salesman New York Store, bds. 109 E. South.
Kelly Patrick, laborer, res. 108 E. Ohio.
Kelly Thomas, currier, res. 11 McCarty.
Kelly William, butcher, bds. 22 Indiana ave.
Kelor John, hackman, res. W. side Noble, bet. Vermont and Michigan.
Kemper Charles, grocer, 12 cor. McCarty and Meridian, res. same.
Kemper J. M., carpenter, res. 122 S. New Jersey.
Kendrick Wm. H., physician, office 33 and res. 35 N. East.
Kennedy Larry, laborer, res. 320 S. Delaware.
Kennedy James, blacksmith, res. 2 Bernard.
Kennedy Joseph, works Dumont & Sinker, res. 21 Benton.
Kennedy John, laborer, res. Indiana ave.
Kennedy Samuel, shoemaker, 38 W. Washington.
Kennedy Thomas, res. 113 E. South.
Kennedy Patrick, 8th Regiment Illinois Volunteers, res. 63 Spring.
Kenney H. T., tailor, res. 34 S. West.
Kennington John, wagoner, res. extreme end Virginia ave.
Kentwell Matthew, foundryman, res. Winston, bet. Ohio and New York.
Kentzel J. S., printer Herald & Era office, bds. 36 East.
Keppel Josiah, res. 67 W. Louisiana.
Kepple Henry, workmen at rolling mill, res. 153 S. Mississippi.
Kepple Martin, clerk Depot Bakery.
Kerin Daniel P., grocer, res. S. E. Michigan Road.
Kerley James, cooper, res. Merrill.
Kern Casper, cabinet maker, res. 172 E. Michigan.
Kern Jacob, porter 26 and 28 W. Washington.
Kern John, tailor, 39 E. Washington, bds. 60 Davidson.
Kern L. D., student, bds. 130 N. New Jersey.
Kerper Charles, saddle and harness maker, res. 21 Indiana ave.
Kesner Henry, shoemaker, res. 64 Bluff Road.
Kesper Peter, foundryman, res. 126 W. Vermont.
Ketchum John L., (K. & Mitchell,) res. 97 E. Merrill.
Ketchum & Mitchell, attorneys at law, Blackford's Building.
Kettenback Henry, grocer, Massachusetts ave., bet. Liberty and St. Clair, res. 216 N. Noble.
Keys Wm., marble dealer, res. Georgia, bet. Missouri and West.

Successive years at Mechanic's Institute, Cincinnati.

INDIANAPOLIS

THE CINCINNATI
TYPE FOUNDRY COMPANY
AND
Printing Machine Works,

Corner Vine & Longworth Streets

BETWEEN FIFTH AND SIXTH,

CINCINNATI, OHIO.

CHAS. WELLS, - - - - Agent.

MANUFACTURE AND FURNISH ALL KINDS OF

PRINTING MACHINERY & FURNITURE,

ELECTROTYPED OR STEREOTYPED.

Specimen Books or Estimates furnished on application.

First Premium awarded the Wheeler & Wilson Sewing Machine for three

Keyser John W., carpenter, res. Tennessee, bet. Second and Third.
Kiby Daniel, cooper, res. Michigan Road.
Kidder J. R., currier for John Fishback.
Kieser Adam, shoemaker, res. Kentucky ave.
Kiger Henry, (K. & Phillips,) U. S. A.
Kiger & Phillips, attorneys at law, Blackford's Building.
Kilberry ——, laborer, res. Mississippi, N. of St. Clair.
Kinder Mrs. M. W., boarding house, 79½ E. Washington.
Kindler Chas., (Ballwig & Kindler,) res. 17 Kentucky ave.
Kinfieng N., tinner Root, Bennett & Co.
King Cornelius, lumber dealer, res. 141 N. Mississippi.
King David, res. 157 W. Mississippi.
King Edward, secretary and treasurer Indianapolis, Pittsburg & Crestline, and cashier Bellefontaine R. R. Lines, res. Meridian, opp. Blind Asylum.
King Francis, Grand Secretary Masonic Lodge, office Masonic Hall Building, res. 72 N. Tennessee.
King Geo., fireman P. & I. R. R., bds. 18 Lord.
King H. L., messenger Adams Express Co., bds. Palmer House.
King Jacob, patern maker, bds. 258 W. Washington.
King James, res. 70 N. Illinois.
King J. B., gas-fitter, res. Mississippi, bet. Michigan and Vermont.
King W. H., clerk Bellefontaine R. R. Line, bds. Bates House.
King W. T., res. 99 Bates.
Kingham Jos., assistant teacher, workshop Blind Asylum, res. 72 St. Joseph.
Kingman Nelson, foreman tin shop Root, Bennett & Co., res. 59 E. New York.
Kingsberry C. G., porter American Express Co., bds. Morris House.
Kingsberry John E., watchmaker, res. 181 Massachusetts ave.
Kingsley Adriel S., res. Duncan.
Kinnan Augustus, stone-cutter for Jason Dame, res. 227 S. Alabama.
Kinney Pat., steward Little's Hotel.
Kinsler Patrick, railroader, res. 204 N. Mississippi.
Kinyer W., laborer for John Fishback.
Kirk E., milliner, 39 N. Pennsylvania, res. same.
Kirkwood Geo., fireman I. & Cincinnati R. R., res. Bates, E. of Cady.
Kirkwood John, res. 108 E. South.
Kirkwood John, fireman, I. & C. R. R., res. 9 Lord.
Kirkil Dol., engineer, res. 100 Louisiana.
Kirland Patrick, 73 S. Meridian, bds. 100 Mississippi.

MIDDLETON, STROBRIDGE & CO.,

Lithographers & Engravers,

64 West Fourth St.,

CINCINNATI, O.

Special attention given to all kinds of work in our line, such as

Maps,
    Portraits,
        Bonds,
           Diplomas,
                Show Cards,
                    Bill Heads,
                        Letter Heads, &c.

ALSO, PUBLISHERS OF

Washington as a Mason,

A beautiful Picture representing Washington surrounded with the emblems of the Order.

ALSO,

ODD FELLOWSHIP,

Beautifully represented, with

A FINE PORTRAIT

Of the Founder of the Order.

AND OTHER PRINTS, &c., &c.

A Wheeler & Wilson Sewing Machine will last a life-time.

Kirlin James, dry goods and groceries, 36 W. Washington, res. cor. Illinois and First.
Kissell J. W., bar-keeper Burt's Dining Saloon, res. Indiana ave.
KISTNER ADAM, proprietor California House, 136 and 138 S. Illinois.
Kistner J. G., boot and shoemaker, 51 S. Illinois, res. same.
Kitchen John M., physician and surgeon, cor. Washington and Meridian, res. 69 N. Pennsylvania.
Klapp Henry, gardener, res. E. National Road.
Klein C. F., book-keeper Martin Hug, bds. same.
Klein Dr. Emil, res. 100 E. New York.
Kliber John Lewis, confectioner, 105 E. Washington, res. same.
Klieger Henry, laborer, res. 101 S. Alabama.
Kline Joseph, clerk 31 S. Meridian, bds. Pyle House.
Klingensmith J. K., bds. 79 W. Maryland.
Klingensmith J., res. 79 W. Maryland.
Klingensmith Israel, bds. 79 W. Maryland.
KLOTZ EMIL, wholesale and retail dealer in fancy goods, notions, &c,. 37 E. Washington, res. 61 Illinois.
Klotz Frank, baker, 186 S. Delaware.
Klotz John, laborer, res. 21 S. Illinois.
Knauf Adam, baker, res. 64 E. St. Joseph.
Knaus Charles, bar-keeper Eagle Saloon, bds. same.
Knainlin Geo., wood sawyer, res. 34 Hosbrook.
Knefler Charles, clerk postoffice, bds. W. H. Campbell.
Knefler Fred., assistant adjutant general, U. S. A.
Kneif John, carpenter, res. 160 N. Liberty.
Knepton James, carver, res. 56 N. Noble.
Knight Elijah, boarding house, res. 19 W. Georgia.
Knight John, coppersmith, res. 72 S. Louisiana.
Knight James, brick-maker, res. 107 S. Missouri.
Knight Jasper N., painter, res. 106 Indiana ave.
Knight John, (Cottrall & K.,) res. 102 E. Louisiana.
Knightly Wm., U. S. service, res. 306 S. Delaware.
Knodle A., (A. K. & Son,) res. 8 Indiana ave.
Knodle Geo., (A. K. & Son,) bds. 8 Indiana ave.
KNODLE A. & SON, manufacturers and dealers in boots and shoes, 32 E. Washington. (See card.)
Knoker Sebastian, baker, res. 213 N. Noble.
Knotts N. K., sign and ornamental painter, 2 N. Pennsylvania, res. 96 E. Market.
Knowlton G. F., salesman 40 E. Washington, res. 140 N. Tennessee.
Knox Asbery, (col.,) barber, res. 59 Kentucky ave.
Knox Francis A., res. Kentucky ave.
Koch Charles, collar maker, 184 S. Pennsylvania.

81,000 Wheeler & Wilson's Sewing Machines in use in this country.

Koch H., grocer, 198 Massachusetts ave., res. same.
Koch Wm., grocery, res. 47 S. East.
Kochman Peter, moulder 268 S. Delaware.
Kœhler John Philip, barber Palmer House hair-dressing saloon, bds. Georgia.
Kœlme Charles, clerk, res. Liberty, bet. New York and Vermont.
Kœstle Jacob, baker, 165 N. Noble, res. same.
Kohn Geo., machinist, bds. Kansas Eating Saloon.
Koiehn John, laborer, res. 118 Union.
Kolb John A., grocer, 69 S. Illinois, res. same.
Kolb Wm., boarding house, 28 and 30 Kentucky ave.
Koldhoff Low., blacksmith, bds. Jack Myer.
Koler John, laborer, res. 71 Elm.
Koontz A., res. N. Illinois.
Koort Frederick, laborer, res. 69 N. Bright.
Kork Charles, printer Indiana Free Press.
Kortyreter Wm., tailor, res. 69 N. Noble.
Kossebaum John G., grocer, 153 Massachusetts ave., res. same.
Kothe William, watchman Washington foundry, res. 69 Davidson.
Kolthoff Henrich, laborer, res. Biddle, near city limits.
Kown James, teamster, cor. Oak and Massachusetts ave.
Krause Philip, laborer, res. 66 E. St. Mary.
Krause Wm., (K. & Wittinberg,) res. S. E. Alabama, bet. Ohio and Market.
Krause and Wittenberg, proprietors German Dry Goods Store, 43 and 45 E. Washington.
Krauth Ernst W., clerk 14 W. Washington, bds. 137 E. Washington.
Kregelo, Blake & Co., planing mill, cor. Canal and W. New York.
Kregelo Chas., (K. Blake & Co.,) res. 132 W. New York.
Kregelo Jacob, carpenter, res. 40 E. St. Clair.
Kregelo David, planing mill, res. 132 N. West.
Kreger Christian, carpenter, bds. 41 N. East.
Kreniger George, grocer, 60 South.
Kretsch Peter, cigars, tobacco, &c., 93 S. Illinois, res. same.
Kreutzer John, tailor, res. Tennessee, bet. Fourth and Fifth.
Krest Charles, laborer, res. 161 N. Liberty.
Krinn Jacob, laborer, res. 106 St. Joseph.
Krome Fred., laborer, res. 76 Huron.
Kroppe Peter, collar maker, 182 S. Pennsylvania.
Kruger Charles, clerk 70 E. Washington, bds. 115 E. Market.
Kruger Wm., works Merritt & Coughlen's woolen factory, bds. 28 Kentucky ave.

The First Premium awarded the Wheeler & Wilson Machine

/Kruger Joseph, cistern builder, res. 115 E. Market.
Krusman Louis, tailor, res. 63 East.
Kruz Christian, carpenter, 9 McCarty.
Kuetemeier Charles, carpenter, res. 142 N. East.
Kuhlmann E. H. L., groceries, 187 W. Washington, res. same.
Kuhn Charles, meat market, res. 107 W. Washington.
Kunil B., cigar maker, 63 E. Washington.
Kurtpeter William, tailor, 63 E. Washington, res. 69 Noble.
Kuschinger Matthew, shoemaker, 64 E. Washington.
Kusick John, grocer, West, bet. Maryland and Georgia.
KUNKELMAN REV. J. A., Eng. Luth., res. 156 N. Pennsylvania.
KUSTER REV. C. E., res. S. New Jersey.

L

Labarre Lewis, moulder, res. 17 S. Illinois.
Labonte Moses, bds. 10 Mississippi.
Lack L., waiter, Louis Lang's.
Ladoy Thomas, boiler maker, res. 259 S. Delaware.
Lafavrie J., grocer, cor Maryland and Illinois, res. same.
Lafayette Railroad Depot, W. North.
Lafever Samuel, bowlderer, res. 140 N. Mississippi.
Lahman Fred, shoemaker at Jones & Vinnedge's, res. E. Nat. Road.
Lahn John, laborer, res. 79 E. Market.
Laing David, Carpenter, res. 20 St. Clair.
Laird Harry, tinner, 11 W. Washington.
Laird W. H., book-keeper, Washington Foundry, res. 140 N. Illinois.
Lake John, (Blanc, Borst & Co.,) res. South of city.
Lake Joseph, carpenter, bds. 85 Indiana ave.
Lake Miss M., fancy store, 38 N. Pennsylvania, res. same.
Lamb Mrs. Mary E., cloak maker, with Miss Moon.
Lamb Peter, porter Morris House, res. 15 Willard.
Lamb Yancy, machinist, res. 20 N. Mississippi.
Lambert William, butcher, 52 S. Delaware.
Lame John P., railroader, res. 237 Indiana ave.
Lamley George, laborer, res. 77 N. East.
Lamotte, tinner, Root, Bennett & Co.
Lancaster H. H., salesman New York Store, bds. C. Scudder's.
Lancaster Washington, shoemaker, 12 S. Illinois, res. same.
LANDON & HASTINGS, printers and engraves, 8 E. Washington.
Landon Albert W., (L. & Hastings.) bds. Morris House.

Landers Thomas, laborer, 96 S. Delaware.
Landers Delilah, (col.,) washer, res. North, bet. Blackford and California.
Landis Milton M., Freight Ag't T. H. & R. R. R., res. 40 S. Pennsylvania.
Landis Jacob, livery stable, 18 Maryland, res. Maryland.
Landis A. C., (wid.,) 104 Virginia ave.
Landragin John, clerk, cor. South and Delaware, res. in rear.
Lane Eda, (col.,) res. 123 E. St. Clair.
Lane Uriah, laborer, res. 170 N. New Jersey.
Lanenberg H. H., grocer, wholesale and retail, 134 W. Washington, res. same.
LANG LOUIS, restaurant and saloon, 13 E. Washington, res. same.
Lang Samuel, tinner, 69 W. Washington, res. Illinois.
Lang Wm. W., book-binder Campbell & Boyle, res. 22 W. St. Clair.
Langdein Joseph, grocery, dealer in fancy goods, 160 E. Washington, res. same.
LANGE ALBERT, Auditor of State, res. 43 W. Michigan.
LANGERBERG H. H., wholesale and retail dealer in groceries and provisions, 134 cor. W. Washington and Mississippi, res. same.
Langsdale J. M. W., (L. & Pattison,) res. E. of city.
Langsdale & Pattison, wholesale and retail grocers, 190 E. Washington.
Larges Michael, laborer, res. 252 Indiana ave.
Lackey Thomas, res. W. Washington.
Latham William H., teacher Deaf and Dumb Asylum, res. 93 E. Ohio.
Latshaw V. K. S., millinery, 22 S. Illinois, res. same.
Lauer Charles, East Empire Saloon, 162 E. Washington, res. 24 N. E. cor. Market and New Jersey.
Lankford Maria, sewing, res. 70 E. St. Mary's.
Langsdale Robert, clerk, 190 E. Washington, bds. Little's Hotel.
Laupheimer Augustus, porter, California House.
Lawrence A. V., res. 164 E. Ohio.
Laurie Wm., salesman New York Store, bds. Morris House.
Law C. L., (wid.,) res. 106 E. McCarty.
Lawler Wm., engineer, Bates House.
Lawless Michael, laborer, res. 90 S. Noble.
Laws C., engineer, res. 137 N. West.
Laws Thomas, teamster, res. N. Blake.
Lawson Elijah, U. S. A., res. 23 S. Illinois.
Lawson Joseph, rear Sentinel Building.
Leach Mrs. Eliza, res. 161 S. Tennessee.

Leappet Henry, sexton, res. 97 Railroad.
Leary Edmond, laborer, S. East.
Leary P. C., grocery, bds. 90 S. Noble.
Leathers W. W., (L. & Carter,) res. cor. Massachusetts ave. and New Jersey.
LEATHERS & CARTER, attorneys at law, 86 E. Washington.
Leavitt D. A., professor of phonography and music, res. Meridian.
Lebking Charles, shoemaker, res. 54 N. Noble.
Lechene Charles, shoemaker, 32 E. Washington.
Lechena Mary A., (wid.,) res. 160 S. Pennsylvania.
Lechsom Morris, peddlar, res. Wabash, bet. Liberty and Noble.
Leck Robt., salesman, New York Store, bds. C. Scudder's.
LEDDIE JOHN, proprietor Little's Hotel Saloon and Restaurant, bds. Little's Hotel.
Lee Benj., clerk M. H. Good's, bds. 31 Indiana ave.
Lee Charles N., chairmaker, res. 60 N. Noble.
Lee E. T., hackman, res. 248 Indiana ave.
Lee H. H., (Luddon & L.,) res. 9 Macy House.
Lee James, salesman, 53 W. Washington, bds. Macy House.
Lee M. G., proprietor Herald and Era, res. 36 East.
Lee William, (Doty & L.,) res. State House Saloon.
Lehr F. A., carpenter, res. 98 N. East.
Lehr Henry, carpenter, res. 165 E. New York.
Lehr Philip, carpenter, 165 E. New York.
Leienberger John, cook Spencer House.
Leiping Fred., U. S. A., res. Elm.
Leisemann William, laborer, res. 186 N. Noble.
Lelly Thomas, tailor, res. 109 W. Michigan.
Lemon J. W. K., conductor Indiana Central R. R. bds. Bates House.
Lemmon Mrs. Jennie, dress maker, res. 34 E. Ohio.
Lemoene Louis, laborer, res. 160 W. Noble.
Lemons William, brick-layer, bds. 159 E. Ohio.
Lempeng John, varnisher, bds. 95 Davidson.
Lendoring Joseph, fireman B. R. R., bds. 91 Railroad.
Lendoring Mrs. H., res. 91 Railroad.
Lenenger Michael, (L. & Ferling,) res. 102 Vermont.
Lenenger & Ferlenger, barbers, under American Express Office.
Lennert Ferdinand, stamp maker, 16½ S. Illinois, res. same.
Lennert Mrs. S., embroidering and stamping, 16½ S. Illinois, res. same.
Lentz Gotleib, butcher, res. 159 Maryland.
Lentz William, wagon driver Union Steam Bakery.
Leonard Michael, laborer, res. 29 South.

For four successive years at the Am. Institute, New York.

Leopold Lewis, cook, 13 S. Illinois.
Lerley Absalom T., brick-layer, res. 48 S. East.
Lerley Joseph, cooper, res. 50 S. East.
Leroy John, bds. Ohio House.
Lesh Andrew, with Wm. Hannaman.
Levi Jacob, tailor, 87 E. Washington, res. same.
Levien S., clerk quartermaster department, res. 22 S. Mississippi.
Levy Joseph, tinner, 69 W. Washington, res. W. Washington.
Levy Mrs. Mary F., (wid.,) res. 74 W. Vermont.
Lewark D. M., teamster, res. Mississippi, bet. First and Second.
Lewis Hiram L., teamster, res. 281 S. East.
Lewis James, bar-keeper Oriental Saloon.
Lewis John, works rolling mill, bds. 19 Willard.
Lewis Thos., secretary for Lunatic and Blind Asylums, res. 55 Meridian.
Lex Lewis, pressman Dodd & Co., res. Vermont, bet. Noble and Davidson.
Lex Jacob, works Dodd & Co., res. Vermont, bet. Noble and Davidson.
Lichtenhein Zach., sutler U. S. A., res. 63 W. New York.
Licket Geo., laborer, res. 238 Madison ave.
Lieber Hiram, gilt frames, mouldings and paintings, Ætna Building, 15 N. Pennsylvania, res. 123 N. Liberty.
Liebrich Louis, porter Robert Browning, res. 172 W. North.
Lietz J., painter, 31 W. Washington, res. Market.
Lightner Daniel, res. 161 S. Tennessee.
Likerd Simon, laborer, res. 3 N. New Jersey.
Lilly J. O. D., (C. G. Perkins & Co.,) res. 69 W. New York.
Linn Ad., laborer, res. cor. Noble and Virginia ave.
Linby A., boot and shoe dealer, res. 17 S. Mississippi.
Lindmann Frank, salesman 101 E. Washington, bds. same.
Lindenbower Wm. H., (Todd & L.,) res. 203 E. St. Clair.
Lindley H. J., book-keeper 39 W. Washington, res. 23 Indiana ave.
Lindley Jacob, wholesale and retail dealer in china, glass and queensware, 16 W. Washington, res. 35 N. Meridian.
Lindley Lemley, conductor Bellefontaine R. R., res. Wabash, bet. Liberty and Noble.
Linn Alex., collar maker Sulgrove & Reynolds, res. alley, bet. Arsenal and W. Market House.
Linn Wm. H., foreman Indiana American.
Linn Winfield S., compositor Indiana American.
Linter John, grocer, res. Indiana ave.
Lintler John, at Lamb's store, res. 273 S. East.
LINTNER C. H. & CO., grocers, 1 Indiana ave.

Lintner C. H., (C. H. L. & Co.,) res. 11 Indiana ave.
Lintner Isaac H., clerk, (J. L. & Son.,) bds. J. Lintner, Indiana ave.
Lintner John H., grocer, 140 E. Washington, res. same.
Lintner J. & Son, grocers, cor. North and Indiana ave.
Lintner Daniel, (J. L. & Son,) res. Indiana ave.
Lintz A., boots and shoes, 39 W. Washington, res. 17 S. Mississippi.
Lintz Conrad, wood chopper, res. cor. Maryland and West.
Lintz John K., salesman 39 W. Washington, bds. 17 Mississippi.
Liscomb E. A., bds. Bates House.
Little Mrs. Mary E., res. 130 N. Alabama.
Little Wilber, bds. 130 N. Alabama.
Little W. T., brass foundry.
LITTLE'S HOTEL, A. H. Hyde, proprietor, cor. New Jersey and Washington.
LITTLE'S HOTEL SALOON AND RESTAURANT, John Ledlie proprietor.
Liver A., grocer, 46 S. Meridian, res. same.
Livsey William, (L. & Co.,) bds. Morris House.
Livsey & Co., brass foundry, Lousiana, near Union Depot.
Lloyd ———, messenger Adams Express Co., bds. Palmer House.
Locke Eric, paymaster U. S. A., res. 40 N. Pennsylvania.
Locke J. (L. & Bro.,) res. 163 N. Pennsylvania.
Locke Joseph, res. 163 N. Pennsylvania.
Locke & Bro., insurance agents, cor. Washington and Meridian.
Lockridge John, cooper, W. Indianapolis.
Lockwood Isaac, pedlar, res. 44 Railroad.
Lockman Chas., grocer, res. cor. Virginia ave. and Cedar.
Logan Bernard, grocer, 129 W. South, res. same.
Logan Thomas, cabinet maker, res. 127 W. South.
Logan Patrick, laborer, res. 179 S. New Jersey.
Lohman Mrs. Pimelia, res. 120 E. Market.
Lohmann E., cigar maker, bds. Macy House.
Lohrmann Paul, saddler at Sulgrove & Reynolds', res. alley bet. St. Clair and Walnut.
Lonergan J. P., machinist, res. 147 N. Tennessee.
LONG REV. GEORGE, minister, res. 33 N. New Jersey.
Long James, with M. H. Good, bds. Palmer House.
Long Joseph, shoemaker, res. 147 N. Pennsylvania.
LONG MATTHEW, undertaker, 28 S. Meridian, res. same.
Long O. F., bar-keeper Morris House Saloon, bds. Morris House.
Long Oliver, engineer, bds. Little's Hotel.
Longenecker Saml., grocer, W. Indianapolis.

Longley John F., chair maker, res. 157 Massachusetts ave.
LOOMIS WM. H., green house and nursery, res. 189 Virginia ave.
Lorchet Peter, laborer, res. E. Maryland.
Lord E. N., (H. A. Fletcher & Co.,) res. 12 W. North.
Lord John M., president Rolling Mill, res. 141 N. Illinois.
Loucks Cornelius, butcher shop, 163 Virginia ave., res. 46 Benton.
Loucks G. W., bds. 46 S. Benton.
Loucks James, carpenter, 194 cor. New Jersey and St. Clair.
Loucks William W., carpenter, res. 123 N. Alabama.
Louden A. A., res. 57 N. Illinois.
Louden James, clerk, res. 140 Virginia ave.
Louder Mrs. Sarah, res. 86 N. Meridian.
Louks David W., city marshal, res. cor. Oak and Cherry.
Lounay Wm., laborer, res. 35 Huron.
Love Gen. John, res. 49 N. Tennessee.
Love William, (Spann & L.,) res. E. Washington.
LOVETT C. D., bar-keeper 220 E. Washington, bds. same.
Low Charles, carpenter, 18 S. New Jersey, res. 148 E. North.
Low Nahum, carpenter, 18 S. New Jersey, res. 148 E. North.
Lowes Bradley, carpenter, res. Spring, bet. Michigan and Vermont.
Lowe Geo., carriage manufacturer, 99 E. Washington, res. Pennsylvania, opp. Blind Asylum.
Lowe John, carpenter, res. 152 N. Delaware.
Lowe Mrs. Margaret, (wid.,) seamstress, res. 51 W. South.
Lowe N., printer, Sentinel Offices, res. 148 North.
Lowman Charles, laborer, res. Winston near Biddle.
Lowman Mrs. Nancy, dress making, res. 58 E. St. Clair.
Lowry George E., clerk, bds. 53 Massachusetts ave.
Lowry Robert, teamster, Ætna Mills.
LOWRY WILEY M., druggist, 49 Massachusetts ave, res. 53 Massachusets ave.
Lubking Charles, shoemaker, res. 54 Noble.
Lucas James, (col.,) whitewasher, res. 149 N. Alabama.
Lucid John, laborer, res. 157 S. Tennessee.
Ludden B. M., (L. & Lee,) res. cor. Maryland and Illinois.
LUDDEN & LEE, drugs and teas, 14 Bates House, N. Illinois.
Ludlow Siles, traveling agent, res. 147 N. Delaware.
Ludlum J. E., res. 230 N. Illinois.
Lue Michael, clerk McKernan & Pierce, bds. 27 Indiana ave.
Lukins Richard, res. 76 S. East.
Luoncy Dennis, traveling agent I. C. R. R., res. 110 W. Georgia.

Lupton William C., Deputy Auditor of State, res. 160 N. Pennsylvania.
Luther Mrs. Caroline, washer, res. 184 N. Delaware.
Lutheran Church, cor. of S. East and Georgia.
Lutheran School House, Georgia, E. of Lutheran Church.
Lutman Samuel, railroader, res. 32 N. Spring.
Luzzatti Abraham, laborer, W. Indianapolis.
Lykins Mrs. Margaret, (wid.,) washer, 83 cor. Pine and Elm.
Lynch G. G., (L. & Kane,) res. 49 Indiana ave.
Lynch Jerry, yard-man Little's Hotel.
Lynch Jerry, laborer, res. 112 S. East.
Lynch John, boarding house, 16 S. Pennsylvania.
Lynch Michael, shoemaker for Thomas A. Connor, 18 Delaware.
Lynch Patrick, engineer, Dumont & Sinker, res. 95 Bates.
Lynch Thos. H., school teacher, res. 14 N. Meridian.
Lynch & Keane, wholesale and retail dry goods, &c., 33 W. Washington.

M

McAdams Hugh H., painter, res. 17 N. Harris.
McAffrey John, teamster, res. 157 W. Maryland.
McAha Margaret, res. 22 on ally, E. of S. East.
McAnulty Peter A., conductor T. H. & R. R. R., res. 39 W. Michigan.
McArthur, John B., miller, res. 152 N. Tennessee.
McArthy Timothy, laborer, res. E. Wyoming.
McBaker Thomas, saloon, W. Pearl, res. 68 E. Michigan.
McBride Michael, peddlar, res. 142 N. Liberty.
McCabe John, clerk Telegraph Restaurant, bds. same.
McCabe Matthew, finisher, Low's carriage shop, res. 5 Forest ave.
McCallian John, machinist, 284 Madison ave.
McCann Dr. S. D., office 29 N. East, res. same.
McCann Patrick, laborer, 182 S. Delaware.
McCann Thomas, 147 S. Delaware.
McCarron George, tailor, res. 168 N. Delaware.
McCarthy Eugene, moulder, bds. National Hotel.
McCarthy M. B., res. 132 S. Alabama.
McCarthy Simon, res: 9 S. Mississippi.
McCarty William, moulder res. 173 E. Ohio.
McCaw Mrs. Nancy, (wid.,) res. 127 N. Mississippi.
McChesney Jeremiah, res. 61 N. Pennsylvania.
McChesney Jacob B., res. cor. Pennsylvania and Virginia ave.

A Wheeler & Wilson Sewing Machine with Hemmer, for $50.

McChesney Wm. L., book-keeper Branch Bank, bds. Pennsylvania.
McClamrock Mrs. Nancy, (wid.,) res. 90 Indiana ave.
McCloud Matilda, (col.,) washer, res. 91 S. Tennessee.
McClure Henry, printer, res. 140 S. East.
McClure Theophilus, printer at Journal Office, res. 93 W. South.
McCollough J. H., student, bds. 130 N. New Jersey.
McConnell James, sup't Union Saloon.
McCool Wm., laborer, res. 239 S. Delaware.
McCord B. R., (McC. & Wheatley,) res. out of city.
McCord Mrs. Hannah, bds. 88 N. New Jersey.
McCORD & WHEATLEY, dealers in all kinds of lumber, laths, &c., 119 S. Delaware.
McCormac Jedediah, carpenter, W. Indianapolis.
McCormack A. D., cutter for E. A. Hall, res. 229 N. Tennessee.
McCormick J. L., carpenter, res. Tennessee, bet. Fifth and Sixth.
McCown Jas. H., harness-maker, 20 W. Washington, res. 89 Massachusetts ave.
McCOY REV. JAMES, Congregational, res. 46 S. Pennsylvania.
McCoy R. B., artist New York Picture Gallery, bds. Farmers' Hotel.
McCoy Theodore, conductor Central R. R., res. 43 E. Georgia.
McCoy Thomas, barber, 145 W. Washington, res. same.
McCoy W. W., res. 127 N. Mississippi.
McCready Nathan, artist, 33 W. Washington.
McCucheon J. C., book-keeper, 25 W. Washington, bds. Mrs. Stewart's, N. Meridian.
McCune Thos., fireman I. & C. R. R., res. cor. Bates and Benton.
McCurdy Geo. W., book-keeper, 56 E. Washington, res. Vermont, bet. Liberty and Biddle.
McDermond J. W., salesman Boston Store, res. 21 W. Michigan.
McDermot Jas., boiler maker, res. 81 W. Maryland.
McDevitt John, clerk Exchange Billiard Rooms, bds. with Mrs. Hoyett.
McDonald Alice, res. 74 N. Missouri.
McDonald C. E., bds. 85 N. Pennsylvania.
McDonald David, attorney at law, office Yohn's Block, res. 85 N. Pennsylvania.
McDonald E. M., clerk 8 N. Pennsylvania, bds. 93 N. Pennsylvania.
McDonald J. E., (McD. & Roach,) res. 93 N. Pennsylvania.

First Premium awarded the Wheeler & Wilson Sewing Machine for three

McDonald Pat., works Rolling Mill, res. 10 Willard.
McDonald & Roache, attorneys at law, Ætna Building.
McDonnough James, inspector U. S. warehouse.
McDoodle Wm., railroader, res. 70 S. Noble.
McDougal John, laborer Rolling Mill, res. 50 S. East.
DeDowel John, bds. 5 Kentucky ave.
McEwan R., conductor T. H. & R. R. R., bds. Bates House.
McElwee John, carpenter, res. 154 N. Mississippi.
McFarland Miss Charlotte, res. 14 E. St. Clair.
McFARLAND JAMES A., clerk Palmer House.
McFarland Laura W., res. 14 E. St. Clair.
McFarland William, baker, bds. 4 S. Meridian.
McGaw John A., stencil cutter, res. 114 N. Mississippi.
McGee Edward, boiler maker, Western Machine Works.
McGenn Charles B., moulder, res. 259 S. Pennsylvania.
McGiffin Samuel, superintendent work department Blind Institute, res. 152 N. Pennsylvania.
McGinnis ——, tailor, 158 W. Washington, res. 162 W. Washington.
McGinnis Christ., tailor, 3 E. Washington.
McGinnis Col. G. F., 11th Ind. volunteers, res. Meridian, N. of city limits.
McGinnis J., grocer, 228 E. Washington, res. 244 E. Washington.
McGinnis Nicholas, tailor, 158 W. Washington, res. same.
McGinnis Owen, merchant tailor and clothier, 39 E. Washington, res. 26 Virginia ave.
McGinnis Peter, tailor, 19 W. Washington, bds. Union House.
McGinnis Stewart, tailor, 39 E. Washington, bds. 26 Virginia ave.
McGinnis Thomas, tailor, 19 W. Washington, bds. Farmers' Hotel.
McGlothlin J. A., gunsmith, res. 232 S. Alabama.
McGray Daniel, laborer, res. 19 E. Georgia.
McHugh Thomas, laborer, res. Jackson, near city limits.
McIntyre Mrs. Catharine, (wid.,) res. Illinois, bet. Second and Third.
McIntyre Chas., wood sawyer, res. 133 N. Tennessee.
McIntyre James, auctioneer, res. 12 N. East.
McIntyre Thos., superintendent Deaf and Dumb Asylum.
McIver John C., (Baker & McI.,) res. 24 S. Illinois.
McKenna John, machinist, res. 69 S. New Jersey.
McKernan James H., (McK. & Pierce,) res. 11 Circle.
McKernan J., law student, bds. 11 Circle.
McKernan & Pierce, real estate and commission agents, 39 W. Washington.
McKibben J. R., carpenter, res. 226 Massachusetts ave.
McKinley Alex., expressman, res. 100 Ft. Wayne ave.

McKinley Harvey, plasterer, bds. 179 E. Market.
McKinley James, res. 148 E. New York.
McKinney David, fireman Terre Haute R. R., bds. 107 S. Tennessee.
McKinney James, clerk 4 S. Meridian, res. 69 S. New Jersey.
McKinney William. (col.,) laborer, res. 141 W. Washington.
McKinnie Henry, clerk Little's Hotel, bds. same.
McKnight Geo., harness maker for Hinesley, res. 8 Willard.
McLain ——, teamster, res. E. National Road.
McLain Joseph, farmer, res. 128 E. Georgia.
McLane Albert, painter and paper hanger, res. 8 W. North.
McLaughlin Captain John A., res. 232 S. Alabama.
McLean's Female Seminary, cor. Meridian and Ohio, Rev. C. Sturdevant, principal.
McLene J., wholesale and retail watches, jewelry, &c., 1 Bates House, bds. same.
McLymont William, clerk 7 N. Pennsylvania, bds. 9 Henry.
McMahan Patrick, laborer, res. 178 S. East.
McMillin Charles, clerk 101 W. Washington, bds. Vermont, bet. West and California.
McMillin Samuel, real estate agent, 31 W. Washington, res. 38 E. Vermont.
McMillin Thomas, engineer Terre Haute R. R., bds. 38 E. Vermont.
McMullen George, engineer, res. near city limits.
McMurray Robert, tobacconist, 35 W. Washington, res. Illinois, bet. Second and Third.
McNamara M., brakeman Indianapolis & Cincinnati R. R., res. 75 S. Alabama.
McNabb Stephen, brick dealer, res. 143 S. Mississippi.
McNally Terry, laborer, res. Elm.
McNeeley John, carpenter, res. 151 N. Mississippi.
McNeely John B., clerk 5 Bates House, Washington, bds. cor. Mississippi and Michigan.
McOuat Andrew, wood sawyer, res. Patterson.
McOuat A. W., (R. L. & A. W. McO.,) res. Loukabee.
McOuat George, bds. N. E. cor. New York and East.
McOuat Mrs. J. S., res. N. E. cor. New York and East.
McOuat Robert L., (R. L. & A. W. McO.,) res. 22 W. New York, cor. Illinois.
McOUAT R. L. & A. W., manufacturers and dealers in stoves, tinware, &c., 69 W. Washington.
McPherson Margaret, res. 18 N. Delaware.
McReady James, boarding house, res. 10 W. Market.
McTaggert, Coffin & Co., pork-packers, office cor. Washington and Delaware.
McTaggert Israel, (McT., Coffin & Co.,) res. 90 E. Market.

McTaggert J. W., bds. Macy House.
McVay Daniel, blacksmith, 203 W. Washington.
McWorkman Jas., late superintendent Blind Asylum.
MACY DAVID, attorney at law, president and superintendent Peru & Indianapolis R. R., office 81 E. Washington, up stairs, res. 78 N. Delaware.
MACY HOUSE, cor. Illinois and Market, J. Edward Redford, proprietor.
Maag Fred., Exchange Billiard Room.
Madden James H., plasterer, res 129 E. New York.
Madison R. R. freight office, South, bet. Delaware and Pennsylvania.
Madison R. R. engine house and shop, S. W. cor. Delaware and Merrill.
Maglen Michael, drayman, res. 70 N. Powell.
MAGNOLIA SALOON, S. A. Flagg, proprietor, 9 S. Illinois.
Maguire Douglass, (Wright, Bates & M.,) res. 38 E. Ohio.
Maguire Harvey, printer Sentinel Office.
Maguire H. P., salesman 6 Bates House, bds. 41 E. Michigan.
Mahoney James, laborer at gas works, res. 36 S. Alabama.
Mahoney Patrick, laborer, res. 210 S. Delaware.
Maier Chas., plow maker at Beard, Starr & Co's., bds. Ohio House.
Mains Samuel, mail agent, res. 59 N. Pennsylvania.
Majes Wm., cooper, bds. Ohio House.
Major Storm, attorney at law, 19½ E. Washington, res. outside city limits.
Maker Geo. W., painter, res. 186 Massachusetts ave.
Maker Thomas, painter, res. 188 Massachusetts ave.
Maloon John, brakeman Terre Haute R. R.
Malone Patrick, works Rolling Mill, res. E. Wyoming.
Maloner Abner, carpenter, res. 107 N. Alabama.
MALOTT V. T., teller Branch of the Bank of the State of Indiana, bds. with J. F. Ramsay.
Manges Frank, cigar maker, ses. 130 S. Delaware.
Manheimer David, salesman Dessar & Bro,, res. 30 N. Mississippi.
Manlove Wm. R., student at law, College Hall, bds. 25 E. Michigan.
Mann Alfred J., carpenter, res. Davidson, bet. New York and Vermont.
Mann Daniel, carpenter, res. 179 Railroad.
Mann James, teamster, res. 95 S. East.
Mann Mrs. Margaret, (wid.,) nurse, res. 207 N. Tennessee.
Mann Samuel, laborer, res. 270 Indiana ave.
Mannfeld Geo., cutter, works Goepper, res. 146 N. East.

For four successive years at the Ohio State Fair.

Mannfeld Julius, tailor, 15 E. Washington.
Mannheimer D., clerk Desser & Bro., res. 30 N. Mississippi.
Manning E. C., wholesale and retail manufacturer and dealer in boots and shoes, 27 S. Illinois, res. same.
Manning Charles, carpenter, res. 137 Railroad.
Manning Thos. S., confectioner, res. 38 W. Ohio.
Mansfield Thos., blacksmith, works 34 Kentucky ave., res. W. side Missouri, S. of South.
Mansur Franklin, pork-packer, bds. 8 E. Vermont.
Mansur J., (W. & J. M.,) bds. Bates House.
Mansur Jeremiah, res. 8 E. Vermont.
Mansur W., (W. & J. M.,) res. 9 Ohio.
Mansur W. & J., pork-packers and provision dealers, 14 S. Meridian.
Many A. J., harness maker, 103 E. Washington, bds. 67 N. Noble.
MANY CHARLES, carpenter, bds. 67 N. Noble.
MANY GERARD, professor of French language, bds. 67 N. Noble.
MANY JOHN B., carpenter and builder, 34 N. Spring, res. 67 N. Noble.
Mapes C. F., hackman, res. 167 E. Ohio.
Marcee Joseph R., saw mill, bet. Little's Hotel and Peru Depot.
Marchant Charles, waiter, Little's Hotel.
Marchant Isaac, Jr., book-keeper Merritt & Coughlin, res. cor. Market and California.
Marchant John, waiter Little's Hotel.
Marcus Elius, carpenter and builder, 59 W. Georgia. res. same.
Marcus Joseph, express wagon, res. 113 E. McCarty.
Marion Agricultural Works, cor. Tennessee and Merrill.
Marker John, cabinet maker, res. 271 S. Delaware.
Markert George, shoemaker, res. 91 St. Joseph.
Markham Thomas, blacksmith, res. 26 Massachusetts ave.
MARLE CHRISTIAN, manufacturer and dealer in boots and shoes, 73 E. Washington, res. 72 Delaware.
Marlin John brick-mason, res. Orient.
Marlin William, salesman New York Store, bds. C. Scudder.
Marmont Hugo, proprietor Jackson House, 136 W. Washington.
Mars Wm. A., gutta percha roofing, res. 97 Virginia ave.
Marry Daniel, railroader, res. W. Elizabeth.
MARSEE REV. JOSEPH, res. 147 E. South.
Marsh Henry, railroader, res. Missouri, S. of South.
Marsh John, laborer, res. 67 N. West.
Marsh Lewis, tailor, res. 10 S. West.
Marshall Benj., laborer, res. S. E. Michigan Road.

The Wheeler & Wilson Hemmer is the only Hemmer that will Fell.

Marshall C. M., manufacturer and dealer in cigars, tobacco, &c., 1 door N. of Exchange Building, res. same.
Marshall Levi, carpenter, res. 77 S. New Jersey.
Martin ——, brakeman Terre Haute R. R., bds. 107 S. Tennessee.
Martin John H., (col.,) cook U. S. A., res. Mississippi.
Martin John W., clerk, bds. 58 N. East.
Martin Joseph, waiter Spencer House.
Martin J. W., deputy Secretary of State, bds. 58 N. East.
Martin L. R., attorney at law, 10 E. Washington, bds. Mrs. McCready's.
Martin Matthew, confectioner Union Steam Bakery.
Martin Michael, cooper, bds. East Street House.
Martin Robert, moulder, res. 113 N. New Jersey.
Martin Robert, chair maker, 328 S. Delaware.
Martin Samuel, laborer, in rear of 17 Virginia ave.
Martin William, bar-keeper, res. 96 N. Mississippi.
Martindale Mrs. Julia A., seamstress, res. 129 N. East.
Martindale Samuel, res. Cherry, near University.
Martz Henry K., mill-wright, res. 99 N. Noble.
Martz Sarah, dress-maker, res. 39 N. Alabama.
Marvel George, toll-gate keeper, Fall Creek bridge.
Maskil Denny, laborer, res. Illinois, bet. Second and Third.
Mason B., messenger American Express Company, bds. Bates House.
Mason Mrs. Louisa, res. 102 E. New York.
MASON MADISON, (col.,) eating saloon, cor. Louisiana and Illinois, res. Washington.
Mason R., engraver, 27 Washington, bds. Spencer House.
Mason Wm. F., school teacher, res. 14 N. Meridian.
MASONIC HALL, cor. W. Washington and Tennessee.
Mastus Philo, wood-sawyer, res. 33 S. Liberty.
Mather John, engineer Lawrenceburg car shop, res. 93 Bates.
Mathews C., bar-tender, res. Wabash, bet. New Jersey and East.
Mathweg John, boot and shoemaker, 51 W. Washington, res. cor. Ohio and Tennessee.
Mattho Wm., salesman 81 and 83 E. Washington, bds. 124 E. Market.
Matthes Clemens, eating and drinking saloon, 163 E. Washington.
Matthews J. W., salesman New York Store, bds. Morris House.
Matthews William, feed store, res. 124 E. Market.
Matthias David, res. 188 S. Tennessee.
Matthias Henry, laborer, res. Elm.
Mattler Anna Mary, Washington House, 80, E. of Union Depot.

81,000 Wheeler & Wilson's Sewing Machines in use in this country.

MATTLER STEPHEN, proprietor Union House, cor. Illinois and South.
Mauldin James, (M. & Co.,) res. Boston.
Mauldin & Co., boots and shoes, 53 W. Washington.
Maxfield George, res. cor. North and Tennessee.
Maxwell Charles, artist, 33 W. Washington, bds. Farmers' Hotel.
Maxwell J. C., bds. Macy House.
MAXWELL S. D., Mayor of city, office Glenns' Block, res. 156 E. Ohio.
May Mrs. Sarah, (wid.,) res. 11 Henry.
May Adam, cooper 58 S. East, res. 81 S. East.
May Edwin, architect and proprietor of May's patent jail, res. 75 N. Pennsylvania.
May John, drayman, res. 119 E. McCarty.
May R. K., with Wm. Sheets, res. 116 W. New York.
MAYER CHARLES, wholesale and retail dealer in fancy goods, notions, &c., 29 W. Washington, res. cor. Illinois and North.
Mayer Christ., carpenter, res. 125 N. Liberty.
Mayer John, drayman, res. 200 Massachusetts ave.
Mayer John F., umbrella manufacturer and dealer, 65 East Washington, res. 63 St. Joseph.
Mayer Joseph, harness maker, 20 W. Washington, bds. Pyle House.
Mayer Mrs. Mary, (wid.,) washer, res. 68 W. Ohio.
Mayer Wilhelm, plow maker with Beard, Starr & Co., bds. Ohio House.
Mayers Xavier, Root's foundry, res. 254 S. Delaware.
Mayhew E. C., (E. C. M. & Co.,) bds. 115 E. Ohio.
Mayhew E. C. & Co., wholesale boots and shoes, Roberts' Block, opp. Union Depot.
Mayhew Parrish, clerk, cor. Washington and Illinois, bds. 160 Tennessee.
Mayhew Royal, res. Michigan Road.
Maynchan Andrew, laborer, res. 245 S. Pennsylvania.
Mays Thomas, shoemaker, res. 102 E. McCarty.
Mead Jas., clerk Skillen's feed store, res. Pine, cor. Fletcher and Forest ave's.
Mears G. W., physician, res. 47 N. Meridian.
Mechreles Henry, carpenter. res. 7 Willard.
Meek Alonzo, engineer I. & C. R. R., res. 24 Huron.
Meek Robert, master machinist I. & C. R. R., bds. 103 S. Alabama.
Meek E. L., suttler U. S. A., bds. Ohio House.
Meerbarger G. W., butcher, bds. 120 N. Mississippi.
Meikel Charles P., printer, Sentinel Office, bds. 65 N. Mississippi.

Meikel Mrs. Catharine, (wid.,) res. 65 N. Mississippi.
Meikel Frederick, book-binder, Journal Office, bds. 65 N. Mississippi.
Meikel Henry P., brewer, bds. 135 W. Maryland.
Meikel John P., brewer, res. 135 W. Maryland.
Meikel's Brewery, W. Maryland.
Meiners Cornelius, saw-mill, res. 219 N. New Jersey.
Meller Dr. W., res. 13 Kentucky ave.
Melville R. B., cutter Glaser & Bros., res. 70 Tennessee.
Merchants' Dispatch, W. T. Clark, ag't, 31½ W. Washington.
Merdick James Y., miller, bds. 179 E. Market.
Meredith S. C., mail ag't Cincinnati R. R., res. 52 N. Blackford.
Meredith Wm. M., printer, Journal Office, res. New Jersey, bet. Michigan and North.
Mermont H., saloon, 136 W. Washington.
MERRILL JOHN F., M. D., eclectic physician, 156 Washington, res. 134 W. New York.
Merrill Samuel, (M. & Co.,) res. S. W. cor. Alabama and Merrill.
MERRILL & CO., publishers, wholesale and retail dealers in books, stationery, &c., Glenns' Block.
Merrimon Ed. S., clerk E. B. Drake & Co., bds. 181 E. Ohio.
Merrimon J. M., (E. B. Drake & Co.,) res. 136 Virginia ave.
Merrit Geo., (M. & Coughlen,) res. 102 West.
Merritt J. G., factoryman, res. 126 W. New York.
Merritt & Coughlen, proprietors Ohio Premium Woolen Factory, W. Washington, near White River Bridge.
Merrymon Edward, painter, res. 181 E. Ohio.
Mersmer Fred., pianist Eagle Saloon, bds. same.
Metaugh John, carpenter, res. 127 W. New York.
METROPOLITAN HALL, cor. Washington and Tennessee, V. Butsch, prop'r.
Metzger A., (A. & J. M.,) 55 E. Maryland.
METZGER A. & J., Union Steam Bakery, 11 N. Pennsylvania.
Metzger George, saw filer, res. 16 E. Michigan.
Metzger J., (A. & J. M.,) res. 11 N. Pennsylvania.
Meyers Charles, blacksmith, bds. 28 Indiana ave.
Meyer Christ., frame maker for H. Leiber, res. Liberty.
MEYER C. J., manufacturer, wholesale and retail dealer in chairs, furniture, &c., 171 E. Washington, res. same.
Meyer Frank, moulder, bds. 124 S. Delaware.
Meyer Geo., F., manufacturer, wholesale and retail dealer in cigars, tobacco, &c., 35 W. Washington, res. 56 W. Vermont.

Meyer Haur, plow maker for Beard, Starr & Co., bds. Ohio House.
Meyer Jacob C., carpenter, res. 181 Indiana ave.
Meyer Ludwig, drayman, res. Davidson.
Meyer Martin, fancy turner, umbrella maker and repairer, 133 E. Washington, res. same.
Meyer Peter, wood sawyer, 266 S. Delaware.
Meyer William, drayman, res. 92 Union.
Michael Philip, U. S. A., res. Central, E. of Liberty.
Michaily John, carpenter, res. Tennessee, bet. Third and Fourth.
Michel Elizabeth, (wid.,) washer, res. 246 Madison ave.
Mietchel Jacob, clerk Glaser & Bros., Bates House.
Michett Robert M., house carpenter, res. 95 St. Joseph.
Mickguin John, laborer, res. 5 Bates.
MIDDLEMAS D. C., wholesale and retail grocer and dealer in wines and liquors, 196 W. Washington, res. same.
Midheffar Henry, drayman, res. 75 Bluff Road.
Mierstedt Augustus, res. 112 W. Vermont.
Mielsch Marris, clerk at arsenal, res. 69 N. Mississippi.
Mifflin James, (col.,) barber, res. 40 West.
Migga Richard, laborer, 250 S. Pennsylvania.
Miller A. R., silversmith, shop 155 E. South.
Miller Andrew, drayman, res. 162 S. Tennessee.
Miller Anthony, carpenter, res. 109 E. Vermont.
Miller Charles G., saloon, cor. Washington and East, res. same.
Miller Christian, carpenter, res. 125 Davidson.
Miller Edward, res. 135 E. Ohio.
Miller Mrs. Emily, (wid.,) res. 155 W. Vermont.
Miller George, laborer, res. E. end Market.
Miller G. W., physician, res. 158 N. Illinois.
Miller Henry, trader, res. 189 S. New Jersey.
Miller Henry, laborer, res. 118 N. Missouri.
Miller Henry W., carpenter, res. 135 N. Noble.
Miller Henry, carpenter, 154 N. East.
Miller J., attorney at law, 84 E. Washington, bds. 44 Pennsylvania.
Miller John, laborer, res. John, near Winston.
Miller Leonard, tailor, res. Pratt, near Delaware.
Miller Mrs. Mary, (wid.,) res. 89 S. Tennessee.
Miller Oliver A., railroader, bds. 107 S. Tennessee.
Miller Randolph, silversmith, res. 75 S. New Jersey.
Miller William, ticket agent Union depot, bds. Charles Kerper 21 Indiana ave.
Miller William, laborer, res. Maryland, bet. West and California.
MILITARY HALL, 24½ E. Washington.

Upwards of 100 W. & W. Machines in use in Ind'p'lis making army clothing.

Mills H. W., (Alford, M. & Co.,) res. 115 E. Ohio.
Milton H. T., U. S. A., res. 254 Indiana ave.
Minock ——, res. 39 N. California.
Minick Hiram, res. 275 S. Delaware.
Minteeth T., carpenter, res. 81 South.
Mitchell Jacob, book-keeper Glaser & Bros., res. 59 Massachusetts ave.
Mitchell Jas. B., (col.,) barber, res. on Canal, N. of Michigan.
Mitchell James L., (Ketcham & M.,) bds. Bates House.
Mitchell Mrs. Mary, (col.,) washer, res. 158 N. Missouri.
Mitchem Nathaniel, (col.,) barber, res. rear of West.
Mitton Geo. A., engineer I. & C. R. R., res. Harrison, E. of Pine.
Mittey Christian, saddler, res. 159 E. New York.
Mittey John C., shoemaker, res. 160 E. New York.
Mock Martin, tailor, 69 E. Washington, res. 178 E. Ohio.
Mode Michael, shoemaker, 73 E. Washington.
Mœsch T. H., confectioner, 76 E. Washington, res. same.
Moffit Dr. John, U. S. A., res. 161 N. Mississippi.
Moffitt John, sr., machinist, Root, Bennett & Co., res. S. New Jersey, bet. South and Merrill.
Moffitt John, jr., printer Journal Office, res. Tennessee, S. of South.
Moffitt Oliver J., printer Sentinel Office, bds. S. New Jersey.
Moffitt Wm., clerk, 22 W. Washington, bds. 21 S. Delaware.
Molding S., carpenter, W. Indianapolis.
Moloney John, U. S. A., res. 169 S. Mississippi.
Moloney Thos., laborer, res. 50 Bates.
Molloy R., flour-packer Carlisle's Model Mills.
Molton D. S., messenger American Express Co., bds. Spencer House.
Monan Jerry, laborer, res. 36 S. Alabama.
Monninger Daniel, La Belle Saloon, cor. Washington and Kentucky ave., res. same.
Monninger C., proprietor Court House Saloon, cor. Washington and Alabama.
Monroe John, carpenter, res. 144 E. McCarthy.
Montague Wm., wagon maker, res. 59 S. New Jersey.
MONTGOMERY CHAUNCEY, Exchange Billiard Rooms, bds. Palmer House.
Montgomery Mrs. Elizabeth, dressmaker and tailoress, res. 65 W. South.
Montgomery Jas., baggageman Union Depot, res. 59 W. Louisiana.
Montgomery Wm., cooper, W. Indianapolis.
Moon Miss Sallie, cloak and dress maker, Ray's Building, 26½ W. Washington, bds. Palmer House.

A Wheeler & Wilson Sewing Machine will last a life-time.

Mooney Jas. E., (M. & Co.,) res. Edinburg, Ind.
Mooney W. W., (M. & Co.,) res. Edinburg, Ind.
MOONEYS & CO., wholesale and retail dealers in leather, hides and oils, Meridian, near Union Depot.
Moore Alex., blacksmith.
Moore Mrs. Deborah D., res. 9 E. Michigan.
Moore G. C., clerk to superintendent public Instruction, bds. 44 N. Pennsylvania.
Moore Isaac, laborer, res. 22 S. Alabama.
Moore J. A., book-keeper Indianapolis Branch Banking Co., res. 9 E. Michigan.
Moore Thomas, salesman 5 W. Washington, bds. 9 E. Michigan.
Moore Thomas, cooper, res. 144 Wood.
Moores Charles W., (Merrill & Co.,) res. E. of Merrill, bet. Alabama and New Jersey.
Morey Harry, works for P. Bannister, bds. 31 Indiana ave.
Morgan David E., works Rolling Mill, res. Missouri, S. of South.
Morgan Dennis, egg-packer, 180 E. Washington.
Morgon Geo., dyer Ohio Premium Woolen Factory.
Morgan John, works Rolling Mill; res. 16 Willard.
Morgan John, brakeman, res. 66 cor. Delaware and South.
Morgan Paulina, (wid.,) res. 21 McCarty.
Morgan Samuel C., merchant tailor and clothier, 27 E. Washington, res. 57 E. New York.
Morgan Sarah, res. 20 N. Mississippi.
Morgenvich Valentine, grocer, 9 Chatham, res. same.
Moriarty Daniel, lamp lighter, res. 174 S. Delaware.
Moriarty Maurice, laborer, res. 204 S. Delaware.
Moritz Sol., (M. Bro. & Co.,) bds. Bates House.
MORITZ BRO. & CO., merchant tailors, clothiers, and dealers in gents' furnishing goods, &c., 3 E. and 19 W. Washington.
Morely A. J., book-binder for William Sheets, bds. Pyle House.
Morningstar Peter, (M. & Gulick,) bds. 28 Pennsylvania.
Morningstar & Gulick, meat market, 8 S. Pennsylvania.
Morris Alex., house and sign painter, bds. 38 W. Market.
Morris Mrs. A. W., (wid.,) res. 53 S. Meridian.
Morris C. G., clerk R. Browning, bds. 50 S. Meridian.
Morris Mrs. Eliza A., res. 38 W. Market.
Morris Harmony, huckster and auctioneer, res. 247 Indiana ave.
MORRIS HOUSE, opp. Union Depot, Henry Whitmore, proprietor.
Morris House Saloon, R. Beebe, proprietor.

MORRIS J. C., photographs, &c., Ray's Building, bds. 38 West Market.
Morris John, res. 50 S. Meridian.
Morris John, shoemaker, res. 67 N. Noble.
Morris L. T., Lieut. U. S. A., bds. 53. S. Meridian.
Morris Sanford, clerk 3 Odd Fellows' Hall, res. 89 N. New Jersey.
Morris Gen. T. A., Pres. I. P. & C. R. R., res. Fort Wayne ave.
MORRIS' TEMPLE OF ART, J. C. Morris, prop'r, Ray's Building.
Morrison Mrs. A. F., res. 32 N. Pennsylvania.
Morrison Charles J., bds. 32 N. Pennsylvania.
Morrison Delia, (wid.,) res. 75 N. Alabama.
Morrison Squire, U. S. A., res. 72 N. Mississippi.
Morrison James, (M. & Ray,) res. Ft. Wayne Road, cor. St. Mary's.
Morrison James, teamster, res. 19 Union.
MORRISON J. A., clerk Palmer House.
Morrison John T., attorney at law, office 26 E. Washington.
Morrison Michael, res. 19 Union.
Morrison W. A., bds. 32 N. Pennsylvania.
Morrison Wm. H., (Alford, Mills & Co.,) res. N. Pennsylvania.
Morrison W. L., salesman, 36 E. Washington, bds. Ft. Wayne ave.
Morrison & Ray, attorneys at law, 26 E. Washington.
Morton James, bds. 10 Mississippi.
Morton John W., rolling mill, res. 19 Willard.
Morton Martin, porter Morris House.
MORTON O. P., Governor State ot Indiana, res. cor. Market and Illinois.
Morton Thomas, res. 95 Virginia ave.
Mosely Albert, watchman Bellefontaine car shop, res. Orient.
Moser Geo., butcher, Wood & Barnett.
MOSES L. W., optician, 20 E. Washington, res. 13 W. Market.
Moses Simon, collar maker for Mooney & Co.
Moss Alfred, engineer B. R. R., res. 143 E. South.
Moss Lewis, machinist, sup't rolling mill, res. Norwood, bet. Illinois and Tennessee.
Mossler Aaron, auction and commission, 10 W. Washington, res. Pennsylvania.
Mossler F. J., auction and commission, 10 W. Washington, res. Pennsylvania.
Mossler Solomon, auction and commission, 10 W. Washington, res. Pennsylvania.

For four successive years at the Am. Institute, New York.

Mots Fred., plow maker for Beard, Starr & Co., bds. Ohio House.
Mothershead Mrs. E. A., res. 49 S. Meridian.
Mottery Fred., clerk Union Steam Bakery.
Moulton Chas. W., engineer, res. 24 Michigan Road.
Mount A. S., (Mooney & Co.,) res. 50 S. Illinois.
Mountain Michael, laborer, 245 S. Pennsylvania.
Mown Patrick, laborer, res. 196 S. East.
Mower John, tailor, res. Elizabeth.
Mowery Andrew, laborer, W. Indianapolis.
Muhlenbeck Miss B. G., (Mrs. A. Baker & Co.,) bds. 26 S. Illinois.
Muir James, wholesale dealer in tobacco and teas, res. 33 W. Market.
Mulcahy Michael, works at Marsee's saw mill, res. 51 S. Noble.
Mullany John, student at law with Thos. A. Hendricks, bds. with John Lynch.
Mulleney Mrs. Mary, (wid.,) res. 53 S. Mississippi.
Muller August, school teacher, res. 110 E. Ohio.
Muller Henry, grocer, 142 N. Noble, res. same.
Muller John A. D., stair builder, res. East, bet. Chestnut and Cherry.
Muller John, importer and wholesale dealer in wines, cigars, &c., 212 E. Washington, res. same.
Mulqueney John, laborer, bds. Tennessee.
Munger Christian, telgraph repairer, res. Illinois, S. of Depot.
Munhall Leander W., blacksmith, bds. 84 N. New Jersey.
Munsell Henry, carriage maker, res. 175 E. Ohio.
MUNSON CHARLES H., (M. & Johnson,) res. 119 E. Ohio.
Munson David, (Locke & M.,) res. 88 E. Market.
Munson Lewis, res. 119 E. Ohio.
MUNSON WM. L., grocery and feed store, 21 N. Alabama, res. same.
MUNSON & JOHNSTON, manufacturers, wholesale and retail dealers in stoves and hardware, 62 E. Washington.
Murdock John J., railroader, res. 149 S. Tennessee.
Murdock Joseph, moulder, res. 43 S. Illinois.
Murphy Nathan L., carpenter, res. East, bet. Liberty and Noble.
Murphy Frank, workman Terre Haute freight depot, res. 164 S. Mississippi.
Murphy Henry, waiter Spencer House.
Murphy James, laborer, res. W. Elizabeth.
Murphy Jesse T., teamster, res. 111 St. Mary's.

CITY DIRECTORY. 177

Murphy John, conductor Terre Haute R. R., bds. 24 Willard.
Murphy John W., (M. & Holliday,) res. 33 E. Ohio.
Murphy Miss Marttia, works at arsenal, bds. 95 W. Market.
Murphy Michael, head waiter Palmer House.
Murphy Milton, engineer Bates City Mills, res. Ohio, bet. Noble and Liberty.
Murphy Patrick, works at Terre Haute freight depot, bds. 24 Willard.
Murphy Rebecca, (wid.,) res. 93 S. Alabama.
Murphy Tobias M., (Barnitz & M.,) res. 43 E. Georgia.
MURPHY & HOLLIDAY, wholesale and retail iron store, 34 E. Washington.
Musgrave Dr. P. D., bds. Tennessee, bet. 5th and 6th.
Musgrave Watson, wool spinner, res. S. Alabama.
Musmire Dedrich, wood sawyer, 336 S. Delaware.
Myer Wm., shoemaker, res. 16 S. Alabama.
Myer John F., umbrella maker, res. 63 E. St. Joseph.
Myer Moses, clothier, 4 W. Washington, res. 116 Ohio.
Myerhoff Henry, laborer, res. 158 S. Alabama.
Myers Christopher, brass moulder at Davis' foundry, res. 159 S. Alabama.
Myers David, cooper, res. 154 N. Noble.
Myers Geo. E., carrier Sentinel, bds. 48 N. Liberty.
Myers Henry, blacksmith, 86 W. Washington, bds. 28 Madison ave.
Myers Jake, bar.keeper American Saloon.
Myers John A., tinner, 62 E. Washington.
Myers Leonard, carrier Sentinel, bds. 48 N. Liberty.
Myers Philip, (Robinson & M.,) res. 81 Davidson.
Myers Wm., works on Railroad, res. 74 E. Georgia.
Myers Wm. H., carrier Sentinel, bds. 48 N. Liberty.

N

Naltner Agedeus, (N. & N.,) res. Meridian.
Naltner Martin, (N. & N.,) res. Meridian.
NALTNER & NALTNER, proprietors Nebraska Saloon, 14 opp. Union Depot.
Nas Lewis, cabinet maker, res. 190 East.
Nathan A., (Moritz, Bro. & Co.,) res. Cincinnati, O.
National Hotel, David Bender, proprietor, W. Washington.
National Saloon and Restaurant, Geo. Rhodius, proprietor, 27 S. Meridian.
Neafly F., watchman, res. S. West.
Neal J. R., clerk 188 E. Washington, res. 30 East.
Neal Jonathan, dealer in provisions, res. 30 N. East.

12

A Wheeler & Wilson Sewing Machine with Hemmer, for $50.

FRANK M. WRIGHT. W. S. DOWNER.

CAPITAL BREWERY.

 **WRIGHT & DOWNER,**

Manufacturers of

PALE STOCK, AMBER,

AND

CHAMPAGNE ALE.

OFFICE AT THE BREWERY,

BLAKE STREET,

NEAR WHITE RIVER BRIDGE,

INDIANAPOLIS, IND.

No. 29 West Washington Street,

INDIANAPOLIS, INDIANA.

Wheeler & Wilson's Sewing Machines awarded the first premium for five

Nealy Hugh, clerk 5 Washington, res. cor. Vine and Plum.
Neas Lewis, carpenter, res. 190 N. East.
NEBRASKA SALOON, 14 opp. Union Depot, Naltner & Naltner, proprietors.
Neeb Charles, bar-keeper Farmers' Hotel.
Neibergale John, carpenter, res. 68 N. Noble.
Neighbors Albert, drayman, bds. 23 Henry.
Neighbors Charles, express wagon. res. 23 Henry.
Neighbors Robert, drayman, res. 35 Union.
NEIMAN MARTIN, Ohio House, 31 W. Market. (See card.)
Nelson E. A., salesman 33 W. Washington, bds. Ohio.
Nelson Henry H., sheriff Supreme Court, office State House, res. 73 N. Mississippi.
Nelson H. L., watchmaker, 24 E. Washington, bds. Pennsylvania.
Nelson Sandy, (col.,) whitewasher and plasterer, res. 78 N. Missouri.
Nelson Thomas, builder, res. 107 W. Ohio.
Nevitt Wm. F., res. 89 E. Michigan.
New John C., res. 102 N. Pennsylvania.
Newcomb Horatio C., (N. & T..) res. 58 N. Alabama.
NEWCOMB & TARKINGTON, attorneys at law, 26 E. Washington.
Newcomer Christian, res. 65 N. Tennessee.
Newcomer F. S., physician, Blake's Building, res. 161 N. Illinois.
Newett John, ostler, bds. Pennsylvania.
NEWELL L. S., teacher, Blind Asylum.
NEWMAN JOHN S., president Indiana Central R. R., res. 31 N. Meridian.
Newman Peter, laborer, res. 149 S. Mississippi.
NEW YORK BAZAAR, Emil Klotz, proprietor, 37 E. Washington.
NEW YORK DRY GOODS STORE, Glenns' Block, W. & H. Glenn & Co., proprietors. (See eng., p. 55.)
New York Picture Gallery, J. D. Crane, proprietor, 19 W. Washington.
Nicholas Willard, printer, Sentinel Office, res. 37 St. Clair.
Nichols T. M., dentist, 18½ S. Meridian, res. same.
Nicholson David, stone-cutter, res. 159 N. New Jersey.
Nicholson J. C., pedlar, res. 27 Union.
Nicholson Wm. T., works Lawrenceburg Car Shop, res. 15 Lord.
Nicholson Wm., stone-cutter, res. South, bet. Missouri and California.
Nicolai Charles, saddler and harness maker, 268 E. Washington, res. same.
Nicolai J., retired merchant, res. 89 W. Washington.

ROBERT BROWNING,

Dealer in

Drugs & Medicines,

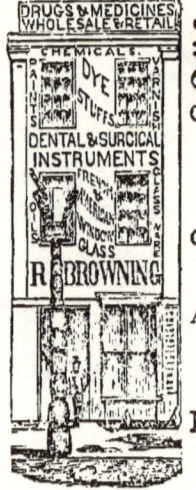

Chemicals, Surgical and Dental Instruments, Paints, Oils, Varnishes, Dye-Stuffs, Window Glass, Glassware,

BRUSHES, PERFUMERY, SPICES,

Coal Oil, Coal Oil Lamps and Fixtures, Cigars, Tobacco, Etc.

All articles warranted as represented, and which we are prepared to sell as low as any other western house.

No. 22 West Washington Street,
INDIANAPOLIS, IND.

ALBERT W. LANDON.   EDWIN L. HASTINGS.

LANDON & HASTINGS,

Plain and Ornamental

Card Printers & Engravers,

No. 8 East Washington Street,
INDIANAPOLIS, IND.

A. KAHN,
WHOLESALE & RETAIL CLOTHIER,

And dealer in

Gents' Furnishing Goods, &c., &c.

No. 2 Palmer House,
INDIANAPOLIS, IND.

The First Premium awarded the Wheeler & Wilson Machine

Nicolai L., meat shop, 119 Massachusetts ave.
Niemann Henry, carpenter, bds. 155 E. Ohio.
Niemann Wm., bds. 157 E. Ohio.
Nienaber Herman, soldier, res. 21 Central.
Niggerman Fred., saloon, 186 E. Washington, res. same.
NIXON REV. J. H., pastor First Presbyterian Church, res. 87 N. Illinois.
Nobbe Henry, printer, Indiana's Home-Life and Camp-Life, res. 144 E. Ohio.
Noble Lewis, farmer, res. Tennessee, bet. Fifth and Sixth.
Noble Geo., harness maker, 20 W. Washington, bds. Pyle House.
NOBLE W. H. L., general ticket agent I. & C. R. R., res. 30 N. Delaware.
Noble Winston P., res. N. side E. Market, E. of Winston.
NOBLE LAZ., Adjutant General State of Indiana, office State House.
Noe Daniel, res. 73 N. New Jersey.
Noel S. V. B., grain dealer, res. 112 N. New Jersey.
Nofsinger Wm. R., physician, E. Indianapolis.
Nohn W., shoemaker, 38 W. Washington.
Nolin Thos., hackman, res. 59 W. Louisiana.
Nolking Charles, laborer, res. 65 E. St. Joseph.
North Myron, res. 19 E. Maryland.
Northway Geo. M., plasterer, res. 94 N. New Jersey.
Northway John, plasterer, res. 146 E. North.
Norwood E. F., pork-packer, res. 26 N. Illinois.
Norwood Mrs. N. N., (wid.,) seamstress, res. 72 W. Maryland.
Null Mrs. Sarah, (wid.,) vest maker, res. 108 W. Vermont.
Nuttneyer Christian, carpenter, res. 151 E. Ohio.

O

Oakey Edward, stone-mason, res. 167 N. New Jersey.
Oakey Philip, carpenter, res. 22 N. New Jersey.
O'Brian Thomas, works Scott & Nicholson, res. 29 Henry.
O'Brian Thomas, stone-cutter, bds. Delaware.
O'Brian Jerry, tinner, 62 E. Washington, res. Delaware.
O'Brien Jeremiah, tinsmith, works Munson & Johnson, res. 200 S. Delaware.
O'Brien Thomas, laborer at Exchange Stables, res. 64 N. Tennessee.
O'Brien Timothy, package agent Indiana Central R. R., bds. Spencer House.
O'Bryan John, laborer, res. 176 S. Alabama.
O'Bryan Patrick, engineer, res. E. Louisiana.

O'Connell Murty, laborer, res. 206 S. Delaware.
O'Conner Michael, jr., street contractor, res. 45 S. Noble.
O'Conner Hugh, shoemaker, bds. Georgia.
O'Conner Mrs. Julia, (wid.,) res. 144 W. Washington, in rear.
O'Connor Michael, laborer, res. 199 E. Ohio.
O'Connor Thomas, boot and shoemaker, 208 S. Delaware.
O'Connor Thomas, laborer, res. 210 S. Delaware, in rear.
ODD FELLOWS' HALL, N. E. cor. Washington and Pennsylvania.
O'Donnell John, laborer, res. 56 Massachusetts ave.
O'Driscoll John, stereotyper for Geo. H. Fleming & Co., bds. Scarry House.
Oehler David, shoemaker, res. 83 S. Meridian.
Oelschlager J. B., salesman 14 W. Washington, res. 111 Ft. Wayne ave.
Ogden Mary, works Widow and Orphan Asylum.
Oglesby J. H., grocer, (W. F. O. & Co.,) res. 91 N. Tennessee.
Oglesby W. F., (W. F. O. & Co.,) bds. 91 N. Tennessee.
O'Harra Frank, laborer, res. 213 S. Alabama.
O'Haver Isaac, book-keeper Patterson's livery stable, res. 148 N. Delaware.
O'Haver N. P., well-digger, res. N. Blake
OHIO HOUSE, M. Neiman, proprietor, 31 W. Market.
Ohio Premium Woolen Factory, Merritt & Coughlen, proprietors, lower arm of canal, S. W. Washington.
O'Hosa Anthony, laborer, res. S. West.
Ohr A. D., clerk Union Depot, res. 41 W. Michigan.
Ohr Henry, janitor at Gymnasium, and scribe Sons of Temperance, res. 48 N. Delaware.
OHR JOHN H., agent Adams' Express, 12 E. Washington, res. 91 E. Ohio.
Ohr M. L., clerk Adams' Express office, bds. Bates House.
Oihler Andrew, watch and clock maker and jewelry repairer, 17 Kentucky ave, res. same.
Okey Joseph B., dealer in patents, res. 144 N. East.
Oltmins H., clerk, 138 W. Washington.
O'Malley Patrick, res. cor. Tennessee and Second.
O'Mara James, driver, Bates House.
O'Neal Patrick, laborer, res. 14 E. Georgia.
O'Neal Tim., laborer, res. near Central car shop.
O'Nell John, laborer, res. 33 E. Market.
ORIENTAL HOUSE, W. J. Elliott, prop'r, Illinois, bet. Maryland and Georgia.
Oriental Saloon, under Oriental House.
O'Riley Timothy, laborer, res. S. Tennessee.
Orlopp Richard, supt. Government stables, res. 117 E. Market.

Ortel Christ., laborer, res. 144 E. Georgia.
Osborn Elizabeth, (wid.,) res. 99 Indiana ave.
Osborn Aaron, U. S. A., W. Indianapolis.
OSGOOD J. B., house, sign and ornamental painter, 16 E. Market, res. 39 W. Maryland.
Osgood J. R., (O. Smith & Co.,) res. 52 S. Meridian.
Osgood, Smith & Co., hub and last factory, S. Union Depot, Illinois.
Oslermon John, clerk, 16 W. Washington, bds. 35 Meridian.
Ossenforth Frederick, laborer, res. Winston, bet. Biddle and North.
Ostermeyer Christian, drayman, res. 137 E. Ohio.
Ostermeyer Fred., (O. & Prange,) res. Plank Road.
Ostermeyer ——., grocer, res. E. National Road.
Ostermeyer Louis, laborer, res. 147 N. Liberty.
Ostermeyer Louis, sr., wood sawyer, res. 145 N. Liberty.
Ostermeyer & Prange, general store, 258 E. Washington.
O'Sullivan Ortho, laborer, res. 204 S. Delaware.
O'Sullivan Patrick, laborer, res. 71 Madison ave.
Oswald Gottfried, laborer, res. 165 Railroad.
Otis W. H., res. 42 S. Pennsylvania.
Ott Fred., brick layer, bds. 159 E. Ohio.
OTT GEORGE, merchant tailor, cleaning, repairing, &c., 106 S. Illinois, res. same.
Ott John, cabinet maker, res. 29 Indiana ave.
Ott Mac, laborer, res. 269 S. East.
Ottan D., cigar store, 159 E. Washington, res. 41 Spring.
Otto William, carpenter, res. 155 E. Ohio.
Ottmanns Hammon, clerk, res. 136 W. Washington.
Otto Philip, works Root, Bennett & Co.
Overhall Thomas, (col.,) ostler, 10 N. Pennsylvania.
Overman Leander, (col.,) cook, res. 123 Indiana ave.
Overstreet Jas. M., laborer, res. Illinois, bet. First and Second.
Owens Nathaniel, plasterer, res. 87 South.
Owings Mrs. Lydia A., sewing, res. Wabash, bet. Liberty and Noble.
Owsley Wm., carpenter, res. 11 N. Ellsworth.
Oyler Wm., U. S. Arsenal, res. 170 S. Alabama.

P

Pace Hardy, res. 300 S. Delaware.
Padlow Robt. J., machinist, Root's foundry.
Paerson J. O., machinist, res. 127 Massachusetts ave.
Paff Wm., carpenter, res. 279 S. East.
Pahler Henry, brewer, 35 S. Illinois.

Paine D. L., foreman Sentinel News Room, bds. at Pyle House.
Painter John, hack driver, res. 227 N. Tennessee.
Palmer Ed. L., book binder for David Braden, res. 40 S. Illinois.
Palmer George, salesman New York Store, bds. 124 E. Michigan.
PALMER HOUSE, J. D. Carmichael, prop'r, cor. Washington and Illinois.
PALMER HOUSE SALOON, Richard F. Young, prop'r, cor. Washington and Illinois.
PALMER HOUSE HAIR-DRESSING SALOON, Henning & Stelzell, propr's.
Palmer N. B., 37 W. Maryland.
Palmer John, supt. freight, Central R. R., res. S. E. Michigan Road.
Palmer T. G., res. 90 N. Illinois.
Paris Mrs. Mary, seamstress, res. 146 Wood.
Parse Wm., wagon maker, res. 136 S. East.
Parish Solomon, res. 104 S. New Jersey.
Parker C. C., clerk, 34 N. Illinois, bds. 23 Indiana ave.
Parker Mrs. Catherine, res. 72 N. East.
PARKER EDGAR, wholesale and retail dealer in notions, fancy goods, &c., 25 S. Illinois, res. same.
PARKER R. R., wholesale and retail dealer in hosiery, notions, &c., 30 W. Washington, bds. 33 N. Meridian.
Parker Wilson, brick layer, res. 103 S. Tennessee.
Parks Hiram, (col.,) cook Little's Hotel.
Parmelee Edward L., telegraphic operator, Ind. Cent. R. R., bds. 38 Pratt.
Parmelee Mrs. Hannah, res. 38 Pratt.
Parmelee Wm. H., ag't Lafayette R. R. freight office, bds. 98 N. Meridian.
Parr Wm., machinist, Western Machine Works.
Parrisette Joseph, confectioneries, 15 N. Illinois, res. same.
Parrish Hardin, bds. Bates House.
PARROTT HORACE, gen'l ticket ag't Ind. Cent. R. R., res. 141 N. Delaware.
Parry Roger, blacksmith, res. 12 Henry.
Parsley A., teamster, res. 161 N. Alabama.
Parson J. L., student, bds. 130 N. New Jersey.
Parsons Charles A., conductor P. & I. R. R., bds. Palmer House.
PARSONS JOHN J., (H. H. Dodd & Co.,) res. 89 N. Tennessee.
Parvin Theophilus, M. D., office 69 N. Alabama, res. same.
Pasco J., boiler maker Bellefontaine car shop, res. 126 E. Georgia.

1862. THE PHŒNIX Insurance Company, OF HARTFORD, CONN.

The Officers and Directors of this Company have the pleasure of presenting to their Agents, and the public generally, their SIXTEENTH SEMI-ANNUAL STATEMENT of the financial condition of the PHŒNIX on the

FIRST DAY OF JANUARY, 1862.

LIST OF ASSETS.

Cash on hand and in bank,..$60,427 58
Cash in hands of Agents, and in course of transmission..........................45,399 40
Bills receivable for loans, secured by personal and collateral security...........28,540 00
"   "   "   "   " Real Estate.............................17,000 00
Real Estate unincumbered...17,500 00

Stocks and bonds as follows, namely:

					Market Value.
50 Shares	United States Trust Company's Stock, New York,				$ 6,000 00
200 "	American Exchange Bank	"	"	"	16,000 00
200 "	Metropolitan	"	"	"	18,400 00
200 "	Manufact'rs and Merchants' Bank	"	"	"	18,000 00
150 "	Continental	"	"	"	11,250 00
428 "	Mechanics'	"	"	"	9,630 00
500 "	Phenix	"	"	"	9,000 00
200 "	Merchants' Exchange	"	"	"	8,000 00
100 "	Merchants'	"	"	"	4,000 00
100 "	Ocean	"	"	"	3,750 00
300 "	Farmers' and Mechanics'	"	"	Hartford,	33,750 00
200 "	City	"	"	"	22,000 00
200 "	Ætna	"	"	"	20,000 00
200 "	Phœnix	"	"	"	19,200 00
200 "	Merchants' and Manufact'rs	"	"	"	18,200 00
200 "	Mercantile	"	"	"	17,000 00
125 "	State	"	"	"	15,250 00
50 "	Hartford	"	"	"	6,500 00
50 "	Conn. River	"	"	"	3,250 00
10 "	Hartford County				450 00
100 "	Citizens'	"	"	Waterbury, Ct.,	10,500 00
38 "	Waterbury	"	"	"	2,090 00
50 "	Niagara District	"	"	St. Cath'r's, C. W.,	5,150 00
250 "	Ontario	"	"	Bowmansville,	10,700 00
100 "	Holyoke Water Power Co.'s	"			10,000 00

20 New Britain Water Bonds,..11,000 00
10 Hartford City Bonds...10,500 00
20 Tennessee State Bonds,..8,700 00
Ohio State Stock of 1870,..1,800 00
Accumulated Interest on Investments,...2,764 75

Total Assets,...$501,701 73
Losses, in course of adjustment, waiting proofs, in suspense, or resisted,.....$30,161
Debts due to Banks, or other Creditors,..none
Losses adjusted and due..none

S. L. LOOMIS, PRESIDENT.
H. KELLOGG, SECRETARY.

J. J. HAYDEN, State Agent Indianapolis, Office corner Washington and Meridian Sts. (OVER.)

A Wheeler & Wilson Sewing Machine will last a life-time.

CHARTER PERPETUAL.

PHŒNIX INSURANCE CO.

OF HARTFORD, CONN.

CASH CAPITAL, - - - - $400,000.

Devoted to Fire Insurance exclusively, and its aim will be to secure a continuance of public confidence, by a prompt and honorable adjustment of all fair claims for loss.

ABSTRACT OF LOSSES PAID

In the Western and Southern States, during the past 5 years, ending January 1st, 1862. A substantial record of a

WELL-TRIED CORPORATION.

$41,690 66	Ohio	$41,690 66
34,640 71	Kentucky	34,640 71
32,644 99	Indiana	32,644 99
77,061 90	Illinois	77,061 90
37,426 82	Michigan	37,426 82
20,843 87	Iowa	20,843 87
47,883 97	Wisconsin	47,883 97
8,653 10	Minnesota	8,653 10
28,261 33	Missouri	28,261 33
9,765 82	Kansas	9,765 82
1,167 00	Nebraska	1,167 00
45,834 90	Tennessee	45,834 90
20,832 55	Mississippi	20,832 55
555 55	Alabama	555 55
22,839 43	Arkansas	22,839 43
3,961 98	Texas	3,961 98

BRANCH OFFICE, 33 WEST THIRD ST. CINCINNATI,

FOR THE FOLLOWING STATES AND TERRITORIES:

Ohio, Wisconsin, Iowa, Tennessee, Indiana, Michigan, Missouri, Mississippi, Illinois, Minnesota, Kentucky, Arkansas, Texas, Kansas, and Nebraska.

☞ Agents appointed; Losses adjusted and paid; Correspondence promptly attended to; Collections made; Insurance blanks furnished to Agents, and the Company's interest in the above States and Territories, under the supervision of

R. H. & H. M. MAGILL, Gen'l Agents.

☞ Agents in all Principal Cities and Towns in Indiana.

Wheeler & Wilson's Sewing Machines warranted for three years.

Pasquier John B., carpenter, res. cor. Michigan and Davidson.
Patterson E. W., stock trader, res. 91 N. West.
Patterson H. J., miller, cor. Washington and Blake.
Patterson James M. livery stables, 34 E. Maryland, res. 104 Massachusetts ave.
Patterson John, laborer, res. 253 S. Delaware.
Patterson John, carpenter, res. S. Illinois.
Patterson John, carpenter, res. N. Meridian.
Patterson John, tailor, res. 175 N. New Jersey.
Patterson John P., traveling ag't, res. 85 N. New Jersey.
Patterson Mrs. M. A. W., (wid.,) bds. 61 W. New York.
Patterson Samuel D., res. S. E. Michigan Road.
Patterson W., attorney at law, 30½ W. Washington, res. 152 E. Ohio.
Patterson Wm., U. S. A., res. 23 S. Illinois.
Pattison, Ray & Fletcher, R. R. City Mill, W. Washington, cor. White River Bridge.
Pattison S. D., (Langsdale & P.,) res. E. of city.
Pattison Samuel J., (P. Ray & Fletcher,) res. out of city.
Pattison Wm. A., bds. Barbour House.
Pauli Henry, carpenter, res. 89 Davidson.
Pauly John, carpenter, res. 107 N. Noble.
Pawen Patrick, boiler maker, res. 209 S. Pennsylvania.
Paxton Mrs. Elizabeth, (wid.,) res. 3 Circle.
Peacock Wm. H., engineer I. & C. R. R., res. E. National Road.
Peak Andrew, cooper, W. Indianapolis.
PEARL STREET SALOON, T. McBaker, proprietor, opp. Johnston's livery stable.
Pearsall P. R., music teacher, res. 26 S. Tennessee.
Pearse Wm., gadener, res. Orient.
Pearsol Wm., farmer, W. Indianapolis.
Peaslee W. A., patent washing machines.
Peat John, laborer, res. 224 N. Alabama.
PECK E. J., President of Terre Haute Railroad, bds. 37 Meridian.
Peck Thomas, foundryman, res. 111 Virginia ave.
Pedicord Mrs. Lydia, boarding house, res. 179 E. Market.
Pedlow James C., blacksmith, res. E. end Market.
Pedrick Mrs. dress-maker, 45 N. Illinois.
Pee Geo. W., salesman 75 W. Washington, bds. 87 N. Meridian.
PEELLE WM. A., Secretary of State, res. 58 N. East.
PEELLE & DAVIS, attorneys at law, over Secretary of State's office.
Peirce James, teamster, bds. 75 N. New Jersey.
Pelton O. H., messenger U. S. Express Company.

81,000 Wheeler & Wilson's Sewing Machines in use in this country.

Pendergast John, carpenter at Byrkit & Beam's, bds. 74 N. Tennessee.
Penders William, laborer, res. 158 N. Delaware.
Penn G. W., clerk at the Institute for the Blind.
Pennell S., painter, res. 165 N. Liberty.
Pentecost M. B., res. 120 N. Alabama.
Perdue M. W., res. 46 Bates.
Peric Sam., bds. 360 N. Tennessee.
Perine Peter, coal dealer, res. 108 N. Pennsylvania.
Perkins ——, laborer, res. 39 Huron.
Perkins C. G., (C. G. P. & Co.,) res. 132 N. Illinois.
Perkins C. G. & Co., wholesale and retail druggists, 14 W. Washington.
Perkins John, cooper, bds. 179 E. Market.
Perkins Mrs. Matilda, (col.,) dress maker, res. 61 Kentucky ave.
Perkins S. E., Judge of Supreme Court, res. 152 W. New York.
PERRIN GEO. K., attorney at law, College Hall, res. 25 E. Michigan.
PERRINE CHARLES O., books and periodicals, Union Depot.
Perrine James B., bookseller, res. N. New Jersey, bet. Market and Ohio.
Perrott Richard E., shoemaker, bds. S. Perrott, 191 Indiana ave.
Perrott Samuel, grocer, 191 Indiana ave., res. same.
Perrott Wm. W., grocer, 115 S. Tennessee, res. same.
Perry Charles, (col.,) barber, 3 N. Illinois, res. Kentucky ave.
Perry Lydia, works at Widows and Orphans' Asylum.
Perry W. M., harness maker, 20 W. Washington, bds. Farmers' Hotel.
Persel August, carpenter, res. cor. Oak and Cherry.
Peru & Indianapolis R. R. Depot, S. New Jersey.
Peter John D., express wagon, res. 107 N. Noble.
Peters Henry, carpenter, res. 146 N. Blake.
Peterson Jefferson, railroader, res. 2 S. Liberty.
Peterson Peter, shoemaker, 73 E. Washington.
Petre John, saloon, 272 E. Washington, res. same.
Petty Julius, farmer, res. 266 Indiana ave.
Peyton William, (col.,) currier, res. 139 N. West.
Pfafflin Theodore, salesman 29 W. Washington, res. 15 W. North.
Pfeiffenber S., bar-keeper, Station House.
Pflager Jacob, tailor, res. 188 E. Ohio.
Pflaker Learhart, waiter at Palmer House, res. 49 E. Maryland.

Pflegan George, laborer, res. 27 N. Noble.
Phelps A. E. saddler, 20 W. Washington, res. 131 N. Meridian.
Phillips Henry N., blacksmith, res. 279 S. Delaware.
Phillips William, clerk at Madison depot, res. 138 E. McCarty.
Phinney Thomas, laborer, res. Canal, S. of South.
Phipps J. M., carriage maker, res. 120 S. Noble.
Phipps Isaac N., real estate agent and notary public, office 28 E. Market, res. 26 E. Market.
Pholer Ludwig, railroader, res. 142 E. Market.
Pickens John, blacksmith, bds. 26 Massachusetts ave.
Pickering Charles H., U. S. A., res. 124 N. West.
PIEL W. F., general store, 240 F. Washington, res. same.
Pierce Winslow S., (McKernan & P.,) res. cor. New York and West.
Pierson L. W., brick layer, res. 112 N. Alabama.
Pierson Stephen D., cutter, 109 E. Ohio.
Pierson William W., liquors, 180 E. Washington, res. 79 N. Noble.
Pigg James, carpenter, res. 42 E. Louisiana.
Pigg Francis, painter, res. 15 N. Harris.
Pike Charles R., works Lawrenceburg car shop, res. S. E. Michigan Road.
Piland A. H., manufacturer of hay, straw and stalk cutters, Indiana ave.
Pitts George W., ice dealer, res. 78 Indiana ave.
Plant George, butcher, res. 193 E. Washington.
Plasnick Christian, cabinet-maker, res. 145 N. Alabama.
Plasnick Henry, blacksmith, bds. 145 N. Alabama.
Ploetringer Hyronimus, wood-sawyer, W. Indianapolis.
Plogstarth Victor, stone mason, res. 164 N. Liberty.
Plummer Hiram, res. 82 E. Market.
Poate Mrs. Jane, nurse, res. 9 Massachusetts ave.
Pohlar Christian, railroader, res. 312 Virginia ave.
Pohlar Wm., laborer, res. 314 Virginia ave.
Pond Fred. S., turner for Spiegel, Thoms & Co., res. 10 Lord.
Pool A. J., freight conductor Peru R. R., res. 37 E. Georgia.
Poorman David, plasterer, res. 93 St. Johns.
Pope Christian, works B. & I. R. R. depot, res. 33 Harrison.
Pope Henry, laborer, res. 117 N. West.
Pope William, (George Hotz & Co.,) bds. California House.
Porter Albert G., Congressman, 109 N. Delaware.
Porter T. R., tailor, res. 81 N. Meridian.
Post Charles, planing mill, res. 164 W. New York.
POST OFFICE, cor. Pennsylvania and Market, A. H. Connor, P. M.

POTTAGE BENJAMIN, wholesale and retail dealer in hardware, &c., 76 W. Washington, res. 91 W. Market.
Pottage Charles, clerk 76 W. Washington, bds. 91 W. Market.
Potter James B., butcher, res. 32 N. Spring.
Potter Joseph, (col.,) laborer, res. Elizabeth.
Pouder Milton, Central Meat Market, 91 E. Washington, res. 60 N. East.
Powel Nicholas, works at peg factory, res. 60 Bluff Road.
Powell David, butcher, cor. Vermont and Massachusetts ave., res. near Camp Morton.
Powell Henry, boot and shoemaker, res. 62 South.
Powell Joseph, workman at Rolling Mill, res. W. Canal.
Powell Wm., traveling agent I. & C. R. R., res. cor. Noble and Harrison.
Power George, laborer, res. Tennessee, bet. Fourth and Fifth.
Power Jacob, wagon maker, res. 31 N. East.
Power Jasper, artist, bds. 31 N. East.
Power Stephen, laborer, res. 21 Benton.
Powers Pat., boiler maker Western Machine Works.
Prange Charles, (Ostermeyer & P.,) res. 258 E. Washington.
Prange Frederick, laborer, res. Davidson, bet. New York and Michigan.
PRATT WILLIAM B., local agent P. & I. R. R., res. 183 E. Market.
Pratt A. H., engineer, bds. Little's Hotel.
Prerzel Henry, moulder, 65 Madison ave.
Preslly John T., engineer, res. 75 East.
Pressel Mrs. Mary, seamstresss, res. 120 E. Michigan.
Pressel Philip, carpenter, res. Plumb, near Cherry.
Pressell William, railroader, res. 70 E. Louisiana.
Preston Elliot, railroader, res. 41 W. St. Clair.
PRETZINGER JACOB, vinegar factory and dealer in liquors, 256 E. Washington, res. same.
Price Mrs. E. J., matron Institute for the Blind.
Price J. R., book-binder Journal Building, bds. Pyle House.
Price Wm. R., finisher, res. Bates, E. of Noble.
Prince John D., porter 36 E. Washington.
Prindle M., superintendent Union Depot, bds. 107 S. Tennessee.
Prine Thomas, bds. Palmer House.
Prinz John, porter, Mills, Alford & Co., bds. 28 Kentucky ave.
Probus Mrs. Anna, (wid.,) washer, res. 173 N. Mississippi.
Prosser Henry, Major 61st (2d Irish) regiment, res. 67 N. Tennessee.
Protzman F., salesman Dessar & Bro., res. 100 Mississippi.

Upwards of 100 W. & W. Machines in use in Ind'p'lis making army clothing.

Protzman Miss J., dress maker, res. 24 N. Mississippi.
Protzman John H., boarding house, res. 24 N. Mississippi.
Prummer Mrs. Eleanor, res. 82 E. Market.
Prummer Wm. H. H., blacksmith, bds. 82 E. Market.
Prunk Dr. D. H., U. S. A., res. 46 Indiana ave.
Pryse Henry, grocer, cor. McCarty and Virginia ave., res. 322 Virginia ave.
Paffling Paul, cook, res. 144 W. Washington, up stairs.
Pullinger John, cabinet maker, res. 146 E. Market.
Puppersoker Gotleib, res. 108 S. Noble.
Purcell Mrs. Sarah, (col.,) washer, res. 139 N. Tennessee.
Purcell William, at woolen factory.
Purdy William, principal Bryant's Commercial College, Ætna Building, bds. Macy House.
Purnell John, cabinet maker, 23 S. Meridian.
Purviance J. H., messenger American Express Co., bds. Morris House.
Pursell Jonathan, shoemaker, res. 78 S. Pennsylvania.
Pursell H., shoemaker, res. 78 S. Pennsylvania.
Pyle John, proprietor Pyle House, 25 cor. Illinois and Maryland.

Q

Quante Fred., cigar maker, bds. Farmers' Hotel.
Quigley Patrick, shoemaker, Garden, bet. Tennessee and Illinois, res. same.
Quimby C. W., (De Ford & Q.,) Roll's Building, S. Illinois.
Quimby Mrs. Hattie, millinery and fancy goods, 20 Illinois, res. same.
Quinn William, clerk Farmers' Hotel.
Quirk Patrick, engineer Bates House.
Quizer Julius, harness maker, 34 W. Washington, res. 175 Massachusetts ave.

R

Ræding A. D., plasterer, res. 13 Loukabee.
Rænart Frederick, tinsmith, res. 61 Bluff Road.
Rafert Henry, res. 193 N. Illinois.
Raffart William, laborer, res. 153 E. Market.
Raffart William, drayman, 242 Madison ave.
Rafferty Arthur, laborer, bds. 169 S. Mississippi.
Rajener Anton, tailor, 158 E. Washington.
RAILROAD PRINTING OFFICE, Cullum & Stanage, proprietors, 19½ W. Washington.

RAMSAY'S BLOCK, cor. Illinois and Maryland.
Ramsay J. F., furniture, &c., 21 S. Illinois, res. 21 W. Maryland.
Ramsay Robert, (col.,) ostler, res. 68 N. Blackford.
Ramsey Mrs., (col.,) washer, res. 147 N. Alabama.
Ramsey Jas. A., clerk Harrisons' Bank, bds. 21 W. Maryland.
Ramsey Thomas, captain night police, res. 41 E. St. Clair.
Ramsey Walter L., (R. & Hanning,) res. cor. Vermont and Ellsworth.
Ramsey & Hanning, plumbers, steam and gas fitters, 85 W. Washington.
Ranaghn James, porter Bates House, res. 123 W. Maryland.
Ranahan Joseph, laborer, res. 240 Indiana ave.
Ranard Eugene, Paris Saloon, E. Washington, res. same.
Rand Bryant, (col.,) barber, res. 68 N. Blackford.
Rand Frederick, (R. & Hall,) res. 162 N. Illinois.
RAND & HALL, attorneys at law, 26 E. Washington.
Randall James W., printer Journal office, bds. S. Mississippi.
Randall John H., printer Journal office, bds. 44 N. Pennsylvania.
Randall N. A., printer Journal office, res. 84 N. East.
Randolph Lott, laborer, W. Indianapolis.
Randolph Reuben, dyer Ohio Premium Woolen Factory.
Rapkey Frederick, 65 cor. McCarty and Madison ave.
Rapp Fred. J., plow manufacturer 154 E. Washington, res. cor. Michigan and Railroad.
Rapp George H., Captain 62d Regiment Indiana Volunteers, bds. Spencer House.
Raschig C. M., tobacconist, 15 E. Washington, res. 111 Vermont.
Rasenneu William, laborer, res. 144 S. Illinois.
Rassner William F., railroader, res. 144 Illinois.
Ratti Francis, res. 92 St. Joseph.
RATTI FRANCIS A., agent Cincinnati daily papers, office 8 Pearl, res. 92 St. Joseph.
Ratti Joseph, printer H. H. Dodd & Co., bds. 92 St. Joseph.
Ranker Thomas, steward Spencer House.
Ray A., works at car shop, res. 32 S. East.
Ray Charles A., (Morrison & R.,) res. 80 N. Illinois.
Ray David, saloon, 32 S. Illinois, res. Pennsylvania.
RAY HOUSE, S. E. cor. Delaware and South, Ray & Lambert, proprietors.
Ray Jacob, assistant bar-keeper, 32 S. Illinois, bds. Pennsylvania.
Ray James M., res. 19 N. Meridian.
Ray James N., clerk U. S. arsenal, res. 91 N. Noble.
Ray Eli, cooper, res. 16 Michigan Road.

The Wheeler & Wilson Hemmer makes hems of any width.

RAY & LAMBERT, proprietors Ray House, 65 South.
Rayford Henry, laborer, res. 156 N. West.
Rayman Henry, clerk Elliott's warehouse, res. 239 S. Alabama.
Raymond J. E., harness maker, 20 W. Washington, bds. Little's Hotel.
Rea John H., clerk U. S. District Court, res. 56 N. Meridian.
Read Earl, salesman 17 W. Washington, bds. Oriental House.
Reaf Anthony, laborer, res. 184 S. Delaware.
Reager John, butcher, res. 61 Madison ave.
Reagger Arnold, works at arsenal, res. 66 Indiana ave.
Reagin Joseph F., wood-chopper, res. bet. Davidson and Railroad.
Reasert John, clerk, res. 120 Delaware.
Reaver Godfrey, stone-cutter, 190 S. Delaware.
Reavil Robert L., coppersmith, res. 64 E. Louisiana.
Rech Henry, clerk 44 Louisiana, bds. 40 Illinois.
Rech Mathias, watchmaker and jeweler, 80 W. Washington, res. same.
Rechman John, laborer, res. 272 S. Delaware.
Reckenmeir Henry, miller, res. 59 E. St. Joseph.
Recker G., clerk for H. Leiber, res. New York.
Recker Hubert L., carpenter, res. E. end of Market.
Reddy Cornelius, railroader, res. 11 Railroad.
Redfield David A., (Hawes & Co.,) 3 N. Illinois, res. 39 E. Michigan.
Redford J. E., res. 35 S. Meridian.
REDFORD J. EDWARD, proprietor Macy House, cor. Illinois and Market.
Redman Mrs., (wid.,) res. 16 S. West.
Redman Dennis, policeman, res. W. South, bet. Mississippi and Missouri.
Redman John, foundryman, bds. 16 S. West.
Redman Wm., teamster, bds. 16 S. West.
Redmond Wm. D., porter New York Store, res. 124 E. Michigan.
Redstone A. E., (R., Bro. & Co.,) res. 35 N. New Jersey.
REDSTONE, BROS. & CO., manufacturers of machinery and agricultural implements, S. Delaware, opp. I. & C. R. R. Depot.
Redstone John H., (R., Bro. & Co.,) res. 35 N. New Jersey.
Redwine Alexander, peddlar, res. 39 McCarty.
Redwine John W., huckster, res. 39 McCarty, in rear.
Reed B. F., res. 62 E. North.
Reed E. R., engraver, 24 E. Washington, res. E. Maryland.
Reed John F., salesman Fancy Bazaar, bds. East.

Reed Joseph H., Pantheon Picture Galllery, Ætna Building, res. 159 N. Pennsylvania.
Reed Mrs. Martha J., res. 54 N. East.
Reed P. Fishe, artist, Ætna Building, res. 159 N. Pennsylvania.
Reed Thad. P., bds. 62 E. North.
Reeder E. C., huckster, res. S. E. Michigan Road.
Reeker G., res. 193 E. New York.
Reese Charles, 26th Ind. volunteers, res. Cherry.
Reese Henry, (Emmerich & R.,) res. 91 W. Washington.
Reeve August, tailor, 63 E. Washington.
Reeves J., tinner, Root, Bennett & Co.
Reeves Wm., soldier, res. 57 S. New Jersey.
Refert Andrew, carpenter, res. Alabama, bet. St. Clair and Wood.
Refert Frederick, carpenter, res. 208 N. Alabama.
Regan Edmund, boiler maker, res. 163 S. Tennessee.
Reger Wm., carpenter, res. 36 Davidson.
Rehling Charles, boots and shoes, 176 E. Washington, res. same.
Reichwein John, laborer, res. 198 Davidson.
Reid Jessie, (wid.)
Reidman Henry, wood sawyer, res. 15 St. Clair.
REILLY JOHN O., dairyman, res. Sugar Grove, 1 mile N. of city.
Reinacher Jacob, laborer, res. 158 N. New Jersey.
Reinault Charles, laborer, res. 66 Elm.
Reinfels Henry, laborer, res. 120 Union.
Reinhardt F., currier for John Fishback.
Reinhardt Joseph P., locksmith and bell hanger, 49 S. Illinois. res. same.
Reinhardt L., shoemaker, res. 48 Massachusetts ave.
Reinken Albert, plasterer, res. 204 N. New Jersey.
Reinken Henry, cigar-maker, 93 Ft. Wayne ave., res. same.
Reinmann Reinhold, saloon-keeper N. Pennsylvania, res. 9 S. Alabama.
Reisert Fred., shoemaker, bds. Delaware.
Reisert John, salesman for Martin Hug, res. 130 Delaware.
Reister John, cooper, res. 239 Massachusetts ave.
Remmington Jacob C., sawyer, res. 36 Spring.
Remus Victor, florist, Fletcher's green house, res. 12 Huron.
Renard John, stone-mason, res. 151 E. New York.
Rench Edward, groceries, &c., 126 S. Illinois, res. same.
Renner F., blacksmith, res. 59 Bluff Road.
Rennington Robert, blacksmith, res. 45 E. Georgia.
Rennon John B., saloon, 242 and 244 E. Washington, res. same.
Rentvel Joseph F., printer, bds. 36 N. East.

CITY DIRECTORY. 195

Rersey S., (col.,) barber, bds. Oriental.
Resener C. F., shoemaker, 194 E. Washington, res. same.
Resener Mrs. Estelle, (wid.,) washer, res. 160 S. Tennessee.
Resener Henry, shoemaker, res. 311 Virginia ave.
Resner William, laborer, res. 37 Union.
Retter John, laborer, res. 89 Bluff Road.
Revel Wm., engineer, res. 27 E. Georgia.
REVELLS REV. W. R., res. 119 N. West.
Revvels A., (col.,) washer, res. alley, cor. New York and Liberty.
Rexford E. M., tinner, 11 W. Washington.
Rey James L., (Redstone, Bro. & Co.,) res. 19 N. Meridian.
Reyer George, saddler, res. 209 N. Alabama.
Reynolds Chesler, laborer, res. near Ash and Cherry.
Reynolds Franklin, freight checker Bellefontaine Depot, res. 107 W. South.
Reynolds Geo., carpenter, res. Illinois, N. of Sixth.
Reynolds John L., bds. 139 N. New Jersey.
Reynolds John, (Sulgrove and R.,) res. 30 W. Ohio.
Reynolds J. W., (R. & Graham,) res. N. Noble.
Reynolds Levi, patent right man, res. 16 Loukabee.
Reynolds Mrs. Mary H., res. 89 N. Noble.
Reynolds Mary, (wid.,) res. 123 N. New Jersey.
Reynolds Mrs. Sarah, res. 170 N. Liberty.
Reynolds Thomas, mill-wright, res. 150 E. North.
Reynolds & Graham, shingle factory, Washington, near Noble.
Rheinhart Valentine, chair maker, res. 59 Madison ave.
Rheinhart Samuel, fireman railroad, res. 61 Bluff Road, in rear.
Rheling Wm., shoemaker, res. 181 S. Delaware.
Rhoads Charles, carpenter, res. 129 W. New York.
Rhoads J. M., physician, res. 145 N. West.
Rhoback Miss S., cloak maker with Miss Moon.
Rhoda A., clerk 20 S. Meridian, res. 148 N. Noble.
Rhodes Jos., (col.,) bell-ringer, res. 136 W. Georgia.
Rhodius George, National Saloon and Restaurant, 27 S. Meridian, res. same.
Ribel David, wood sawyer, res. 128 W. Maryland.
Rice Solomon, salesman 16 E. Washington, bds. N. New Jersey.
Ricer John, clerk, 130 S. Delaware.
RICHARDS JOHN, Palmer House Saloon, res. 17 Indiana ave.
Richards James, laborer, res. N. Blake.
Richard John, carpenter, res. Chestnut, bet. New Jersey and East.
Richards Richard, stone-cutter, res. 110 N. Missouri.

13

350 families in Indianapolis and vicinity use Wheeler & Wilson.

Richardson A. A., tinner at Root, Bennett & Co.
Richardson Jas., cooper, W. Indianapolis.
Richardson John, cigar maker, 12 N. Pennsylvania, bds. Mrs. Cook.
Richardson Warren, book-keeper and compilor of directories, bds. Oriental House.
Richey Mrs., bds. 18 N. East.
Richmann Charles, (R. & Buchanan,) res. 12 Fletcher's ave.
Richmann & Buchanan, wagon makers, 111 E. Washington.
Richmond Jos. S., express messenger, res. 24 S. Meridian.
Richmond J. S., messenger American Express Company, res. 119 Market.
Richter August, stone mason, res. 315 Virginia ave.
Richter E. J., shoemaker, 161 E. Washington, res. same.
RICHTER FLORANCE, Florance's Saloon, 13 N. Illinois, bds. Palmer House.
RICHTER FREDERICK, (R. & Roggs,) res. 114 E. Washington.
Richter Henry, grocer, res. Illinois, bet. Second and Third.
Richter Henry, saw miller, res. 175 S. Mississippi.
Richter & Roggs, merchant tailors and clothiers, 144 E. Washington.
Richter William, stone mason, res. 41 Hosbrook.
Richter Julius, tinner, Root, Bennett & Co.
Rick August, clerk 91 W. Washinton, bds. same.
Rickards Thomas, carpenter, shop 86 S. Delaware, res. 138 Market.
Ricker R. E., superintendent T. & R. R. R., res. 93 N. Tennessee.
Rickets William H., book-binder Campbell & Boyles, bds. Illinois.
Riddle Sarah, (wid.,) res. 111 W. Michigan.
Ridefaran James, laborer, res. last house, E side, S. Delaware.
Rider Henry, laborer, res. 127 W. Michigan.
Rief Fred., waiter Little's Hotel, res. 23 Henry.
Riemenschneider Herman, grocer 47 N. New Jersey, res. same.
Riffer Jacob, tailor 10 S. Pennsylvania.
Rifle Dick, butcher, res. Washington.
Rifle John, tailor, res. 9 Virginia ave.
RIGGS JOHN, proprietor Riggs' meat market, 32 N. Illinois, bds. Macy House.
RIGGS' MEAT MARKET, 32 N. Illinois, John Riggs, proprietor.
Riggs Simpson, (R. & David,) res. 83 South.
Riggs & David, meat market, 6 S. Meridian.
Rihl Charles H., mason, res. 38 N. California.

Riley B. F., ice dealer, res. 92 W. New York.
Riley James, porter Bates House, res. 23 Elizabeth.
Riley Martin W., printer Journal office, res. Walnut, bet. Illinois and Meridian.
Ringer John Q. A., car repairer Peru R. R., res. 108 St. Johns.
*Ringer Mrs. Mary A., res. 116 N. East.
Rinihan James, porter Bates House.
Ripkerds Thomas, carpenter, res. 138 E. Market.
Ripport John, saloon, E. Washington.
Risner Anthony, drayman, res. 15 McCarty.
Ritter Peter, stone cutter for W. W. James & Co., res. cor. South and Missouri.
Ritzinger Frank, clerk Fletcher's Bank, bds. 124 E. Ohio.
Ritzinger Frederick, secretary insurance company, res. 124 E. Ohio.
Ritzinger J. B., clerk Fletcher's Bank, bds. 124 E. Ohio.
Roach A. C., corresponding and general agent, Yohn's Block, bds. Morris House.
Roach Charles, railroader, res. 10 Bates.
Roache A. L., (McDonald & R.,) res. 97 N. Pennsylvania.
Roales James, farmer, res. 71 N. East.
Roback Eli, book-binder, bds. 7 W. Walnut.
Roback Henry, moulder, bds. 7 W. Walnut.
Roback Mrs. Sarah, res. 7 W. Walnut.
Robins H. R., attorney at law, res. 14 E. Ohio.
Roberts Jos. T., attorney at law, 18 E. Washington, bds. National Hotel.
Roberts Mrs. Catharine, res. Alabama, cor. Market.
Roberts Thos. A., machinist, P., C. & I. R. R.
Roberts Dwight, wholesale and retail grocer, cor. Washington and Illinois, res. 160 Tennessee.
Roberts Edward, (col.,) in the army, res. 65 S. Noble.
Roberts M., messenger American Express Company, bds. Bates House.
Roberts T. G., salesman 10 W. Washington, bds. Spencer House.
ROBERTS REV. TURNER, (col.,) res. 54 N. Blackford.
Roberts Warrington, sergeant 26th Indiana volunteers, res. 129 N. Liberty.
Robins Charles, superintendent R. R., res. 249 S. Alabama.
Robins E. P., expressman, res. 12 W. St. Clair.
Robinius Francis, (R. & Myers,) res. Noble.
Robinius & Myers, boots and shoes, 206 E. Washington.
*Robinius Frank, shoemaker, res. 121 N. Noble.
Robinson Charles S., carpenter, res. Tennessee, bet. First and Second.

For four successive years at the Am. Institute, New York.

ROBINSON CHAS. B., assistant superintendent P. & I. R. R., res. 249 S. Alabama.
Robinson Edward, blacksmith, res. 162 Indiana ave.
Robinson G., painter, 36 N. Pennsylvania.
Robinson Matthew B., teamster, res. 91 E. Market.
Robinson Richard B., miller Carlisle's Model Mills.
Robinson Robert W., carpenter, res. 68 N. Missouri.
Robinson Thornton F., res. Duncan, bet. Delaware and Alabama.
Robinson William, plasterer, res. 225 S. Alabama.
Robinson William H., res. S. E. cor. Alabama and Ohio.
Robinson Mrs. Elizabeth, (wid.,) W. Indianapolis.
Robson Mrs. C. F., res. 86½ N. Pennsylvania.
ROCKEY H. S., dealer in coal oil and lamps, 13 S. Meridian, res. 118 N. West.
Rockey John, clerk 13 S. Meridian, bds. 118 N. West.
Rockwell C. B., sutler 11th regiment, res. 87 N. Tennessee.
ROCKWELL R. E., agent M. & I. R. R., bds. 75 N. Alabama.
Rockwood W. O., treasurer I. & C. R. R., res. 30 S. Tennessee.
Roda Anthony, laborer, res. 148 N. Noble.
Rodavard Henry, grocer, Indiana ave., res. same.
Roderus Andrew, barber, bds. opp. Madison depot.
Rodolph Martin, laborer, res. Water, N. of McCarty.
/ Roesch Charles, tinner, bds. cor. Washington and Liberty.
Roford Charles, res. 119 N. Meridian.
Rogers Benjamin F., railroader, res. 128 E. St. Clair.
Rogers Dr. H., res. 14 E. Ohio.
Rogers Mrs. Fanny, (wid..) res. alley, rear of 73 Missouri.
Rogers I. W., res. 108 E. McCarty.
Rogers George, taxidermist, bds. 112 Mississippi.
Roggs Rudolph, (Richter & R.,) res. 144 E. Washington.
Rohren Martin, res. 65 Benton.
Rolfing Christian, laborer, res. 150 N. Noble.
Roll Isaac H., res. cor. Illinois and Vermont.
Roll William H., paper hangings and shades, 16 S. Illinois, res. 71 W. Maryland.
Roll Joseph, res. 145 N. New Jersey.
Rolla Henry, tinner, Root, Bennett & Co.
ROLLING MILL, S. Tennessee, S. of R. R. tracks, office 8 Blake's Row.
Rooker Alfred J., painter, res. 104 Indiana ave.
Rooker George, painter, res. 158 N. West.
Roop John, weaver, res. S. Calfornia, bet. Maryland and Georgia.
Roos Emanuel, butcher, bds. 89 S. Illinois.
Roos Jacob, (R. & Schmalzreed,) res. 91 S. Illinois.

ROOS & SCHMALZREED, dealers in all kinds of fresh and salt meats, 89 S. Illinois.
ROOT, BENNETT & CO., manufacturers and dealers in stoves, tin-ware, sheet-iron, &c., 66 E. Washington.
Root Charles H., (R., Bennett & Co.,) res. 80 N. Meridian.
Root Deloss, (E. B. Drake & Co.,) res. 33 N. Meridian.
Root J. B., (R., Bennett & Co.,) bds. 80 N. Meridian.
Root Samuel, laborer, res. 178 S. Alabama.
Rose A. D., Captain in 26th regiment, U. S. A. res. 110 N. East.
Rose Franklin, engineer I. & C. R. R., res. cor. Bates and Benton.
Rose J. G., plumber, bds. cor. Vermont and Ellsworth.
Rosebrock Frederick, grocer, res. 283 S. Delaware.
Rosebrock Herman H., grocery, res. 168 Virginia ave.
Rosemeyre Charles, wood-dealer, res. 65 Hosbrook.
Rosemeyre Charles, Jr., wood-dealer, bds. 65 Hosbrook.
Rosener Herman, peg and last factory, res. 127 N. Liberty.
Rosengarten Henry, druggist, 172 E. Washington, res. 46 N. Delaware.
Rosenthal A., wholesale dealer in foreign and domestic liquors, and manufacturer of cigars, 38 opp. Union Depot, res. Missouri.
Rosenthal Samuel, clerk 38 opp. Union Depot, bds. Missouri.
Ross Bascomb, bds. N. M. Ross.
Ross Jas., grocer, res. 36 Indiana ave.
Ross J. H., coal merchant, res. 174 N. Tennessee.
Ross Norman M., res. Broad Ripple Road.
Ross Reuben, pump-maker, res. 12 S. West.
Rosset Theo., butcher, res. 63 Hosbrook.
Roth Louis, with Lou. Lang, bds. same.
Rothrock Valentine, res. 147 Virginia ave.
Rouchette Dela Bretique Arthur, res. extreme E. end of Maryland.
Roupp William, merchant tailor, 105 E. Washington, res. same.
Routier Anoltole, carpenter, res. 65 Elm.
Routier John E., carpenter, bds. 65 Elm.
Routier P., carpenter, res. 65 Huron.
Rowe Austin, engineer Central R. R., res. 55 Benton.
Rowe Samuel, gunsmith, bds. 80 N. New Jersey.
Rozier Aaron, laborer, res. 132 W. New York.
Rubush Alexander, brick-layer, res. 203 N. Noble.
Rubush Jacob, brick-layer, res. 62 N. East.
Rubush Fletcher, carpenter, res. 59 N. Noble.
Rucker Dr. J. S., res. 58 W. Vermont.

Upwards of 100 W. & W. Machines in use in Ind'p'lis making army clothing.

RUCKLE N. D., merchant tailor and agent for Williams & Orris' $25 sewing machines, E. Market, opp. Post-office, res. Second, bet. Illinois and Meridian.
Ruckle N. R., Captain Co. E, 11th regiment Indiana Volunteers.
Ruckwein Philip, clerk Union Hall.
Rue Mrs. Martha, W. Indianapolis.
Rumann August, express driver, res. 131 E. Washington.
Rundle Charles, shooting gallery 29½ S. Meridian.
Runnion William, (Hays & R.,) bds. Mrs. Kinder.
Runnels John, res. S. E. cor. Ohio and Tennessee.
Rusch Fred. P., produce and commission merchant, 81 and 83 Masonic Hall, res. Virginia ave.
Rusche Peter, stone cutter, res. Wyoming.
Ruschaupt Aug., clerk German Dry Goods Store.
Ruschaupt F., (R. & Bals,) res. 61 New Jersey.
Ruschaupt & Bals, wholesale and retail dealers in wines, whiskies and brandies, 82 E. Washington.
Russell James L., clerk in postoffice, res. cor. Maryland and Merrill.
Russell James, U. S. A., res. 14 Michigan Road.
RUSSELL JOHN S., policeman, res. 284 Delaware.
Russell Levi, laborer, res. 111 E. McCarty.
Russell Nicholas, res. 42 Bates.
Russell Samuel, laborer, res. 21 Railroad.
Russman Charles, German boarding house, 119 E. Washington.
Ruswenkel John, cigar-maker, res. 123 N. East.
Ruth Adolph, clerk W. Washington, bds. same.
Rutz F. A., bar-keeper Crystal Palace saloon, bds. same.
Ryan Mrs. Ellen, (wid.,) res. Georgia, bet. Tennessee and Illinois.
RYAN J. B., (C. A. Elliott & Co.,) res. 100 Mississippi.
Ryan John, railroader, res. 120 E. Market.
Ryan John, U. S. A., res. 42 Liberty.
Ryan John, laborer, res. 198 S. Delaware.
Ryan Michael, railroader, res. 103 Railroad.
Ryan Patrick, laborer, res. 110 S. East.
Ryan Mrs. Peggy, (wid.,) res. 16 S. East.
Ryan R. J., Lieut. Colonel 35th regiment Indiana Volunteers.
Ryan T. F., wholesale wines, liquors and tobacco agency, bds. 32 Kentucky ave.

S

Sackett C. O., printer H. H. Dodd & Co., bds. 79½ E. Washington.
Sage John, moulder, res. 25 Henry.
Sahm Ludwig, carpenter, res. 88 Ft. Wayne ave.
Sahm Lugfried, clerk, 84 W. Washington, bds. 15 W. Ohio.
ST. CHARLES SALOON, E. Haas, proprietor, 86 E. Washington.
St. Johns Church, Georgia, bet. Tennessee and Illinois.
St. John E., salesman 16 S. Illinois, bds. 71 W. Maryland.
St. Johns Female Seminary, cor. Tennessee and Georgia.
ST. MARYS SISTERS OF PROVIDENCE, school cor. Georgia and Tennessee.
ST. NICHOLAS SALOON, Eurich & Schaffer, proprietors, 7 N. Illinois.
Sales Al., ostler for Wm. Wilkison.
Sample Samuel C., carpenter, res. 192 E. St. Clair.
Sanders John, (col.,) laborer, res. 68 W. Vermont.
Sanders John, carpenter, res. 148 N. Liberty.
Santo Edward, bar-keeper Verandah Saloon, bds. same.
Sapp W. D., clerk Morris House.
Sauar John, laborer, res. 30 Union.
Saubum Joseph B., painter, res. 53 S. Pennsylvania.
Saum Jacob, brick-layer, res. 23 Central.
Sawyer John S., book-keeper C. Donaldson 71 W. South, bds. New Jersey, bet. South and Merrill.
Sayles Horatio, blacksmith, res. S. E. Michigan Road.
Scalheimer Wm., huckster, W. Indianapolis.
Scarry House, John Scarry, proprietor, 20 N. Pennsylvania.
Scarry John, proprietor Scarry House, 20 N. Pennsylvania.
Schaaf Abel, laborer, res. 49 N. Noble.
Schad George, laborer, res. 52 Davidson.
Schad Gotlieb, wagon-maker, res. 52 Davidson.
Schaffer Michael, dyer, 31 Virginia ave.
Schaffer C., (Eurich & S.,) res. W. Georgia.
Schaffner Jacob, laborer, res. 219 N. Noble.
Schaub George, shoemaker, res. 125 Noble.
Schaub Henry, bar-keeper, bds. 6 W. Washington.
Schaub Henry, proprietor Central restaurant, 6 W. Washington, res. 137 Noble.
Schaub Peter, expressman, res. 123 N. Noble.
Scheader C., laborer, res. 130 N. Noble.
Scheer Fred., proprietor Station House, opp. Union Depot.
Schilling Henry, laborer, res. 292 Virginia ave.
Schilring Nicholas, baker and cook, res. 158 N. Liberty.
Schindler Robert, salesman 26 and 28 W. Washington.

Schlatthamer Valentine, cabinet-maker, res. 75 Davidson.
Schley Allan, tinner 11 W. Washington, bds. 24 N. Pennsylvania.
Schley George J., printer Journal office, res. 24 N. Pennsylvania.
Schley Mrs. G. M., res. 24 N. Pennsylvania.
Schley John, printer H. H. Dodd & Co., bds. 82 N. Delaware.
Schloer Christian, shoemaker, res. 74 Ft. Wayne ave.
Schmalzried Charles, (Roos & S.,) res. 91 S. Illinois.
Schmidt Frederick, brewer, res. 299 S. Delaware.
Schmidt Philip, shoemaker, 7 N. Meridian.
Schmitt A., house and sign painter, 103½ E. Washington.
Schmitt John, cigar maker, bds. Bluff Road.
Schnable John, wood-sawyer, res. cor. Tennessee and First.
Schnell Zacharias, flower garden, res. 78 Pratt.
SCHNEIDER REV JOHN, methodist, res. 122 E. Ohio.
Schnues Charles, shoemaker, bds. 51 S. Illinois.
Schnuckler T. H., res. 155 Massachusetts ave.
Schnull A., (A. & H. S.,) res. Alabama, bet. Market and Ohio.
Schnull H., (A. & H. S.,) res. Alabama, bet Market and Ohio.
SCHNULL A. & H., wholesale grocers, produce and commission merchants, whisky, wines, &c., cor. Washington and Delaware.
Schofield Thos. B., (T. B. S. & Co.,) bds. 24 N. Mississippi.
SCHOFIELD THOS. B. & CO., manufacturers of vinegar, &c., 49 E. South.
SCHONACKER HUBERT J., professor of music, bds. Spencer House.
SCHOPPENHORST WILLIAM, dealer in groceries, produce, liquors, feed, &c., 101 E. Washington, res. same.
SCHOTT JOSEPH, dealer in groceries, provisions, &c., 117 E. Washington, res. same.
Schouzer R., saw-filer, 62½ E. Washington.
Schowe Fred., works T. H. engine house, res. 291 Virginia ave.
Schrader Anthony, laborer, res. 144 N. Liberty.
Schrader Henry, adjutant 26th Ind. volunteers.
Schrader John, machinist, res. 148 E. Market.
Schramm Charles, clerk, res. 105 E. Vermont.
Schramm J. C. A., clerk City Treasurers Office, res. Vermont, bet. East and New Jersey.
Schreck Mrs. Mary, sewing, res. 143 N. Noble.
Schroder Frederick, cooper, res. 192 N. Noble.
Schuessler Conrad, laborer, res. 152 N. New Jersey.
Schuldmeir Fred., salesman 144 E. Washington, res. same.

Schuler Geo. J., salesman New York Store, bds. Morris
  House.
Schuler Joseph, butcher, res. 209 S. Pennsylvania, up stairs.
Schulmyer Frederick, laborer, res. 55 E. St. Mary.
Schumm Julius, teacher of the German and English free
  school, res. 69 N. Delaware.
Schunneman Wm., laborer, res. 82 Bluff Road.
Schuster Theodore, U. S. service, res. 51 McCarty.
Schuyler F. J., printer Sentinel Office, bds. 44 N. Pennsyl-
  vania.
Schwal Henry, printer Indiana Free Press.
Schwameier Christian, laborer, res. 164 E. Michigan.
Schwamire Wm., cooper, res. 187 N. Noble.
Schwarty Christian, cartman, res. Phipps.
Schwarty Michael, U. S. A., 35 Huron.
Schwico Charles, salesman Fitzgibbon & Co., res. 87 Un-
  ion.
Schwico Fred., porter Fitzgibbon & Co., bds. 87 Union.
Schwegel Len., harness maker, res. 102 Pennsylvania.
Schweinhart Peter, grocery, 253 Indiana ave., res. 251 In-
  diana ave.
Schwomeyer Henry, cooper, res. 180 N. Noble.
Schyler Geo., bar-keeper Exchange Restaurant.
Scott Almon, teamster, res. 69 Spring.
Scott Charles, laborer, res. 123 Bluff Road.
Scott Henry M., student at law with Harrison & Fishback,
  bds. 127 N. Alabama.
Scott John, salesman New York Store, res. 191 N. Illinois.
Scott John, (col.,) wood sawyer, res. Illinois, bet. Second
  and Third.
Scott, Nicholson & Co., stone and marble yard, Kentucky
  ave.
Scott Adam, (S., Nicholson & Co.,) res. East.
Scribner Geo. B., jun., hatter, bds. Ohio House.
Scudder Caleb., boarding house, 46 W. Market.
Scudder Michael R., constable, res. 92½ N. New Jersey.
Seafart Louis, meat market, 77 E. Washington, res. S. Del-
  aware.
Seaman Edwin, agent Wm. Sheets, res. 18 W. Ohio.
Seaman Wm., blacksmith, res. 27 N. Spring.
Sears Andrew, laborer, res. 207 S. Pennsylvania.
Sears Martin, laborer, bds. 207 S. Pannsylvania.
Sears Thomas, laborer, bds. 209 S. Pennsylvania.
Seasel S., salesman 8 E. Washington, bds. Morris House.
Seay Abraham, U. S. A., res. 60 Indiana ave.
Secrets Charles, brick-mason, res. 205 S. Alabama.
Seele Henry, laborer, res. 174 N. Liberty.
Secrist H., confectioner, res. 26 S. Meridian.

The Wheeler & Wilson Hemmer is the only Hemmer that will Fell.

Seibert Samuel, blacksmith, 252 E. Washington, res. 3 N. Liberty.
Seidensticker, Adolph, attorney at law, 91 E. Washington, res. 41 N. Noble.
Seiter R., cooper, res. 116 E. Market.
Seiver John A., (Church & Co.,) res. Cumberland.
SELESTIAL SHOE SHOP, Thomas Dugan, proprietor, Blake's Building, fourth story.
Sell Pat., U. S. A., res. 103 W. South.
Semmelink Wm., carpenter, res. 157 E. Ohio.
Semmons J. H., (J. H. S. & Co.,) res. 23 S. Illinois.
Semmons J. H. & Co., opticians, 23 S. Illinois.
Senior Mrs. Parthenic, washer, res. 90 Massachusetts ave.
SENOUR REV. F., presbyterian, bds. 140 N. Tennessee.
Senour J. F., wholesale and retail druggist, 5 Bates House, W. Washington, res. 140 N. Tennessee.
Sergant E. M., at Bellefontaine car shop, res. 19, alley E. of S. East.
Sergent Ezro, foreman Bellefontaine car shop, res. 19 N. East.
Sergent F. L., blacksmith. res. 161 N. Liberty.
Serger A., salesman 3 E. Washington, bds. Oriental House.
Server Augugtus, clerk at Mansur's pork-house, res. 59 N. Mississippi.
Server Franklin, at Mansur's pork-house, res. 59 N. Mississippi.
Server Elliott, butcher, 56 Davidson.
Servison Wm., Lafayette R. R.
Severance F. M., machinist, res. 157 N. Liberty.
Severin Henry, grocery, 207 N. New Jersey, res. same.
Sewel Joseph, U. S. A., res. 13 Elm.
Seybold Allis, res. 121 E. Ohio.
Seybold Jas. K., marble yard, cor. Market and Delaware, res. 68 N. Mississippi.
Shachnacy Thos., musician, res. 243 S. Pennsylvania.
Shade B. W., salesman New York Store, bds. 106 Tennessee.
Shafer Cornelius, saloon, Illinois, res. 166 S. Tennessee.
Shafer Simon, res. 67, alley in rear of 70 N. Mississippi.
Shane Michael, laborer, res. 55 E. St. Joseph.
Shaneberger D. H., clerk Adams Express office, bds. 93 E. Ohio.
Sharer John, carpenter, res. Elizabeth.
Sharp Geo., cigar maker, 35 W. Washington, bds. Spencer House.
Sharp Stephen, res. 101 Meek.
Sharpe E., book-keeper Indianapolis Branch Banking Co., bds. 95 N. Pennsylvania.

SHARPE J. K., manufacturer and dealer in boots and shoes, leather, &c., also, hats, caps and furs, 88 and 90 E. Washington, res. E. Washington, outside city limits.
Sharpe Thos. H., (Fletcher & S.,) res. 95 N. Pennsylvania.
Sharpless P., book-keeper 86 W. Washington, res. 102 N. Meridian.
Shaub John, wood sawyer, res. 129 N. Noble.
Shaughnessy Mrs. J., dress maker, res. 131 S. Alabama.
Shaw Henry, laborer, res. 169 S. Alabama.
Shaw J. P., res. 78 Madison ave.
Shaw Patrick, clerk 49 South, bds. Jefferson House.
Shaw Victor, plasterer, res. Michigan, bet. Liberty and Noble.
Shawver C. J., saddler, 20 W. Washington, bds. 54 Indiana ave.
Shay Jerry, laborer, res. 23 alley E. of S. East.
Shay Thomas, laborer; res. cor. Plum and Cherry.
Shayler Henry, laborer, res. 139 S. Alabama.
Shea Roger, laborer, res. 105 W. New York.
Shea Cornelius, laborer, res. 105 W. New York.
Shea James, laborer, res. 166 S. Mississippi.
Shead M., tailor, res. Vermont, bet. Liberty and Noble.
Shearer David, plow maker at Beard, Starr & Co., bds. Ohio House.
Shearer Frederick, chair maker, res. 71 E. Merrill.
Shearer George, engineer Bellefontaine R. R., res. 336 S. Delaware.
Shearer Mary, (wid.,) res. 336 S. Delaware.
Sheehan Mary, (wid.,) res. 192 S. Delaware.
Sheets Wm., blank book manufacturer, &c., 77 W. Washington, res. cor. Pennsylvania and Ohio.
Shehan Daniel, laborer, res. 143 W. Alabama.
Shekel Christian, laborer, res. 230 S. Alabama.
Shellenberger John, pattern maker, res. 142 N. New Jersey.
Sheppard Mrs., cloak maker, with Miss Moon.
Sherbern Asa, engineer T. H. R. R., bds. 107 S. Tennessee.
Sherbern William, engineer T. H. R. R., res. 99 W. Maryland.
Sheridan John W., tailor, res. West, bet. Maryland and Georgia.
Sherman George, grocer, cor. Pennsylvania and North, res. cor. Meridian and New York.
Sherman Gustavus, res. 29 N. Meridian.
Sherman Paul, harness maker, 20 W. Washington, res. 44 Indiana ave.
Shewver Alex., carpenter, res. 21 Chatham.
Shigert Fred., Turner Hall, res. cor. Kentucky ave. and S. Tennessee.

Shilcott John, carpenter, bds. cor. Tennessee and First.
Shillett Henry, res. 22 N. Mississippi.
Shilling Charles, works Bellefontaine freight depot, res. 138 Davidson.
Shire Maurice, laborer, rear of 241 S. Pennsylvania.
Shipmire Charles, drayman, res. 193 E. St. Clair.
Shippey Mrs. J. C., house-keeper C. B. Rockwell, 87 N. Tennessee.
Shively L. H., millwright, res. 110 E. South.
Shmidt H., Corporation Garden, E. National Road.
Shoecraft Siles, (col.,) barber, res. 22 Loukabee.
Shoemaker Fred., piano maker, res. 98 W. Maryland.
Shoemaker Henry, res. 58 N. Noble.
Shoemaker John, bds. 98. W. Maryland.
Shoemaker Mary, (wid.,) res. 115 E. Maryland.
Shober Jacob, laborer, res. 214 S. Alabama.
Shomberg Wm., shoemaker, on alley between Market and Washington.
Shopp Elizabeth, (wid.,) res. 26 Union.
Shore Fred, blacksmith, res. 101 Water.
Shore John railroader, res. 110 S. Noble.
Shore Wm., brick mason, res. 101 Water.
Short F. C., student, bds. 130 N. New Jersey.
Short John, meat market, 208 W. Washington, res. same.
Shortridge A. C., teacher, near Oak.
Shortridge A. F., res. 118 N. Illinois.
Shotte Charles, butcher, bds. 22 Indiana ave.
Shotts George, brewer, bds. 135 W. Maryland.
Shoub Jacob, shoemaker, res. 238 Massachusetts ave.
Shouse Greenberry, teamster, W. Indianapolis.
Shrader F., shoemaker, 38 W. Washington.
Shrader John A., res. back of 70 N. Mississippi.
Shriner Wm., tanner, 78 Madison ave.
Shroeck Geo., carpenter, res. 248 Indiana ave.
Shuer John, res. 35 N. Noble.
Shuler Fred., currier for J. K. Sharpe.
Shulmyer L. C., clerk, 72 E. Washington, res. 163 N. New Jersey.
Shulty John, peddler, res. cor. Orient and National Road.
Shwevel Daniel, saddler, res. 201 S. Pennsylvania.
Siberd Hiram, blacksmith, res. 91 S. East.
Sibert Cicero, mechanic, bds. 75 E. Market.
Sibert David, blacksmith, res. 75 E. Market.
Sibert Mrs. Sarah, res. 8 Chatham.
SICKELS REV. WM., Presbyterian, res. 170 N. Illinois.
SIEGRIST SIMON, pastor St. Mary's German Catholic Church, 46 S. Delaware.
Siemon Christ., laborer, res. 151 N. Noble.

Sikes John, engineer Terre Haute R. R., bds. 107 S. Tennessee.
Simcox John W., saddler, 138 N. East, res. same.
Simmons Henry, grocer, res. 37 cor. Tennessee and Indiana ave.
Simms James, laborer, res. 222 S. Alabama.
Simon A. F., grocer, E. National Road.
Simon G., (G. S. & Son.) res. Cincinnati.
SIMON G. & SON, clothiers, 1 S. W. cor. Washington and Meridian.
SINGER I. M. & CO., sewing machines, 3 Odd Fellows' Hall, Washington.
Simon Lewis, barber, res. 56 S. East.
Simon Peter, currier, res. 141 E. Market.
Simon Reese, grocer, 104 N. Noble, res. same.
Simons Miss Sallie, cloak maker with Miss Moon.
Simonson George A., school teacher, res. 87 Massachusetts ave.
Simonson Col. S., U. S. A., bds. Bates House.
Simpson F. F., (Danforth & S.,) res. 83 N. Illinois.
Simpson John, U. S. A., bds. Morris House.
Simpson John, laborer, W. Indianapolis.
Simpson Mrs. Lavina, boarding, res. 27 Indiana ave.
SIMPSON M. & R., wholesale and retail dealers in wines and liquors, groceries and country produce, cor. South and Delaware.
Simpson N., grocery and saloon, 162 and 164 W. Washington, res. same.
Simpson Richard, (M. & R. S.,) cor. S. and Delaware, bds. Bates House.
Simpson Wm., U. S. A., res. 83 cor. Pine and Elm.
Sims John, carpenter, res. 20 St. Clair.
Sims Wm., res. New York, near Canal.
Sinker Edward, (Dumont & S.,) res. 101 Virginia ave.
Sipp Charles A., machinist, res. 43 N. New Jersey.
Skilly Mrs. T., (wid.,) boarding house, S. Meridian.
Skillen J., (J. S. & Bro.,) res. cor. West and Market.
Skillen R. G., (J. S. & Bro.,) res. 250 W. Washington.
Skillen J. & Bro., wholesale and retail grocers, 248 W. Washington.
Skinner Wm. H., engineer Central R. R., res. 55 S. Noble.
Slack A. H., salesman Fancy Bazaar, bds. 83 New York.
Slatter Charles, carpenter, res. 71 N. East.
Slaughter Milton, carpenter, res. 21 E. Georgia.
Sleek Alex., wood sawyer, res. 124 E. Michigan.
Slein Joseph, shoemaker, 64 E. Washington.
SLOAN E. W., sup't Am. Express Co., res. 97 N. Tennessee.

Sloan Geo. W., clerk, 22 W. Washington, res. 101 N. Tennessee.
Sloan John, cabinet maker, res. 83 S. Tennessee.
Sloan John N., bds. 97 N. Tennessee.
Slugger Henry, laborer, res. 271 S. East.
Small David, carpenter, res. 139 Massachusetts ave.
SMALL REV. GILBERT, Associate Reform, res. 40 N. Delaware.
Small Jerome N., clerk, 155 E. Washington, bds. Michigan Road, E. of city.
Small R. A., foreman Lawrenceburg car shop, res. S. E. Michigan Road.
Smalwood John, res. 32 N. Noble.
Smidt Obed, drum head manufacturer, res. 47 S. New Jersey.
Smith Albert, laborer, bds. 52 Huron.
Smith A. C., compositor with Cullum & Stanage, bds. Little's Hotel.
Smith Andrew J., works Lawrenceburg car shop, res. 54 Bates.
Smith Andrew conductor, Peru R. R., res. 241 S. Alabama.
Smith Anne, teacher, res. 36 E. Ohio.
Smith Hon. Caleb B., Secretary of Interior, Washington, res. cor. New York and California.
Smith Christian, stone cutter, (Smith, Ittenbach & Co.,) 180 South Delaware.
Smith Cyrus, teacher, res. cor. Ash and Cherry.
Smith Ellen, (wid.,) res. 107 S. Alabama.
Smith E. M., carpenter, res. 99 W. Maryland.
Smith E. R., bds. Scarry House.
SMITH FRANCIS, real estate agent, 37 E. Washington, res. 58 S. Tennessee.
Smith Frank, clerk Beebe & Hawes, bds. 44 Indiana ave.
Smith Frederick, grocery, 126 N. Mississippi, res. same.
Smith George, printer, res. 12 N. New Jersey.
Smith George, baker, 200 W. Washington, bds. same.
Smith George, blacksmith at Drew's carriage shop, bds. Ohio House.
Smith George, laborer, res. 97 Railroad.
Smith George T., clerk, Werden & Co., bds. 115, N. New Jersey.
Smith G. W. B., printer Sentinel Office, res. 12 N. New Jersey.
Smith Mrs. Hannah, res. 36 E. Ohio.
Smith Henry C., salesman, 25 W. Washington, bds. 53 Indiana ave.
Smith Henry, res. 196 N. Illinois.
Smith Hugh F., (S. & Stevenson,) bds. 21 S. Delaware.

Smith Hugh H., shoemaker, res. 19 Alabama.
Smith Isaac, foreman Mansur & Ferguson's cooper shop, W. Indianapolis.
SMITH, ITTENBACH & CO., stone yard, 170 S. Delaware. (See card.)
Smith Jacob, ambrotype and photograph artist, 8 Glenns' Block, res. 142 New York.
Smith Jacob, blacksmith, 312 S. Delaware.
Smith James, laborer, res. 118 S. New Jersey.
Smith James, railroader, res. 135 N. Liberty.
Smith James H., clerk Merrill & Co., bds. Mrs. Smith.
Smith John, wire worker, 266 S. Delaware.
Smith John, railroader, res. 161 Virginia ave.
Smith John, stone cutter, res. E. National Road.
Smith John, shoemaker, 32 E. Washington, res. 9 E. North.
SMITH REV. JOHN C., Methodist, res. 115 N. New Jersey.
Smith John C., carpenter, res. cor. St. Clair and James.
Smith John G., blacksmith, res. 84 N. New Jersey.
Smith J. W., Phœnix Saloon, 15 W. Washington, res. same.
Smith Jonathan, printer, Journal Office, bds. 9 E. North.
Smith Joseph, finisher, Lawrenceburgh car shop, res. Elm.
Smith Lawrence, porter Bellefontaine R. R. res. Meridian.
Smith Leonard, currier for Mooney & Co.
Smith Leo, laborer, res. 12 Meridian.
Smith M. C., dry goods, res. 139 N. Alabama.
Smith Mrs. M. C., (wid.,) boarding, res. 44 S. Pennsylvania.
Smith Mrs. Mary Elizabeth, (wid.,) res. 48 Michigan Road.
Smith P. G., salesman Fancy Bazaar, bds. Mrs. Kinder.
Smith Richard, teamster, res. 51 Union.
Smith Samuel F., (Osgood, S. & Co.,) res. 42 S. Meridian.
Smith Sophia, dress maker, res. 86 Pratt.
SMITH STEPHEN, city bill poster, card and circular distributor, res. 102 N. Mississippi.
Smith Theo. M., salesman Bee-Hive, bds. Macy House.
Smith Thomas, res. cor. Washington and Alabama.
Smith Wm., chandler, res. 36 N. California.
Smith Wm., butcher, res. 151 Massachusetts ave.
Smith Wm., bar-keeper Phœnix Saloon, 15 W. Washington.
Smith Wm., res. 37 N. Delaware, cor. Ohio.
Smith Wm. C., R. R. City Mills, res. 33 W. Ohio.
Smith Wm. Frank, clerk 22 Washington, res. $102\frac{1}{2}$ N. Meridian.
Smith Wm. H., clerk J. S. Dunlop, bds. 84 N. New Jersey.
Smith Wm. Q., coal dealer, res. 38 N. East.
Smith Wm. S., fish dealer, res. 192 N. Illinois.
Smither H. G., clerk Hogshire & Hunter, bds. 53 Indiana ave.

For four successive years at the Ohio State Fair.

Smither Jas. W., mail agent I. & C. R. R., bds. 53 Indiana ave.
Smither John, res. 53 Indiana ave.
Smithmeyer John M., bds. 79½ E. Washington.
Smock Abraham, driver hose carriage, bds. Marion engine house.
Smock George W., laborer, res. 196 N. New Jersey.
Smock M. L. C., butcher, bds. 28 S. Pennsylvania.
Smock Mrs. Nancy, (wid.,) seamstress, res. 17 Huron.
Smock Peter, clerk 56 E. Washington, res. Alabama, bet. Maryland and Georgia.
Smock Peter, clerk, res. 196 N. New Jersey.
Smock Richard W., laborer, 138 S. East.
Smock Wm. C., deputy county clerk, res. 123 E. New York.
Smydes Frederick, blacksmith, res. cor. Water and McCarty.
Snapp Mrs. Abigal, hair-braider, res. 160 E. New York.
Snapp Charles, watch maker, 1 Bates House.
Snider Conrad, carpenter, res. Vermont, bet. Liberty and Noble.
Snider Geo. W., laborer, res. N. Noble, bet. Vermont and New York.
Snider Paul, laborer, res. 64 Bluff Road.
Snow Isaac, tailor, res. 34 E. Louisiana.
Snyder Conrad, laborer, res. E. Wyoming.
SNYDER DAVID E., cashier Branch Bank of the State of Indiana, bds. S. Pennsylvania.
Snyder John, moulder, res. S. Alabama.
Snyder L., (W. & L. S.,) res. Maryland, opp. Pyle House.
Snyder W., (W. & L. S.,) res. 95 Mississippi.
Snyder W. & L., meat market, 29 S. Meridian.
Soewell Henry, grocer, res. 16 N. New Jersey.
Soewell Henry M., (Spencer & S.,) res. 18 N. New Jersey.
Sogamier August, porter A. & H. Schnull.
Solomon Charles, cigar maker, 30 S. Illinois, bds. same.
Solomon J., (J. & M. S.,) res. 30 S. Illinois.
Solomon J. & M., manufacturers, wholesale and retail dealers in cigars and tobacco, 30 S. Illinois.
Solomon M., (J. & M. S.,) res. 30 S. Illinois.
Sondenegger Fidel, porter Branch Bank.
Sorter William, chair maker, res. 72 N. Mississippi.
Southard J. P., wholesale and retail boots and shoes, 19 E. Washington, res. 68 Vermont, cor. Alabama.
Southard M. R., salesman 19 E. Washington, res. 10 St. Clair.
Spalding John W., carriage maker, res. 72 N. Alabama.
Spann John S., (S. & Love,) res. 73 N. Pennsylvania.
SPANN & LOVE, real estate and insurance agents, cor. Washington and Meridian. (See card outside.)

CITY DIRECTORY. 211

Spaht Bernard, res. 46 S. Delaware.
Spear Frederick, drayman, res. 103 E. South.
Spears Mrs. Priscilla, (col.,) carpet weaver, res. 63 S. Noble.
Speckman H., cigar store, 57 S. Illinois, res. Georgia, bet. Illinois and Tennessee.
Speigel Augustus, (S., Thoms & Co.,) res. 121, cor. Liberty and Vermont.
Speigel Christian, (S., Thoms & Co.,) res. cor. East and North.
SPEIGEL, THOMS & CO., wholesale and retail manufacturers and dealers in furniture, &c., 73 W. Washington.
Spenn James R., butcher, res. 106 Davidson.
SPENCER HOUSE, M. Harth, proprietor, cor. S. Illinois and Louisiana.
Spencer House Saloon, M. Harth, proprietor.
Spencer James, (col.,) eating saloon, res. 135 N. Tennessee.
Spencer Milton, (S. & Soewell,) res. 132 E. Market.
Spencer Stephen, wholesale and retail dealer in hats, caps, furs, &c., 32 W. Washington, res. 10 W. Market.
Spencer & Soewell, grocers, 202 E. Washington.
Spicer Bloomfield M., carpenter, res. 26 Michigan Road.
Spielhoff Henry, carpenter, res. 49 McCarty.
Splan James, coal-hauler, res. 57 S. West.
Spol John, peddler, res. E. National Road.
Spongenburg Dedrick, shoemaker, res. 109 E. South.
Spotts William, (Elliott & S.,) res. 6 Fletcher ave.
Sprandel George, res. 106 W. Vermont.
Spratt Mrs. Martha, seamstress, res. 139 N. Alabama.
Spraw George, waiter Spencer House.
Spray Kezug, laborer, res. 83 S. Meridian.
Spring Adam, stone-cutter, res. 48 N. Noble.
Spressee Elizabeth, (wid.,) res. 267 S. Delaware.
Springer David, carpenter, res. 5 Chatham.
Springer Martin B., moulder, res. 178 E. Ohio.
Springsteen Abram, brick-mason, res. 111 E. Market.
Springsteen Jefferson, painter, res. 31 Spring.
Springsteen John, bar-keeper Kentucky Union Saloon, bds. 31 Spring.
Sproule W. R., salesman, 22 S. Illinois, bds. same.
Sprow Mrs. Louisa, washer, res. 82 E. Vermont.
Staats George D., superintendent Odd Fellows' Hall, res. 6 Michigan.
Staats & English, painters, 6 S. Meridian.
Stacy ——, laborer, res. 162 N. Blake.
Stagg C. W., law student, bds. 76 W. New York.
Stagg Mrs., (wid.,) res. 76 W. New York.

350 families in Indianapolis and vicinity use Wheeler & Wilson.

Stahlhuth Chas., carpenter, res. First, bet. Meridian and Illinois.
Staker Franklin, U. S. A., res. cor. Maryland and Delaware.
Stall Jake, butcher, 200 E. Washington.
Stallard Mrs. Clara, res. 151 E. Ohio.
STANAGE S. W., (Cullum & S.,) res. 72 N. Alabama.
Stanage ——, stock-trader, res. N. Mississippi.
STAPP J. H., real estate and general intelligence office, W. Washington, res. Drake's Edition, Illinois, bet. Second and Third.
Stark Gustaves, carpenter, res. 81 Ft. Wayne ave.
Starr James M., plow manufacturer, 86 cor. Tennessee and Washington.
Starr John C., carpenter, res. 101 W. South.
STATE HOUSE SALOON, opp. State House, Doty & Lee, proprietors.
Staten Mrs. Mary A., (wid.,) res. 201 Indiana ave.
Stater Christ., laborer, res. 92 E. McCarty.
Station House, Fred. Scheer, proprietor, Illinois, opp. Depot.
Stature James, laborer, res. 283 S. East.
STAUB JOSEPH, merchant tailor, 69 E. Washington, res. 110 N. Noble.
Staulman Frederick, laborer, res. 119 E. South.
Stauss Gustave, finisher car shop, res. Market, near Cady.
Stebbins John, laborer, res. 141 S. Alabama.
Stedman Dr. E. P., office and res. 40 Massachusetts ave.
Stedman Percival, clerk freight depot I. & C. R. R., res. 117 S. Alabama.
Steegman Charles, grocer, res. 205 S. Delaware.
Steele Wm. H., carpenter, res. 159 N. East.
Steenberg L, bar-keeper Palmer House Saloon, bds. 17 Indiana ave.
Sterling Samuel, clerk, res. 195 S. Illinois.
STERN REV. M. G. J., German Reformed, res. 15 N. Alabama.
STEFFENS C. W. & CO., mathematical, optical and instrument makers, 8 Blackford's Building.
Steffens Charles W., (C. W. S. & Co.,) res. 55 E. Ohio.
Steffens E. F., (C. W. S. & Co.)
Steiner Jacob, res. 156 N. East.
Steinhilber Martin, laborer, res. 149 E. Market.
Steinmann Geo., tailor, res. S. Meridian.
Steinmann John, tailor, S. Meridian, res. same.
Steinnuller Geo., cigar maker, bds. Union Hall.
Steinwenter Andrew, works Rolling Mill, res. 68 E. St. Joseph.
Stelhorn Christian, carpenter, res. 176 N. Noble.

Steller Wm., bar-keeper Washington Hall Saloon, res. 160 Alabama.
Stelzell John, (Henning & S.,) res. 13 North.
Stem Frederick, Justice of the Peace, Judah Block, res. cor. Market and Cady.
Steobler Michael, teamster, res. 45 Spring.
Stephens George W., U. S. service, res. 43 S. Illinois.
Stephens Samuel, U. S. service, res. 43 S. Illinois.
Stephens Levi B., brick-maker, 256 Madison ave.
Steub Joseph, tailor, res. 110 N. Noble.
Stevens Alexander D., printer, Dodd & Co., bds. 78 S. East.
Stevens Geo. P., sutler 39th Indiana volunteers, bds. 95 N. Tennessee.
Stevens Marinda C., (wid.,) res. 78 S. East.
Stevens S. H., salesman Perrine's news stand, Union Depot, bds. 78 S. East.
Stevenson C. S., paymaster U. S. A., res. 94 N. West.
STEVENSON REV. DAVID, presbyterian, res. 248 N. Illinois.
Stevenson John, cooper, res. Missouri, bet. Vermont and Michigan.
Steward Jacob, laborer, res. 344 S. Delaware.
Steward Joshua, laborer, res. Virginia ave.
Steward Andrew, laborer, res. W. Elizabeth.
Stewart Axton, (col.,) cook Palmer House, res. 137 N. Tennessee.
Stewart Charles G., (Bowen, S. & Co.,) res. 99 N. New Jersey.
Stewart J. Austin, clerk I. McTaggart, bds. Morris House, rooms McOuat's Block.
Stewart James, cooper, res. Indiana ave.
Stewart John A., brakeman T. H. R. R., res. 221 N. Mississippi.
Stewart R. R., printer Witness Office, res. 39 W. Ohio.
Stewart Sophia W., res. 99 N. New Jersey.
Stewart T. W., clerk American Express Co., bds. 121 E. Market.
STEWART REV. THOMAS H., baptist, res. Davidson, bet. Vermont and Michigan.
Stewberry Charles, carpenter, res. 201 S. Delaware.
Stibing Philip, laborer, res. 119 N. Noble.
Sticker Fred., painter, res. 32 N. Noble.
Stiedel George, file-maker, res. 55 N. Noble.
Stiematz John, moulder, res. 63 Madison ave.
Stiles John, baker, Union Steam Bakery.
Stillhorn Frederick, carpenter, res. 144 Davidson.
Stilz Daniel, laborer, res. 89 Ft. Wayne ave.
STILZ J. GEORGE, agricultural implement and seed store, 74 E. Washington, res. S. E. of city limits.

For four successive years at the Am. Institute, New York.

Stilz Wm. P., clerk 74 E. Washington, res. S. E. of city limits.
Stine Joseph, shoemaker, res. 63 Madison ave.
Stiffelbean Susan, res. 56 E. St. Marys.
Stirk James, wagon-maker, res. 157 N. Liberty.
Stockwell Daniel, wheat-buyer, res. S. E. Michigan Road.
Stoelting Frederick, grocer, S. W. cor. North and West.
Stoff John, ostler, 10 N. Pennsylvania.
Stoffer John, railroader, res. 54 S. Noble.
Stokely Benjamin, machinist, res. 36 N. Noble.
Stokes Richard, carpenter at Byrkit & Beam's, bds. 74 N. Tennessee.
Stokes Jarvis, baggage master I. & C. R. R., bds. 3 Virginia ave.
Stolger Fred., carpenter, res. 99 Railroad.
Stollberg August, tailor, res. 183 E. Vermont.
Stolte Henry, carpenter, bds. 281 S. Delaware.
Stolte Wm., clerk, res. 281 S. Delaware.
Stone Bertrand, clerk 76 W. Washington, bds. 10 W. Market.
STONE W. O., (V. K. Hendricks & Co.,) bds. 10 W. Market.
Stoneman Wm. C., book-keeper, M. Fitzgibbon & Co., bds. 33 N. Meridian.
Stote H. A., railroader, res. 135 E. McCarty.
Stotle William, salesman 81 and 83 Masonic Hall, res. cor. Delaware and McCarty.
Stott Amos, wood-sawyer, res. 87 Davidson.
Stout Benjamin G., res. 100 N. Tennessee.
Stout Carhart, coal agent, res. 101 S. Tennessee.
Stout David L., bks. Tennessee.
Stout O. B., (O. B. Stout & Bros.,) res. 18 Delaware.
Stout Ira H., U. S. A., res. 15 Hosbrook.
Stout John R., (O. B. S. & Bros.,) bds. 100 N. Tennessee.
STOUT O. B. & BROS., wholesale and retail grocers, 42 W. Washington.
Stout O. H., physician, bds. 100 N. Tennessee.
Stout R. C., (O. B. S. & Bros.,) res. 117 W. Maryland.
Stout Remson, carpenter, res. 101 S. Tennessee.
STOVER REV., United Brethren, res. Orient.
Stowell M. A., (Willard & S.,) bds. Bates House.
Strachan G. C., salesman New York Store, res. 11 W. North.
Stranhenmueller John, baker Union Steam Bakery.
Strange William R., notary public and commissioner of deeds, res. 108 E. Vermont.
Straup F. W., cook Union Hall.
Straup Sol., salesman 19 W. Washington, bds. Morris House.
Strecher Howard, R. R. poster.

The Wheeler & Wilson Hemmer makes hems of any width.

Strecher Mrs. Sarah, res. 84 N. Meridian.
Stretcher Jacob, carpenter, res. 121 Ft. Wayne ave.
Streight A. D., Colonel 51st regiment Indiana Volunteers.
Strickler Samuel, butcher, res. 76 Kentucky ave.
Stringer William H., grocery 77 N. Meridian, res. 27 N. Meridian.
STRINGFELLOW REV. HORACE, Episcopal, res. cor. Circle and Meridian.
Stringfield Woodford, attorney at law, res. 152 N. Pennsylvania.
Strip Peter, railroader, res. 11 E. Georgia.
Strobel J., shoemaker, res. Fourth, bet. Tennessee and Mississippi.
Stropner F., tailor, 15 E. Washington.
Struble John, waiter Spencer House.
Stuck John, farmer, 287 Virginia ave.
Stuck Mathias, laborer, res. 277 S. East.
Stuck Peter, teamster, res. 277 Virginia ave.
Stuck William, laborer, res. 267 S. East.
Stucke Charles, cooper, res. 27 N. Spring.
Stuckmeyer John H., joiner, res. 301 Virginia ave.
Stump Henry, stone mason, res. 228 N. Alabama.
Stumph J. B., city assessor, office Glenns' Block.
STUMPH JOHN, contractor and stone mason, res. 125 Illinois.
Stumpf George, bricklayer, res. 73 Davidson.
Stumpf John H., laborer, res. 148 N. East.
Stundon Thomas, laborer, res. 43 E. Louisiana.
STURDEVANT REV. C., principal M'Lean's seminary, res. same.
Sturdevant Miss C., teacher M'Lean's seminary, bds. same.
Sturm Capt. H., ordinance department, res. 40 N. Mississippi.
Sturm Robert, ordinance department, 40 N. Mississippi.
Suar Albert, watchman Mad. engine house, res. 123 Bluff Road.
Suart John, nursery, 43 McCarty.
Sudbrock Frank, wood sawyer, res. 120 Davidson.
Sueso Charles, tailor, 69 E. Washington.
Sufferen Prof. Wm. J., music teacher, Ætna Building.
Suiney Patrick, laborer, res. 265 S. Delaware.
Sulgrove B. R., editor Daily Journal, res. 87 W. South.
Sulgrove Eli C., harness maker, alley bet. New York and Ohio.
Sulgrove George, bds. 117 N. Alabama.
Sulgrove J. B., saddle and harness maker, 74 E. Washington, res. 72 Kentucky ave.
Sulgrove James W., jr., clerk, 20 W. Washington, bds. 57 W. Maryland.

Upwards of 100 W. & W. Machines in use in Ind'p'lis making army clothing.

Sulgrove James, (S. & Reynolds,) res. 57 Maryland.
Sulgrove John M., saddle and harness maker, 20 W. Washington, bds. 59 Maryland.
Sulgrove Joseph B., harness maker, 44 E. Washington, bds. 59 W. Maryland.
Sulgrove Milton M., saddler, 20 W. Washington, res. cor. Ohio and Illinois.
SULGROVE & REYNOLDS, wholesale and retail dealers in saddlery hardware, harness, &c., 20 W. Washington.
Suitt James B., foreman Washington Foundry.
Sullevan Timothy, laborer, res. 147 E. Ohio.
Sullivan Daniel, shoemaker, res. 48 Indiana ave.
Sullivan Daniel, laborer, res. 12 S. East.
Sullivan John, laborer, res. 5 Bates.
Sullivan James, works at rolling mill, cor. Missouri and Canal.
Sullivan John B., carpenter, res. 40 Pratt.
Sullivan Patrick, railroader, res. Indiana ave.
Sullivan W. H., book-keeper, 74 W. Washington, bds. 125 N. Illinois.
SULLIVAN WILLIAM, justice of the peace, College Hall, res. 107 N. Meridian.
Sully Robert, salesman New York Store, bds. 124 E. Michigan.
Sulzer Mike, salesman 46 E. Washington, bds. Pennsylvania.
Summers Albert B., carpenter, res. N. James.
Summer August, laborer, res. 125 Bluff Road.
Summers Benjamin, res. 16 Georgia.
SUMNER WILLIAM & CO., agents Wheeler & Wilson's sewing machines, 19 W. Washingtan.
Sunderegger Frank, house and sign painter, 69 Madison ave.
Sunfield William, carpenter, res. 109 W. South.
Sunnyfield Wm., teamster, res. 36 S. Noble.
Sure Lewis, saw filer, E. Wyoming.
SUTHERLAND JAS., sec'y White River Valley Ins. Co., office 19 W. Washington, bds. Morris House.
Sutherland J. W., blacksmith, Western Machine Works, res. 38 S. Noble.
Supthan J., works Geisendorff's Store, res. 80 W. Georgia.
Sutro Mrs. Elizabeth, res. 32 N. Spring.
Sutton Joseph, plasterer, res. 136 N. Alabama.
Swagert Peter, carpenter, res. 92 N. East.
Swain James, res. 29 N. Illinois.
Swanke Wm. B., cooper, res. 90 S. East.
Sweed H. A., (col.,) barber, bds. Little's Hotel.
Sweeny John, foreman cigar store, res. 18 N. Illinois.

First Premium awarded the Wheeler & Wilson Sewing Machine for three

Sweet John, tailor for Staub, 59 E. Washington, bds. 28 Kentucky ave.
Sweetser James N., attorney at law, 19½ E. Washington, res. 50 Pennsylvania.
Sweinhart Augustus, shoemaker for J. K. Sharpe.
Sweinhart Edmond, shoemaker, res. 68 E. St. Mary's.
Sweinhart Wm., cutter for J. P. Gramling, res. 165 N. Alabama.
Swico Charles, laborer, res. 87 Union.
Swier Charles, laborer, res. 25 Chatham.
Swift Martin, cash boy, 70 E. Washington, bds. 51 N. Liberty.
Swift Mrs. Mary, res. 52 N. Liberty.
Swincharte Amos, tinner, res. 84 N. Alabama.
Swinebacke Jacob, butcher, res. 241 S. Delaware.
Swomine Charles, drayman, res. 87 Bluff Road.
Syerup Henry, grocer, 119 N. East, res. same.
Sym J., engineer Western Machine Works.
Symons Henry W., carpenter, res. 38 E. St. Clair.

T

Taffe George, policeman, res. 122 N. East.
Taggart Samuel, mill-wright, office 98 S. Delaware, res. 64 Mississippi.
Talbot John M., res. 66 N. Tennessee.
Talbot Richard L., (Alford, Mills & Co.,) res. 54 W. Vermont.
TALBOTT JOHN T., (Dodd, T. & Parsons,) bds. Palmer House.
Talbott R. C., grocery, 101 W. Washington, res. 161 W. Vermont.
Talbott W. H., (W. H. T. & Co.,) res. cor. Meridian and Ohio.
Talbott W. H. & Co., wholesale and retail dealers in watches, jewelry, silverware, &c., 24 E. Washington.
Talkington Robert, brick-mason, res. cor. New York and Railroad.
Tallett Charles, saddler, bds. Washington.
Tarkington John S., (Newcomb & T.,) res. 35 E. Ohio.
TARLTON & KEEN, wholesale and retail grocers, and dealers in country produce, 8 S. Meridian.
Tarlton J. A., (T. & Keen,) res. cor. Maryland and Illinois.
Tarters James, laborer, Rolling Mill, res. bet. Madison ave. and Union.
Tary James, laborer, res. 101 E. Louisiana.
Tansey Mrs. Esther, res. 72 W. Michigan.

Tapking Frederick H., (T. & Becker,) res. Liberty, bet. Vermont and Michigan.
/TAPKING & BECKER, merchant tailors and clothiers, 63 E. Washington.
/Tapting John, cabinet maker, res. 65 N. New Jersey.
TATUM REV. DAVID, Friends' Society, cor. East and Cherry.
Taylor Calvin, (T. & T.,) res. 175 Massachusetts ave.
Taylor D. M., deputy auditor, bds. Barbour House.
Taylor Israel, salesman 75 W. Washington, res. 57 Massachusetts ave.
Taylor Jesse, res. 154 N. Delaware.
Taylor N. B., (T. & T.,) res 109 N. Alabama.
Taylor Mary, (wid.,) dress maker, res. 196 N. Alabama.
Taylor Robert A., brick-layer, res. 175 Massachusetts ave.
Taylor Robert R., carpenter, res. Market, opp. Fourth Ward School House.
Taylor Thos. W., painter, res. 112 N. Mississippi.
Taylor W. H., tinner, 182 E. Washington, res. 121 E. Market.
Taylor & Taylor, attorneys at law, 30½ W. Washington.
Teal N., physician and surgeon, 5 Blake's Building, res. N. Illinois.
Teals Robert M., manufacturer of boots and shoes, 7 N. Meridian, bds. cor. Market and Circle.
Tearcy Mrs. Pamilla, (wid.,) W. Indianapolis.
Tearney Martin, blacksmith, res. 53 S. New Jersey.
Teckenbrock Christian, blacksmith, res. Maryland, bet. Delaware and Alabama.
Teckenbrock Wm. H., laborer, res. 155 S. Alabama.
Teeney Abraham, cooper, res. 35 S. Liberty.
Teepe Harman, striker Washington Foundry, res. Virginia ave.
Teeple Henry, carpenter, res. S. E. Michigan Road.
Telegraph Restaurant, 12 opp. Union Depot, H. Walls, proprietor.
Telken H. G., cigar maker, bds. 41 Spring.
Tellcamp John, soldier, res. 150 S. New Jersey.
Temple Thomas, works 22 Kentucky ave., bds. 28 Kentucky ave.
TenEyck J. A., (J. A. & R. F. T.,) res. California, bet. New York and Vermont.
TenEyck J. A. & R. F., boot and shoemakers, 260 W. Washington.
TenEyck John, shoemaker, res. 86 Indiana ave.
TenEyck Nelson, shoemaker, res. cor. Maryland and California.
TenEyck R. F., (J. A. & R. F. T.,) res. California, bet. New York and Vermont.

81,000 Wheeler & Wilson's Sewing Machines in use in this country.

SINGER'S
Letter A Machine,

Is the best Machine in the World for Family Sewing and Light Manufacturing Purposes.

Price, [with Hemmer and beautifully ornamented,] **$50.**

We would ask for our Letter "A" Machines, the special attention of Vest Makers and Dress Makers, and all those who want Machines for light manufacturing purposes. They embody the principles of the Manufacturing Machines, making, like them, the interlocked stitch, and are destined to be as celebrated for family Sewing and light manufacturing purposes as our Manufacturing Machines are for manufacturing purposes in general.

Family Sewing Machines are valuable in proportion to to the number of things they dan do well. See what ours can do before making a purchase.

There is no doubt as to the value of our Machines for manufacturing purposes, but it is only of late that the public began to learn that the essential elements of a machine best adapted to the heaviest work, would also be the elements to be embodied in a Family Machine. It is now well understood that our Letter "A" Machine is the only Family Machine yet offered to the public which has simplicity, rapidity, durability, and certainty of correct action. While, as a general thing, the sewing-machine people are candid enough to acknowledge that our machines are unequalled for manufacturing purposes, they are almost sure to assert, in the same breath, that Singer's Letter "A," or Family Machines, are not as good as theirs! This is a mere trick of the trade, and we confidently invite those interested in the subject to examine for themselves, and see what our Letter "A" Family Machines, with all the recent improvements, are capable of doing. While they will sew the most delicate material to perfection, as already stated, they are also adapted to light manufacturing purposes, and this, be it remembered, can not be said of any of the other Family Machines yet offered to the Public.

Office 3 Odd Fellows' Hall,
INDIANAPOLIS.

Singer's Hemmer WILL FELL. Do not be deceived. Come and see it. [OVER.]

The Wheeler & Wilson Hemmer is the only Hemmer that will Fell.

GREAT REDUCTION IN THE PRICES
OF
SINGER & CO.'S
STANDARD MACHINES,

Well known to be the best for Manufacturing Purposes:

No. 1, Shuttle Machine, formerly sold at $90, - - Reduced to - - $70.
No. 2, "   "   formerly sold at $100, - - Reduced to - - 75.

The Nos. 1 and 2 Machines are of great capacity and application for manufacturing purposes.

Our No. 3 Machines are especially adapted to all kinds of light and heavy leather work, in carriage trimming, boot and shoe making, harness making, etc., etc. They are of extra size, with an arm long enough to take under it and stitch the largest sized dashes. There is scarcely any part of a Trimmers' stitching that cannot be better done with them than by hand; so, too, the saving of time and labor is very great. The table of these machines is 24 inches long, and the shuttle will hold six times as much thread as the shuttle of those used for tailoring purposes. The large machines work as fast as small ones.

We have always on hand, Binding Gauges, Silk Twist, Linen and Cotton Thread on spools, Best Machine Oil in Bottles, etc., etc.

We manufacture our own Needles, and would warn all persons using our machines not to buy any others. We know that there are needles sold of the most inferior quality, at higher prices than we charge for the best. The needles sold by us are manufactured especially for our machines. A bad needle may render the working of the best machine almost useless. Our customers may rest assured that all our Branch Offices are furnished with the "genuine article."

In case of small purchases, the money may be sent in postage stamps, or bank notes.

☞ Correspondents will please write their names distinctly. It is all important that we should, in each case, know the Post Office, County, and State.

☞ All persons requiring information about Sewing Machines, their sizes, prices, working capacities, and the best methods of purchasing, can obtain it by sending to us, or any of our Branch Offices for a copy of

"I. M. Singer & Co.'s Gazette,"

Which is a beautiful Pictorial Paper entirely devoted to the subject.—It will be sent gratis.

☞ We have made the above reduction in prices with the two-fold view of benefiting the public and ourselves. The public have been swindled by spurious machines made in imitation of ours. The metal in them, from the iron casting to the smallest piece, is of poor quality. Their makers have not the means to do their work well. They are hid away in secret places, where it would be impossible to have at their command the proper mechanical appliances. It is only by doing a great business, and having extensive manufacturing establishments, that good machines can be made at moderate prices. The best designed machines, badly made, are always liable to get out of order, and are sure to cost considerable trouble and money to keep them in repair.

The qualities to be looked for in a machine, are: certainty of correct action at all rates of speed, simplicity of construction, great durability, and rapidity of operation, with the least labor. Machines to combine these essential qualities, must be made of the best metal and finished to perfection. We have the ways and means, on a grand scale, to do this.

The purchasers of machines, whose daily bread it may concern, will find that those having the above qualities not only work well at rapid as well as slow rates of speed, but last long in the finest possible working order. Our machines, AS MADE BY US, will earn more money with less labor than any others, whether in imitation of ours or not. In fact, they are cheaper than any other machines as a gift.

I. M. SINGER & CO.,
458 Broadway, New York.

Indianapolis Office, 3 Odd Fellows' Hall,
WASHINGTON ST.

☞ LOCAL AGENTS WANTED.

A Wheeler & Wilson Sewing Machine will last a life-time.

Tennis Wm. H., salesman, Bee-Hive, res. 95 Tennessee.
Terhune Mrs. M. A., seamstress, res. 151 N. Liberty.
Terrell W. H. H., Military Secretary to Governor Morton, bds. Bates House.
TERRE HAUTE & RICHMOND R. R., Engine House, Louisiana, near West.
TERRE HAUTE & RICHMOND R. R., Freight Office, Louisiana, bet. Tennessee and Mississippi.
Tetaz Henry L., grocer, 162 E. Market.
Thalman Isaac, laborer, res. 180 E. Ohio.
Thalman Isaac, book-keeper, Hoosier Woolen Factory, res. Washington.
Thalman John, baker, 27 N. Alabama, res. West, cor. Alabama and Ohio.
Thatcher Amos, teamster, res. 15 Georgia.
Thayer George, clerk 30 W. Washington.
Thayer S., salesman 8 W. Washington, res. 145 Market.
Thayer Semira, boarding house, res. 28 Benton.
Theodore Thomas, bricklayer, res. 125 N. East.
Theyer Daniel, editor Free Press, res. 145 and 147 E. Market.
Thistler Nicholas, currier, res. 12 McCarty.
Thistlethwait Rachael, (wid.,) res. 149 Virginia ave.
Thomas Charles, clerk 31 W. Washington, bds. 31 N. Noble.
Thomas Edward, baggage master, res. 70 Bluff Road.
Thomas George, laborer, res. 61 N. Noble.
Thomas Henry, dairy-man, near University.
Thomas L., teamster, W. Indianapolis.
Thomas Louis L., carpenter, res. 110 N. Mississippi.
Thomas M., Sister of Providence, cor. Georgia and Tennessee.
Thomas Mrs. M. J., (Mrs. M. J. T. & Co.,) 46 W. Washington.
Thomas Mrs. M. J. & Co., wholesale and retail dealers in millinery and fancy goods, 46 W. Washington.
Thomas John, manager of Rolling Mill, res. 57 W. South.
Thompson Mrs., physician, res. 74 N. Illinois.
Thompson Daniel J., sergeant 11th regiment Indiana volunteers, res. 128 N. Noble.
Thompson Eli, carpenter, res. 133 W. New York.
THOMPSON H., bakery, 4 S. Meridian, res. same.
Thompson Capt. James, 17th regiment Indiana volunteers.
Thompson James C., conductor Peru R. R., bds. Palmer House.
Thompson John, huckster, res. 51 Huron.
THOMPSON MARY, (wid.,) dry goods and groceries, cor. Delaware and South, res. in rear.

The Wheeler & Wilson Hemmer is the only Hemmer that will Fell.

Thompson Milton, carpenter, res. 59 E. St. Mary.
Thompson Richard M., machinist I. & C. R. R. shop, res. 167 S. Noble.
Thompson Wm. C., physician, U. S. A.
Thomson Mrs. Anne, (Mrs. A. T. & Son,) res. Henry.
THOMSON MRS. ANNE & SON, books, periodicals, newspapers, &c., Pennsylvania, S. of Postoffice.
Thomson Wm., (Mrs. A. T. & Son,) bds. Henry.
Thoms F., (Spiegel, T. & Co.,) res. 29 N. Liberty.
Thornberry Wm., res. 134 N. Alabama.
Thorne John, butcher, res. 101 E. Georgia.
Thornly Orian, machinist, res. 35 McCarty.
Thorp Caliph, brick-maker and mason, res. 10 Michigan Road.
Thorpe John D., deputy sheriff, office Court House, res. 39 E. Market.
Tiblei Charles, saloon, res. 116 S. Noble.
Ticke Henry, in Lawrenceburg car shop, res. S. E. Michigan.
Tilford A. L., salesman Spiegel, Thoms & Co., res. 192 N. Mississippi.
Tilford J. M., pres't Indianapolis Journal Co., res. 67 N. Meridian.
Tilford J. W., mailing clerk at Journal Office, bds. Macy House.
Tilly Gilbert, stone cutter for Jason Dame, res. Delaware, near South.
Tilly Joseph, retired druggist, res. 128 S. Delaware.
Tilman Mrs. E., (col.,) washer, res. 143 N. Tennessee.
Timmermann H., street contractor, res. 153 Railroad.
TINDALL REV. GEO. P., presbyterian, res. 87 N. Pennsylvania.
Tindall Henry, res. 172 N. Tennessee.
Tindall Mrs. J. M., (wid.,) bds. 168 N. Tennessee.
Tindall N., cigars and tobacco, 12 N. Pennsylvania, res. 168 N. Tennessee.
Tine Gotib, drayman, res. N. bet. St. Clair and St. Joseph.
Tiney Frederick, laborer, res. 127 E. New York.
Tinke J. F., machinist, res. 31 McCarty.
Tisdale Walker H., salesman New York Store, res. 17 Massachusetts ave.
Tisler N., currier for John Fishback.
Titcomb Daniel, clerk, res. 48 E. Market.
Tittman Alex., machinist, res. Kentucky ave.
Toley Murty, laborer, res. 208 S. Delaware, in rear.
Todd Chas. W., professor McLean's Seminary, res. 132 N. Tennessee.
Todd B. M., (T. & Lindenbower,) res. 203 E. St. Clair.

Todd Kate, (wid.,) boarding, 39 W. Vermont.
Todd & Lindenbower, real estate agents, 6 S. Pennsylvania.
Tomlinson J. M., (T. & Cox,) bds. cor. Meridian and St. Clair.
Tomlinson S. D., res. 11 W. Ohio.
Tomlinson & Cox, City drug store, 18 E. Washington.
Tompkins William, boss carder Ohio Premium Woolen Factory.
Toohey M. A., clerk 39 W. Washington, bds. with Mrs. Simpson.
Toole Martin, laborer, res. 177 S. East.
Toolwater Charles, tinner, 62 E. Washington.
Topp Frank, shoemaker, 7 N. Meridian.
Torbett Oliver B., attorney at law, office Temperance Hall.
Torrel Wm., at Bates House, res. 184 S. East.
Totton Stewart, salesman New York Store, bds. Morris House.
Touson James, machinist, res. 111 S. New Jersey.
Tousey Eliza, res. 31 N. Ellsworth.
TOUSEY GEO., pres't Branch of the Bank of the State of Indiana, res. 31 N. Delaware.
Tousey Oliver, (T. & Byram,) res. 39 N. Meridian.
Tousey Zalman, salesman 70 E. Washington, res. 12 W. New York.
TOUSEY & BYRAM, wholesale and retail dry goods, &c., 70 E. Washington.
Tout Henry F., brick mason, res. 215 N. Alabama.
Tout Isaac, brick mason, res. Illinois, cor. Second.
Tout Z. F., with J. W. Copeland.
Towe & Sons, carpenters, 18 S. N. Jersey, res. 148 E. North.
Townsend J. M., auditor Bellefontaine R. R., res. 20 N. Meridian.
Traucemenns John, cigar maker, 130 S. Delaware.
Trask George K., stump puller, res. 44 Pratt.
Traub Charles, varnisher, Speigel, Thoms & Co., res. N. Old Bellefontaine car shop.
Traub Israel, painter, res. 214 N. Alabama.
Traub John, laborer, res. 152 E. Market.
Traver G. M., salesman Bee-Hive Store, res. 32 Meridian.
Travis Albert, teamster, res. 130 E. North.
Trayser Geo., piano manufacturer, res. 98 W. Maryland.
Treundelman Henry, laborer, res. 60 Huron.
Trester John, hackman, res. 21 N. Ellsworth.
Treter John, stone mason, res. 174 N. East.
Treub Conrad, well digger, res. 117 Ft. Wayne ave.
Trimble Joseph P., business ag't Indiana American and notary public, res. 91 N. Alabama.

Successive years at Mechanic's Institute, Cincinnati.

Trindle Samuel, conductor Terre Haute R. R., bds. 107 S. Tennessee.
Trout John, baker for H. M. Haynes.
Trucksess John, blacksmith, res. 62 Kentucky ave.
Trump Jacob, brick layer, res. 103 N. Noble.
Trust J., salesman. 4 W. Washington, bds. Ohio.
Tudor Mrs. Hattie, dress maker, res. 53 N. East.
Tull Thomas, res. 119 S. New Jersey.
Tully House, S. Illinois, near Union Depot, William Tully, Agent.
Tully William, agent Tully House, S. Illinois, near Union Depot.
Tupp Charley, carpenter, res. 86 Huron.
Turner A., (col.,) barber, 15½ W. Washington, res. Tennessee, cor. Georgia.
Turner Mrs. Ann, (col.,) res. North, bet. Blackford and California.
Turner C., laborer, res. S. E. Michigan Road.
Turner James, township trustee, office Court House, res. 121 S. Alabama.
Turner Lewis, res. 161 S. Delaware.
Turner William, brick-layer, res. 65 E. Merrill.
Turner William H., (Grosvenor & T.,) res. 270 N. Illinois.
Turquin Martin, res. 138 E. New York.
Tutewiler Charles, tinsmith, bds. 65 Massachusetts ave.
Tutewiler Henry, with J. W. Adams, boots and shoes, 53 W. Washington, bds. 65 Massachusetts ave.
Tutewiler John W., with Geisendorff & Co., 63 W. Washington, bds. 65 Massachusetts ave.
Tuttle B. F., wholesale and retail grocer, 27 W. Washington, res. 83 Meridian.
Tuttle Dennis, res. 7 Madison ave.
Tuttle G. P., salesman 27 W. Washington, bds. with Mrs. Kellogg.
TYLER LEWIS H., proprietor Bee-Hive dry goods store, bds. 95 Tennessee.
Tyler Mrs. R. D., boarding house, 95 N. Tennessee.
Tyner Charles, shoemaker, bds. 50 N. Liberty.
Tyre George, Captain in Railroad Regiment, res. 105 Virginia ave.

U

Uhl T., cigar maker. 15 E. Washington, bds. Spencer House.
Uhlendorff George, bar-keeper Little's Hotel Saloon.
Umbersall John, deputy marshal, res. 147 S. Alabama.

A Wheeler & Wilson Sewing Machine with Hemmer, for $50.

Underhill Robert F., proprietor Underhill's flouring mill, S. part of city, near Bluff Road, res. 43 E. Michigan.
United States Arsenal, W. Washington, Capt. H. Sturm, superintendent.
UNITED STATES EXPRESS COMPANY, cor. Meridian and Washington, J. Butterfield, agent.
United States Forage Depot, 150 S. Delaware.
United States Warehouse, cor. Meridian and Louisiana, J. W. Bryson, superintendent.
Union Engine House, 5 South.
UNION HALL, Matthew Emmenegger, proprietor, 107, 109, 111 and 113 E. Washington.
UNION HOUSE, Stephen Mattler, proprietor, cor. Illinois and South.
Union Railway Company, office Union Depot.
UNION STEAM BAKERY, A. & J. Metzger, proprietors, 11 N. Pennsylvania.
Unrisan J. A., laborer, res. E. Wyoming.
Unthank Wm., saddler, 34 W. Washington.
UPFOLD GEORGE, Rt. Rev. Bishop, Protestant Episcopal Church, res. 51 N. Tennessee.
Uphaus Henry, shoe shop, 188 S. Delaware, res. in rear.

V

Vahle Henry, foundryman, 56 South.
Vajen Charles D., Quartermaster Camp Morton, bds. Pyle House.
Vajen J. H., wholesale and retail hardware, &c., 21 W. Washinhton, res. 94 S. Illinois.
Valner Conrad, laborer, res. 89 Bluff Road.
Vanantwerp George W., clerk, res. 22 N. Liberty.
Vanarmaker Adam, tailor, res. 7 Willard.
Vanbergen Wm., bds. 128 N. Tennessee.
Vanbergen Wm. H., carpenter, res. 45 W. Michigan.
Vanblaricum Benjamin, fisherman, res. W. Indianapolis.
Vanblaricum Jesse, wagon maker, res. 177 W. Washington.
Vanblaricum Michael, laborer, W. Indianapolis.
Vanblaricum Wm. J., teamster, res. 49 W. South.
Vancomp Gilbert, res. 110 W. Ohio.
Vance Lawrence M., res. E. Washington, cor. Cady.
Vance Thomas P., railroader, res. 131 N. Liberty.
Vance Thomas, cabinet-maker, res. bet. Liberty and Noble.
Vandegrift Benj., printer, res. 85 N. Mississippi.
Vandegrift Mrs. Charlotte, (wid.,) res. 11 W. St. Clair.
Vandegrift Harry, res. 33 Kentucky ave.
Vandegrift J. A., trunk maker, bds. 11 W. St. Clair.

Vandegrift W. H., telegraph messenger, bds. 33 Kentucky ave.
Van Deusen C., railroader, res. 24 N. Liberty.
VAN HOUTEN & GRAHAM, wholesale and retail grocers, 34 N. Illinois.
Vanlaningham Lemuel, sec'y Indianapolis Gas Light and Coke Co., res. 65 N. Alabama.
Vanlaningham Menervie, res. 198 N. New Jersey.
Vannide Philip, laborer, res. 197 N. Noble.
Vanriper John H., agent, res. 53 N. New Jersey.
Vanslack Nathan, laborer, W. Indianapolis.
Varcharld Nicholas, laborer, res. 23 E. Georgia.
Varus Jane, (wid.,) res. 20 S. East.
Vater Mrs. Eleanor P., res. 41 W. Walnut.
Vater Thos. J., U. S. Surveyor, res. 45 W. Walnut.
Vater Septimius, printer, bds. 41 W. Walnut.
Vatter Marion, machinist, res. 18 Union.
Vaugh Jacob M., carpenter, res. 152 N. Mississippi.
Veach Nelson, carpenter, res. 132 E. St. Clair.
Verandah Saloon, John Bussey prop'r, opp. Union Depot.
Vestal Mrs. Sophia, (col.,) washer, Michigan, bet. Missouri and West.
Vetter A., manufacturer and dealer in furniture, 97 E. Washington, res. 168 Pennsylvania.
Vetter John, cabinet-maker, res. 185 S. Pennsylvania, shop in rear.
Vick Harvey, (col.,) whitewasher, res. 138 W. Ohio.
VICKERS W. B., wholesale and retail druggist, Odd Fellows' Hall, res. 6 Alvord's Block, S. Pennsylvania.
Victor Mrs. Catharine, sewing, res. 89 N. Alabama.
Victor Louis, grocer, res. 53 N. Noble.
Vigo Henry, laborer, res. 13 E. Georgia.
Vincent Felix A., actor at Metropolitan Hall.
Vincent George D., carpenter, res. 124 Davidson.
Vincent Wm. H., carpenter, res. 91 Davidson.
Vinnedge J. A., groceries and provisions, 8 N. Pennsylvania, res. 85 S. Pennsylvania.
Vinnedge J. D., (Jones, V. & Co.,) res. 41 E. Washington.
Vinton Almus E., (Hasselman & V.,) res. 30 N. Pennsylvania.
Virt John W., harness maker, 44 E. Washington.
Visnerr Leonard, clock maker, res. 64 Davidson.
Vœgtle Jacob, stoves and Tinware, 177 E. Washington, res. same.
Vogel Henry, carpenter, res. E. Market.
Vogt Bernard, musician, res. 108 N. Noble.
Voight ——, laborer, res. S. E. Michigan Road.
Voight David, harness maker, res. Dennison, cor. Leonard.

Voight Henry, salesman 133 E. Washington, res. 113 Michigan.
Voight H. L., (H. L. V. & Co.,) res. 67 S. Illinois.
VOIGHT H. L. & CO., confectioners, 67 S. Illinois.
Voldt Albert, clerk, bds. 24 E. Georgia.
Vollinger Joseph, clerk Spencer House.
Volman Garret, wood sawyer, res. 340 S. Delaware.
Volmer Charles, wholesale wines and liquors, 65 W. Washington, res. 141 N. Noble.
Volmer Otto P., distiller, 159 E. St. Clair, res. same.
Volz Eliza, res. 230 N. New Jersey.
Volz John W., works Rolling Mill, bds. 230 N. New Jersey.
Vonderseir John, laborer, res. 25 S. Illinois.
VONNEGUT CLEMENS, dealer in foreign and domestic hardware, leather, &c., 142 E. Washington, res. same.
Voorhees A. L., res. 97 N. Illinois.
Voorhees Jacob, plasterer, res. Ft. Wayne ave., near Corporation line.

W

Wachter Lawrence, shoemaker, res. 131 Bluff Road, in rear.
Waddell Miss Eliza, dress maker, res. 7 E. North.
Waddell John, salesman German Dry Goods Store.
Wade John R., bar-keeper 32 S. Illinois.
Wagner James, shoemaker, res. S. Delaware.
Wagner Frank, laborer, res. 193 S. Pennsylvania.
Wagner Henry, miller, bds. Michigan, bet. New Jersey and East.
Wagoner Henry, cooper, res. 110 E. McCarty.
Wagoner John, laborer, res. W. Indianapolis.
Waidigh John, sup't Widow and Orphan Asylum.
Wainright Samuel, tinner, res. 32 N. Meridian.
Walber Jake, cigar maker, bds. Spencer House.
Walden Elijah, (col.,) laborer, res. Mississippi, bet. First and Second.
Walden Wm., (col.,) white-washer, res. 131 N. West.
Walden Wm., works Rolling Mill, res. cor. West and Canal.
Waldo E. G. B., real estate agent and notary public, 38½ W. Washington.
Waldo Mrs. Mary, res. 63 W. Louisiana.
Waldo Azer, works for Root, Bennet & Co., res. Mississippi, bet. Louisiana and South.
Waldo Geo., tinner, Root, Bennet & Co., bds. Mississippi, bet. Louisiana and South.
Waldo Robert, clerk, 66 E. Washington, bds. Mississippi, bet. Louisiana and South.

Waldo William, U. S. A., bds. Mississippi, bet. Louisiana and South.
Walk Anthony, shoemaker, res. 150 E. Market.
Walk Julius, watchmaker, under Spencer House.
WALK LOUIS, boarding house, 14 W. Georgia.
Walker L., shoemaker, res. Bluff Road.
Walker W. F., pruning and carpentering, res. 188 Ind. ave.
Walker Thomas, salesman 3 W. Washington, bds. Macy House.
Walkup A. E., conductor Jeffersonville R. R., bds. Palmer House.
Wall Thomas, U. S. A., res. N. Mississippi.
WALLACE ALEX. G., county recorder, office County Building, res. 86 E. Market.
WALLACE ANDREW, wholesale grocer and commission merchant, cor. Virginia ave., and Delaware, res. 34 N. Delaware.
Wallace Mrs. Beuleh, dress-maker, res. 79 Massachusetts ave.
Wallace George C., assistant county recorder, bds. 86 E. Market.
Wallace George E., clerk and book-keeper for Andrew Wallace, res. 35 N. Alabama.
WALLACE JAMES, copyist, res. 176 N. New Jersey.
WALLACE J. ANDY, deputy sheriff, res. 18 N. Alabama.
Wallace Samuel, brick-layer, res. 176 N. New Jersey.
WALLACE WILLIAM, clerk Circuit and Common Pleas Courts, office Court House, res. 121 N. Delaware.
Wallace William, works Lawrenceburg car shop, res. 43 Hosbrook.
WALLACE WILLIAM JOHN, county sheriff, opp. county office building, res. 18 N. Alabama.
Wallace Mrs. Zerelda, res. 139, cor. Massachusetts ave. and New Jersey.
Waller B., boot and shoemaker, 150 W. Washington, res. same.
Waller John, blacksmith, res. 32 S. Liberty.
Waller Mrs. Louisa, boarding house, res. 31 Indiana ave.
WALLICK JOHN F., manager Western Union Telegraph Company, 1 N. Meridian, bds. 10 W. Market.
Wallick Samuel, bds. 10 W. Market.
Wallingford Mrs. Catherine, res. 138 N. East.
Walls H., Telegraph Restaurant, 12 opp Union Depot, res. same.
Wally Matthew, blacksmith, bds. 26 Massachusetts ave.
Walmsley John, tailor, res. 58 E. Michigan.
Walpole Bryan C., notary public, 2 second floor old Sentinel Building, res. 156 N. Illinois.

WALPOLE R. L., (T. D. & R. L. W.,) res. cor. Vermont and Meridian.
WALPOLE THOS. D., (T. D. & R. L. W.,) res. 156 N. Illinois.
WALPOLE T. D. & R. L., attorneys at law, 2d floor old Sentinel building.
Walsh Honora, (wid.,) res. 17 S. Delaware.
Walsh Maurice, works in Quartermaster's Department, res. 194 S. Delaware.
Walsh Wm., laborer, res. 71 Madison ave.
Walstetter G., grocery, W. Washington, near bridge, res. same.
Walters Andrew, teamster, res. Harrison E. of Pine.
Walton Wm. P., distiller, res. 19 Kentucky ave.
Waltzman Fred., cook at Oriental House.
Wampner Henry, works Lawrenceburg car shop, res. 29 Harrison.
Wainwright Samuel, stoves and tinware, 11 S. Illinois, res. cor. New York and Meridian.
Wanderly Henry, brick mason, res. Davidson, bet. Ohio and Market.
Wands A., boot and shoemaker, 12 S. Meridian, res. 131 N. Pennsylvania.
Wanger Wm., painter, res. 215 N. New Jersey.
Wanpaner A. F., teamster, res. 15 Harrison.
Wands John, laborer, res. cor. McCarty and Greer.
Wands Robert, machinist, res. Greer near McCarty.
Warren Chas. E., bds. Ohio House.
Ward D. L., messenger American Express Co., bds. Palmer House.
Ward Ed., ostler Johnston's livery stable.
Ward Gabriel, res. 262 Indiana ave.
Ward Homer, conductor B. & I. R. R., bds. Bates House.
Ward John, laborer, res. 181 S. New Jersey.
Ward John, laborer, res. Elizabeth.
Ward John, laborer, res. 105 Madison ave.
Wardell Miss M., teacher McLean's Seminary, bds. same.
Ware R., conductor, res. 75 W. South.
Warner Chas., wholesale liquor dealer, res. 66 N. Mississippi.
Warner Charles G., printer Sentinel office, res. cor. Indiana ave. and Tennessee.
Warner Edwin R., bricklayer, res. 180 N. East.
Warner Geo., bar-keeper Kansas eating saloon, bds. same.
Warner A. George, laborer, res. 109 McCarty.
Warner Mrs. Sarah, tailoress, res. 178 N. East.
Warren Geo. S., bds. Mrs. Kinder.
Warweg Henry, wood chopper, res. 25 Harrison.

15

INDIANAPOLIS

Pure Coin Silver Ware,

All Styles and Varieties kept on hand,

AND MADE TO ORDER ON SHORT NOTICE.

McLENE'S JEWELRY STORE IN THE BATES HOUSE Is the Place for Bargains in WATCHES, JEWELRY OR SILVERWARE.

AGENCY FOR THE SALE OF THE AMERICAN WATCH. In all Styles, at Manufacturers' Prices.

Clocks, Canes, Military Goods, AND GAS FIXTURES.

FINE TABLE AND POCKET CUTLERY,

ENGRAVING
Done in the Finest Style.

WATCHES, CLOCKS AND JEWELRY,
Repaired on short notice and in the best manner.

Wheeler & Wilson's Sewing Machines have been awarded the First Premium

WASHINGTON FOUNDRY MACHINE SHOP, Hasselman & Vinton, proprietors, opp. Union Depot.
Washington Hall, 78 Washington.
Washington House, 83 South Meridian.
Washington James, salesman New York store, res. New York.
Wasmuth Louis, tailor, 39 E. Washington, res. New Jersey.
Wasson J. H., agent Ohio River Salt Co., N. W. cor. Washington and Meridian.
Waters Wm. W., dealer in brick, res. 73 W. South.
Watjen H. J., clerk, 22 W. Washington, bds. 102 N. Illinois.
Waters John G., city clerk, office Glenns' Block, res. 110 E. Market.
Waters Patrick, shoemaker, res. 82 Meridian.
Watson J. M., machinist, Lawrenceburgh car shop, res. E. National Road.
Watson J. P., printer Wm. Sheets, res. cor. Maryland and Missouri.
Watson Samuel, book-keeper, res. W. Maryland.
Watson Samuel W., book-keeper Harrison's bank, res. 138 N. Illinois.
Watson Wm., tinner Root, Bennett & Co.
Watson Wm. P., clerk General Ticket Office Indiana Cent. R. R., bds. 139 N. New Jersey.
Way Truman, road master Peru & Ind. R. R., res. 115 E. McCarty.
Wayman A., blacksmith, res. 160 S. East.
Weakley J. A., tinner, 71 E. Washington, res. 97 W. New York.
Wear James W., marble dealer, res. 86 S. East.
Weasthesteer John, American Saloon, 25 S. Meridian, res. same.
Weaver C. C., clerk 6 Bates House, bds. 147 N. Illinois.
Weaver E. A., harness maker, 20 W. Washington, res. 172 S. Alabama.
Weaver Frederick, laborer, res. 173 Railroad.
Weaver William H., (W. & Williams,) res. 147 N. Illinois.
WEAVER & WILLIAMS,, undertakers 72 W. Washington.
Webb Thomas B., (Cady & Co.,) bds. Oriental House.
Webber Henry, laborer, res. 250 S. Pennsylvania, in rear.
Webber John G., tailor, 84 E. Washington.
Webster G. S., machinist, 262 W. Washington, res. 114 W. Vermont.
Webster G. C., clerk 22 S. Meridian, res. Maryland, bet. Pennsylvania and Virginia ave.
Webster Geo. C. jr., clerk 22 S. Meridian, bds. Maryland.
Webster J. H., fireman, res. 43 Massachusetts ave.
Wechsler David, butcher, 128 N. Alabama, res. same.

Weekley Patrick, works Rolling Mill, bds. 188 S. Tennessee.
Weeks Richard, laborer, res. 17 S. Alabama.
Weeks W. H., (W. & Cox,) bds. Mrs. Kinder.
WEEKS & COX, Metropolitan Photograph, Daguerreotype, and Ambrotype Gallery, College Hall.
WEKLE LUKAS, boots and shoes, 179 E. Washington, res. same.
Weghorst Henry, gardener, S. E. of Corporation Line.
Wehn Christian, tanner, res. 234 Madison ave., in rear.
Weeble John Edward, barber, Bates House Hair Dressing Saloon, res. 188 N. Illinois.
Weigle Gotleib, currier, res. 65 N. Noble.
Weikert John, salesman 21 W. Washington, res. 118 N. Alabama.
Weiland Wm., laborer, res. 69 Bluff Road.
Weilenmann Jacob, laborer, res. John, near Winston.
Weir J. W., (W. & Bro.,) res. 86 East.
Weir Wm., (W. & Bro.,) bds. Macy House.
Weir & Bro., City Marble Works, 13 Virginia ave.
Weise John, brick-layer, res. St. Joseph, bet. Meridian and Pennsylvania.
Weisenbaugh John, assistant, Farmers' Hotel.
Welsh Pat., bar-keeper Bates House Saloon, bds. Delaware.
Welsh Thos., blacksmith, Western Machine Works.
Welden Margaret, bds. 13 N. New Jersey.
Weldentherler F. T., eating saloon, 183 E. Washington, res. same.
Welking Henry, shoemaker, res. 37 Noble.
Weller Levi, clerk Exchange Billiard Rooms, bds. 20 Michigan.
Wells G. A., dentist, 15 E. Washington, res. same.
Wells Haden, teamster, res. 15 Chatham.
Wells Wm. F., saw mill, Massachusetts ave., near city limits, res. 85 E. New York.
Wenger George M., grocer, 20 N. Noble, res. same.
Wentz W. W., passenger conductor I. & C. R. R., res. 99 S. New Jersey.
Werbe L. F., groceries, &c., 185 W. Washington, res. same.
Werbe C. G., notary public, 95½ E. Washington
Werby Charles, salesman at Fancy Bazaar, bds. Spencer House.
Werden E., (W. & Co.,) res. Pittsfield, Mass.
WERDEN & CO., booksellers and stationers, 26 E. Washington.
Werner Jacob, varnisher Speigel, Thoms & Co., res. 95 E. Washington.

The Wheeler & Wilson Hemmer makes hems of any width.

Wert Joseph, boot and shoemaker, 6 S. Meridian, res. 63 N. Alabama.
Wesling Conrad, drayman, res. Michigan, bet. Noble and Railroad.
West Geo. H., res. 47 W. Michigan.
West Joseph, shoe shop, 6 S. Pennsylvania, res. 63 S. Alabama.
Western Machine Works, Dumont & Sinker, proprietors, S. Pennsylvania.
WESTERN UNION TELEGRAPH COMPANY, John F. Wallick, manager, 1 N. Meridian.
Weston James A., railroader, res. 24 S. Alabama.
Wethus Michael, laborer, res. 84 N. Tennessee.
Wetmore S. F., printer Journal office, bds. cor. Market and Circle.
Wetsell George C., porter Little's Hotel.
Wheeling Charles, wagon maker, 156 S. Delaware, res. bet. Alabama and New Jersey.
Wheatley John, book-keeper, bds. Ray House.
Wheatley William M., Colonel 26th regiment Ind. Vols., res. 108 E. Ohio.
Wheeler Joseph, (col.,) cook Little's Hotel.
Wheeler Rachael, (col.,) res. 111 W. North.
Wheeler Walter, engineer, bds. Little's Hotel.
Wheitzell Adolph, waiter Spencer House.
WHITCOMB JERRY G., freight agent Jeffersonville R. R., res. 50 E. Market.
White ——, (col.,) laborer, res. Harris.
White A. M., school teacher, res. 151 N. East.
White Charles, laborer, res. 124 N. Mississippi, up stairs.
White Jacob, laborer, res. 104 E. McCarty.
White James, wood dealer, res. 86 Huron.
White Jeremiah, wood sawyer, res. W. Elizabeth.
White Jesse (col.,) laborer, res. 126 W. Georgia.
WHITE RIVER VALLEY INSURANCE COMPANY, Isaac E. Johnson, President; Jas. Sutherland, Sec'y; office 19 W. Washington.
White Washington, (col.,) railroader, res. 57 W. Georgia.
Whitehead Christian, laborer, res. 270 N. New Jersey.
Whitehead Moses, wagon-maker, res. 144 N. Mississippi.
Whitehead Nathaniel, carriage-maker, bds. 144 N. Mississippi.
Whitehead Thomas, miller, Ætna Mills.
Whitehead William, miller, Ætna Mills.
Whiteman Peter, wood-cutter, res. 155 Railroad.
Whitemore John B., railroader, res. Davidson, near Ohio.
Whiting Miss Helen, teacher McLean's Seminary, bds. same.

Upwards of 100 W. & W. Machines in use in Ind'p'lis making army clothing.

Whitmore Henry, proprietor Morris House, opp. Union Depot.
Whitney C. C., telegraphic operator, bds. 24 S. Meridian.
Whitney F., telegraph office, bds. 10 W. Market.
Whitney J. B., operator Western Union Telegraph Co., bds. 10 W. Market.
Whitney William Jr., conductor Indiana Central Railway, bds. Palmer House.
Whitridge Samuel, painter, bds. 181 N. New Jersey.
Whitridge William, house and sign painter, 86½ E. Washington, res. 181 N. New Jersey.
Whitsit Jesse, res. 244 Virginia ave.
Whitsitt John B., engineer P. & I. R. R., res. 18 Lord.
Whitt James, clerk 21 S. Illinois, bds. Oriental House.
Whitten John, railroader, res. 38 S. Liberty.
Whitton James, clerk 3 W. Washington.
Wholer Martin, U. S. A., res. 192 S. Tennessee.
Wick W. W., attorney at law, 95 E. Washington.
Wickert John, clerk for J. H. Vajen, res. 118 N. Alabama.
Wiedrichs William, cigars and tobacco, 63 E. Washington, res. same.
Wiedenhorn Joseph, hair-braider, res. 46 E. Market.
Wienner J. J., varnisher for Speigel, Thoms & Co., res. 95 E. McCarty.
Wiggins Charles P., (W. & Chandler,) bds. Bates House.
Wiggins H. D., machinist, res. 53 W. Vermont.
WIGGINS & CHANDLER, foundry and machine shop, 262 W. Washington.
Wiland Christ., switchman Central Depot, res. 20 Union.
Wilcox W. H., res. 18 N. Illinois.
Wild John, saloon, res. Wabash, bet. New Jersey and East.
WILDE O. J., manufacturer, wholesale and retail dealer in furniture, &c., 71 S. Illinois, res. same.
Wilds Samuel, clerk 59 W. Washington, res. 7 Chatham.
Wile Frederick, currier, res. 46 N. Noble.
Wiley D., M. D., bds. Macy House.
Wiley William Y., real estate agent, 10 E. Washington, res. 32 E. New York.
Wilke Henry, drayman, res. Liberty, bet. New York and Vermont.
Wilking Henry, shoemaker, res. 37 N. Noble.
Wilkins John, res. 34 E. Market.
Wilkins Willard, res. 83 N. Illinois.
Wilkison Daniel S., grocer, cor. North and East, res. 149 N. East.
Wilkison Jacob, teamster for peg and last factory, res. 133 S. Tennessee.

CITY DIRECTORY. 235

Wilkinson Wm., livery and sale stables, 10 E. Pearl, res. 119 S. Alabama.
Willard A. B., salesman 26 and 28 W. Washington, res. 66 E. New York.
Willard A. G., (W. & Stowell,) res. 92 Massachusetts ave.
WILLARD & STOWELL, wholesale and retail dealer in music and musical instruments, 4 Bates House, Washington.
Willard William, teacher Deaf and Dumb Asylum.
Willett Wm., works in grocery, res. 188 N. Alabama.
Willets Jacob S., res. 69 Ft. Wayne ave.
Willets Wm. P., clerk, bds. 69 Ft. Wayne ave.
William Franklin, (col.,) whitewasher, res. 119 Indiana ave.
Williams Christian, laborer, res. 165 S. Alabama.
Williams Charles, (Weaver & W.,) res. 20 W. Michigan.
Williams Charles, carpenter, res. 11 N. Liberty.
Williams Daniel G., (Werden & Co.,) res. cor. Michigan and Pennsylvania.
Williams David N., works Rolling Mill, res. 13 Union.
Williams Geo., butcher, cor. New York and Massachusetts ave., res. 60 N. Delaware.
Williams G. D., clerk 63 W. Washington, res. 87 Illinois.
WILLIAMS REV. GIBBON, superintendent Indianapolis Female Institute, res. 34 E. Michigan.
Williams Hubbard, house-painter, res. 1 Huron.
Williams John, works Rolling Mill, res. Missouri, S. of South.
Williams James, machinist, bds. 46 California.
Williams Jas. L., tinner, 182 E. Washington, bds. Meridian.
Williams J. T., book-binder, res. 46 N. California.
Williams Kate, res. 48 E. New York.
Williams Miss N. H., dealer in millinery goods, 22 S. Illinois, res. same.
Williams O., clerk, 63 W. Washington, res. 134 N. Illinois.
Williams Philip, harness maker, res. 155 N. East.
Williams Rees R., engineer, res. 165 S. Tennessee.
Williams Samuel (col.,) eating house, Indiana ave. bet. Missouri and West.
Williams Mrs. Susan, res. 51 N. Liberty.
Williams Wm., tailor, res. 24 Stephen.
Williams Wm. (col.,) barber, basement Little's Hotel, bds. same.
Williamson, J. D., editor Herald & Era, res. Philadelphia.
Williamson L. B., (W. & Haugh,) res. 118 E. Vermont.
Williamson & Haugh, manufacturers iron railing, 2 N. Delaware.
Williamson Marshal D., dealer in lumber, res. 114 N. East.
Williamson Sheridan, plasterer, res. Mississippi N. of St. Clair.

Successive years at the United States Fair.

Willis Clark, plasterer, res. 50 N. East.
Wilmot Horace, salesman, 820 W. Washington, bds. 115 N. Pennsylvania.
Wilmot Saml., dealer in hats, caps and furs, 8 W. Washington, res. 115 N. Pennsylvania.
Wilmot T. H., salesman 8 W. Washington, bds. 115 N. Pennsylvania.
Wilson Abner, foreman press-room Journal office, bds. 58 S. Penn.
Wilson A. J., marble mantle maker, res. 10 N. Delaware.
Wilson C. G., sash painter, res. 174 S. Mississippi.
Wilson Daniel, res. 55 S. Pennsylvania.
Wilson Edward, laborer, res. Market bet. West and California.
Wilson James, carpenter, res. Indiana ave.
WILSON J. B., wholesale and retail hardware, 60 W. Washington, res. 266 N. Illinois.
Wilson J. Colman, telegraphic operator, T. H. & R. R. R. Depot, res. 15 S. Illinois.
Wilson John R., laborer, res. 137 N. West.
Wilson John, baker, bds. 4 S. Meridian.
Wilson John, plasterer, res. 183 E. Ohio.
Wilson John, laborer, res. 128 W. Georgia.
Wilson John H., miller, res. 135 Bluff road.
Wilson Jonathan, res. 64 E. North.
Wilson J. S., dealer in lumber, bds. 167 E. Ohio.
Wilson Jos. B., miller Carlisle's Model Mills.
Wilson L. B., civil engineer, res. 63 W. Maryland.
Wilson Mrs. G. (wid.,) seamstress, res. 53 Huron.
WILSON O. M., attorney at law and notary public, cor. of Washington and Meridian, res. Tennessee bet. Georgia and Maryland.
Wilson Mrs. Rebecca, nurse, res. 121 N. New Jersey.
Wilson Sanford B., boarding-house, res. E. National Road.
Wilson Stephen P., plasterer, 250 Madison ave.
Wilson T. K., salesman, 61 Blake's Block, bds. 266 Illinois.
Wilson Thomas, laborer, res. 114 S. New Jersey.
Wilson W., watchman Madison depot, res. 272 S. Delaware.
Wilt J. F., currier for J. K. Sharpe, res. 46 E. Ohio.
Wilt John, American Eating Saloon, 168 E. Washington, New Jersey.
Winchel Mrs. E. A., seamstress, res. 148 E. New York.
Wineburger J. C., Depot Bakery, opp. Union Depot, res. Georgia.
Wineburger H., clerk Depot Bakery.
Wingate J. F., grocery 165 Virginia ave., res. 151 Virginia ave.
Winkel Fred., teamster Carlisle's Model Mills.

81,000 Wheeler & Wilson's Sewing Machines in use in this country.

Winkler Valentine, stone mason, res. 57, cor. McCarty and Bluff Road.
Winkler V., currier for John Fishback.
Winsor John, car trimmer Lawrenceburg car shop, res. cor. Bates & Cady.
Winter David E., painter, res. 122 E. Market.
Winans Samuel, printer Indiana American.
Winegar G., ostler bds. Farmers' Hotel.
Wingate E. H., merchant.
Wipple Charles W., res. 44 E. Louisiana.
Wirz Jacob, U. S. A., res. 52 South.
Wise Charles, carpenter, res. 145 E. Ohio.
Wise William, agent Dayton ale, 74 W. Washington, res. 94 N. Illinois.
Wiseman Mrs. B. A., (wid.,) res. 83 N. Pennsylvania.
Wishmire Anthony, laborer, res. 148 E. Ohio.
Wishmire Christian F., res. Davidson, near saw mill.
Wishmire John, res. 25 East.
Wissert John, express-man, res. 181 E. Market.
Witte Lou., assistant book-keeper Branch Bank, bds. 93 W. Washington.
Wittenberg Charles, (Krause & W.,) res. 111 E. Ohio.
Witness, (weekly,) M. G. Clarke and Co., proprietors and publishers, office Odd Fellows' Hall.
Wocher Ferdinand, (Egner & W.,) bds. Union Hall.
Woelz Charles A., confectioner, res. Michigan, bet. Liberty and Noble.
WOERNER PHILIP, dealer in groceries, liquors and ale, 78 W. Washington, res. same.
Woerner Philip F., clerk 78 W. Washington, bds. same.
Wolf Catherine, (wid.,) res. 124 S. Delaware.
Wolf Mrs. Isabella, seamstress, res. cor. East and Ohio.
WOLF WILSON S., attorney at law and notary public, 7 Glenns' Block, bds. Pyle House.
Wolfe Charles, harness maker for Sulgrove & Reynolds, res. alley, bet. Arsenal and W. Market House.
Wolfe Louisa, (wid.,) washer, res. 246 Madison ave.
Wolff Robert, gunsmith, works 17 Kentucky ave., bds. 28 Kentucky ave.
Wolfram A. T., printer Journal Office, bds. 101 N. New Jersey.
Wolfram C. A., printer, res. 101 N. New Jersey.
Wolfram Mrs. Sarah, res. 101 N. New Jersey.
WOLTZE W. E., watchmaker and jeweler, 164 E. Washington, res. same.
WOOD A. D., wholesale and retail dealer in hardware, stoves, &c., 71 E. Washington, res. 164 N. New Jersey.

A Wheeler & Wilson Sewing Machine with Hemmer, for $50.

WOOD ALEX., dealer in groceries, provisions, country produce, &c., 129 N. Illinois, res. 127 N. Illinois.
Wood B., surgeon dentist, 42 N. Pennsylvania, res. same.
Wood E. A., (W. & Barnett,) res. outside city limits.
Wood E. R., (J. G. W. & Sons,) res. St. Joseph, bet. Pennsylvania and Meridian.
Wood Jacob, pump maker, W. Indianapolis.
Wood James, surveyor, res. 127 N. Illinois.
Wood James N., surveyor, bds. 127 N. Illinois.
Wood James M., paper maker, res. 146 W. Ohio.
Wood J. G., (J. G. W. & Sons,) res. St. Joseph, bet. Pennsylvania and Meridian.
Wood John F., clerk postoffice, res. 161 E. Market.
Wood John M., (W. & Foudray,) res. 53 N. Pennsylvania.
Wood J. G. & Sons, house joiners and cabinet makers, 9 Virginia ave.
Wood J. W., (J. G. W. & Sons,) res. St. Joseph, bet. Pennsylvania and Meridian.
Wood Levi, 31st Indiana Volunteers, res. 37 E. Michigan.
Wood Mrs., (wid.,) res. 57 N. Pennsylvania.
Wood Wm., res. 140 N. Pennsylvania.
Wood Wm. D., saddler, 34 W. Washington.
Wood Wm., brick mason, res. W. Indianapolis.
Wood Mrs. Zyrena, (wid.,) res. 178 S. Tennessee.
WOOD & BARNETT, meat market, 157 E. Washington.
WOOD & FOUDRAY, livery and sale stables, 10 N. Pennsylvania.
Woodford Margaret, (col.,) washer, res. 21 Virginia ave.
Woodruff Mrs. Adeline, tailoress, res. 232 N. New Jersey.
Woolen Wm. M., grocer, res. 82 W. Vermont, cor. Mississippi.
Woolf Erasmus, cooper, res. N. Blake.
Woollen Milton, farmer, res. 147 N. West.
WOOLLEN WM. W., attorney at law and notary public, College Hall, bds. 149 West.
Word Henry, laborer, res. 113 W. Michigan.
Wordsworth William, manufacturer of woolen goods at Yount's factory, bds. 74 N. Tennesse.
Worland William, provision and feed store, 37 Virginia ave., res. in rear.
Worth A., secretary of I. & C. R. R., res. 246 S. Alabama.
Worth J. C., auctioneer, res. 125 Ft. Wayne ave.
Wasmont Louis, tailor, res. 5 N. New Jersey.
Wathers John, res. 100 Bates.
Wren Edmond, wagon-maker, res. 51 S. New Jersey.
Wren Michael, laborer, bds. 184 S. Tennessee.
Wren Thomas, contractor, res. S. Alabama.
Wrenn John, carpenter, res. 192 S. Delaware.

CITY DIRECTORY. 239

Wright Aaron, res. W. Indianapolis.
Wright Arthur L., deputy treasurer, res. 92 N. Alabama.
Wright Asa, painter, bds. 10 N. Mississippi.
Wright Augustus S., homeopathist, res. 136 N. Illinois.
Wright C. A., real estate agent, Temperance Hall.
WRIGHT, BATES & MAGUIRE, wholesale grocers, 6 Bates House.
Wright C., pump maker, res. 128 S. Noble.
Wright Esther, family sewing, res. 191 N. New Jersey.
Wright Frank M., (W. & Downer,) res. 143 N. Pennsylvania.
Wright George, ostler, res. 77 N. Noble.
Wright Hiram, blacksmith, Bellefontaine car shop, res. 74 Benton.
Wright Jacob T., county auditor, office county buildings, res. 117 N. Delaware.
Wright John C., (W., Bates & Maguire,) res. 30 N. Meridian.
Wright Matilda, dressmaker, 10 N. Mississippi.
Wright M. H., physician and surgeon, res. cor. Meridian and Ohio.
Wright R. M., foreman shoe shop, Deaf and Dumb Asylum, res. S. E. Michigan road.
Wright Thomas, salesman, New York store, bds. Spencer House.
Wright Thos. C., billiard saloon, 16 W. Georgia, bds. Oriental House.
Wright Wesley, bar-keeper, Magnolia saloon, res. 10 Mississippi.
Wright W. H., messenger Adams' Express, res. 175 Alabama.
Wright Wm. G., pump-maker, res. 28 Huron.
WRIGHT CHRIST., Eagle Saloon, 138 E. Washington, res. same.
WRIGHT & DOWNER, brewers of Downer's champagne ale, Blake, near Patterson's Mill
Wundrum William, tailor, 63 E. Washington.
Wust John, wood-turner, res. 97 Ft. Wayne ave.
Wyatt Monroe, bar-keeper, bds. 10 Mississippi.
Wygart W. D., farmer, res. 76 W. Maryland.
Wyse Mrs., washer, res. 103 Railroad.
Wysong Christopher, brick-layer, res. Illinois, S. of Pogue's Run.

Y

Yager William, cooper, res. 166 N. Noble.
Yandes Daniel, res. 64 N. Pennsylvania.

Successive years at Mechanic's Institute, Cincinnati.

Yandes D., Jr., (Y. & Co.,) res. 64 N. Pennsylvania.
Yandes Frederick, blacksmith, res. 99 Bluff Road.
Yandes George, salesman 38 E. Washington, res. 64 Pennsylvania.
YANDES SIMON, attorney at law, 19½ E. Washington.
Yandes & Co., wholesale and retail dealers in hides and leather, 38 E. Washington.
Yarbrough Peter, railroader, res. 35 S. Noble.
Yarger John, meat market, 200 E. Washington, res. one mile E. of city.
Yarger K., butcher, 200 E. Washington.
Yeager Christ., grocery, 215 E. Washington, res. same.
Yeager John, file cutter, bds. 166 S. Alabama.
Yewell Solomon, book-keeper, res. 193 S. Pennsylvania.
Yohn James C., paymaster U. S. A., res. 74 N. Delaware.
York E. D., driver American Express Company, bds. Morris House.
Yost Thos., bds. 69 W. South.
Yot John, waiter for Louis Lang.
Young Christ., patern maker, res. 80 Vermont.
Young Granville, bds. 11 S. Mississippi.
Young Geo. D., machinist, res. 68 S. New Jersey.
Young Dr. J. S., bds. Ohio House.
Young H. H., school teacher, res. cor. Ash and Cherry.
Young Julius, tailor, bds. 103½ E. Washington.
Young N. R., book-keeper, bds. 13 S. Illinois.
YOUNG RICHARD F., Palmer House Saloon, cor. Washington and Illinois, bds. 101 W. New York.
Young Sules D., printer, bds. cor. Ash and Cherry.
YOUNG MEN'S CHRISTIAN ASSOCIATION, Ray's Block.
Youngerman Charles, blacksmith, res. 16 N. Delaware.
Youngerman Charles F., stone cutter, 168 S. Delaware.
Youngerman George, blacksmith, bds. East Street House.
Youngerman George, saloon, cor. Washington and Delaware, res. 209 Washington.
Youngerman Mrs. Mary, res. 86 Massachusetts ave.
Youtsey Thomas, laborer, res. 229 S. East.

Z

Zabel Charles, cabinet-maker, bds. 73 S. Illinois.
Zehringer Landilien, cabinet-maker, res. 121 N. Noble.
ZEIGLER WILLIAM, Boston Store, 10 E. Washington, res. 71 N. Meridian.
Zellers Henry, mattress-maker, bds. 63 W. Louisiana.
Zimmerman Christopher, gravel-roofing, res. 130 E. Market.

Zimmerman Joseph, tailor 31 Virginia ave., res. same.
Zink Henry, barber, bds. Mississippi, bet. South and Canal.
Zipperle John, shoemaker, W. Indianapolis.
Zoick William, tailor, bds. 54 N. Noble.
Zumbush Theodore, jeweler, 128 South, up stairs.
Zurick William, tailor, 144 E. Washington.

PEARL STREET SALOON

Opposite O. W. Johnson's Livery Stable,

INDIANAPOLIS, IND.

Wines, Liquors and Cigars

Of every description always on hand.

THOS. McBAKER, Prop'r.

For four successive years at the Ohio State Fair.

JACOB ELDRIDGE,
REAL ESTATE AGENT
AND
Commission Merchant,
No. 13 SOUTH ILLINOIS ST.,

Four doors S. of Palmer House, East side, up stairs,

INDIANAPOLIS, INDIANA,

Will attend to the buying and selling of Indiana and Western Lands, Pay Taxes, Examine Titles, Negotiate Trades, Exchange Goods for Land, and Land for Goods.

All Correspondence Promptly Attended to,

IF ACCOMPANIED WITH A STAMP TO PAY POSTAGE.

C. BEATTY, Assistant.

RAY HOUSE,

Two Squares South-East of Union Depot, corner of Delaware and South Streets,

INDIANAPOLIS, IND.

RAY & LAMBERT, Proprietors.

STEPHEN SMITH,
THE OLD AND RELIABLE
BILL POSTER,
INDIANAPOLIS, IND.

☞ **LEAVE ORDERS** at either of the Printing Offices.

RESIDENCE, No. 102 NORTH MISSISSIPPI ST.

Wheeler & Wilson's Sewing Machines warranted for three years.

REDSTONE, BROS. & CO.,
Redstone Machine Works,

Delaware Street, Opp. Cincinnati Freight Depot,

Have constantly on hand and for sale a large variety of Machines, for which they have the exclusive right to manufacture.

PORTABLE STEAM ENGINES,

Reapers and Mowers, Sawing Machines, Shingle Machines, Straw Cutters, Power Pumps, Single or Double Horse Power Saw Mills, and

CHEAP HORSE POWERS,

Can be supplied at the above Works.

Every Machine Warranted.

CERTIFICATES

Of some of our well-known citizens who have used the Redstone Sawing Machine:

INDIANAPOLIS, December 3, 1861.

This is to certify that we have been using Messrs. Redstone, Bros. & Co.'s Sawing Machine over six months, and find that it will accomplish easily an equal amount of work with less than one-fifth the power necessary to run a circular saw large enough to do the same kind of work, and we take pleasure in recommending it to those who have use for a Sawing Machine, easily adapted to hand or other motive power, on the farm or in the workshop.
OSGOOD, SMITH & CO.

BROOKVILLE, March 14, 1861.

Messrs. Redstone, Bros. & Co.:

We are well pleased with the Sawing Machine we got from you, it is certainly ahead of anything we have ever seen for cross-cutting timber. It cuts very rapidly and as true as a straight edge, and with less power than any other machine that we have ever seen.
MORGAN & MEANS.

INDIANAPOLIS, February 13, 1862.

Messrs. Redstone, Bros. & Co.:

GENTS: I have been using one of your Sawing Machines about three months, and do unhesitatingly pronounce it all that it is recommended, and would say that one-horse power is enough to run it. The cutting of wood with your machine is mere pastime—the handling of the wood being all that seems like work.
JOHN BUCHANAN.

INDIANAPOLIS, February 15, 1862.

Messrs. Redstone, Bros. & Co.:

GENTS: We are using one of your Sawing Machines and can recommend it as the best machine in use for sawing.
DAVID M. COMPTON,
HIRAM KENWORTHY.

Many other references may be had by calling at the shop, where the machines may be seen.

The Wheeler & Wilson Hemmer is the only Hemmer that will Fell.

WHEELER & WILSON'S
SEWING MACHINES.

More than 81,000 of the Wheeler & Wilson Machines are in successful operation in this Country.

It is used universally—for all purposes. Families, Tailors, Hat Binders, Dressmakers, Shirt Manufacturers, in fact all who want a Sewing Machine that will do its work *well and rapidly*, use

WHEELR & WILSON.

It is made light and strong—no superfluous parts to mar its beauty or distract the operator.

There is no purpose for which a Sewing Machine is required that will test its capacities in the same degree, as for Family Sewing—from the airy tissue and light Swiss to the heavy cassimers or coarse homespun. It is this peculiar adaptation to the use in a family that has won for the Wheeler & Wilson such a

WORLD-WIDE REPUTATION,

And caused so many to be sold.

Its mechanism is perfection.
  Its appearance is elegant.
    Its uses without limit.
      Its admirers innumerable.

Any person of ordinary capacity can, in an hour's practice, acquire a perfect knowledge of it. It is so constructed that the wear is but slight, the motion being rotary. It can be used an ordinary life-time without needing any repairs or a single part replaced.

We Warrant all Machines Three Years.

We invite all who want a Sewing Machine to examine and test the Wheeler & Wilson.

WILLIAM SUMNER & CO.,
DEALERS IN THE WEST.
C. C. CLAFLIN, Agent,
Office No. 19 W. Washington Street,
INDIANAPOLIS, INDIANA,

A Wheeler & Wilson Sewing Machine will last a life-time.

BUSINESS MIRROR.

Containing the Name and Location of principal Business Men; in the City, under the particular Trade or Profession in which they are engaged.

Accoucher and Midwife.
Thompson Mrs., 74 N. Illinois.

Academy for Boys.
Hay's, under Masonic Hall.

Agents, Ale and Porter.
Barnard J., Chicago Champaign Ale, S. Meridian.
Wise Wm., Dayton Ale, 74 W. Wash.

Agent American Bible Society.
Armstrong Rev. W. P., 186 N. Ill.

Agent Cincinnati Newspapers.
Ratti F. A., 8 Pearl.

Agents, Insurance.
(*See Insurance.*)

Agents, Knitting Machine.
Harlin, J. J., 6½ W. Washington.

Agents, Patent Right.
Bussell E. T., 19 S. Mississippi.

Agents, Real Estate.
(*See Real Estate.*)

Agent, School Books.
Grant Geo. H., 18 W. Washington.

Agents, Sewing Machine.
(*See Sewing Machines.*)

Agricultural Implements.
Beard, Starr & Co., 2 N. Tenn.
Binkley Sam'l, S. Mississippi.
Grosvenor & Turner, 84 W. Wash.
Marion, cor. Tennessee & Merrill.
Redstone, Bros. & Co., S. Delaware, opp. I. & C. R. R. offices.
Stiltz J. George, 74 E. Washington.
Wiggins & Chandler, 202 W. Wash.

Architects.
Bohlen D. A., Ætna Building.
Costigan F., Oriental House.
Curzon Joseph, Journal Building.
Hodgsen Isaac, 14 Yohn's Block.
May Edwin, 75 N. Pennsylvania.

Artists, Portrait and Scenic.
Cox J., Ray's Building.
Dunlap James, 137 E. Washington.
Glessing T. B., 62 N. Tennessee.
Gulick Samuel.
Reed P. Fishe, Ætna Building.

Artists, Photograph, Ambrotype and Daguerreotype.
Bruening E. & J. B., 6½ E. Wash.
Crane J. D., 19 W. Washington.
Fish A. A., N. W. cor. Meridian and Washington.
Hays & Runnion, 32½ E. Wash.
Johnson C. A., 33 W. Washington.
Kellogg & Davis, 8½ E. Washington.
Morris C. J,, 26½ W. Washington.
Reed J. H., Ætna Building.
Smith Jacob, 8 Glenns' Block.
Weeks & Cox, College Hall.

Artists' Materials.
Crapo R. P. & Co., Journal Building.
Leiber H., N. Pennsylvania.
Perkins G. C. & Co., 14 W. Wash.

Attorneys at Law.
Barbour & Howland, Dunlop's Building.
Beal J. A., 6 Glenns' Block.
Bowles Thos. H., 10 E. Washington.

350 families in Indianapolis and vicinity use Wheeler & Wilson.

Brown Ignatus, 19½ E. Washington.
Brown P. A., 24 E. Washington.
Buff H. G., res. 177 South
Bufkins J. C., 43½ E. Washington.
Burns W. V.. 38½ W. Washington.
Campbell W. L., Sinking Fund Building.
Carter Geo., 86 E. Washington.
Caven John, 19½ E. Washington.
Clark Edward, 24½ E. Washington.
Colley Sims A., 10½ S. Meridian.
Coulon Chas., Cumberland.
Davis E. A., Kentucky ave.
De Ford & Quimby, 35 E. Wash.
Duncan Robt. B., Hubbard's Block.
Dye John T., Blackford's Building.
Elliott Byron K., 24½ E. Wash.
Ellsworth Henry, S. Meridian.
Ferguson Kilby, 24½ E. Wash.
Fishback W. P., 62 E. Washington.
Fuller J. M., 14 E. Ohio.
Gordon Geo. E., Odd Fellows' Hall.
Hall R. H., 26½ E. Washington.
Hamilton J. W., Blackford's Building.
Hamlin C., 18½ E. Washington.
Hammond U. J., 19½ E. Washington.
Harrison & Fishback, 62 E. Wash.
Henderson Wm., Ætna Building.
Hendricks Thos. A., Ætna Building.
Hoefger S. B., 19½ E. Washington.
Howland J. D., Dunlop's Building.
Johnson Isaac E., 4 Blake's Building.
Ketchum & Mitchell, Blackford's Building.
Kiger & Phillips, Blackford's Building.
Leathers & Carter, 86 E. Wash.
Macy David, cor. Washington and Delaware.
McDonald D., Yohn's Block.
McDonald & Roache, Ætna Building.
Major S., 19½ E. Washington.
Martin L. R., 10½ E. Washington.
Morrison J. T., 26 E. Washington.
Morrison & Ray, 26 E. Washington.
Miller J., 84 E. Washington.
Mitchell J. L., Blackford's building.
Newcomb & Tarkington, 26½ E. Washington.
Patterson W., 30½ E. Washington.
Peelle & Davis, over Sec'y State's office, Kentucky ave.
Perrin G. K., College Hall.
Quimby C. W., 35 E. Washington.
Rand & Hall, 26½ E. Washington.

Ray C. A., 26 E. Washington.
Roberts Jos. T., 18 E. Washington.
Robbins H. R., 14 E. Ohio.
Seidensticker A., 91 E. Washington.
Smith Francis, 37 E. Washington.
Stringfield W., 152 N. Pennsylvania.
Sweetser J. N., 19½ E. Washington.
Tarkington J. S., 26½ E. Wash.
Taylor & Taylor, 30½ W. Wash.
Torbett O B., Temperance Hall.
Walpole & Walpole, 18 E. Wash.
Wick W. W., 95 E. Washington.
Wilson O. M., S. E. cor. Wash. and Meridian.
Wolf Wilson S., 7 Glenns' Block.
Woollen W. M., College Hall.
Yandes Simon, 19¼ E. Washington.

Auction and Commission.

Featherston & Barker, 56 E. Wash.
Mossler Bros., 10 W. Washington.

Bakers.

Boolman Fred., 87 E. Washington.
Brown J. W., 150 N. New Jersey.
Cunningham F. P., 43 N. Illinois.
Depot Bakery, J. C. Wineberger.
Fenling Joseph, 201 E. Washington.
Foos Thos. J., 84 N. Mississippi.
Ganter C., 181 E. Washington.
Gray Wm., 64 South.
Grein John, 214 E. Washington.
Gutkeucht W., 134 Illinois.
Haas Geo., 246 W. Washington.
Haynes H. M., 40 W. Washington.
Huff John E., 200 W. Washington.
Metzgar A. & J., 11 N. Penn.
Thompson H., 4 S. Meridian.
Union Steam Bakery, A. & J. Metzger, proprietors, 11 N. Penn.
Wineburger J. C., opposite Union Depot.

Bank Locks, Iron Doors, &c.

Williamson & Haugh, 2 N. Del.

Banks.

Bank of the State, cor. Illinois and Kentucky ave.
Branch of the Bank of the State, cor. Meridian and Washington.

Bankers.

Fletcher's Banking Office, 30 E. Washington.
Fletcher & Sharpe, banking office, S. W. cor. Penn. and Wash.

Wheeler & Wilson's Sewing Machines have been awarded the First Premium

CITY DIRECTORY. 247

Harrisons', 19 E. Washington.

Barbers.

Brandum Samuel, Oriental House.
Close & Bros., 4 N. Pennsylvania.
Ferdinand Z., 62 South.
Frankenstein G., Morris House.
Franklin Wm. H., under Branch Bank, cor. Meridian and Wash.
Fisher Benjamin, cor. Louisiana and Illinois.
Geetig Henry, Odd Fellows' Hall.
Henning & Stelzell, Bates House and Palmer House.
Lenenger & Ferling, under Am. Express Office.
Shoecraft Silas, 60 E. Washington.
Turner A., 15½ W. Washington.
Williams Wm., Little's Hotel.

Basket Makers.

Burgner John, 17 Chatham.
Cutting A., 117 N. Delaware.

Bazaars.

Baldwin J. H., 6 E. Washington.
Mayer C., 29 W. Washington.
New York, E. Klotz, prop'r., 37 E. Washington.
Parker Edgar, 25 S. Illinois.

Beef and Pork Packers.

Ferguson & Mansur, opp. Madison Depot.
McTaggart I., office cor. Del. and Washington.
Mansur W. & I., 14 S. Meridian.

Bell and Locksmiths.

Livsey & Co., Louisiana, near Union Depot.
Reinhardt J. P., 49 S. Illinois.

Bill Poster.

Smith Stephen, slate at Printing offices.

Billiard Saloons.

Bush Jacob, 248 E. Washington.
Exchange, C. Montgomery, N. Ill.

Blacksmiths.

Berryman John, near cor. Cady and Washington.
Brotz John, 86 W. Washington.
Burns John, 158 S. Delaware.
Forshee G. W., 34 S. Pennsylvania.

Gates John J., 14 S. New Jersey.
Geisel Geo., 49 Ft. Wayne Ave.
Geisel Henry, 158 S. Delaware.
Hillman Wm., 306 Virginia Ave.
Seibert Samuel, 252 E. Washington.
Smith John G., 36 Kentucky Ave.
Youngerman Chas., 122 S. Del.

Blacksmiths' Tools.

Murphy & Holliday, 34 E. Wash.

Blank Book Manufacturers and Book Binders.

Braden Wm., 24 W. Washington.
Campbell & Boyle, 37 E. Wash.
Dodd H. H. & Co., 18 E. Washington.
Douglass James G., Journal Building.
Sheets Wm., 77 W. Washington.

Boarding Houses.

Bright Mrs. E., 45 N. Pennsylvania.
Coen John, 107 S. Tennessee.
Collman Henry.
Cook Mrs. J., 44 N. Pennsylvania.
Donnan Mrs. B., 74 N. Tennessee.
Edward E., 53 S. Illinois.
Elder Wm. G., 89 E. Market.
Hanraman P., 184 S. Tennessee.
Holmes Mrs. Mary, 51 N. East.
Hoyt H., 27 S. Delaware.
John Charles, 199 E Washington.
Kinder Mrs. M. W., 79½ E. Wash.
Knight Elijah, 19 W. Georgia.
Kolb Wm., 28 and 30 Kentucky ave.
Lynch John, 16 S. Pennsylvania.
McReady Jas., 10 W. Market.
Pedicord Mrs. Lydia, 179 E. Market.
Protzman J. H., 24 N. Mississippi.
Pyle House, J. Pyle, prop'r, cor. Maryland and Illinois.
Russman C., 119 E. Washington.
Scarry House, 20 N. Pennsylvania.
Scudder C., 46 W. Market.
Simpson Mrs. L., 27 Indiana ave.
Skilly Mrs. T., S. Meridian.
Smith Mrs. M. C., 44 S. Penn.
Tylor Mrs. R. D., 95 N. Tennessee.
Walk Louis, 14 W. Washington.
Waller Mrs. Louisa, 31 Indiana ave.

Boiler Makers.

Dumont & Sinker, S. Penn., near Union track.
Hasselman & Vinton, opp. Union Depot.

Bonnet Bleachers.

Conaty J. B., 22 S. Illinois.

For four successive years at the Am. Institute, New York.

INDIANAPOLIS

Copeland J. W., 8 E. Washington.

Book Publishers.

Asher & Co., 3 Odd Fellows' Hall.
Clarke & Co., Odd Fellows' Hall.
Dodd H. H. & Co., 18 E. Washington.
Perrine C O., Union Depot.
Merrill & Co., Glenns' block.
Streight A. D., Yohn's Block.

Booksellers and Stationers.

Asher & Co., Odd Fellows' Hall.
Bowen, Stewart & Co., 18 W. Wash.
Clarke & Co., Odd Fellows' Hall (up stairs.)
Merrill & Co., Glenns' Block.
Perrine C. O., Union Depot.
Thompson Mrs. A. & Son, N. Penn.
Werden & Co., 26 E. Washington.

Boots and Shoes, Wholesale.

Hendricks V. K. & Co., 76 W. Wash.
Mayhew E. C. & Co., Roberts' Block, (opp. Union Depot.)

Boots and Shoes, Retail.

Aldag Aug. & Co., 137 E Wash.
Bruner Chas., 38 W. Washington.
Busch C., 188 W. Washington.
Cady & Co., Glenns' Block.
Cooper Joshua, 53 E. Washington.
Cook Wm., 189 E. Washington.
Davis James, 187 E. Washington.
Doggett Richard, 3 Indiana ave.
Dugan Thos., Blake's Building, 4th story.
Evans J. L. & W. N., 3 Bates House, Washington.
Grout J. B., 3 W. Washington.
Gutkneght R., 124 N. Mississippi.
Heffer August, 103 W. Washington.
Hoffman Henry, 27 Union.
Jones, Vinnedge & Co., 17 W. Wash.
Karrle Joseph, 64 E. Washington.
Kistner J. G., 51 S. Illinois.
Knodle A. & Son, 32 E. Washington.
Lancaster W., 12 S. Illinois.
Lintz A., 80 W. Washington.
Lubking C., 184 E. Washington.
Manning E. C., 27 S. Illinois.
Marle Ch., 73 E. Washington.
Mathweg John, 51 W. Washington.
Maudlin & Co., 53 W. Washington.
Rehling C., 176 E. Washington.
Richter E. J., 161 E. Washington.
Robinus & Myers, 206 E. Wash.
Sharp J. K., 88 and 90 E. Wash.

Southard J P., 19 E. Washington.
Teals R. M., 7 N. Meridian.
TenEyck J. A. & R. F., 260 W. Wash.
Waller B., 150 W. Washington.
Wands A., 12 S. Meridian.
Wands J. & Son, 65 E. Washington.
Wekle Lukas, 179 E. Washington.
West Joseph, 6 S. Pennsylvania.

Bowling Alleys.

Bush Jacob, 248 E. Washington.
Gymnasium, cor. Mer. & Maryland.
Wright Thos. C., Georgia, bet. Illinois and Meridian.

Brass and Bell Founders.

Davis J. W. & Co., S. Delaware.
Livsey & Co., Louisiana, near Depot.

Brewers.

Harting & Bros., 25 S. Illinois.
Meikel's, W. Maryland.
Wright & Downer, Blake, near Patterson's Mill.

Brick Makers.

McNabb Stephen, 143 S. Miss.
Waters W. W., 73 W. South.

Brokers, Bill and Note.

Cain John, 18 E. Washington.
Fletcher S. A. & Co., 30 E. Wash.
Gatling R. J., Blackford's Building.
McKernan & Pierce, 29½ W. Wash.
Wiley W. Y., 10½ E. Washington.

Broom Makers.

Cutting A., 177 N. Delaware.
Holman M. C., 152 N. Pennsylvania.
Jones Fleming, Illinois N. of Sixth.

Building Stone.

Scott, Nicholson & Co., Kentucky ave.
Smith, Ittenbach & Co., 170 S. Del.

Butchers and Meat Markets.

Blane, Borst & Lake, Bates House, Illinois.
Bouf John, cor. Ill. and Ind. ave.
Boyd James, cor. North and Penn.
Cook Richard, 3 N. Illinois.
Crimer Henry, cor. East and North.
Davis Thomas, 6 S. Alabama.
Duvall Joseph P., 260 Madison ave.
Ennis Louis, E. Washington.
Gaff Andrew, Noble, near Market.

The Wheeler & Wilson Hemmer makes hems of any width.

CITY DIRECTORY.

Greeger J. W., Central Meat Market.
Hahn Louis, 105 W. Washington.
Hyde & Wethers, 173 E. Wash.
Jones Wm., 122 S. Illinois.
Kuhn Charles, 107 W. Washington.
Loucks C., 163 Virginia ave.
Morningstar & Gulick, 8 S. Penn.
Nicolai C., 119 Massachusetts ave.
Pouder M., 91 E. Washington.
Powell David, cor. Vermont and Massachusetts ave.
Riggs John, 32 N. Illinois.
Riggs & David, 6 S. Meridian.
Roos & Schmalzreed, 89 S. Illinois.
Seafart Louis, 77 E. Washington.
Short John, 208 W. Washington.
Snyder W. & L., 29 S Meridian.
Wechsler D., 128 N. Alabama.
Williams George, cor. New York and Massachusetts ave.
Wood & Barnett, 157 E. Washington.
Yarger John, 200 E. Washington.

Butter and Egg Packers.

Everson Geo. P., Metropolitan Hall, W. Washington.
Holmes Sam'l, 188 E. Washington.
Morgan Dennis, 180 E. Washington.

Cancer Doctors.

Haugh Adam, 6 N. Meridian.
Howard E. & Son, 52 S. Illinois.

Carpenters and Builders.

Avery John L., cor. North and Ala.
Balinger E. M., 150 N. East.
Beehimer S. B., 28 E. Georgia.
Bland Hiram, 166 S. New Jersey.
Bracken Thos. A., St. Joseph, bet. Illinois and Meridian.
Braning Humphrey, 295 S. Del.
Bronson R. T., 103 N. Alabama.
Brouse Andrew, 60 E. New York.
Buchannan Cyrus F., 14 S. West.
Busswell John, 90 S. Delaware.
Byrkit & Beam, 60 S. Tennessee.
Carter Henry, W. Georgia.
Coffman Jacob, 171 S. New Jersey.
Coffman S. J., 163 N. Mississippi.
Collins John, 37 S. Illinois.
Colestock Henry, 22 W. North.
Comegys Levi, 62 N. Delaware.
Cook J. M., 111 E. New York.
Cox Jefferson R., 188 S. East.
Derringer David, Howard.
Ebert John, 32 Kentucky ave.
Eden C, 86 E. Ohio.

Ely Ephraim, W. Indianapolis.
Emmerson R., 141 W. Ohio.
Fatout J. L. & M. K., 109 Indiana ave.
Fearnley & Greer, 68 S. Delaware.
Feary J. E., 7 Virginia ave.
Flaig M. V., Kentucky ave.
George Otis, at Theater,
Gordon C. L., S. Missouri.
Hearth John G., 127 N. East.
Helwig Charles, 113 E. Ohio.
Hiles Isaac, 156 W. Vermont.
Holland John, 217 S. Delaware.
Hornaday J. E., 150 N. Alabama.
Howes Henry, 50 Indiana ave.
Keely Wm., 62 E Michigan.
Loucks Jas., 194 New Jersey.
Low C. & N., 18 S. New Jersey.
Many John B., 34 N. Spring.
Marcus Elias, 59 W. Georgia.
Michett R. M., 95 St. Joseph.
Nelson Thomas, 107 W. Ohio.
Rickards Thomas, 86 S. Delaware.
Routier A., 65 Elm.
Sims John, 20 St. Clair.
Spicer B. M., Market opposite Post Office.
Taylor R. R., W. Market.
Towe & Sons, 18 S. New Jersey.
Wood J. G. & Sons, 9 Virginia ave.

Carpets and Matting.

Fletcher H. A. & Co., 26 and 28 W. Washington.
Glenn W. & H. & Co., Glenns' block
Tousey & Byram, 70 E. Washington.
Zeigler Wm., 10 E. Washington.

Carpet Weaver.

Spears Mrs. P., 63 S. Noble.

Carriage Makers.

Drew S. & Son, East Market square.
Gaston H. R. & Co., Kentucky ave.
Harding Thomas W., cor. Maryland and Delaware.
Lowe George, 99 E. Washington.
Munsell Henry, 175 E. Ohio.

Carriage Trimming.

Murphy & Holliday, 34 E. Wash.

China, Glass and Queensware.

Hawthorn & Buchanan, 83 E. Wash.
Lindley Jacob, 16 W. Washington.

Cigar Box Maker.

Greenwald H., 79 Davidson.

Upwards of 100 W. & W. Machines in use in Ind'p'lis making army clothing.

INDIANAPOLIS

Cigars and Tobacco.
Augleman Wm., 35 W. Washington.
Frost J. M., 95 E. Washington.
Heidlinger J. A., 3 Palmer and 10 Bates House.
Henninger & Co., 42 E. Washington.
Henninger Chas. & Co., 87 S. Ill.
Hunt C. C., 61 E. Washington.
Kretsch Peter, 93 S. Illinois.
McMurray Robert, 35 W. Wash.
Marshall C. M., N. Illinois, next to Exchange Building.
Meyer G. F., 35 W. Washington.
Otan D., 159 E. Washington.
Raschig C. M., 15 E. Washington.
Richardson John, 12 N. Penn.
Rosenthal A., 38 Louisiana.
Solomon J. & M., 30 S. Illinois.
Speckman, 57 S. Illinois.
Tindall N., 12 N. Pennsylvania.
Wiedrichs. Wm., 63 E. Washington.

Cistern Builders.
Kruger Joseph, 115 E. Market.

Clairvoyant Physician.
Howard S. W., 13 S. Mississippi.

Cloak and Mantilla Maker.
Moon Miss Sallie, 26½ W. Wash.

Clothiers.
(*See also Merchant Tailors.*)
Buedenz H. & Co., 144 W. Wash.
Criqui M., 84 E. Washington.
Dessar Bros., 4 E. Washington.
Glaser Bros., Bates House.
Gœpper F., 15 E. Washington.
Gramling J. & P., 41 E. Wash.
Kahn A., 2 Palmer House.
Kahn Jacob, 46 E. Washington.
McGinnis Owen, 30 E. Washington.
Moritz Bro. & Co., 3 E. and 19 W. Washington.
Myer Moses, 4 W. Washington.
Richter & Roggs, 144 E. Wash.
Simon G. & Son, 1 W. Washington.
Tapking & Becker, 63 E. Wash.

Coal Dealers.
Armstrong & Perine, 12 W. Mary'd.
Butsch Valentine, South, opp. Madison Depot.
Burk John, office 31 W. Wash.
Ross J. H., office New York Grocery.
Smith W. Q., S. Delaware.

Coal Oil and Lamps.
Browning Robert, 22 W. Wash.

Rockey H. S., 13 S. Meridian.
Tomlinson & Cox, 18 E. Wash.
Vickers W. B. & Co., Odd Fe'lows' Hall.

Comb Maker.
Gardiner Rich. C., 25 N. Alabama.

Commercial College.
Bryant's, Wm. Purdy, prin'l, Ætna Building.

Commission Merchants.
Bugby L. M., cor. Railroad and Del.
Donaldson C. S., 71 W. Washington.
Fitzgibbon M. & Co., cor. Meridian and Louisiana.
Gallup W. P. & E. P., 74 W. Wash.
Glazier Chas., 16 S. Meridian.
Grosvenor & Turner, 84 W. Wash.
Hahn C. F., 41 N. Alabama.
Rusch F. P., 83 W. Washington.

Confectioners.
Cunningham F. P., 43 N. Illinois.
Daggett W., 22 S. Meridian.
Haynes H. M., 40 W. Washington.
Huff John E., 200 W. Washington.
Kleber John L., 105 E. Washington.
Moesch T. H., 76 E. Washington.
Parrisette J., 15 N. Illinois.
Voight H. L. & Co., 67 S. Illinois.

Contractors.
Stumph John.
Timmerman H., 153 Railroad.

Coopers.
Burton Geo. K., 78 N. West.
May Adam, 58 S. East.

Coppersmiths.
Cottrell & Knight, 94 S. Delaware.
Munson & Johnson, 62 E. Wash.

Daguerrean Goods.
Crapo R. P. & Co., Journal building.
Perkins G. C. & Co., 14 W. Wash.

Daguerrean Artists.
(*See Artists.*)

Dentists.
Frink S. C., 4 Yohn's Block.
Hunt P. G. C., E. Market, bet. Pennsylvania and Delaware.
Johnston J. F., 11 E. Maryland.
Nichols T. M., 18½ S. Meridian.
Wells G. A., 15 E. Washington.
Wood B., 42 N. Pennsylvania.

First Premium awarded the Wheeler & Wilson Sewing Machine for three

CITY DIRECTORY. 251

Distiller.

Volmer Otto P., 159 E. St. Clair.

Dress Makers.

Danniels Mrs. C. F., 60 N. Delaware.
Fahnestock Mrs., 18 S. Illinois.
Farrell Mrs. C. J., 21 S. Delaware.
Foulke Mrs. E., 79 Massachusetts ave.
Healy Mrs., 11 N. Alabama.
Johnson Mrs., 12½ S. Pennsylvania.
Lemmon Mrs. Jennie, 34 E. Ohio.
Lowman Mrs. N., 58 E. St. Clair.
Martz S., 39 N. Alabama.
Montgomery Mrs. E., 65 W. South.
Pedrick Mrs., 45 N. Illinois.
Perkins Mrs. M., (col.,) 61 Kentucky ave.
Protzman Miss J., 24 N. Miss.
Shaughnessy Mrs. J., 131 S. Ala.
Tudor Mrs. H., 53 N. East.

Drugs and Medicines.

Browning Robert, 22 W. Wash.
Eguer & Wocher, 81 E. Washington.
Frauer J. C., 185 E. Washington.
Hannaman William, 40 E. Wash.
Lowry W. M., 49 Massachusetts ave.
Ludden & Lee, 14 N. Illinois, Bates House.
Perkins G. C. & Co, 14 W. Wash.
Rosengarten H., 172 E. Washington.
Senour J. F., 5 Bates House, W. Washington.
Tomlinson & Cox, 18 E. Wash.
Vickers W. B., Odd Fellows' Hall.

Dry Goods.

Bee-Hive Store, L. H. Tylor, prop'r, cor. Meridian and Washington.
Boston Store, Wm. Zeigler, 18 E. Washington.
Callinan D. J., 28 E. Washington.
Cook Wm. & Co., 189 E. Washington.
Flatuer & Jackson, 75 E. Wash.
Fletcher H. A & Co., 26 and 28 W. Washington.
Geisendorf G. W. & Co., 63 W. Wash.
German Store, Krause & Wittenberg, 43 and 45 E. Washington.
Good M. H., 5 E. Washington.
Kirlan James, 36 W. Washington.
Lynch & Keane, 33 W. Washington.
New York Store, Glenn W. & H. & Co., Glenns' Block, E. Wash.
Tousey & Byram, 70 E. Wash.

Dry Goods, Wholesale.

Crossland J. A., 75 W. Washington.

Dyers and Cleaners.

Bouchet Ed., N. Illinois.
Harris E., Paris Dye House, 19 S. Meridian.
Harris Joseph, 38 S. Illinois and E. Washington.
Heaf August, 10 S. Pennsylvania.
Kall Lewis, 93 E. Washington.

Edge Tool Maker.

Kellogg Newton, W. Washington, (near bridge.)

Embroidery.

Lennert Mrs. Sarah E., 16½ S. Ill.

Engravers on Wood.

Byrkit S. M., 19 W. Washington.
Fahnestock John, 19½ W. Wash.
Landon & Hastings, 8½ E. Wash.

Express Companies.

Adams, 12 E. Washington, John H. Ohr, agent.
American, cor. Meridian and Wash., J. Butterfield, agent.
Merchants' Despatch, 31 W. Wash., W. T. Clark, agent.
United States, cor. Meridian and Washington, J. Butterfield, agent.

Fancy Goods.

Baldwin J. H., 6 E. Washington.
Callinan D. J., 28 E. Washington.
Klotz Emil, 37 E. Washington.
Lake Miss M., 38 N. Pennsylvania.
Mayer Chas, 29 W. Washington.
Parker R. R., 30 W. Washington.

File Works.

Benjamin D. O. & Son, S. Penn.

Florists and Gardeners.

Loomis W. H., 189 Virginia ave.
Klapp Henry, E. National Road.
Weghorst H., S. E. of Corp'n Line.

Flour and Feed Dealers.

Carlisle John & Son, 68 W. Wash.
Church J. A. & Co., 5 S. Delaware.
Heckman C., 266 E. Washington.
Jordan Thos., 18 S. Meridian.
Mathews Wm., 124 E. Market.
Rusch Fred. P., 83 W. Washington.
Worland Wm., 37 Virginia ave.

INDIANAPOLIS

Flouring Mills.

Ætna Mills, J. Skillen & Bro., W. Washington.
Bates City, cor. Noble and Washington, J. W. Jeffries.
Capital Mills, cor. Market and Missouri, J. P. Evans & Co.
Carlisle John, 254 W. Washington.
Identical, T. Hudnut, S. Penn.
Pattison, Ray & Fletcher, W. Wash. (near bridge.)
Underhill R. F., Bluff road.

Foundries and Machine Shops.

Dumont & Sinker, S. Pennsylvania, E. Union Depot.
Redstone Bros. & Co., S. Delaware, opp. Cin. R. R. office.
Root, Bennett & Co., S. of Union Track.
Washington Foundry, Hasselman & Vinton, opp. Union Depot.
Wiggins & Chandler, 262 W. Wash.

Fruit Preserving House.

Williams, VanCamp & Co., Ohio, N. of Paper Mill.

Furniture.

Dohn Phillip, 21 S. Meridian.
Fisher Andrew, 78 E. Washington.
Gimbael Martin, 147 E. Washington.
Heitkum Chas., 61 E. Washington.
Ingersoll H. W., 78 E. Washington.
Jose N., 4 S. Pennsylvania.
Meyer C. J., 171 E. Washington.
Ramsey J. F., 21 S. Illinois.
Speigel, Thoms & Co., 73 W. Wash.
Vetter A., 97 E. Washington.
Wilde O. J., 71 S. Illinois.

Fur Agents.

Gregory David, 9 W. Washington.

Gas Fixtures.

Cottrell & Knight, 94 S. Delaware.
McLene J., Bates House.

Gas Fitters and Plumbers.

Cottrell & Knight, 94 S. Delaware.
Dunn J. C., 24 Kentucky ave.
Livsey & Co., near Union Depot.
Ramsey & Hanning, 85 W. Wash.

Gents' Furnishing Goods.

(*See Clothing.*)

General Stores.

Cook William & Co., 189 E. Wash.
Ostermyer & Prange, 258 E. Wash.
Piel W. F., 240 E. Washington.

Gilders and Picture Framers.

Crapo R. P. & Co., Journal Building.
Lieber H., 15 N. Pennsylvania.

Grain and Produce Dealers.

Bugby L. M., cor. Railroad track and Delaware.
Cassady Isaac N.
Elliott Thos. B., cor. S. Alabama and Cincinnati R. R.
Everson George P., 42 W. Maryland.
Glazier C., 16 S. Meridian.
Rusch Fred. P., 83 W. Washington, Masonic Hall.

Grocers, Wholesale.

Alford, Mills & Co., 36 E. Wash.
Birch & Farmer, 79 E. Washington.
Culver Elihu, 142 W. Washington.
Danforth & Simpson, 3 N. Penn.
Elliott C. A., cor. Meridian and Maryland.
Emmerich & Reese, 91 and 93 W.
Fitzgibbon M. & Co., Meridian, opp. Union Depot.
Holland J. W., 72 E. Washington.
Holmes C. L., 31 W. Washington.
Hogshire & Hunter, 25 W. Wash.
Langsdale & Patterson, 190 E. Wash.
Lannenberg H. H., 134 W. Wash.
Oglesby W. F. & Co., 59 W. Wash.
Schnull A. & H., cor. Wash. & Del.
Skillen J. & Bro., 248 W. Wash.
Stout O. B. & Bros., 42 W. Wash.
Wallace Andrew, cor. Virginia ave. and Delaware.
Wright, Bates & Maguire, 6 Bates House, Washington.

Grocers, Retail.

Avells M., 277 S. Delaware.
Barnitt Thos., 170 E. Washington.
Beebe & Hawes, 9 W. Washington, and 9 N. Illinois.
Birch & Farmer, 79 E. Wash.
Boyd D. M., 39 S. Meridian.
Brado Thomas, cor. East S. Vir. ave.
Brah L., 46 Ft. Wayne ave.
Brand J. G., 25 Bluff road.
Bretz Adam, 44 Louisiana.
Brinker Aug., 94 W. New York.
Brotz A., 82 S. Illinois.
Brown J. G., 150 N. New Jersey.

81,000 Wheeler & Wilson's Sewing Machines in use in this country.

CITY DIRECTORY. 253

Burch William, Orient.
Butsch George M., 173 S. Delaware.
Christy Albert, 14 Louisiana.
Christy A., cor. Ills. and Md.
Clem & Bros., cor. Massachusetts ave. and Alabama.
Collup Fred., 166 E. Washington.
Crug G., 24 E. Washington.
Culver Elihu, 142 W. Washington.
Danforth & Simpson, 3 Odd Fellows' Hall, Pennsylvania.
Dougherty Charles, 245 S. Delaware.
Emmerich & Reese, 91 and 93 W. Washington.
Ennes Philip, 229 Massachusetts ave.
Feeling F. W., 125 E. South.
Gahm John, cor. North and Indiana ave.
George James, 132 W. Washington.
Gold Adam, W. Washington, opp. Hoosier Woollen Factory.
Green George, cor. Tennessee and South.
Harlington Patrick, 50 E. La.
Harman Valentine, W. Indianapolis.
Harris Joseph.
Harrington Patrick, 58 South.
Hart James, 230 E. Washington.
Hawes & Co., 3 N. Illinois.
Hensan Charles, 50 Bluff Road.
Helin John, 104 Davidson,
Hinde E., 155 E. Washington.
Hofmeister & Nicholas.
Hogshire & Hunter, 25 W. Wash.
Hohl C. C., 77 E. Washington.
Holmes C. L., 31 W. Washington.
Holland J. W., 72 E. Washington.
Jenkins A. W., cor. Penn. & North.
Jerard, Ittenbach & Co., 180 S. Delaware.
Johnson G. W., Mississippi, cor. St. Clair.
Johnson J. F., 31 S. Meridian.
Johnson William, 167 S. Tennessee.
Keeley W. H., cor. Market & Noble.
Kemper Charles, cor. McCarty and Meridian.
Kerin D. P., S. E. Michigan Road.
Kettenback Henry, Massachusetts ave., bet. Liberty and St. Clair.
Kirlan James, 36 W. Washington.
Koch H., 198 Massachusetts ave.
Kolb John A., 69 S. Il"nois.
Kossebaum J. G., 153 Massachusetts ave.
Kuhlmann E. H. L., 187 W. Wash.

Kusick John, West, bet. Maryland and Georgia.
Kreniger George, 60 South.
Lafavrie J., cor. Maryland & Illinois.
Langdien Joseph, 160 E. Wash.
Lannenberg H. H., 134 W. Wash.
Langsdale & Pattison, 190 E. Wash.
Liver A., 46 S. Meridian.
Lintner C. H. & Co., 1 Indiana ave.
Lintner J. H., 140 E. Washington.
Lintner John & Son., cor. North and Indiana ave.
Lockman C., cor. Virginia ave. and Cedar.
Logan B., 129 W. South.
Longnecker Sam'l., W. Indianapolis.
McGinnis J., 228 E. Washington.
Middlemas D. C., 196 W. Wash.
Morganvich V., 9 Chatham.
Muller H., 142 N. Noble.
Munson W. L., 21 N. Alabama.
Oglesby W. F. & Co., 59 W. Wash.
Perrott Samuel, 191 Indiana ave.
Perrott W. W., 115 S. Tennessee.
Pryse Henry, cor. McCarty and Vir. ave.
Rench Edward, 126 S. Illinois.
Richter Henry, Illinois, bet. Second and Third.
Riemenschneider H., 47 N. N. J.
Roberts Dwight, cor. Wash. and Ill.
Ross James, 36 Indiana ave.
Schoppenhorst Wm., 101 E. Wash.
Schott Joseph, 117 E. Washington.
Schweinhart P., 253 Indiana ave.
Severin H., 207 N. New Jersey.
Sherman George, cor. Pennsylvania and North.
Simpson N., 162 & 164 W. Wash.
Simmons Henry, cor. Ind. ave. and Tennessee.
Simpson M. & R., cor. South & Del.
Skillen J. & Bro., 248 W. Wash.
Smith Fred., 126 N. Mississippi.
Spencer & Soewell, 202 E. Wash.
Stout O. B. & Bros., 42 W. Wash.
Stringer Wm. H., 77 N. Meridian.
Talbott R. C., 101 W. Washington.
Tarlton & Keen, 8 S. Meridian.
Thompson Mary, cor. Del. and South.
Tuttle B. F., 27 W. Washington.
VanHouten & Graham, 34 N. Ill.
Vinnedge J. A., 8 N. Pennsylvania.
Wenger G. M., 20 N. Noble.
Wesbe L. F., 185 W. Washington.
Wingate J. F., 165 Virginia ave.
Woerner Philip, 78 W. Washington.

A Wheeler & Wilson Sewing Machine with Hemmer, for $50.

INDIANAPOLIS

Wood A., 129 N. Illinois.
Woolen W. M., 82 W. Vermont.
Yeager Christ., 215 E. Washington.

Gunsmiths.

Balwig & Kindler, 17 Ky. ave.
Beck C., 15 S. Meridian.
Beck Samuel, 86 E. Washington.

Hardware and Cutlery.

City Hardware Store, 12 W. Wash.
Pottage Benjamin, 76 W. Wash.
Vajen J. H., 21 W. Washington.
Vonnegut Clemens, 142 E. Wash.
Wilson J. B., 61 W. Washington.
Wood A. D., 71 E. Washington.

Hats, Caps and Furs.

Baker & McIver, 22 E. Washington.
Bamberger H., 16 E. Washington.
Brown W. P., 20 Kentucky ave.
Sharp J. K., 88 and 90 E. Wash.
Spencer William, 32 W. Wash.
Wilmot Samuel, 8 W. Washington.

Hat Manufacturer.

Brown W. P., 20 Kentucky ave.

Harness Maker.

(*See Saddle and Harness.*)

Hides and Leather.

(*See Leather Stores.*)

Hoop Skirt Manufactory.

Goldston & Carfunkle, 12 S. Penn.

Hosiery and Trimmings.

Parker R. R., 30 W. Washington.

Hominy Mills.

Darby John, R. R. City Mills.

Hotels and Proprietors.

Bates House, William Judson, cor. Washington and Illinois.
Batty House, J. H. Batty, 31 N. Ala.
California House, A. Kistner, 138 S. Illinois.
East St. House, Hahn H., cor. East and South.
Farmers' Hotel, H. E. Buchrig, cor. Illinois and Georgia.
Jackson House, H. Marmont, 136 W. Washington.
Little's Hotel, A. R. Hyde, cor. Washington and New Jersey.

Macy House, J. E. Redford, cor. Ill. and Market.
Morris House, H. Whitmore, opp. Union Depot.
National, D. Bender, W. Wash.
Ohio House, M. Neiman, 31 W. Market.
Oriental House, W. J. Elliott, S. Ill.
Palmer House, J. D. Carmichael, S. E. cor. Wash. and Illinois.
Ray House, Ray & Lambert, S. E. cor. Del. and South.
Spencer House, M. Harth, cor. Illinois and Louisiana.
Tully House, S. Illinois, Wm. Tully.
Union Hall, 107, 109, 111, 113 E. Washington.
Union House, S. Mattler, S. Illinois.

Ice Dealers.

Butsch John, 48 W. South.
Parrisette J., 15 N. Illinois.
Pitts G. W., 78 Indiana ave.
Riley B. F., 92 W. New York.

Insurance.

Anderson G. P., 44 N. Pennsylvania.
Davis C. B., Odd Fellows' Hall.
Dunlop J. S., N. W. cor. Meridian and Washington.
Hayden J. J., Blackford's Block, cor. Meridian and Washington.
Henderson Wm., Ætna Building.
Locke & Bro., Blackford's Building.
Spann & Love, S. W. cor. Washington and Meridian.
White River Valley Insurance Company, 19 W. Washington.

Iron Railing.

Williamson & Haugh, 2 N. Delaware.
Dumont & Sinker, S. Pennsylvania.

Iron, Steel and Nails.

Murphy & Holliday, 34 E. Wash.
Root, Bennett & Co., 66 E. Wash.

Intelligence Office.

Stapp J. H., W. Washington.

Justices of the Peace.

Curtis Andrew, 39 E. Washington.
Fisher Charles, Yohn's Block.
Stem Frederick, Judah's Block.
Sullivan William, College Hall.

Wheeler & Wilson's Sewing Machines awarded the first premium for five

CITY DIRECTORY.   255

Lard, Oil, Soap and Candles.
Joachime August., 93 W. Maryland.

Lath Machines.
Redstone, Bros. & Co., S. Delaware, opp. Cincinnati R. R. office.

Last and Peg Manufacturers.
Osgood, Smith & Co., S. Illinois.

Law Book Publishers.
Dodd H. H. & Co., 18 E. Washington.
Merrill & Co., Glenns' Block.

Lightning Rods.
Munson David, 62 E. Washington.

Lime and Cement.
Butsch Valentine, South, opp. Madison Depot.

Leather and Hide Dealers.
Fishback John, 30 S. Meridian.
Mooneys & Co., S. Meridian.
Sharpe J. K., 88 and 90 E. Wash.
Yandes & Co., 38 E. Washington.

Livery and Sale Stables.
Allen & Hinesley, Pearl, rear Palmer House.
Brinkman & Ruschaupt, 17 S. Del.
Burrows G. W., 14 N. Pennsylvania.
Crouch G. W. & J. C., 24 S. Penn
Hall Charles W. & Co., Exchange Building, N. Ill., opp. Bates House.
Johnston O. W., 11 & 13 W. Pearl.
Landis Jacob, 18 W. Maryland.
Pattersen J. M., 34 E. Maryland.
Wilkison William, 10 E. Pearl.
Wood & Foudray, N. Pennsylvania.

Locksmiths.
Isensee A. F. W., 17 Kentucky ave.
Reinhardt J. P., 49 S. Illinois.

Lumber, Lath and Shingles.
Brown Philip, 275 Mass. ave.
Byrkit & Beam, 60 S. Tennessee.
King Cornelius, 141 N. Mississippi.
Kregelo, Blake & Co., cor. Canal & New York.
McCord & Wheatley, 119 S. Del.
Reynolds & Graham, E. Washington, near Noble.

Machine Shop.
Dumont & Sinker, cor. Penn. and Railroad.

Redstone Bros. & Co., S. Delaware.
Washington Foundry and Machine Shop, Hasselman & Vinton, opp. Union Depot.
Wiggins & Chandler, 262 E. Wash.

Marble Works.
Dame Jason, 67 E. Washington.
Downey M., 127 E. Washington.
James W. W. & Co., 58 S. Meridian.
Keys Wm., Georgia, bet. Missouri and West.
Seybold J. K., cor. Market and Del.
Scott, Nicholson & Co., Kentucky ave.
Weir & Bro., 13 Virginia ave.

Mathematical Instruments.
Steffens C. W. & Co., 8 Blackford's Building.

Matress Maker.
Evers John, 191 E. Washington.

Medical Books.
Streight A. D., Yohn's Block.
Werden & Co., 26 E. Washington.

Merchant Tailors.
Beudenz H. & Co., 144 W. Wash.
Bippus John, 16 N. Pennsylvania.
Criqui M., 84 E. Washington.
Deruham Max, agent 1 W. Wash.
Dessar & Bro., 6 E. Washington.
Gerstner A. G., 158 E. Washington.
Glaser & Bros., 2 Bates House.
Goepper F., 15 E. Washington.
Goodman Anthony, 16 N. Penn.
Gramling J. & P., 41 E. Washington.
Hotz George & Co., 69 S. Illinois.
Johnson John, 48 S. Illinois.
McGinnis Owen, 39 E. Washington.
Morgan S. C., 27 E. Washington.
Moritz, Bro. & Co., 3 E. and 19 W. Washington.
Ott George, 106 S. Illinois.
Richter & Roggs, 144 E. Wash.
Roupp William, 105 E. Washington.
Ruckle N. D., E. Market, opp. P. O.
Staub Joseph, 69 E. Washington.
Steinman G. & J., S. Meridian.
Tapking & Becker, 63 E. Wash.
Walker William, 2 Odd Fellows' Hall, Washington.

Milliners and Dress Makers.
(See also Dress Makers.)
Baker Mrs. A. & Co, 24 S. Illinois.

Successive years at Mechanic's Institute, Cincinnati.

Bidin C. W., 165 E. Washington.
Copeland J. W., 8 E. Washington.
Fahnestock Mrs. O., 18 S. Illinois.
Kirk E., 39 N. Pennsylvania.
Latshaw V. K. S., 22 S. Illinois.
Quimby Mrs. H., 20 S. Illinois.
Thomas Mrs. M. J. & Co., 46 W. Washington.
Williams Miss N. H., 22 S. Illinois.

Mill-Wright and Manufacturer of Bolting Cloths.

Taggart Samuel, 98 S. Delaware.

Music and Musical Instruments.

Willard & Stowell, 4 Bates House, Washington.

Music Teachers.

Allen Mrs. A. C., 38 E. New York.
Brummer Charles, 12 E. Michigan.
Hines E., Dancing Academy, 71 Indiana ave.
Newell L. S., Blind Asylum.
Pearsall P. R., 26 S. Tennessee.
Schonacker H. J., Spencer House.
Suffern Wm. J., Ætna Building.

News Depots.

Keating J. J., 19 S. Illinois.
Perrine C. O., Union Depot.
Thompson Mrs. A. & Son, N. Penn.

Newspapers and Periodicals.

Christian Record, A. D. Goodman, weekly, Journal Building.
Free Press (German), R. Henninger, weekly, 83 E. Washington.
Herald & Era, M. G. Lee, weekly, 2 S. Meridian.
Humorist, Landon & Hastings, monthly, 8 E. Washington.
Indiana American, T. A. Goodwin, daily and weekly, 11 E. Pearl.
Indiana Home-Life and Camp-Life, G. H. Fleming & Co., weekly, G. H. Fleming editor, 18 E. Wash.
Indianapolis Journal Co., daily and weekly, Journal Building, J. M. Tilford prest., B. R. Sulgrove ed'r.
Indiana State Sentinel, daily and weekly, Elder, Harkness & Bingham, proprietors, 2 S. Meridian.
Indiana School Journal, monthly, Journal Building, Prof. G. Hoss, editor and proprietor.

Indiana Volksblatt (German), weekly, J. Boetticher, 130 E. Wash.
The Witness, M. G. Clarke & Co., Odd Fellows' Hall.

Notaries Public.

Anderson G. P., 44 N. Penn.
Bowles Thos. H., 10 E. Washington.
Brown Ignatius, 19½ E. Washington.
Deford W. R., 35½ E. Washington.
Dunlop John S., N. W. cor. Meridian and Washington.
Dunn Jacob P., Indianapolis Branch Banking Co.
Elliott B. K., 24½ E. Washington.
Ferguson K., 24½ E. Washington.
Hamlin C., 18½ E. Washington.
Harrison & Fishback, 62 E. Wash.
Hayden J. J., Blackford's Block.
Howland L., Dunlop's Building.
Perrin G. K., College Hall.
Phipps I. N., 28 E. Market.
Seidensticker A., 91 E. Washington.
Smith Francis, 37 E. Washington.
Taylor N. B., Temperance Hall.
Walpole Bryan C., 18 E. Wash.
Werbe C. G., 95½ E. Washington.
Wiley W. Y., 10 E. Washington.
Wilson O. M., S. W. cor. Meridian and Washington.

Nurseries.

Beechwood Nursery, office 44 N. Pengsylvania, J. F. Hill & Co.
Pearce Wm., cor. Orient and Michigan Road.
Woodlawn Green House, W. H. Loomis, 180 Virginia ave.

Occulist and Aurist.

Gustin L., cor. Louisiana & Illinois.

Opticians.

Moses L. W., 20 E. Washington.
Semmons & Co., 23 S. Illinois.

Orchestral Bands.

Gresh B. F., 17 Kentucky ave.
Hahn H., East Street House.
Hines E., 71 Indiana ave.

Oysters, Agents.

Barnard J., 20 S. Meridian.
Beebe & Hawes, 9 W. Washington.
M. Hug, 14 E. Washyhington.

Paint and Color Works.

Drake E. B. & Co., 47 South.

The First Premium awarded the Wheeler & Wilson Machine

CITY DIRECTORY. 257

Painters and Glaziers.

Beale J., 175 E. South.
Cook M. R., 31 S. Meridian.
Fertig Frank, 6 E. Washington.
Winter D. M., S. Meridian.
Greuzard L. S., 136 E. Washington.
Jenkins E., rear of Bates House.
Knotts N. K., 2 N. Pennsylvania.
McLane Albert, 8 W. North.
Osgood J. B., 16 E. Market.
Rooker A. J., 104 Indiana ave.
Schmitt A., 103½ E. Washington.
Statts & English, 6 S. Meridian.
Traub J., 214 N. Alabama.
Whitridge Wm., 86½ E. Wash.

Paper Mill.

Sheets Wm., W. Market.

Paper Dealers.

Bowen, Stewart & Co., 18 W. Wash.
Braden William, 24 W. Wash.
Sheets William, 77 W. Washington.

Paper Hangers.

Beale J., 175 E. South.
Brown James, 135 N. Alabama.
Coen John, 107 S. Tennessee.
Dain R. C.

Patent Medicines.

Acher Frank, 101 S. New Jersey.
Frost J. M., 95 E. Washington.

Patent Solicitors.

Russell E. T., 19 S. Mississippi.
Redstone J. H., S. Delaware, opp. Cin. R. R. office.

Photographic Artists.

(See *Artists, Ambrotype, Photograph, and Daguerrean*.)

Physicians.

Abbett Chas. H., 20 Virginia ave.
Abbett L., 20 Virginia ave.
Athon Jas. S., 82 N. New Jersey.
Backesto J. P., 28 N. Illinois.
Barnes H. F., Blake's Building.
Barnitz J. W., 148 N. Illinois.
Bell Miletus, 124 N. Delaware.
Bobbs J. S., over Harrison's Bank.
Boyd J. T. (Homeopathic), 108 Ind. ave.
Bradford A., Ohio House, Market.
Bullard Talbot, 23 S. Meridian.
Bullard Wm. B., 23 S. Meridian.
Burnham N. G. (Eclectic), 4 Yohn's Block.
Bush Geo. B., 143 Virginia ave.
Corliss C. (Homeo.), 7 E. Maryland.
Dickson J. L. (Eclectic), 135 S. Ala.
Dorsey N. J., 48 N. Pennsylvania.
Dougherty L., California, bet. Wash. and Market.
Dunlap Livingston, 12 Virginia ave.
Ewing J. & D., 18 Virginia ave.
Fahnestock S., Glenns' Block, res. 71 N. Alabama.
Fishback Charles, 22 E. Market, res. 48 E. New York.
Funkhouser D., (J. & F.,) 5 S. Mer.
Gall A. D., 37 N. New Jersey.
Gaston John M., 22 E. Market.
Gustin L., cor. Louisiana & Georgia.
Homburg, Ray's Building.
Jameson & Funkhouser, 5 S. Mer.
Keely Isaac I., 62 E. Michigan.
Kendrick William H., 33 and 35 N. East.
Kitchen J. M., S. W. cor. Washington and Meridian.
Klein Emil, 100 E. New York.
Ludden B M., 14 N. Illinois.
McCann S. D., 29 N. East.
Mears G. W., 47 N. Meridian.
Merrill John F., (Eclectic,) 156 W. Washington.
Miller G. W., 158 N. Illinois.
Musgrave P. D., N. Tennessee, bet. Fifth and Sixth.
Newcomer F. S., 161 N. Illinois.
Nofsinger William R., E. Indianapolis.
Parvin T., 69 N. Alabama.
Prunk D. H., 46 Indiana ave.
Rhoads J. M., 145 N. West.
Rogers H., 14 E. Ohio.
Rucker J. S., 58 W. Vermont.
Stedman E. P., 40 Mass ave.
Stont O. H., 101 N. Tennessee.
Teal N., 5 Blake's Building.
Thompson Mrs., 74 N. Illinois.
Thompson W. C., Market, opp. P. O.
Wright Augustus S., (Homeo.,) 136 N. Illinois.
Wright M. H., cor. Meridian & Ohio.

Piano Fortes.

Ames James, 1 Blake's Row, up stairs.
T₁eyser G., manf'r, 98 W. Maryland.
Willard & Stowell, Bates House, W. Washington.

For four successive years at the Ohio State Fair.

Piano Forte Tuners.

Herring Philip, at Willard & Stowell's.
Schonacker H. J., bds. at Spencer House.

Planing Mills.

Byrkit & Beam, S. Tennessee.
Hill G. W., cor. East and Georgia.
Kreglo, Blake & Co., cor. Canal and W. New York.

Plow Makers.

Beard, Starr & Co., 2 N. Tennessee.
Wiggins & Chandler, 262 W. Wash.

Plumbers.

(See Gas Fitters.)

Powder Agents.

Gallup W. P., 74 W. Washington.
Hinde E., 155 E. Washington.

Portrait Painters.

Cox Jacob, Ray's Building.
Dunlap James, 136 E. Washington.
Hays & Runnion, 32½ E. Wash.

Printers, Book and Job.

Cameron W. S., 8 Pearl.
Dodd H. H. & Co., 18 E. Washington.
Elder, Harkness & Bingham, S. Meridian, opp. old Postoffice.
Journal Company, Journal Building.

Printers, Job.

Capital Job Office, Wm. S. Cameron, 8 Pearl.
Cullum & Stanage, 19½ W. Wash.
Dodd H. H. & Co., 18 E. Washington.
Elder, Harkness & Bingham, 2 S. Meridian.
Journal Company, Journal Building.
Landon & Hastings, 8 E. Wash.

Pork Packers.

McTaggart & Coffin, office cor. Washington and Delaware.
Mansur W. & I., 14 S. Meridian.

Produce Dealers.

Carlisle John & Son, Model Mills, E. Washington.
Emmerich & Reese, 91 and 93 W. Washington.

Everson Geo. V.
Hahn C. F., 41 N. Alabama.
Rusch Fred. P., 81 and 83 W. Wash.

Pump Makers.

Childers J. P., rear German Catholic Church.
Giel Conrad, 216 E. Washington.
Hasket Elijah, 26 Kentucky ave.

Real Estate Agents.

Barnitz & Murphy, 8 Temp. Hall.
Boes Wm., 261 S. Pennsylvania.
Eldridge Jacob, 13 S. Illinois.
Ellsworth H., S. Meridian.
Ferguson Kilby, 24½ W. Wash.
Gatling R. J., Blackford's Building.
Hamlin L. H. & C., 3d floor old Sentinel Buildings.
McKernan & Pierce, 30½ W. Wash.
McMillin Samuel, 31 W. Wash.
Phipps Isaac N., 28 E. Market.
Smith Francis, 37 E. Washington.
Spann & Love, S. W. cor. Washington and Meridian.
Stapp J. H., W. Washington.
Todd & Lindenbower, 6 S. Penn.
Waldo E. G. B., 38½ W. Wash.
Wiley W. Y., 10 E. Wasnington.
Wright C. A., Temperance Hall.

Restaurants.

(See also Saloons.)

Burt's, A. S. Burt, proprietor, 13 S. Illinois, (no liquors sold.)

Rolling Mill.

Indianapolis Rolling Mill, cor Merrill and Mississippi.

Saddle and Harness Makers.

Andra John, 171 E. Washington.
Blair James, 198 W. Washington.
Hereth J. C., 103 E. Washington.
Hinesley A. J., 34 W. Washington.
Nicolai C., 268 E. Washington.
Simcox J. W., 138 N. East.
Sulgrove J. B., 73 E. Washington.
Sulgrove & Reynolds, 20 W. Wash.

Saddlery Hardware.

Hinesly A. J., 34 W. Washington.
Mooneys S. & Co., 75 S. Meridian.
Sulgrove J. B., 44 E. Washington.
Sulgrove & Reynolds, 20 W. Wash.

Wheeler & Wilson's Sewing Machines warranted for three years.

Saloons.

American, 25 S. Meridian.
Astor, Fey & Rammon, 9 N. Penn.
Beck Ed., 44 W. Washington.
Blaes N., 48 S. Delaware.
Burk Eli, W. Indianapolis.
Burk George, 13 W. Washington.
Burt's Restaurant, 13 S. Illinois.
Bush & Hannum, 53 and 55 S. Ill.
Carroll's Saloon, 11 N. Illinois.
Caylor Santford, 220 E. Washington.
Central Restaurant, 6 W. Wash.
City Saloon, 53 and 55 S. Illinois.
Court House, cor. Wash. and Alabama, C. Monninger, proprietor.
Crystal Palace, E. Beck, proprietor, 44 W. Washington.
Cummings James, 194 W. Wash.
Dietz Adam, cor. Alabama and Fort Wayne ave.
Dietz Davis, 78 and 380 W. Washington.
Doty & Lee, opp. State House.
Eagle Saloon, 130 E. Washington.
East Empire, C. Lauer, proprietor, 162 E. Washington.
Empire, R. Beebe, proprietor, 23 W. Washington.
Eurich & Schaffer, St. Nicholas Saloon, 7 N. Illinois.
Exchange, C. W. Hall, proprietor, N. Illinois.
Faber August, 73 S. Illinois.
Farmers', cor. Illinois and Georgia.
Florence's, F. Richter, proprietor, 13 N. Illinois.
Frenzell J. P., Kansas saloon, 83 and 85 S. Illinois.
Happe George, 81 S. Meridian.
Hofmeister Chris., 75 E. Wash.
Hug Martin, 14 E. Washington.
Johnson B. F., 212 W. Washington.
La Belle, D. Monninger, cor. Wash. and Kentucky ave.
Lang Louis, 13 E. Washington.
Little's Hotel, John Ledlie, prop'r.
Magnolia, 9 S. Illinois, S. A. Flagg, proprietor.
Matthes C., 163 E. Washington.
Mason M., cor. Illinois & Louisiana.
Miller Charles G., cor. Washington and East.
Morris House, R. Beebe.
National, 27 S. Meridian, G. Rhodius, proprietor.
Nebraska, Naltner & Naltner, proprietors, 14 Louisiana.
Niggerman Frederick, 186 E. Washington.
Oriental, S. Illinois.
Palmer House, R. Young, prop'r.
Paris, Eugene Ranard, proprietor, E. Washington.
Pearl Street, Thomas McBaker, proprietor.
Rennon J. B., 242 & 244 E. Washington.
St. Charles, 86 E. Washington, E. Haas, proprietors.
St. Nicholas, 7 N. Illinois, Eurich & Schaffer, proprietor.
State House, opp. State House, Doty & Lee, proprietors.
Station House, opp. Union Depot, F. Scheer, proprietor.
Telegraph Restaurant, 12 Louisiana, H. Walls, proprietor.
Union Hall, 107, 109, 111 and 113 E. Washington, M. Emmenegger.
Union, M. Hunter, proprietor, 81 E. Washington.
Verandah, opp. Union Depot, John Bussey, proprietor.
Wright C., 138 E. Washington.
Youngerman G., cor. Washington and Delaware.

Salt Agency.

Wasson J. H., N. W. cor. Washington and Meridian, Ohio River Salt Company.

Sash, Doors and Blinds.

Barr Jacob, 86 N. Alabama.
Byrkit & Beam, 60 S. Tennessee.
Kreglo, Blake & Co., cor. New York and Missouri.

Saw Manufacturer.

Atkins E. C., 155 S. Illinois.

Saw Mills.

Hill G. W., cor. East and Georgia.
Marsee J. R., near P. & I. Freight Depot.
Wells William F., Massachusetts ave., near city line.
Wishmire C. F., 189 N. Davidson.

Schools, Private.

Bronson G. W., Fifth Ward School House.
Carroll Miss Belle, Ohio, bet. Pennsylvania and Delaware, under Associate Reformed Church.

The Wheeler & Wilson Hemmer is the only Hemmer that will Fell.

Many Gerrad, (French school) 69 N. Noble.

Scales and Safes.
Gallup W. P. and E. P., 74 W. Wash.

Seal and Press Makers.
Ballard Austin, 5 Circle.

Seed Stores.
(See *Agricultural*.)

Sewing Machines.
Grover & Baker, J. J. Harlan, Yohn's Building.
Singer I. M. & Co., J. F. Elliott, 3 Odd Fellows' Hall, E. Wash.
Wheeler & Wilson, C. C. Claflin, 19 W. Wash.
Williams & Orvis, N. D. Ruckle, agent, E. Market, opp. Post Office.

Shingle Manufacturers.
Redstone Bros. & Co., S. Delaware.
Reynolds & Graham, E. Wash. near Noble.

Silver Smiths.
(See *Watchmakers and Jewelry*.)

Stair Builders.
Chester A. A., Duncan bet. Del. and Alabama.
Muller John A. D., East bet. Chestnut and Cherry.

Stereotype Foundry.
Fleming G. H. & Co., 18½ E. Wash.

Stock Brokers.
(See *Brokers, Bill and Note*.)

Stone Yard.
(See *Building Stone*.)

Stoves and Tinware.
Cox Charles, 11 W. Washington.
Frankem I. L., 49 & 51 E. Wash.
Goldsberry L. D., 182 E. Wash.
McOunt R. L. & A. W., 69 W. Wash.
Munson & Johnson, 62 E. Wash.
Pottage Benjamin, 76 W. Wash.
Root, Bennett & Co., 66 E. Wash.
Voegtle, Jacob, 177 E. Washington.
Wainwright S., 11 S. Illinois.
Wood A. D., 71 E. Washington.

Straw Goods.
(See *Millinery*.)

Sugar Mills.
(See *Agriculture*.)

Surveyors.
Hosbrook D. B., 108 N. Mississippi.
Wilson L. B., 63 W. Maryland.
Wood James, 3 Blake's Building.

Tanners.
Fishback John, 30 S. Meridian.
Sharpe J. K., 90 E. Washington.
Yandes & Co., cor. Washington and Benton.

Tea Dealers.
Donaldson C. S., 71 W. Washington.
Daggett W., 22 S. Meridian.
Ludden & Lee, 14 N. Illinois, Bates House.
Muir James, 33 W. Market.

Telegraph Office.
1 N. Meridian.

Tin Plate & Tinners' Tools.
(See *Hardware and Coppersmiths*)

Trunk and Valise Manufacturers.
Becker H., 30 W. Washington.
Sulgrove & Reynolds, 20 W. Wash.

Umbrella Makers.
Mayer John F., 65 E. Washington.
Meyer Martin, 133 E. Washington.

Undertakers.
Gruenstein Geo., 114 E. Market.
Long Matthew, 28 S. Meridian.
Weaver & Williams, 72 W. Wash.

Veterinary Surgeons.
Blauvelt Daniel, 23 S. Delaware.
Ellerby J., 10 N. Pennsylvania.

Vinegar Manufacturers.
Pretzinger Jacob, 256 E. Wash.
Schofield T. B. & Co., 49 South.

Wagon Manufacturers.
Bristor S. M., Kentucky ave.
Burk Eli, W. Indianapolis.
Munsel & Son, Wabash, bet. Liberty and Noble.
Richmann & Buchanan, 111 E. Wash.

A Wheeler & Wilson Sewing Machine will last a life-time.

CITY DIRECTORY. 261

Vanblaricum J., 177 W. Washington
Wheeling C., 156 S. Delaware.

Wall Paper and Window Shades.

Bowen, Stewart & Co., 18 W. Wash.
Roll W. H., 16 S. Illinois.
Werden & Co., 26 E. Washington.

Watches and Jewelry.

Beck John A., Odd Fellows' Hall.
Bell A., 37 W. Washington.
Bingham W. P. & Co., 20 E. Wash.
Craft W. H., 2 Odd Fellows' Hall.
Daumont S. H., 9 S. Meridian.
Decker J. B., 184 E. Washington.
Feller George, 67 W. Washington.
French Charles G., 37 W. Wash.
Ferguson C. A., 7 W. Washington.
Gridley F., Bates House, Wash.
McLene J., 1 Bates House.
Oihler Andrew, 17 Kentucky ave.
Rech M., 80 W. Washington.
Talbott W. H. & Co., 24 E. Wash.
Walk Julius, Spencer House.
Woltze W. E., 164 E. Washington.

Watch Material.

Bingham W. P. & Co., 20 E. Wash.
Talbott W. H. & Co., 24 E. Wash.

Whip Manufactory.

Holdskom C., 20 W. Washington.

Wines and Liquors.

Brinkmeyer J. C. & Co., 82 W. Washington.

Hug Martin, 140 W. Washington.
Middlemas D. C., 196 W. Wash.
Muller John, 212 E. Washington.
Pierson W. W., 180 E. Washington.
Pretzinger Jacob, 256 E. Wash.
Rosenthal A., opp. Union Depot.
Ruschaupt & Bals, 82 E. Wash.
Ryan T. F., 73 S. Meridian.
Schnull A. & H., 81 and 83 E. Wash.
Simpson M. & R., cor. South and Delaware.
Volmer C., 67 W. Washington.

Wood and Willow Ware.

Baldwin J. H., 8 E. Washington.
Klotz Emil, 37 E. Washington.
Mayer Charles, 29 W. Washington.

Wood Dealers.

Johnson C. R., Ohio House.
Keating L. M., 20 Elm.
Rosmyre C., 65 Hosbrook.

Woolen Factories.

Hoosier, G. W. Geisendorff & Co., prop'rs, W. Wash., near bridge.
Ohio Premium, Merritt & Coughlen, proprietors, W. Washington.
Wadsworth William, E. Wash.

Yankee Notions and Toys.

Baldwin J. H., 6 E. Washington.
Crossland J. A., 75 W. Washington.
Klotz Emil, 37 E. Washington.
Mayer Charles, 29 W. Washington.

350 families in Indianapolis and vicinity use Wheeler & Wilson.

CHURCHES AND PASTORS.

CHURCHES.	LOCATION.	PASTOR'S NAME.	RESIDENCE.
First Presbyterian	N. E. cor. Circle and Market	Rev. G. H. Nixon	87 N. Illinois.
Second do	N. W. cor. Circle and Market	Rev. G. P. Tindall	87 N. Pennsylvania.
Third do	Cor. Illinois and Ohio	Rev. G. C. Heckman	134 N. Tennessee.
Fourth do	Cor. Market and Delaware	Rev. A. L. Brooks	89 E. Ohio.
Fifth do	New Jersey, bet. Wash. and Maryland	Rev. G. Long	33 N. New Jersey.
Associate Reformed Presbyterian	Ohio, W. of Delaware	Rev. Gilbert Small	40 N. Delaware.
Congregational	Meridian, N. of Circle	Rev. N. A. Hyde	10 E. Market.
Asbury Chapel, Methodist	New Jersey, S. of Louisiana	Rev. Joseph Marsee	147 E. South.
Roberts Chapel do	Cor. Pennsylvania and Market	Rev. Jacob Colclazer	35 N. Pennsylvania.
Strange Chapel do	Tennessee, S. of Vermont	Rev. James Havens	107 N. Tennessee.
Wesley Chapel do	S. W. cor. Circle and Meridian	Rev. C. D. Battelle	2 Circle.
North St. Chapel do	North, W. of Alabama	Rev. Elijah Whitten	
African do	Georgia, bet. Canal and Mississippi	Rev. W. R. Revells	119 N. West.
do do	Ohio, E. of New Jersey	Rev. John Schinder	122 E. Ohio.
Episcopal (Christ Church)	N. E. cor. Meridian and Circle	Rev. H. Stringfellow, Jr	Adjoining church.
Baptist (Masonic Hall)	Are building cor. Penn. and New York	Rev. Henry Day	Cor. Meridian & Merrill
African Baptist	Missouri, near New York	Rev. Moses Broyals	
Christian	Cor. Ohio and Delaware	Rev. Perry Hall	
First Evangelical Lutheran	Cor. Alabama and New York	Rev. J. A. Kunkleman	156 N. Pennsylvania.
Second do	Pennsylvania, bet. St. Clair and Pratt	Rev. G. A. Exline	Ill. bt. Second & Thir d
German United Evangelical	Ohio, bet. Illinois and Meridian	Rev. Herman Quintus	Basement of church.
German Lutheran	New Jersey, bet. Wash. and Maryland	Rev. Chas. Fricke	13 N. East.
German Reformed	Alabama, S. of Market	Rev. M G. J. Stern	15 N. Alabama.
German Evangelical	New Jersey, bet. Market and Ohio	Rev. M. Kreuger	Rear of church.
United Brethren	Georgia, bet. Tennessee and Illinois	Rev. Thos. Evans	27 N. Liberty.
St. Johns, Catholic	Maryland, bet. Pennsylvania and Delaware	Rev. A. Bessolnes	Adjoining church.
St. Mary's do	College Hall	Rev. Simon Siegrist	46 S. Delaware.
Universalist		Rev. B. F. Foster	8 Virginia ave.
Friends, Orthodox	Cor. Delaware and St. Clair	David and Hannah Tatum	E. St. Joseph.

Wheeler & Wilson's Sewing Machines have been awarded the First Premium

STREET DIRECTORY.

The leading Streets are named East, West, North and South, taking Meridian Street for one basis, and Washington for the other. The Streets printed in Capitals are the most important ones in the City.

Agnes, N. and S., N. W. of City.
ALABAMA, N. and S., three blocks E. of Circle.
Ann, from Rolling Mill to McCarty.
Arch, from Jackson to Noble, N. E. of city.
Arizona, S. of Utah.
Ash, N. of Car Works, N. E. of city.
Athon, from Rhode Island to Indiana ave.
Barnhill, from North to Davis.
Bates, from Noble to eastern limits, S. of city.
Benton, from Harrison to Central Track, E. of Noble.
Bicking, from Delaware to East, S. of city.
Blackford, from New York to North, three blocks W. of Canal.
Blake, N. and S., from Washington to Indiana ave., near W. limits.
Bright, from New York to North, N. W. of city.
Broadway, N. of Car Works, N. E. of city.
Buchanan, S. E. of city, 3 blocks N. of Morris.
Cady, from Harrison to Central Track, E. of Benton.
California, from New York to North, two blocks W. of Canal.
Catharine, from West to Canal, S. of Merrill.
Cedar, Fletcher's Addition, S. E. of city.
Center from Dunlop to Ellen, N. W. of city.
Charles, from St. Clair to Peru track.
Chatham, from Massachusetts ave. to St. Clair, E. of East.
Cherry, from Fort Wayne ave. to Ash, near Northern boundary.
Christian ave., 1 block N. of city limits.
Coburn, S. E. of city, 1 block N. of Morris.
Coe, from Fall Creek to Hiawatha, N. E.
Cottrell, from Georgia to Louisiana, W. of Canal, S. W.
Cross, from Peru Track to City line, N. E.
Curve, from Bellefontaine Car Works, N. E. to city limits.
Dacota, from White River to Morris, W. of West.
Davidson, N. and S., E. of Railroad.
Davis, from N. W. city line to Fall Creek.
DELAWARE, N. and S., two blocks E. of Circle.
Douglass, from New York to Michigan, N. W. of city.
Dougherty, S. E. of city, 2 blocks N. of Morris.
Duncan, from Delaware to New Jersey, continuation of Garden.

Dunlop, from Madison ave. 3 blocks S. of Morris.
East, N. and S., five blocks E. of Circle.
East Second, W. of city line.
Elizabeth, from Indiana ave. to Blake, N. W. of city.
Elk, Fletcher's Addition, S. E. of city.
Ellen, from North to Indiana ave.
Ellis, from Maryland S. W. of West.
Elm, from Noble S. E. of Fletcher's Addition.
First, Northern city boundary.
Fifth, five blocks N. of city limits.
Fletcher's Avenue, Fletcher's addition, S. E. of city.
Forest ave., Fletcher's Addition, S. E. of city.
Forest Home ave., S. of N. W. C. University.
FORT WAYNE AVENUE, from North running N. E. to city limits.
Fourth, four blocks N. of city limits.
Franklin, from Morris S. two blocks, E. of Madison ave.
Garden, from Canal to Delaware, six blocks S. of Circle.
George, from Merrill to Garden, W. of Illinois.
GEORGIA, E. and W., three blocks S. of Circle.
Greer, between McCarty and Virginia ave.
Grove, from Virginia ave. to city line.
Harris, N. and S., N. W. of city.
Harrison, from Noble to Eastern limits, S. of Ind. & C. R. R.
Henry, from Canal to Mississippi, S. of South.
Hiawatha, N. and S. W. of City Hospital.
High, from McCarty S., E. of Delaware.
Hosbrook, Fletcher's Addition, S. E. of city.
Howard North, from First to Seventh, W. of Lafayette Railroad.
Howard South, from Morris S. E. of Madison ave.
Huron, Fletcher's Addition, S. E. of city,
ILLINOIS, N. and S., one block W. of Circle.
INDIANA AVENUE, N. W. Diagonal.
Jackson, N. of Car Works, N. E. of city.
James, N. W. of city.
Japan, from Morris S. 3 blocks E. of Madison ave.
John, from Peru track to city limits.
Kansas, from Bluff Road to West, S. of city line.
KENTUCKY AVENUE, S. W. Diagonal.
Liberty, N. and S., six blocks E. of Circle.
Locke, from North to Indiana ave.
Lord, from Noble to Eastern limits, S. of I. and C. R. R.
LOUISIANA, E. and W., four blocks S. of Circle.
Loukabee, from East to Liberty, bet. Vermont and New York.
McCarty, from River to Virginia ave,, S. of city.
McGill, from Louisiana to South, W. of Mississippi.
McKernan, from Buchanan to Morris, 3 blocks E. of East.
Madison ave., from South to city line, S. E. Diagonal.
Margaret, S. side of City Hospital.
Maria, from Smith to Locke.
MARKET, E. and W., through Circle.
MARYLAND, E. and W., two blocks S. of Circle.
MASSACHUSETTS AVENUE, N. E. Diagonal.
Maxwell, from North to Davis.
Meek, from Noble to Eastern limits, S. of Indiana Central R. R.
MERIDIAN, N. and S., through Circle.
Merrill, from Kentucky ave. to Virginia ave., seven blocks S. of Circle.
MICHIGAN, E. and W., four blocks N. of Circle.

MICHIGAN ROAD, N. E. and S. W., through the city.
Mill, from Fifth to Seventh, W. of Howard.
Minerva, N. and S., N. W. of city.
Minnesota, W. of Canal from Morris, S.
MISSISSIPPI, N. and S., three blocks W. of Circle.
MISSOURI, N. and S., along Canal.
Morris, Southern boundary line.
Nebraska, from Madison ave. 4 blocks S. of Morris.
NEW JERSEY, N. and S., four blocks E. of Circle.
NEW YORK, E. and W., two blocks N. of Circle.
Noble, N. and S., seven blocks E. of Circle.
North ave., N. of N. W. C. University.
NORTH, E. and W., five blocks N. of Circle.
Oak, N. of Car Works, N. E. of city.
OHIO, E. and W., one block N. of Circle.
Orient, from Pennsylvania to Fort Wayne ave., S. of St. Joseph.
Oxford, from Peru Track to city line.
Patterson, N. and S., N. W. of city.
PENNSYLVANIA, N. and S., one block E. of Circle.
Pine, Fletcher's Addition, S. E. of city.
Pittsfield, continuation of Mill to Lafayette Railroad Track.
Plum, N. of Car Works, N. E. of city.
Powell, from Michigan to North.
Pratt, from Illinois to Fort Wayne ave., N. of Blind Asylum.
Railroad Avenue, N. and S., between Pennsylvania and S. Delaware.
Railroad Street, N. and S., along Bellefontaine R. R. track.
Ray, from Canal to Railroad, S. of city.
Rhode Island, from Blake to Western limits, N. of city.
St. Clair, from Indiana ave. to Massachusetts ave., N. of Blind Asylum.
St. Joseph, from Illinois to Fort Wayne ave., N. of Blind Asylum.
St. Mary, E. from Meridian, Northern city boundary.
School, from South to Virginia ave., W. of Noble.
Second, two blocks N. of city limits.
Seventh, seven blocks N. of city limits.
Short, from Morris to Dougherty, W. of Virginia ave.
Sinker, from Alabam to New Jersey.
Sixth, six blocks N. of city limits.
Smith, from Rhode Island to Indiana ave.
SOUTH, E. and W., five blocks S. of Circle.
TENNESSEE, N. and S., two blocks W. of Circle.
Texas, from Madison ave. W. 6 blocks, S. of Morris.
Third, three blocks N. of city limits.
VERMONT, E. and W., three blocks N. of Circle.
Vine, from Jackson to Ash, N. E. of city.
VIRGINIA AVENUE, S. E. Diagonal.
Union, from McCarty to Morris, E. of Bluff Road.
University ave., E. of N. W. C. University.
Utah, S. of Wisconsin.
Walnut, from Canal to Massachusetts ave., N. of Blind Asylum.
WASHINGTON, E. and W., one block S. of Circle.
Watters, from McCarty to Virginia ave.
WEST, N. and S., one block W. of Canal.
Western ave., continuation of Fort Wayne ave.
Wilkins, from Canal to Railroad, S. of city.
Willard, from Garden to Merrill, W. of Tennessee.
Williams, between McCarty and Virginia ave.
Wilson, from North to Davis.

Upwards of 100 W. & W. Machines in use in Ind'p'lis making army clothing.

Winston, N. and S., near Eastern limits.
Wisconsin, from Bluff Road to River, S. of Kansas.
Wright, from Buchanan to Morris, 2 blocks E. of East.
Wyandot.
Wyoming, from Delaware to High, S. of city.

L. B. WILLIAMSON.   E. HAUGH'

WILLIAMSON & HAUGH,
Manufacturers of
WROUGHT AND CAST IRON RAILING,
Verandahs, Bank Vaults, Iron Shutters, Iron Stairs, plain and ornamental. Builders of E. May's Patent Iron Jail. Also, manufacturers of

WHEELER'S PATENT WATER DRAWER.

NO. 2 N. DELAWARE ST., INDIANAPOLIS.

N. B. Bolts of all sizes made to order.

GEO. W. PITTS,
Wholesale and Retail

DEALER IN ICE,

Office and residence No. 78 Indiana Avenue,

INDIANAPOLIS.

First Premium awarded the Wheeler & Wilson Sewing Machine for three

APPENDIX.

CITY GOVERNMENT.

ANNUAL ELECTION SECOND TUESDAY IN MAY; COUNCIL MEETS EVERY OTHER SATURDAY NIGHT.

CITY OFFICERS FOR 1862.

Mayor—S. D. MAXWELL.
Treasurer—JOSEPH K. ENGLISH.
Clerk—JOHN G. WATERS.
Marshal—DAVID W. LOUCKS.
Deputy Marshal—JOHN UMBERSAW.
City Engineer—JAMES WOOD, SR.
Assistant Engineer—JAMES WOOD, JR.
Street Commissioner—JOHN A. COLESTOCK.
Market Master—THOMAS J. FOOS.
Assessor—JOHN B. STUMPH.
City Attorney—JAMES M. SWEETSER.

COUNCILMEN.

First Ward—Sims A. Colley; Samuel M. Sibert.
Second Ward—T. P. Haughey; Andrew Wallace.
Third Ward—W. Clinton Thompson; Vacancy.
Fourth Ward—George W. Geisendorff; John Blake.
Fifth Ward—E. H. L. Kuhlman; Stephen McNabb.
Sixth Ward—Austin H. Brown; Alex. Metzger.
Seventh Ward—S. A. Fletcher, Jr.; Charles Richmann.
Eigth Ward—Jas. M. Buchanan; Hiram N. Wright.
Ninth Ward—Henry Geisel; Christ. F. Wishmeyer.

WATCHMEN.

Chief of Police, T. A. Ramsey.
First Ward, Thomas D. Amos; George Taffe.
Second Ward, John S. Bray; Haldin Davis.
Third Ward, Hannibal Taffe; Charles E. Carter.
Fourth Ward, James P. Catterson; Wm. H. Fitch.

Successive years at the United States Fair.

Fifth Ward, Michael Gallivan; Fred. Scheigert.
Sixth Ward, Henry Paul; John S. Russell.
Seventh Ward, A. E. Catterson; H. S. Adams.

Sealer of Weights and Measures, James Loucks.

Keeper of Cemetery, James W. Alred.

INDIANAPOLIS STEAM PAID FIRE DEPARTNENT.

Chief Fire Engineer, Joseph W. Davis.

STEAM COMPANY No. 1, Located on Washington street.

Engineer, Frank Glazier. | *Driver of Engine Team*, Aug. Nagle.
Fireman, John M. Davis. | *Driver of Hose*, Charles Rhoads.

Hosemen, George Webster, Leonard Gay, Eli Thompson, Danl. Locks.

Company No. 1 have four horses.

STEAM COMPANY No. 2, Located on corner of Massachusetts Avenue.

Engineer, Charles E. Curtis. | *Driver of Engine*, Lafe Doughty.
Fireman, E. H. Webster. | *Driver of Hose*, Abe Smock.

Hosemen, Chas. Anderson, Fred. Heinebaugh, Jas. Pierce, Geo. Williams.

Company No. 2 have five horses.

STEAM COMPANY No. 3, Located on South street, between Delaware and Alabama streets.

Engineer, Daniel Glazier. | *Driver of Engine*, J. Calahan.
Fireman, Ralph Hunter. | *Driver of Hose*, Samuel Blythe.

Hosemen, Henry Busher, Columbus Gray, Casper Freshour, J. Redman.

Company No. 3 have three horses.

HOOK AND LADDER COMPANY, Located on New Jersey street, north of Washington.

Driver, Henry Kincil.

SCHOOL TRUSTEES.

First Ward, Oscar H. Kendricks. | *Fifth Ward*, James Sulgrove.
Second Ward, D. V. Culley. | *Sixth Ward*, Louis W. Hasselman.
Third Ward, James Green. | *Seventh Ward*, vacant.
Fourth Ward, Dr. Elliott. |

81,000 Wheeler & Wilson's Sewing Machines in use in this country.

CENTER TOWNSHIP OFFICERS.

Constables, Michael Scudder, Jeptha Bradley, W. Woolen.
Township Trustee, James Turner.

MARION COUNTY OFFICERS.

Judge of Common Pleas Court, Chas. Ray.
Clerk of Circuit and Common Pleas Court, William Wallace.
Sheriff, Wm. J. Wallace.
Recorder, Alex. G. Wallace.
Treasurer, John L. Brown.
Auditor, Jacob T. Wright.
Coroner, Garrison W. Alred.
Surveyor, Oliver W. Voorhies.

COURTS.

UNITED STATES CIRCUIT COURT.

Held at the U. S. Court-room, Post Office Building, on the third Mondays of November and May in each year.

Circuit Judge, —— Swan.   *Circuit Clerk,* John H. Rea.

UNITED STATES DISTRICT COURT.

Held at the U. S. Court-room, Post Office Building, on the third Mondays of November and May of each year. Clerk's office at the State Bank Building.

District Judge, Elisha M. Huntington,   *District Clerk,* John H. Rea, *District Attorney,* John Hannah.

UNITED STATES MARSHALS.

Marshal, D. G. Rose.
Deputy Marshals, I. S. Bigelow, A. M. Ruter.

SUPREME COURT OF INDIANA.

Court meets in State House fourth Mondays in May and November.

Judges—Andrew Davidson, J. L. Worden, James M. Hanna, Samuel E. Perkins.
   Clerk, John P. Jones.   *Sheriff,* Henry H. Nelson.

COURTS OF MARION COUNTY.

MARION CIRCUIT COURT.

Meets at Court House, Indianapolis, fourth Mondays in March and September.

Judge Fifth Judicial Circuit, Fabius M. Finch.
Clerk, William Wallace.   *Sheriff,* William J. Wallace.

A Wheeler & Wilson Sewing Machine with Hemmer, for $50.

INDIANAPOLIS

MARION COURT OF COMMON PLEAS.

Judge, Charles A. Ray.
Clerk, William Wallace.   *Sheriff*, William J. Wallace.

POST OFFICE.

In new Government Building, S. E. cor. Pennsylvania and Market streets.

Postmaster, A. H. Conner.
Clerks, E. A. Elder, William H. Campbell, John Fish, John F. Wood, George W. Joseph, Jas. B. Hill, David W. Barnitt, John A. Buchanan, D. J. Charles, Jas. A. Russell, John Farrell, Charles Knefler, George M. Sweetser, Joseph F. Dougherty, Benton C. Vandegrift, George G. McChesny, John F. Owings, John S. Duncan, Samuel E. Frazee.
Porters, Jacob Reinacher and Maurice Healey.

MASONIC ORDERS.

GRAND COMMANDERY OF KNIGHTS TEMPLAR.

The next annual conclave of the Grand Commandery of Knights Templar of the State of Indiana, will be held at Fort Wayne, on the first Tuesday in April, 1862.

GRAND OFFICERS.

Sir Solomon D. Bayless, of Fort Wayne, R. E. Grand Commander.
Sir Rev. John W. Sullivan, of Jeffersonville, V. E. D. G. Commander.
Sir John A. Hutton, of New Albany, Grand Generalissimo.
Sir Harvey G. Hazlerigg, of Thorntown, Grand Captain General.
Sir Rev. Thomas R. Austin, of New Albany, Grand Prelate.
Sir Henry C. Lawrence, of Lafayette, Grand Senior Warden.
Sir Samuel McElfatrick, of Fort Wayne, Grand Junior Warden.
Sir Charles Fisher, of Indianapolis, Grand Treasurer.
Sir Francis King, of Indianapolis, Grand Recorder.
Sir Wm. Hacker, of Shelbyville, Grand Standard Bearer.
Sir Joseph Johnson, of Fort Wayne, Grand Sword Bearer.
Sir Wm. M. Smith, of Connersville, Grand Warden.
Sir Henry Colestock, of Indianapolis, Grand Captain Guard.

GRAND COUNCIL OF ROYAL AND SELECT MASTERS.

The Grand Council of Royal and Select Masters of the State of Indiana will hold the next annual communication at Lafayette, at 9 o'clock A. M., on the Tuesday before the fourth Monday of May, 1862.

Wheeler & Wilson's Sewing Machines awarded the first premium for five

GRAND OFFICERS.

Comp. Wm. Hacker, of Shelbyville, M. Puissant Gr. Master.
Comp. Thomas Pattison, of Aurora, D. Puissant Gr. Master.
Comp. Thomas R. Austin, of New Albany, T. Ill. Gr. Master.
Comp. Chauncey Carter, of Logansport, Gr. P. C. of Work.
Comp. Henry Goodlander, of Connersville, Gr. Capt. Guards.
Comp. Charles Fisher, of Indianapolis, Grand Treasurer.
Comp. Francis King, of Indianapolis, Grand Recorder.
Comp. Rev. Franklin A. Hardin, of Newcastle, Gr. Chaplain.
Comp. Henry Colestock, of Indianapolis, Gr. S. and Sentinel.

GRAND CHAPTER OF THE STATE OF INDIANA.

The Grand Royal Arch Chapter of the State of Indiana will hold its next annual communication at Lafayette, at 2 o'clock P. M., on the Tuesday before the fourth Monday of May, 1862.

GRAND OFFICERS.

Comp. George W. Porter, of New Albany, M. E. Gr. High Priest.
Comp. John Taylor, of Lafayette, E. D. Grand High Priest.
Comp. Erastus W. H. Ellis, of Goshen, E. Grand King.
Comp. Philip Mason, of Connersville, E. Grand Scribe.
Comp. Joseph Johnson, of Fort Wayne, Grand Capt. of Host.
Comp. Henry Goodlander, of Connersville, Grand R. A. Capt.
Comp. Rev. Franklin A. Harding, of Newcastle, Gr. Chaplain.
Comp. Charles Fisher, of Indianapolis, Grand Treasurer.
Comp. Francis King, of Indianapolis, Grand Secretary.
Comp. Henry Colestock, of Indianapolis, Grand Guard.

GRAND LODGE OF THE STATE OF INDIANA.

The Grand Lodge of Indiana holds its annual communication at the Masonic Hall, in the city of Indianapolis, at 2 o'clock P. M., on the fourth Monday of May, 1862.

GRAND OFFICERS.

M. W. Thomas R. Austin, of New Albany, Grand Master.
R. W. John B. Fravel, of Laporte, D. G. Master.
R. W. Eleazer Malone, of Centerville, G. S. Warden.
R. W. Henry D. Washburn, of Newport, G. J. Warden.
R. W. Charles Fisher, of Indianapolis, Gr. Treasurer.
R. W. Francis King, of Indianapolis, Gr. Secretary.
Bro. Rev. John Leach, of Laporte, Gr. Chaplain.
Bro. Thomas Carnahan, of Lafayette, Gr. Lecturer.
Bro. Wm. Hacker, of Shelbyville, Gr. Marshal.
Bro. Wm. J. Willard, jun., of Millersville, G. S. Deacon.
Bro. Wm. W. Clinedenst, of Centreville, G. J. Deacon.
Bro. Henry Colestock, of Indianapolis, G. Tyler.

RAPER COMMANDERY, No. 1.

Chartered 1850. Stated meetings fourth Wednesday of each month.

Sir Ephraim Colestock, G. C.
Sir John M. Bramwell, G.
Sir Wm. H. Lingenfelter, C. G.
Sir Samuel Campbell, T.
Sir Charles Fisher, R.
Sir Levi Gustin, St. B.

Successive years at Mechanic's Institute, Cincinnati.

Sir Thomas H. Lynch, P.
Sir Francis King, S. W.
Sir Wm. J. Millard, J. W.

Sir C. F. Brown, Sw'd B.
Sir Calvin Fletcher, jr., W.
Sir Henry Colestock, S.

COUNCIL.

Indianapolis Council, No. 2, at Indianapolis.

Meets first Monday in each month.

John M. Bramwell, I. I. L. L.
Israel Conklin, A. I. I. L. L.
Geo. W. H. Riley, P. C. W.
Francis King, C. G.

Samuel Campbell, T.
Charles Fisher, R.
Henry Colestock, S.

CHAPTER.

Indianapolis Chapter, No. 5, at Indianapolis.

Meets first Friday of each month.

John M. Bramwell, H. P.
Ephraim Colestock, K.
Samuel Campbell, S.
Francis King, C. H.
Israel Conklin, P. S.
Roger Parry, R. A. C.

James H. Seybold, G. M. 3d V.
Joseph R. Haugh, G. M. 2d V.
———— ————, G. M. 3d V.
James Sulgrove, T.
Charles Fisher, S.
Henry Colestock, G.

MARION LODGE, No. 35.

Chartered 1853. Meets at Masonic Hall, third Wednesday in each month.

John M. Bramwell, W. M.
Wilson S. Wolf, S. W.
Ebenezer Sharpe, J. W.
Joseph R. Haugh, T.

Francis King, S.
Roger Parry, S. D.
William R. Foster, J. D.
Henry Colestock, T.

CONCORDIA LODGE, No. 178.

Chartered May, 1855. Meets at Masonic Hall the second Wednesday in each month.

OFFICERS.

Geo. F. Meyer, W. M.
Frank Damme, S. W.
———— Bernhauer, J. W.
August Braininger, S.

Charles Lauer, T.
Christ. Meyer, S. D.
———— ————, J. D.

CENTER LODGE, No. 23.

Chartered 1846. Meets at Masonic Hall first Wednesday of each month.

Aaron D. Ohr, W. M.
John M. Kerper, S. W.
W. T. Clark, J. W.
Isaac H. Roll, T.

Charles Fisher, S.
Charles E. Holland, S. D.
Peter H. D. Bandey, J. D.
Henry Colestock, T.

The First Premium awarded the Wheeler & Wilson Machine

INDEPENDENT ORDER OF ODD FELLOWS.

R. W. G. ENCAMPMENT, I. O. O. F., OF INDIANA,

Was instituted on the 10th of December, 1847, and convenes at Odd Fellows' Hall, Indianapolis, on the third Monday preceding the third Tuesday of May and November of each year.

OFFICERS.

L. M. Campbell, M. W. G. Patriarch, Danville.
J. A. Moorman, M. E. G. High Priest, Winchester.
F. R. A. Jeter, R. W. G. Senior Warden, Brookville.
B. W. Smith, R. W. G. Junior Warden, North Madison.
E. H. Barry, R. W. G. Scribe, Indianapolis.
T. P. Haughey, R. W. G. Treasurer, Indianapolis.
Christopher Toler, W. G. Sentinel, Madison.
Jacob T. Williams, D. G. Sentinel, Indianapolis.
T. B. McCarty, } G. Reps. to G. L. U. S., { Wabash.
J. T. Sanders, } { Jeffersonville.
R. S. C. Maccoun, Alt. G. Rep. G. L. U. S., Danville.
C. W. Elmore, Alt. G. Rep. G. L, U. S., Crawfordsville.

GRAND LODGE OF INDIANA.

The R. W. Grand Lodge of I. O. O. F. of Indiana, was instituted on the 14th of August, 1837, and convenes at Odd Fellows' Hall, Indianapolis, on the third Tuesday of May and November of each year.

OFFICERS.

W. H. Dixon, M. W. Grand Master, Jeffersonville.
T. W. Watkins, R. W. D. Grand Master, Terre Haute.
Dennis Gregg, R. W. Grand Warden, New Albany.
E. H. Barry, R. W. Grand Secretary, Indianapolis.
T. P. Haughey, R. W. Grand Treasurer, Indianapolis.
Thomas Underwood, G. Rep. G. L. U. S., Lafayette.
James E. Blythe, G. Rep. G. L. U. S., Lafayette.
James Burgess, Alt. G. Rep. G. L. U. S., Danville.
J. Y. Allison, Alt. G Rep. G. L. U. S., Madison.
Rev. T. G. Beharrell, R. W. Grand Chaplain, Moore's Hill.
W. C. Lupton, R. W. Grand Marshal, Indianapolis.
R. L. Higginbotham, R. W. Grand Conductor, Delphi.
G. A. Milnes, Grand Sentinel, Crooked Creek.
S. Frazier, Grand Herald, Greenwood.

METROPOLITAN ENCAMPMENT, No. 5.

Meets first and third Mondays of each month.

Chief Patriarch, Levi Marshall.	Scribe, Thomas Farley.
High Priest, John G. Pendergast.	Per. Scribe, John G. Waters.
Senior Warden, Joseph Kingham.	Treasurer, H. A. Fletcher.
Junior Warden, Thomas Kelley.	

MARION ENCAMPMENT, No. 35.

Meets second and fourth Mondays of each month.

Chief Patriarch, W. J. Fisher. | Scribe, R. H. Stokes.

For four successive years at the Ohio State Fair.

High Priest, David Mathias. | Per. Scribe, —— ——.
Senior Warden, W. P. Noble. | Treasurer, J. B. Root.
Junior Warden, H. E. P. Talbott. |

TEUTONIA ENCAMPMENT No. 57.

Meets second and fourth Fridays of each month.

Chief Patriarch, Chas. Richmann. | Scribe, G. Stous.
High Priest, Christian Off. | Per. Scribe, —— ——.
Senior Warden, Joseph Staub. | Treasurer, Ernest Despa.
Junior Warden, Wm. Langenberg. |

CENTRE LODGE, No. 18.

Meets every Tuesday evening.

John G. Pendergast, N. G. | H. A. Fletcher, T.
Henry Allen, V. G. | A. W. Fuqua,
Thomas Farley, R. S. | W. H. Jones, } Trustees.
John G. Waters, P. S. | H. A. Fletcher,

PHILOXENIAN LODGE, No. 44.

Meets every Wednesday evening.

Joseph Staub, N. G. | Joseph R. Hough, T.
Daniel G. Gilmore, V. G. | George D. Staats,
David Anderson, R. S. | Andrew Wallace, } Trustees.
Joseph S. Watson, P. S. | Thomas J. Vater,

CAPITAL LODGE, No. 124.

Meets every Friday evening.

W. R. Wright, N. G. | John F. Wallick, P. S.
W. H. Weeks, V. G. | A. J. Hincsley, T.
J. B. Root, R. S. |

GERMANIA LODGE, No. 129.

Meets every Thursday evening.

Frederick Rushschaupt, N. G. | John C. Brinkmeyer, Treas.
Christian Karle, V. G. | Charles Richmond,
John Kistner, Sec. | Alexander Metzger, } Trustees.
Tobias Bender, Per. Sec. | John B. Stumph,

INDIANAPOLIS ROLLING MILL COMPANY.

Officers.

President and Superintendent, John M. Lord.
Treasurer, Aquilla Jones.
Secretary, C. B. Parkman.
Manager, John Thomas.
Directors, John M. Lord, James Blake, John Thomas, Aquilla Jones.
Weight Master and Shipping Clerk, James R. Blake.

Wheeler & Wilson's Sewing Machines warranted for three years.

INDIANAPOLIS GAS LIGHT AND COKE COMPANY.

OFFICERS.

President, D. S. Beaty.
Secretary and Collector, Lem Vanlanningham.
Directors, D. S. Beaty, E. Peck, D. V. Cuily, S. A. Fletcher, I. Mansur.

BANKS.

BANK OF THE STATE OF INDIANA.

Office cor. Illinois and Kentucky ave. Capital paid in, about $3,100,000.
President, Hugh McCullough. *Cashier*, James M. Ray.

BRANCH OF THE BANK OF THE STATE OF INDIANA.

Office N. E. cor. Meridian and East Washington. Capital $225,000.
President, George Tousey. *Cashier*, David E. Snyder.

BANKERS.

INDIANAPOLIS BRANCH BANKING COMPANY.

Corner Pennsylvania and Washington.
President, C. Fletcher. *Cashier*, Thomas H. Sharp.

S. A. FLETCHER.

No. 30 East Washington. Open from 8 A. M. until 4 P. M.

A. & J. C. S. HARRISON.

19 East Washingson.

EDUCATIONAL.

McLEAN FEMALE INSTITUTE.

Rev. Charles Sturdevant, A. M., President.
Charles N. Todd, A. M., Professor of Chemistry, Greek and Latin.
Mons. Gerard Many, Professor of French Language.
Miss Sturm, Teacher of German Language.
Mrs. Sarah Starling, Teacher of Drawing and of Painting in Oil and Water Colors.
Miss E. J. Gildersleeve, Miss M. Elmina Jewel, Miss M. Helen Whiting, and Miss Mary Warsdell, Teachers of General Literature in the English Department.
Professor Charles Brummer and Miss Clara M. Sturdevant, Teachers of Vocal and Instrumental Music.
James Anderson, Stewart.
Mrs. H. Anderson, Housekeeper.

The Wheeler & Wilson Hemmer is the only Hemmer that will Fell.

NORTH-WESTERN CHRISTIAN UNIVERSITY.

A. R. Benton, A. M., President, Professor of Ethics and Greek.
G. W. Hoss, A. M., Professor Mathematics.
S. K. Hoshour, A. M., Professor Latin and Modern Languages.
R. T. Brown, M. D., A. M., Professor Natural Sciences.
A. C. Shortridge, Professor Preparatory Department.

INDIANAPOLIS FEMALE INSTITUTE.

North-East of corner Pennsylvania and Michigan.

Rev. Gibbon Williams, Superintendent.

BOARD OF INSTRUCTION.

Miss E. A. Williams, Principal, and Teacher of Mental and Moral Science and Latin.
Miss Fannie Snow, Teacher of Mathematics and Natural Science.
Miss Lucy Tinsley, Teacher of Music.
Miss M. A. Ford, Teacher of the Primary Department.
Miss Fannie Vanhoughten, Teacher of Penmanship.

HAY'S ACADEMY FOR BOYS.

Under Masonic Hall, South Tennessee Street.

Rev. L. G. Hay, Principal.

SAINT JOHN'S ACADEMY. (Catholic.)

Adjoining the Catholic Church, North-East cor. Tennessee and Georgia.

Conducted by the Sisters of Providence.

Mary Ambrose, Superioress.

HALLS AND PUBLIC BUILDINGS.

Ætna Building, Pennsylvania, between Washington and Market.
Blackford's Building, South-East corner Meridian and Washington.
College Hall, South-West corner Washington and Pennsylvania.
Court House and County Offices, Court House Square, Washington, bet. Dealware and Alabama.
Glenns' Block, Washington, between Meridian and Pennsylvania.
Journal Building, corner Circle and Meridian.
Macy & McTaggart's Building, Washington, corner of Delaware.
Masonic Hall, South-East corner Washington and Tennessee.
Metropolitan Hall, (Theater,) N. E. corner Washington and Tennessee.
Military Hall, North side Washington, between Meridian and Pennsylvania.
Odd Fellows' Hall, North-East corner Washington and Pennsylvania.
Ramsey's Block, South Illinois, between Maryland and Georgia.
Ray's Building, North side Washington, between Meridian and Illinois.
Sentinel Building, (old,) Washington, between Meridian and Pennsylvania.
Sinking Fund Office, corner Pennsylvania and Virginia ave.

A Wheeler & Wilson Sewing Machine will last a life-time.

State Bank, corner Illinois and Kentucky ave.
State House, Washington, between Tennessee and Mississippi.
Temperance Hall, North side Washington, between Meridian and Illinois.
Union Depot, Louisiana, between Meridian and Illinois.
Union Hall, South side Washington, between Delaware and Alabama.
United States Court House and Post Office, corner Market and Pennsylvania.
Yohn's Building, North-East corner Washington and Meridian.

LIBRARIES.

INDIANA STATE LIBRARY.

R. D. Brown, *Librarian.* For the use of Judges and State officers. Office hours from 9 A. M. till 4 P. M. No. of volumes, about 20,000.

MARION COUNTY LIBRARY.

Under the charge of nine Trustees. This institution was organized under the special law of 1843. No. of volumes, .1,700. John W. Hamilton, *Librarian..* Office in Court House. Terms, 75 cents a year for two books, 50 cents for one book. Open Saturdays from 9 to 12 A. M. and 1 to 3 P. M.

CENTER TOWNSHIP LIBRARY.

Court House. No. of volumes, 1000. Open on Saturdays from 2 to 5 P. M. Terms free.

RAILROADS.

BELLEFONTAINE RAILROAD LINE.

Office North-west corner Meridian and Louisiana.

OFFICERS.

President and Superintendent, John Brough.
Assistant Superintendent, John Canby.
Gen'l Ticket Agent, J. M. Townsend.
Gen'l Freight Agent, Lucien Hills.
Cashier, Edward King.
Auditor, J. M. Townsend..

INDIANA AND ILLINOIS CENTRAL RAILWAY COMPANY.

Office 24½ East Washington.

OFFICERS.

President and Treasurer, Edmund Clark.
Secretary, B. K. Elliott.

350 families in Indianapolis and vicinity use Wheeler & Wilson.

INDIANAPOLIS AND CINCINNATI RAILROAD.

Offices on South Delaware, South of the Railroad track.

Officers.

President and Superintendent, Henry C. Lord.
Assistant Superintendent, J. W. Mills.
Treasurer, W. O. Rockwood.

Secretary, A. Worth.
Gen'l Ticket Agent, W. H. L. Noble.
Gen'l Freight Agent, G. L. Barringer.

INDIANA CENTRAL RAILWAY.

Offices corner Delaware and Virginia avenue.

Officers.

President, John S. Newman.
Superintendent, H. C. Carey.
Treasurer, Samuel Hanna.

Gen'l Ticket Agent, H. Parrott.
Gen'l Freight Agent, W. A. Bradshaw.

JEFFERSONVILLE RAILROAD.

Office 43 South Street.

Officers.

President, D. Ricketts.
Superintendent, A. S. Crothers.
Gen'l Ticket Agent, Thomas Carse.

Gen'l Freight Agent, James Ferrier.
Freight Agent, Indianapolis, J. G. Whitcomb.

LAFAYETTE AND INDIANAPOLIS RAILROAD.

Officers.

President, W. F. Reynelds.
Superintendent,

General Agent, Indianapolis. W. H Parmelee.

MADISON AND INDIANAPOLIS RAILROAD.

Office 43 South Street.

Officers.

President, F. H. Smith.
Superintendent, D. C. Branham.
Treasurer, Thomas Pollock.

Gen'l Ticket Agent, T. P. Mathews.
Gen'l Agent, Indianapolis, R. E. Rockwell.

TERRE HAUTE AND RICHMOND RAILROAD.

Offices Louisiana, West of Union Depot.

Officers.

President, E. J. Peck.
Superintendent, R. E. Ricker.
Secretary, Charles Wood.

Gen'l Freight Agent, Indianapolis, M. M. Landis.

Wheeler & Wilson's Sewing Machines have been awarded the First Premium

CITY DIRECTORY. 279

PERU AND INDIANAPOLIS RAILROAD.

Offices cor. Delaware and Washington.

OFFICERS.

Superintendent and General Agent, David Macy.
Assistant Sup't, C. B. Robinson
Treasurer and General Ticket Agent, Theodore P. Haughey.

General Freight Agent, L. N. Andrews.
Freight Agent, Indianapolis, W. B. Pratt.

INDIANAPOLIS TYPOGRAPHICAL UNION, No. 1.

Meets the last Saturday night in every month, in the Ætna Building.

OFFICERS.

President, Daniel L. Paine.
Vice President, D. M. Cantrell.
Recording Secretary, Alexander D. Stevens.
Corresponding Secretary, George J. Schley.

Financial Secretary, John Schley.
Treasurer, M. H. Halpin.
Guardian, Martin W. Riley.
Executive Committee, C. O. Sackett, William Bodenhamer, G. W. B. Smth, E. Cullum.

YOUNG MEN'S CHRISTIAN ASSOCIATION.

Organized November, 1854. Rooms located in Ray's Building. Library open Saturday and Tuesday evenings. Regular monthly meetings, every third Monday in each month. Entrance fee, $1.00.

OFFICERS.

President, Dr. T. Parvin.
Vice Presidents, one from each Evangelical Church represented.
Recording Secretary, Carlos Dickson.

Corresponding Secretary, F. A. W. Davis.
Treasurer, Wm. H. Smith.

STATE BENEVOLENT INSTITUTIONS.

INDIANA INSTITUTE FOR EDUCATING THE DEAF AND DUMB.

Located one and a half miles east of the city on the National Road.

OFFICERS.

President, A. Wallace.
Trustees, J. M. Kitchen, M. D., J. Burt, M. D.

Sup't, Thomas MacIntire, A. M.
Stewart, W. R. Foster.
Matron, Miss Taylor.

For four successive years at the Am. Institute, New York.

INSANE ASYLUM.

Located on the National Road, two miles West of the City.

OFFICERS.

President, A. Wallace.
Commissioners, T. H. Jameson, J. W. Moody.
Sup't, W. H. Woodburn, M. D.

1st Assistant, J. S. Dunlap, jr., M. D.
2d Assistant, Dr. Craven.
Stewart, Wm. M. French.

INDIANA INSTITUTE FOR EDUCATING THE BLIND.

Located on North, between Pennsylvania and Meridian Streets.

OFFICERS.

President, A. Wallace.
Trustees, John Beard, William M. Smith.
Sup't, Wm. M. Churchman.
Matron, Mrs. Price.

Teachers Literary Department, Granville Ballard, Mrs. Moore.
Teachers Music Department, L. S. Newell, Miss Dyer.

The Wheeler & Wilson Hemmer makes hems of any width.